# THE USBORNE BOOK OF THE
# EARTH

## Contents

| | |
|---|---|
| Planet Earth | Page 1 |
| Ecology | Page 49 |
| Energy & Power | Page 97 |
| Weather & Climate | Page 145 |
| Index | Page 192 |

First published in 1992 by Usborne
Publishing Ltd, Usborne House, 83-85
Saffron Hill, London EC1N 8RT, England

Copyright © 1992 Usborne Publishing

The name Usborne and the device ꝏ
are Trade Marks of Usborne Publishing
Ltd.

Printed in Spain

# PLANET EARTH

Fiona Watt
Edited by Corinne Stockley
Designed by Stephen Wright

Illustrated by Kuo Kang Chen, Chris Shields and Aziz Khan
Scientific advisors: Steve Stone and Mike Collins

# Contents

3  About this book
4  The Earth in space
6  The structure of the Earth
8  The seas and oceans
10  Earth movements and earthquakes
12  Volcanoes
14  The Earth's atmosphere
16  Weather
18  Climates
20  Rocks and minerals
22  The changing planet
24  Glaciation
26  Rivers
28  Water under the ground
30  The work of the sea
32  Deserts
34  The living world
36  The human population
38  The Earth's energy resources
40  Antarctica
42  Controlling the future
44  Earth facts
45  Useful addresses
46  Glossary

We are extremely grateful to Ben and Melissa Collins, and the teachers and pupils of Edenbridge Middle School, Edenbridge, Kent and Sherwood Park Primary School, Tunbridge Wells, Kent, for constructing, testing and making suggestions on all the various activities and experiments which appear in the book. We are also grateful to the British Antarctic Survey and Greenpeace for their help in compiling information and statistics for pages 40-41.

# About this book

The Earth has gradually changed over millions of years to become the complex planet we know today. This book explains how many of the Earth's features and landscapes were formed, such as volcanoes, glaciers and deserts. It also looks at the various processes which continue to shape the Earth's surface, such as the action of rivers, the sea and the weather.

Throughout the book there are examples of many ways in which we use the Earth's resources, such as coal, minerals and energy from the Sun. It also shows the fragile balance which exists between the natural world and human activities. It looks at a wide variety of plant and animal species and how they survive in different environments around the world.

## Using the glossary

The glossary on pages 46-47 is a useful reference point. It gives detailed explanations of the more complex terms used in the book, and introduces some new ones.

## Useful addresses

On page 45, there is a list of addresses of museums and organizations who may be able to provide you with more information about the Earth and its resources.

## Activities and projects

Special boxes like this one are found throughout the book. They are used for experiments and activities which will help you to understand different aspects of physical geography.

All the experiments and activities have clear instructions and are easy to do. You may need to buy some of the equipment at an electrical or hardware shop.

This scene shows an African grassland, or savannah, and some of the many species of animal which live there. Few people live in these areas because the climate is not suitable for farming. For more information about different climates, see page 19.

# The Earth in space

The planet Earth seems enormous to us, but it is really just a tiny part of the Universe. The Universe consists of billions of stars, planets and moons, as well as vast areas of emptiness. No one knows how big it is, and astronomers think it is still expanding. They believe it was formed about 20,000 million years ago when all the matter, which was once packed together in one place, was thrown into space by a massive explosion. Galaxies formed in the clouds of dust and gas which spread out. It is thought that the Earth was formed about 4,600 million years ago.

## Galaxies, stars and planets

A galaxy is an enormous cluster of thousands of millions of stars and planets. Galaxies can be different shapes, such as spirals. There are over 6,000 million known galaxies.

The Milky Way is a small part of one galaxy, but it is still made up of millions of stars and planets. It has a disc-like shape, formed by 'arms' spiralling out from a central cluster of stars.

The Solar System is a very tiny part of the Milky Way. It is made up of the Sun and the nine major planets. Each planet follows its own elliptical (oval-shaped) path, or orbit, around the Sun. Thousands of asteroids (balls of ice, dust and gas), also travel around the Sun.

The Earth is the fifth largest planet in the Solar System. From space it appears as a blue planet, covered with swirling clouds.

The Universe is so enormous that distances cannot be measured in the normal way, so they are measured in light years. One light year is the distance light travels in a year (9,500 billion kilometres).

The Sun is the centre of the Solar System. It is a not a planet, but a star. Stars send out light and heat energy. This is produced by chemical changes in the very centre, or core, of the star.

The temperature and pressure in the core of the Sun are so high that hydrogen gas is turned into helium gas, giving off huge amounts of energy.

Mercury. Extremely hot, about 500°C in the daytime and −175°C at night. Almost no atmosphere. Rocky surface.

Earth. Temperature range of 60°C to −90°C. Atmosphere of mainly nitrogen and oxygen. 75% of surface covered by water.

Venus. Very hot, about 480°C. Thick, dense atmosphere – clouds of carbon dioxide which trap Sun's heat. Rocky, cratered surface.

Mars. Freezing temperatures. Atmosphere mainly carbon dioxide. Red, rocky surface.

Asteroids. Irregular-shaped lumps of rock which travel around the Sun.

## The spinning planets

As each planet orbits the Sun, it rotates about its axis (an imaginary line running through it). The Earth spins around once every 23 hours and 56 minutes. Venus takes 243 Earth days to rotate, whereas Uranus takes only 11 hours.

Axis (imaginary line)

The Earth rotates in this direction.

## Exploring the planets

Exploration by unmanned space craft, such as the American space probes Viking and Voyager and the Russian probe Venera, has revealed information about the surface and atmosphere of the planets in the Solar System. From the information sent back from space, scientists have worked out what it may be like on each planet.

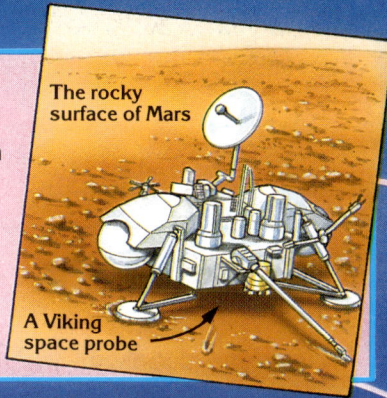

The rocky surface of Mars

A Viking space probe

Pluto. Smallest planet. Thought to have no atmosphere and thick icy crust surrounding core.

Neptune. Receives little light from Sun, so extremely low temperatures. Thought to have rocky core covered in ice crust.

Jupiter. Largest planet, mostly made up of clouds of gas and ice crystals. Atmosphere of hydrogen and helium. Tiny particles and rocks form a ring around it.

Uranus. Blue-green planet due to atmosphere of methane. Very low temperatures. May have solid core. Nine known rings circle the planet.

Saturn. Enormous ball of hydrogen and methane gas, with solid core. Circled by rings of thousands of blocks of ice.

## The unique planet

The Earth is the only known planet where living things, as we know them, can exist. It is neither too hot nor too cold and contains just the right mixture of gases and water needed by plants and animals.

The Earth's atmosphere is the only one to contain nitrogen and oxygen. Living things need to breathe or absorb oxygen and nitrogen to build their cells. The atmosphere also helps to reflect harmful radiation from the Sun back into space.

Green plants use the Sun's energy to make their own food in a process called photosynthesis. Animals cannot make their food, so they must eat plants, or other animals.

Without the Sun's energy, life on Earth could not exist. The Earth is the only planet in the Solar System which receives the right amount of light and heat to support life.

**A tropical rainforest supports thousands of species of plants and animals.**

# The structure of the Earth

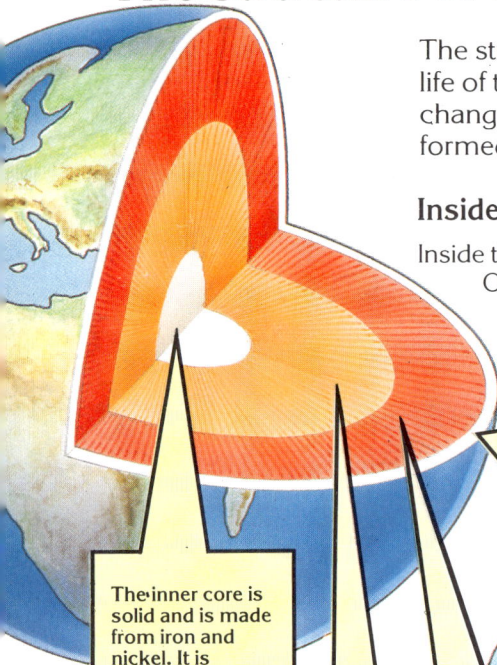

The structure, atmosphere and natural life of the Earth have gradually changed, or evolved, since it was formed. The planet's rocks provide geologists (people who study rocks and their formation) with information about changes to the surface and structure of the Earth.

## Inside the Earth

Inside the Earth are several layers of rock. One way scientists have worked out what these are like is by studying shock waves from earthquakes (see pages 10-11).

The crust is a relatively thin layer, between 6km and 70km thick. It is thickest under mountains. The oceanic crust lies below the oceans and runs under the continental crust, which forms the land.

The·inner core is solid and is made from iron and nickel. It is extremely hot (about 5,000°C).

The outer core is made from molten (liquid) metal. As the Earth rotates, this layer moves around very slowly, producing the Earth's magnetic field.

The Earth's crust

Ocean

Oceanic crust

Mantle

Mountains

Continental crust

The mantle is the layer of rock below the crust. It is about 3,000km thick. Areas of the mantle are so hot that the rock has melted to form a thick, treacle-like substance called magma (see page 12).

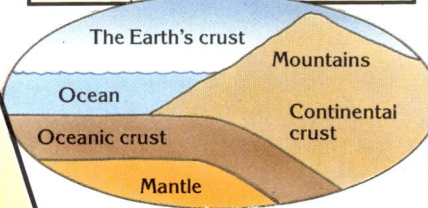

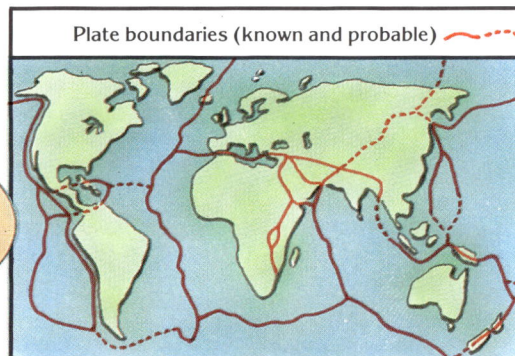

## Continental plates

The Earth's crust is divided into large pieces, or continental plates, which move around very slowly. If they move apart, magma comes up, cools and forms new rock. If they collide, they either rise up, or one is pushed below the other. Plates can also slide sideways against each other.

Plate boundaries (known and probable)

Plates moving apart

Plates moving together

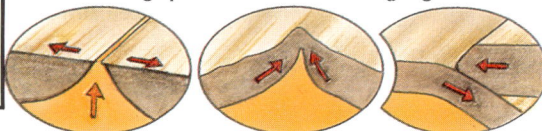

## Moving continents

If you look at a world map, you will see that the shapes of the continents seem to match each other like the pieces of a giant jigsaw puzzle. Some scientists think the continents were once joined together (about 200 million years ago), forming one massive land they call Pangea. They think the continental plates gradually drifted apart, making the land split up to form today's continents.

Evidence for the existence of Pangea comes from fossils, the remains of dead plants and animals preserved in rock. Fossils of the same creatures have been found on continents thousands of kilometres apart. For example, fossils of Lystrosaurus, a plant-eating reptile, have been found in South Africa, Asia and Antarctica. This suggests that these continents were once joined.

Some people do not think Pangea ever existed. They say that animals travelled across strips of land, or land bridges, which once existed between the continents. Others think they travelled across the oceans on clumps of floating plants.

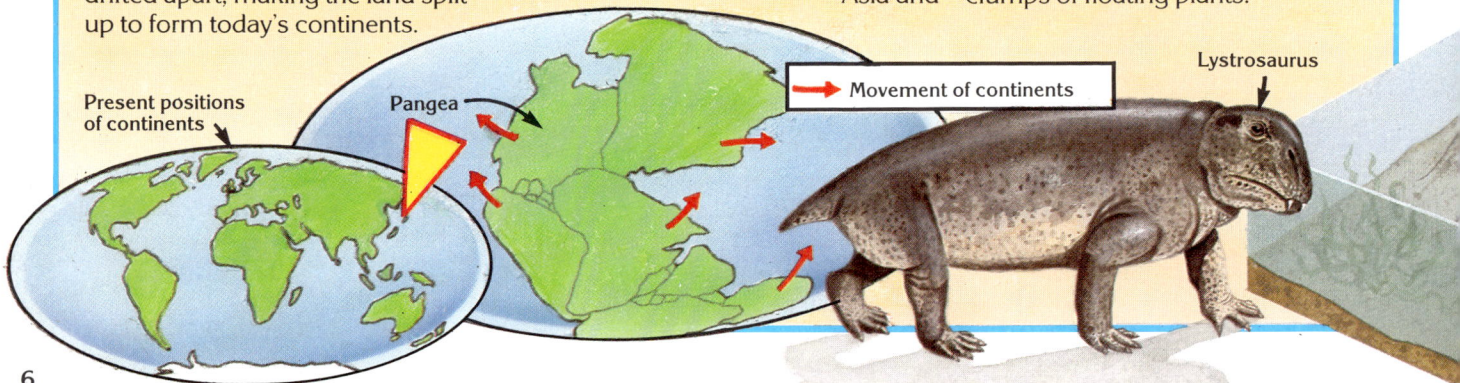

Present positions of continents

Pangea

Movement of continents

Lystrosaurus

## Hunting for fossils

Fossils are often found in rocks such as limestone, shale and slate. A good place to find them is where layers of rocks are exposed, for example where a new road is being built. Always ask permission before digging. You may also find fossils in the debris at the foot of a cliff. Differences in colour, shape and type of rocks are all clues to look for. To get the fossils out, you will need a geologist's pick and a chisel. You could record your discoveries in a notebook.

Belemnites

This is the part you usually find.

Crinoid or sea lily

Use a chisel to split a rock by inserting it along the grain of the rock.

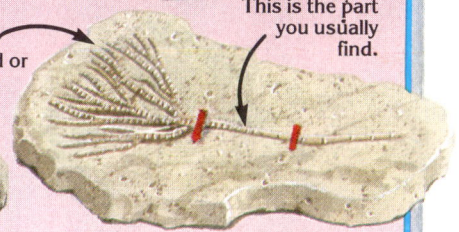

Rock

Some fossils you may find:

Ammonites

## The ever-changing Earth

About 4,600 million years ago, the Earth was covered with fiery volcanoes which sent out gases, molten rocks, and water vapour. A crust of rock formed as the surface cooled. Water vapour condensed and fell as rain, and shallow seas gradually covered the surface.

Over millions of years the Earth went through many stages. The first simple plant and animal life was found in the shallow seas.

When land appeared, simple plants were the first to live there. Later, when swamps covered much of the surface, the first animals came out onto the land. They had developed special limbs, and organs for breathing air.

Homo Erectus or "upright man" (may have developed into modern humans)

Ice Age

Small mammals

2 million years ago

Reptiles called dinosaurs (many were enormous)

65 million years ago

These animals and plants are not drawn to scale.

135 million years ago

The development of life on Earth

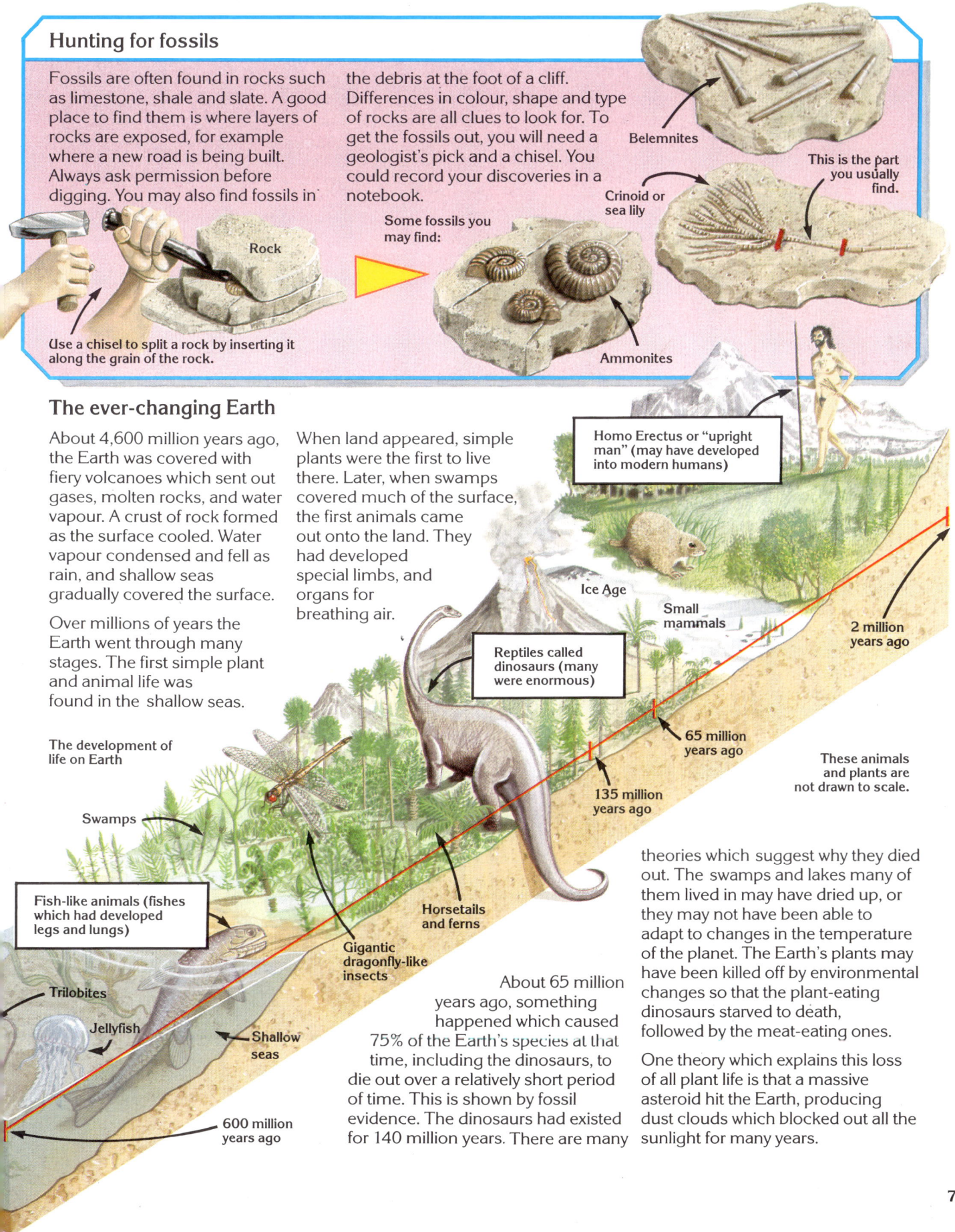

Swamps

Fish-like animals (fishes which had developed legs and lungs)

Horsetails and ferns

Gigantic dragonfly-like insects

Trilobites

Jellyfish

Shallow seas

600 million years ago

About 65 million years ago, something happened which caused 75% of the Earth's species at that time, including the dinosaurs, to die out over a relatively short period of time. This is shown by fossil evidence. The dinosaurs had existed for 140 million years. There are many theories which suggest why they died out. The swamps and lakes many of them lived in may have dried up, or they may not have been able to adapt to changes in the temperature of the planet. The Earth's plants may have been killed off by environmental changes so that the plant-eating dinosaurs starved to death, followed by the meat-eating ones.

One theory which explains this loss of all plant life is that a massive asteroid hit the Earth, producing dust clouds which blocked out all the sunlight for many years.

# The seas and oceans

Almost three-quarters of the Earth's surface is covered by vast oceans and smaller seas. They supply the Earth's atmosphere with water vapour which rises to form clouds (see pages 16-17). They also influence the weather and climates of the world because winds are warmed or cooled as they pass over them.

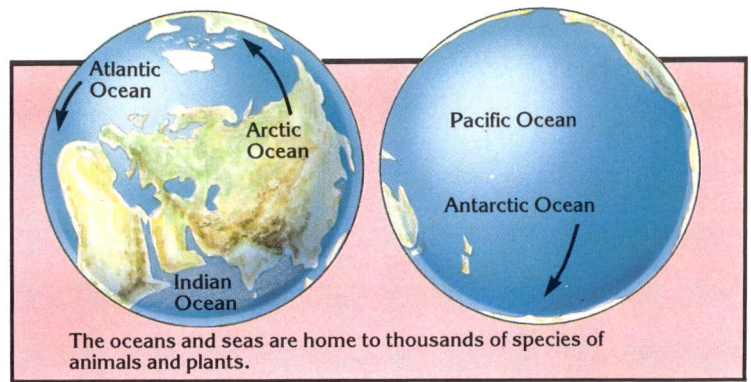

The oceans and seas are home to thousands of species of animals and plants.

The main ocean currents of the world

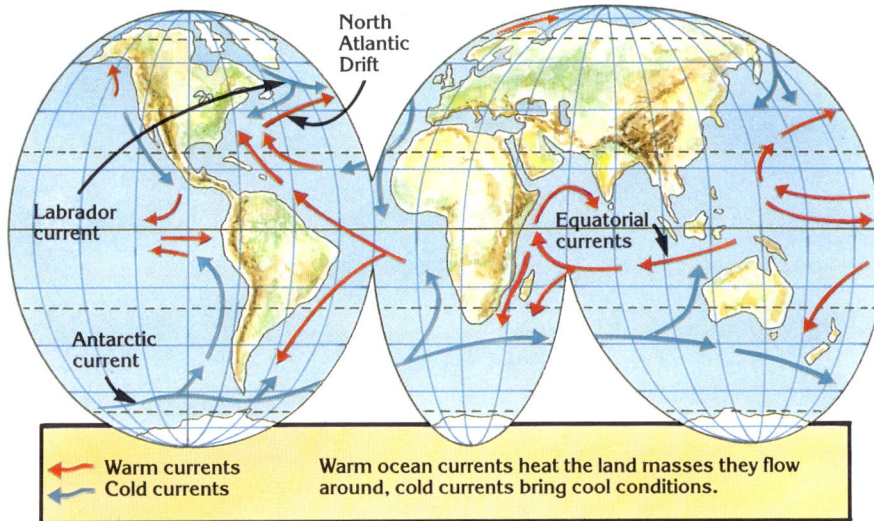

Warm ocean currents heat the land masses they flow around, cold currents bring cool conditions.

→ Warm currents
→ Cold currents

## Ocean currents

Ocean water travels around the world in currents. Surface currents form as the wind pushes the surface along. They follow the direction of the prevailing winds (the commonest winds which blow in an area). Warm currents flow near the surface where the Sun heats the water. Cold currents flow deep in the ocean, often moving in a different direction to surface currents.

All currents influence the climates of lands in their path. For example, Iceland lies in the flow of the North Atlantic Drift, or Gulf Stream, and is warmer in winter than places further south.

## The ocean floor

The ocean floor has many mountains, hills, valleys and deep trenches. Many of the ridges and trenches run along the boundaries of the continental plates.

The longest mountain range in the world, the Mid-Atlantic Ridge, lies in the Atlantic Ocean. Along the ridge, molten rock rises through cracks in the ocean floor and solidifies or hardens, as it meets the cold water.

Deep trenches in the ocean floor occur where one plate disappears below another. The deepest trench, the Mariana Trench in the Pacific Ocean, plunges 11,033m below sea level. If Mount Everest (8,843m) stood in the trench, its summit would still not reach up to the ocean floor.

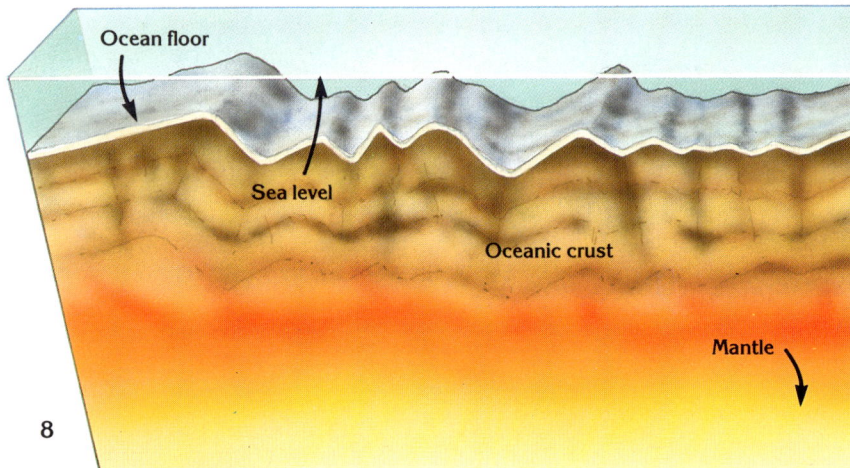

Ocean floor

Sea level

Oceanic crust

Mantle

## Tropical cyclones

Warm ocean currents can cause tropical cyclones (called hurricanes in America and typhoons in the Far East). These are fierce storms, with strong winds which form massive waves up to 25m high. The moist, warm air rises and cools, forming clouds.

Cooler air from the ocean surface rushes into the space left by the rising warm air and begins to spiral around. Wind speeds increase and land which lies in the cyclone's path is hit by the fierce storm.

Tropical cyclones can reach 320km per hour

## The frozen ocean

In the far north, ice covers much of the Arctic Ocean. When the water freezes, ice forms on the surface. As the wind blows, the ice moves and forms slabs, or floes. These join together to make a field of pack ice, hundreds of kilometres across.

Ships which travel in polar regions have reinforced hulls to cut a path through the ice.

## Volcanic islands

Underwater volcanoes are formed when molten rock rises to the surface through cracks in the oceanic crust and solidifies as it comes into contact with the cold, deep ocean water.

Where there are violent eruptions, large amounts of lava build up and the volcanoes appear above the surface as islands.

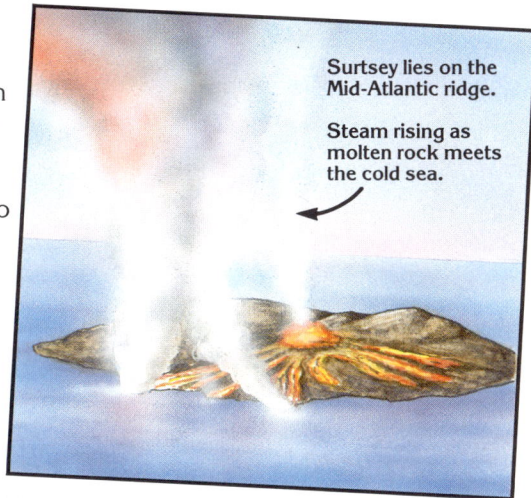

Surtsey lies on the Mid-Atlantic ridge.

Steam rising as molten rock meets the cold sea.

▲ Off the coast of Iceland, in 1963, fishermen thought they saw a boat on fire. It turned out to be eruptions from an underwater volcano. In just ten days, the volcano grew almost 200m above sea level, forming a new island which was named Surtsey.

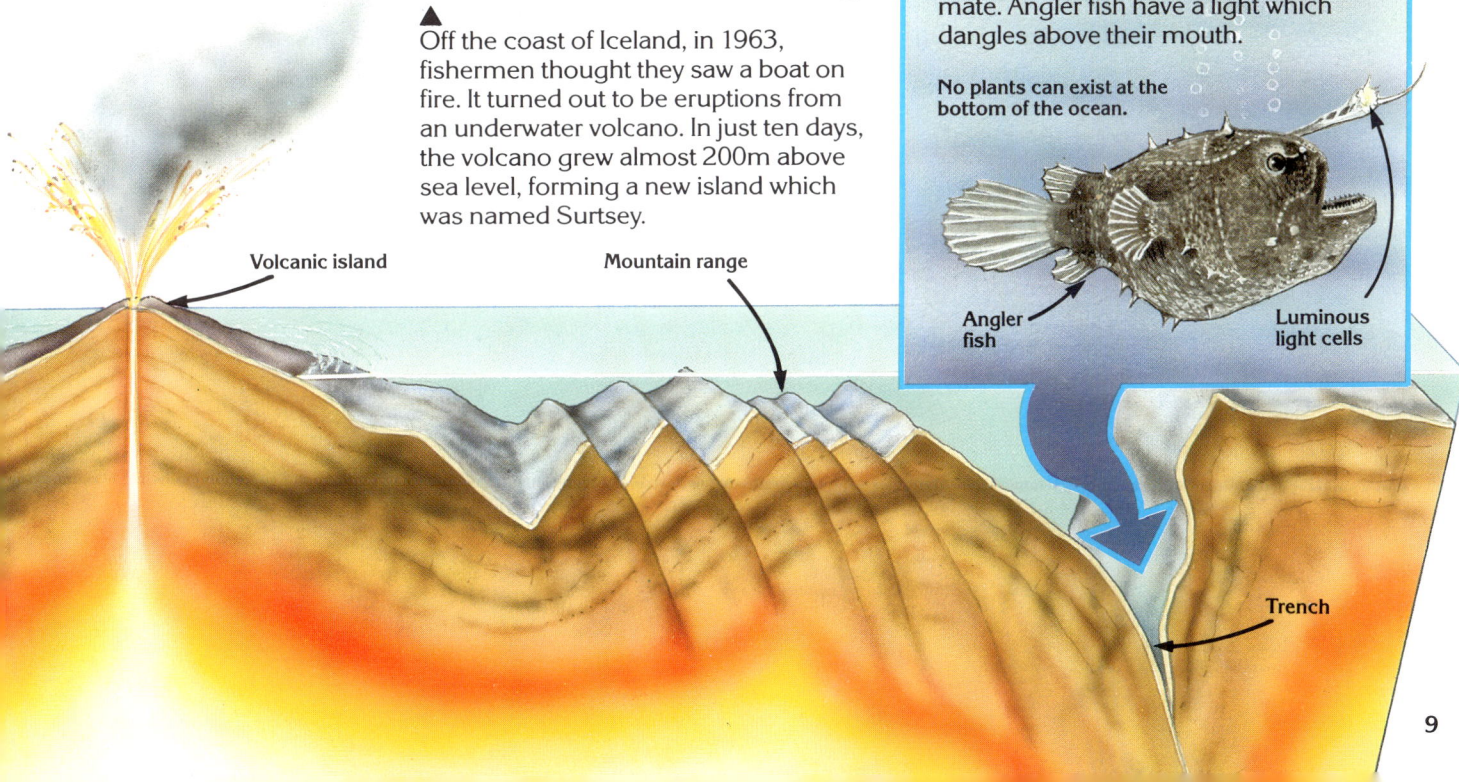

Volcanic island

Mountain range

## Life in the oceans

Sea water contains oxygen, which is vital for all the animals which live in the oceans. The oxygen comes from seaweeds and phytoplankton (tiny single-celled plants). Like all green plants, these use the Sun's energy to make food, producing oxygen.

Because they need sunlight, all plants live near the surface of the oceans, so most animals live there too, as there is plenty of oxygen and food.

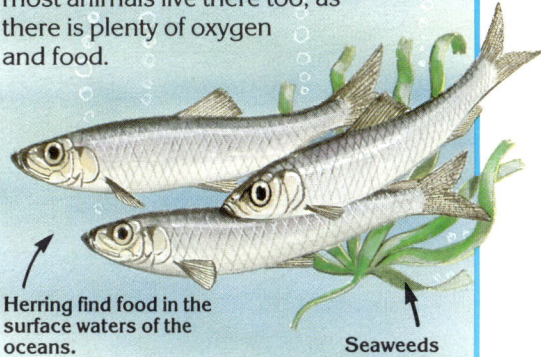

Herring find food in the surface waters of the oceans.

Seaweeds

No light from the surface reaches the depths of the oceans, so plants cannot live there. This means the deep water contains very little oxygen, so the animals which live there have special breathing systems. They feed on debris which falls from the water above.

Some fish have special light cells which they use to attract their prey or to find a mate. Angler fish have a light which dangles above their mouth.

No plants can exist at the bottom of the ocean.

Angler fish

Luminous light cells

Trench

# Earth movements and earthquakes

As the Earth's continental plates move together or apart, or slide sideways (see page 6), pressure, or stress, is exerted all across the layers of rocks which make up the plates. Although most rocks are hard, the pressure may cause them either to bend, making wave-like formations called folds, or to break, causing a line of weakness called a fault.

## Folds

Folds occur when pressure which builds up in the crust makes the rock crumple up. This may happen at the plate edges or further inside the plates. The crumpled rock may rise to form mountain ranges, such as the Himalayas and the Alps.

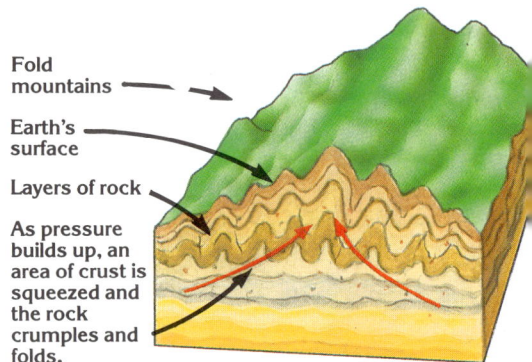

Fold mountains

Earth's surface

Layers of rock

As pressure builds up, an area of crust is squeezed and the rock crumples and folds.

## Faults

Faults are cracks, found throughout the crust. The major ones are found at plate boundaries. The main types are normal, reverse and tear faults.

Any movement of the plates has its greatest effect at faults because they are lines of weakness. If the pressure created by the movement is released suddenly, an earthquake may occur. San Francisco and Los Angeles both lie on the San Andreas fault, a tear fault in California.

Types of fault   A normal fault is created when tension builds up as the crust is pulled apart.

Fault

Fault

Tension

Areas either side slip downwards as faults appear.

Tear faults form as pieces of crust slide in opposite directions.

Fault

Reverse faults are created as the crust is squeezed, or compressed.

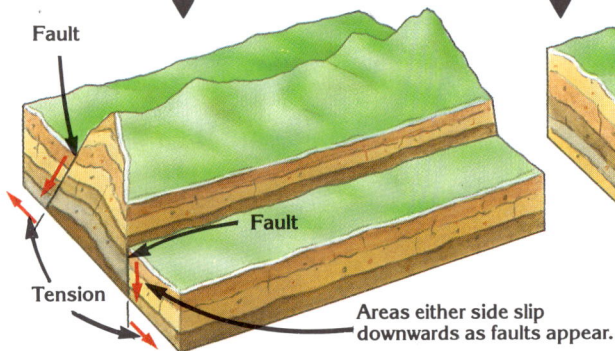

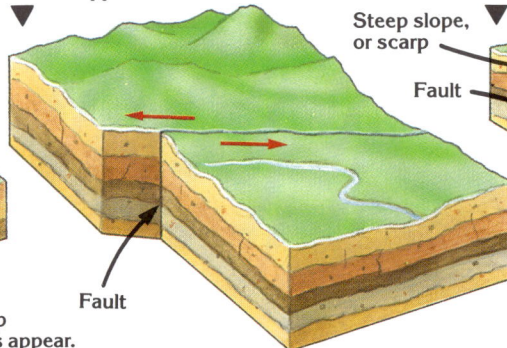

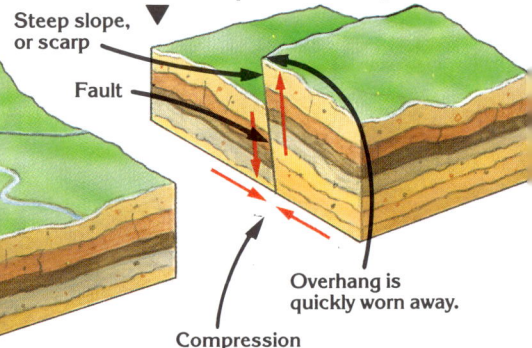

Steep slope, or scarp

Fault

Overhang is quickly worn away.

Compression

## Making a vibration detector

Earthquake vibrations are detected by special machines. You can make your own vibration detector to use around your home.

### What you will need

30cm hacksaw blade
4.5 volt battery
Small light bulb and holder
3x12cm lengths of single core wire (ask for help to strip 2cm at the ends)
Two pieces of wood (approx. 40cm x 10cm x 1cm and 4cm x 2cm x 1.5cm)
A screw
A drawing pin
Strong glue

### What to do

1. Stick the small block of wood to the larger piece, as shown.

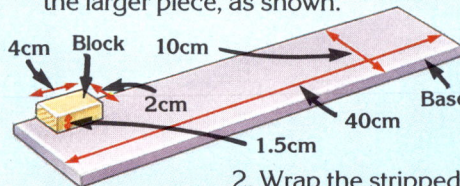

4cm   Block   10cm
2cm
40cm
1.5cm
Base

2. Wrap the stripped end of one wire around the screw, and screw one end of the hacksaw blade to the block.

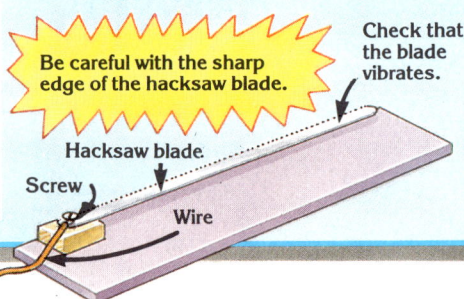

Be careful with the sharp edge of the hacksaw blade.

Check that the blade vibrates.

Hacksaw blade

Screw

Wire

3. Wrap one end of another wire around the drawing pin and push it into the base below the free end of the blade. Attach the other end of the wire to the bulb holder.

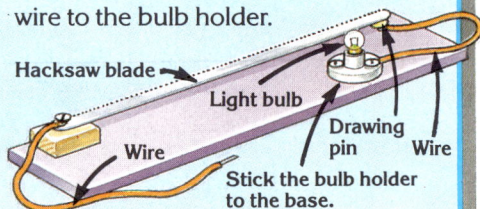

Hacksaw blade

Light bulb

Drawing pin   Wire

Wire

Stick the bulb holder to the base.

4. Attach the last wire to the bulb holder (second connection) and the two loose ends to the battery. When vibrations make the blade touch the pin, the bulb will light.

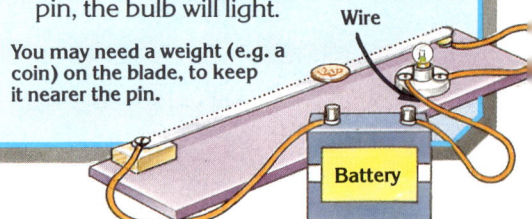

You may need a weight (e.g. a coin) on the blade, to keep it nearer the pin.

Wire

Battery

# Earthquakes

Earthquakes occur when there is a sudden release of pressure, for instance when plates slip suddenly. The point in the crust or upper mantle where this happens is called the focus. Vibrations, or shock waves, pass outwards through the rocks.

Earthquakes have most effect at the epicentre, the point on the surface directly above the focus. They are often followed by weaker aftershocks as the rocks resettle. The areas most likely to suffer are those which lie on plate boundaries.

Every year over 500,000 earthquakes take place, but only a few cause severe damage. It is hard to predict where or when they will occur, although there are some signs which may come before an earthquake, such as a series of small shocks.

## Measuring earthquakes

Seismologists (scientists who study Earth movements) use two different scales to measure earthquakes.

The Richter scale is based on the amount of energy produced at the focus. This is worked out using a seismometer, a device which measures surface vibrations. Each step up the Richter scale is about 30 times greater than the last.

The San Francisco earthquake of 1989 measured 7.1. It destroyed sections of the Bay Bridge and made the upper layer of an interstate road collapse.

The Mercalli scale is based on eyewitness observations (see below). The Armenian earthquake of 1988, which destroyed whole towns, rated 10.7 on the Mercalli scale.

### The Mercalli scale

1 Not felt.

2 Felt by a few people, and on upper floors of buildings.

3 Hanging objects swing.

4 Windows and objects rattle.

5 Liquids spill, objects fall over.

6 Felt by everyone. Pictures fall off walls, windows break.

7 Difficult to stand, buildings damaged.

8 Towers and chimneys collapse.

9 General panic, cracks appear in the ground.

10 Severe damage to buildings and bridges.

11 Railway lines bend, underground pipes break.

12 Nearly everything damaged, large areas of land slip and move.

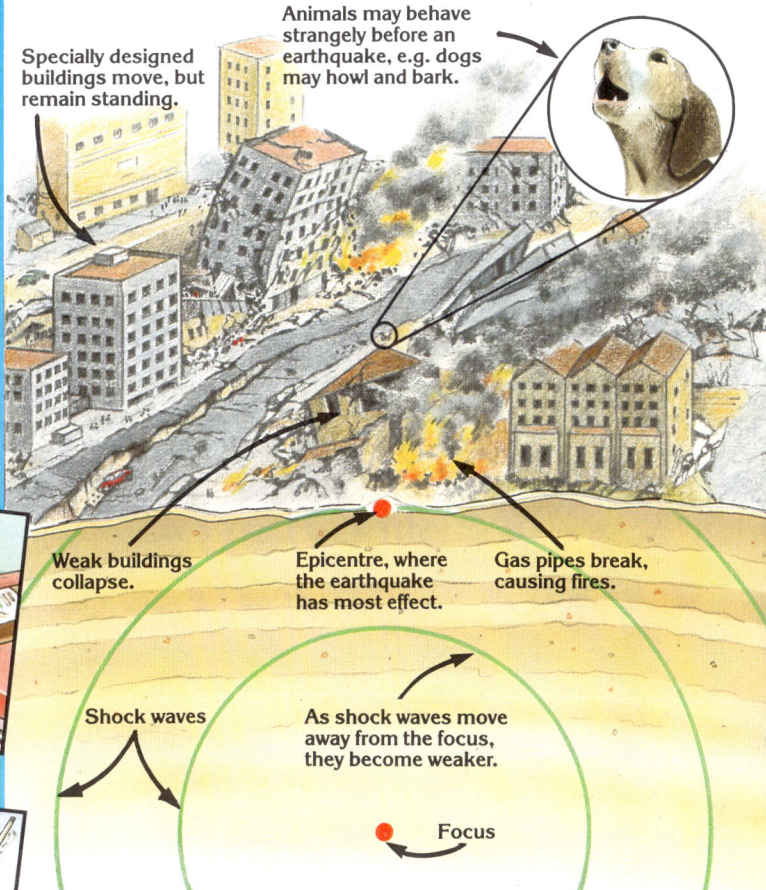

Animals may behave strangely before an earthquake, e.g. dogs may howl and bark.

Specially designed buildings move, but remain standing.

Weak buildings collapse.

Epicentre, where the earthquake has most effect.

Gas pipes break, causing fires.

Shock waves

As shock waves move away from the focus, they become weaker.

Focus

## Tsunamis

When an earthquake's focus is under the sea, the vibrations create waves called tsunamis. These are often known as tidal waves, but they are not caused by tides. By the time they reach land they may be many metres high and cause severe flooding.

Tsunamis can cross oceans, causing damage to areas thousands of kilometres away from an epicentre.

Tsunamis up to 30m high can crash onto coasts.

# Volcanoes

Volcanoes, like earthquakes, are usually found in areas near the boundaries of continental plates. When pressure builds up below the crust, magma (molten rock) and gas are forced up into weak areas.

The magma may cool and solidify in the crust, or it may break through onto the surface, where it is called lava. It may emerge through thin cracks, called fissures, or be forced out through a wider pipe, where it builds up to form a volcano.

Inside an erupting volcano

Steam, dust and gas rise into the upper atmosphere.

Volcanic blocks and bombs (rock fragments thrown out from the volcano)

Falling ash

If the vent is blocked by solidified lava, a secondary cone may form on the side of the volcano.

Crater

Vent (above ground level)

When magma cools below the surface, dykes or sills may be formed.

Dykes are formed in near-vertical cracks which cut across layers of rock, or strata.

Sills are sheet-like formations which lie along the strata.

The magma rises up the pipe and into the vent.

Pipe (below ground level)

Magma chamber

## The shape of volcanoes

The shape of a volcano depends on the type of lava, how far it flows and the strength of the eruption. Viscous lava is thick and sticky, and cools quickly around the vent, solidifying and building up steep-sided cones. Non-viscous lava is thin, runny lava. It may flow for several kilometres before it cools.

When an eruption stops, magma in the vent and crater solidifies, forming a plug. Live volcanoes may be active, erupting fairly frequently, or dormant, resting for a long time between eruptions. Dead, or extinct, volcanoes will not erupt again.

Shield volcanoes are formed from non-viscous lava. They are low and flat.

Alternate layers of viscous lava and ash form steep-sided cones, called composite volcanoes.

## Types of eruptions

When pressure builds below the crust, gas and magma explode through the pipe and vent of a volcano. This throws out dust, ash and rocks. Sometimes an eruption will be so violent that the whole volcano blows up, leaving a large crater called a caldera.

Not all eruptions are violent. When the lava is runny, gases escape easily and the lava flows or spurts from the vent.

Shield volcanoes in Hawaii produce spurting fountains of runny lava.

The gases in viscous magma escape with force, causing an explosion in the chamber or pipe. Ash is thrown high into the air.

## Predicting volcanic eruptions

It is difficult to predict when an eruption will occur, as each one is different. In the past, certain signs have been noted, such as bulges appearing on the side of a volcano, but nowadays more accurate predictions are possible. Scientists use satellites to detect "hotspots" below the surface.

## Hot springs, geysers and fumaroles

In areas of volcanic activity, hot zones of the mantle lie relatively near the surface. Water in the ground is heated by the surrounding hot rocks. It bubbles up through cracks, forming hot springs.

Geysers are springs which send out jets of steam and water under pressure. Volcanic gases are given off from vents in the ground called fumaroles.

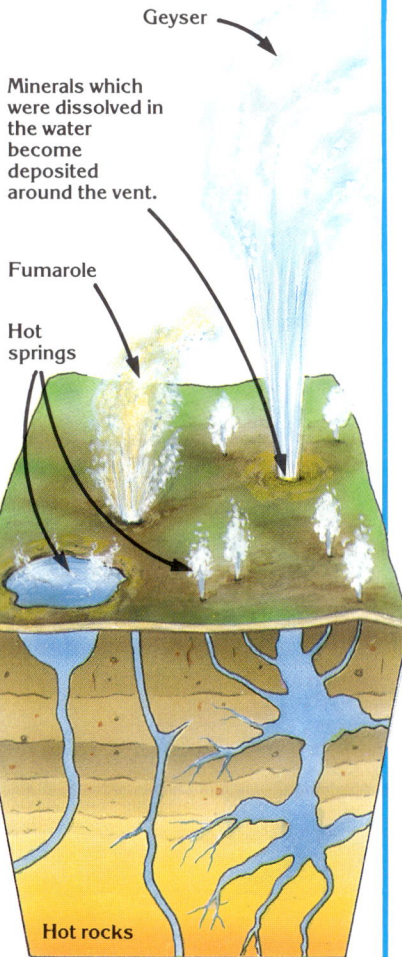

Geyser

Minerals which were dissolved in the water become deposited around the vent.

Fumarole

Hot springs

Hot rocks

## Vesuvius

In AD79, Vesuvius, a volcano in Italy, suddenly erupted. Hot ash and poisonous gas spread over nearby towns and cities. One city, Pompeii, lay under 6m of volcanic ash until it was discovered in 1711. The ash had protected the city, preserving the buildings and leaving things exactly as they had been when Vesuvius erupted. Vesuvius has erupted many times since then, but not as violently as in AD79.

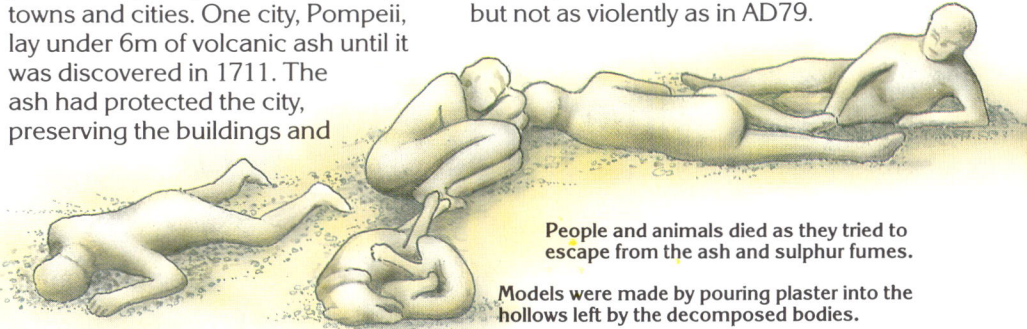

People and animals died as they tried to escape from the ash and sulphur fumes.

Models were made by pouring plaster into the hollows left by the decomposed bodies.

## Benefits from volcanoes

Rocks which come from volcanoes are known as igneous rocks (see page 20). Many contain valuable ores and minerals, such as diamonds, gold and copper. Despite the constant threat of eruptions, many people use the fertile soil on the slopes of volcanoes for farming.

## Making a model volcano

To make a model volcano which will erupt safely, you will need bicarbonate of soda (sodium bicarbonate), washing-up liquid, three tablespoons of vinegar, red food colouring, a test tube or some other tube-like container, cotton wool and sand or fine soil.

### What to do

1. Place a teaspoonful of bicarbonate in the tube. Add warm water so that it is a third full. Shake the mixture thoroughly.

Place your thumb over the end when you shake the mixture.

Test tube

2. Add five drops of washing-up liquid and three drops of food colouring (to make your 'lava' look real). Mix the liquid.

Put some cotton wool in the neck of the tube.

3. Using the sand or soil, build a volcano round the tube, until it is level with the top.

The plug stops the sand getting into the mixture.

Sand or soil

Foam 'lava'

4. Remove the plug and pour in the vinegar from a small container. The new mixture will fizz up and out, like lava bubbling from a volcano.

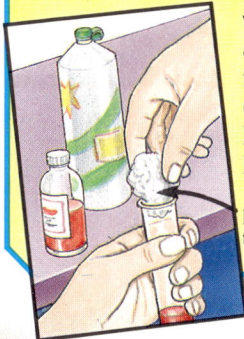

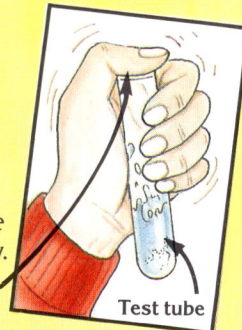

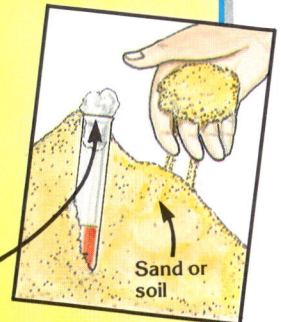

# The Earth's atmosphere

The atmosphere is a mixture of gases which surrounds the planet, stretching from the surface to over 900km into space. It protects the Earth from the harmful rays of the Sun and also contains the gases vital to all living things. The atmosphere traps heat from the Sun, warming up the air near the surface and creating the weather.

## The composition of the atmosphere

The main gases which make up the Earth's atmosphere are nitrogen (78%) and oxygen (21%). There are also traces of carbon dioxide and other gases. Water exists in the atmosphere as water vapour, as droplets in clouds and as ice crystals.

## The layers of the atmosphere

The atmosphere is divided into layers (though there are no sharp boundaries). The temperature changes through the layers (see below – read up from the bottom).

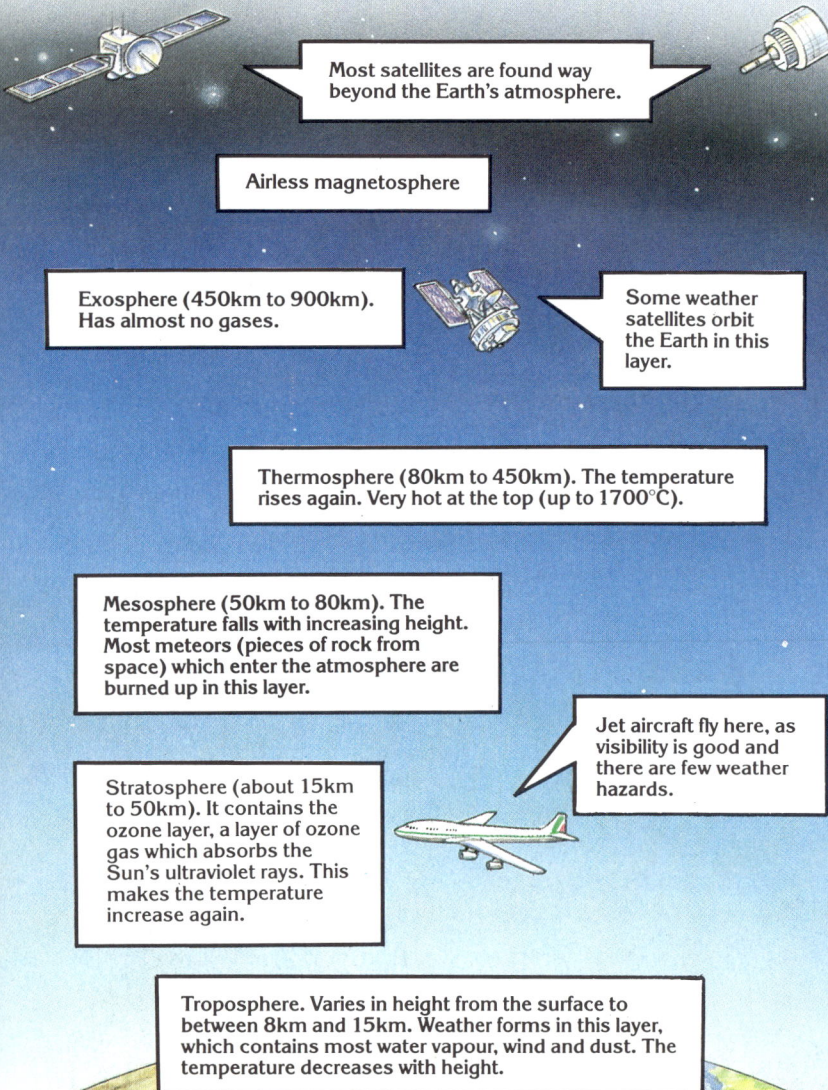

Most satellites are found way beyond the Earth's atmosphere.

Airless magnetosphere

Exosphere (450km to 900km). Has almost no gases.

Some weather satellites orbit the Earth in this layer.

Thermosphere (80km to 450km). The temperature rises again. Very hot at the top (up to 1700°C).

Mesosphere (50km to 80km). The temperature falls with increasing height. Most meteors (pieces of rock from space) which enter the atmosphere are burned up in this layer.

Jet aircraft fly here, as visibility is good and there are few weather hazards.

Stratosphere (about 15km to 50km). It contains the ozone layer, a layer of ozone gas which absorbs the Sun's ultraviolet rays. This makes the temperature increase again.

Troposphere. Varies in height from the surface to between 8km and 15km. Weather forms in this layer, which contains most water vapour, wind and dust. The temperature decreases with height.

## Air pressure

Although you cannot feel it, the layers of the atmosphere exert a force, or pressure, on the Earth's surface. Air pressure is greatest on the surface and decreases as you rise through the layers. It is affected by the temperature of the land or sea, so places at the same height do not always have the same pressure. Low pressure often brings wet weather, and high pressure is linked with fine weather.

## Making a model barometer

Air pressure is measured on a barometer. To make a model barometer which shows changes in air pressure, you will need a wide-mouthed jar, a balloon, a drinking straw, an elastic band and some card.

**What to do**

1. Cut the neck off the ▶ balloon and stretch the balloon over the mouth of the jar, so that it is taut.

Fix the balloon in place with the rubber band.

2. Cut one end of the straw to make a point. Fix the other end to the middle of the stretched balloon using some sticky ▶ tape.

Straw pointer

Make sure the straw is horizontal and that it is touching the balloon.

Sticky tape

3. Place the card behind the jar so that the pointer is touching the card, and mark the position of the pointer. Draw a scale above and below this mark. Tape the card to the jar, with the mark in line with the pointer.

▼

As the air pressure rises, the extra pushing force will push down on the balloon, and the pointer will move up the scale.

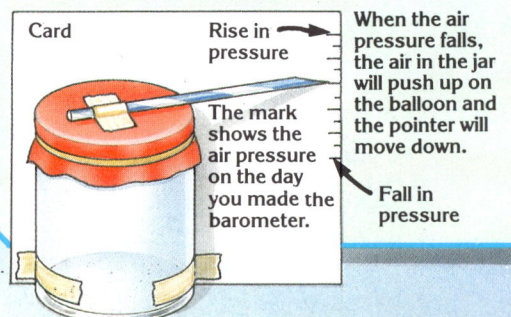

Card

Rise in pressure

The mark shows the air pressure on the day you made the barometer.

Fall in pressure

When the air pressure falls, the air in the jar will push up on the balloon and the pointer will move down.

## Movement of air in the atmosphere

Differences in temperature and pressure cause the air in the lower layers of the atmosphere to move, forming the world's winds. They blow from areas of high pressure towards low pressure areas. In many places there are local winds, caused by differences between the temperature of the land and sea. High mountains also affect local winds.

The main pressure belts and winds of the Earth

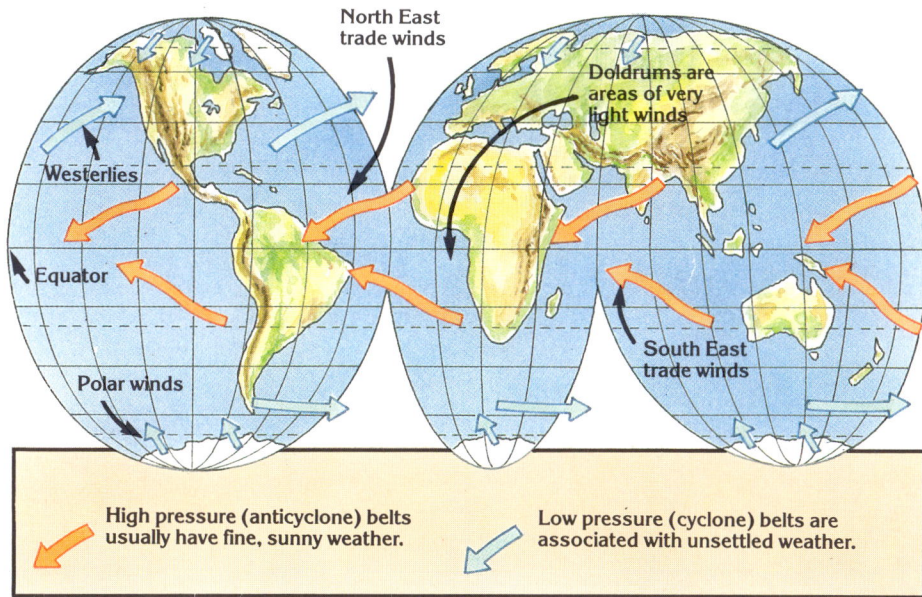

North East trade winds

Doldrums are areas of very light winds

Westerlies

Equator

Polar winds

South East trade winds

High pressure (anticyclone) belts usually have fine, sunny weather.

Low pressure (cyclone) belts are associated with unsettled weather.

## The greenhouse effect

Heat energy from the Sun is trapped by carbon dioxide and other gases in the atmosphere. This process is called the greenhouse effect because it occurs in much the same way as glass traps heat in a greenhouse.

The amount of carbon dioxide in the atmosphere is increasing as fossil fuels (see pages 38-39) are burnt. World temperatures are rising as more heat is trapped. This is known as global warming.

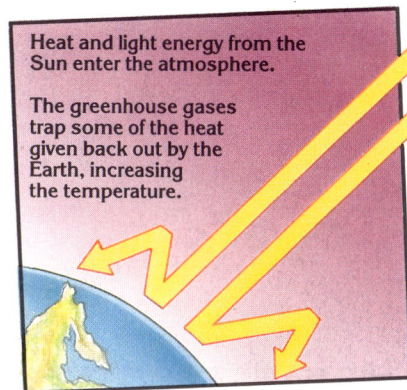

Heat and light energy from the Sun enter the atmosphere.

The greenhouse gases trap some of the heat given back out by the Earth, increasing the temperature.

## Ozone in the atmosphere

The ozone layer is found in the stratosphere. It is a layer of ozone gas which absorbs much of the Sun's ultraviolet radiation, preventing it from reaching the Earth.

Scientists have found that gases called CFCs (chlorofluorocarbons), destroy ozone gas. They are used in some aerosol cans and refrigerators. Holes have been discovered in the ozone layer above the Arctic and Antarctica. These may increase the amount of ultraviolet radiation which reaches the Earth.

Surface ozone is produced in the lower atmosphere, by a chemical reaction between sunlight and the exhaust fumes from cars. Normally it disperses through the atmosphere, but if a layer of cold air is trapped beneath warm air, it becomes concentrated and causes photochemical smog. Unfortunately, surface ozone cannot replace holes in the higher ozone layer.

Photographs taken from satellites show the hole in the ozone layer above Antarctica.

The size of the hole changes, but scientists think it is growing.

Efforts are being made to control the exhaust fumes from cars.

Air pollution has decreased since smokeless fuels were introduced in cities.

Photochemical smog causes eye irritations and some people find breathing difficult.

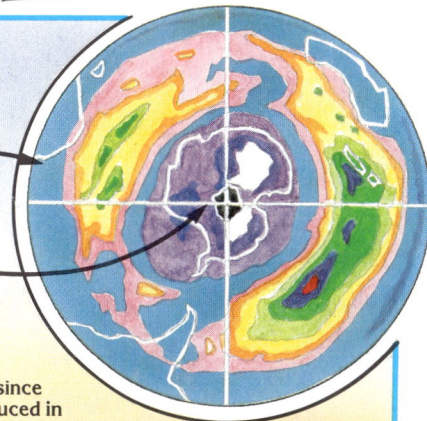

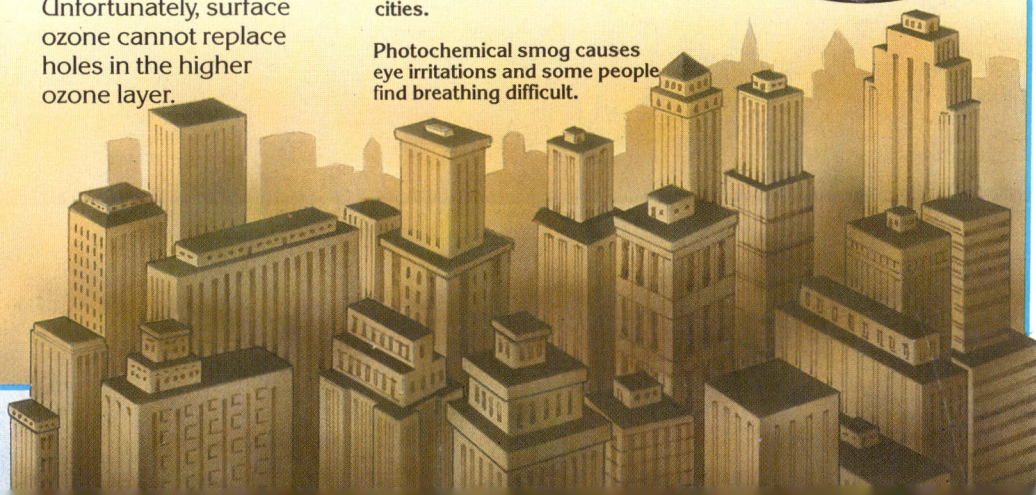

15

# Weather

Weather is the daily condition of the atmosphere at a particular place at any one time. It changes from day to day and from place to place and is a combination of temperature, precipitation (rain, snow, sleet or hail), humidity (the amount of water vapour in the air), wind and sunshine. Winds are important as they help to circulate the air in the atmosphere around the world (see page 15).

## The seasons

The seasons are caused by the amount of heat and light energy the Earth receives from the Sun. The seasons change due to the way parts of the Earth receive direct sunshine at different times of the year. The Earth is tilted at an angle, and as it orbits the Sun, a different half, or hemisphere, gradually receives more direct sunlight. It is summer in the hemisphere which receives most sunlight and winter in the other. Areas near the equator have no real variations in the seasons. This is because the Sun is almost directly overhead throughout the year.

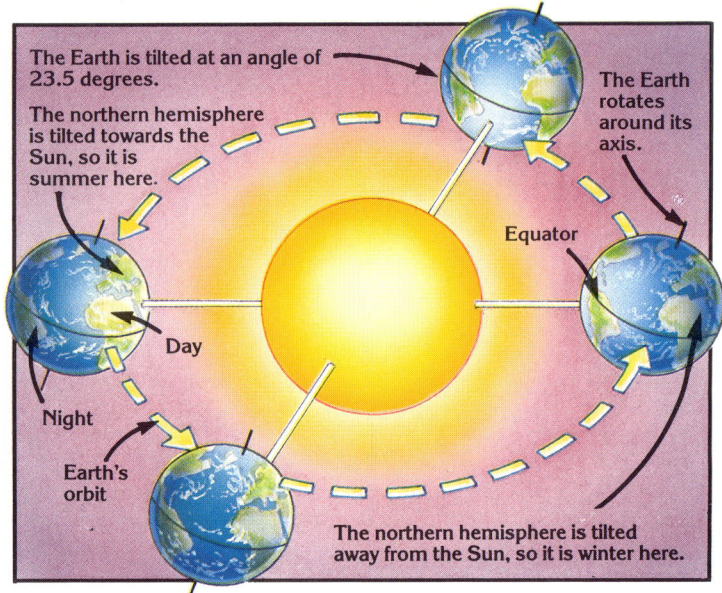

The Earth is tilted at an angle of 23.5 degrees.

The northern hemisphere is tilted towards the Sun, so it is summer here.

The Earth rotates around its axis.

Equator

Day

Night

Earth's orbit

The northern hemisphere is tilted away from the Sun, so it is winter here.

## Making a rain detector

To make a detector that will buzz when it rains, you will need some kitchen foil, a clothes peg, a sugar lump, a buzzer, a 4.5 volt battery and 220cm of single core wire cut into 2 x 1m and 1 x 20cm pieces (with 2cm stripped at each end).

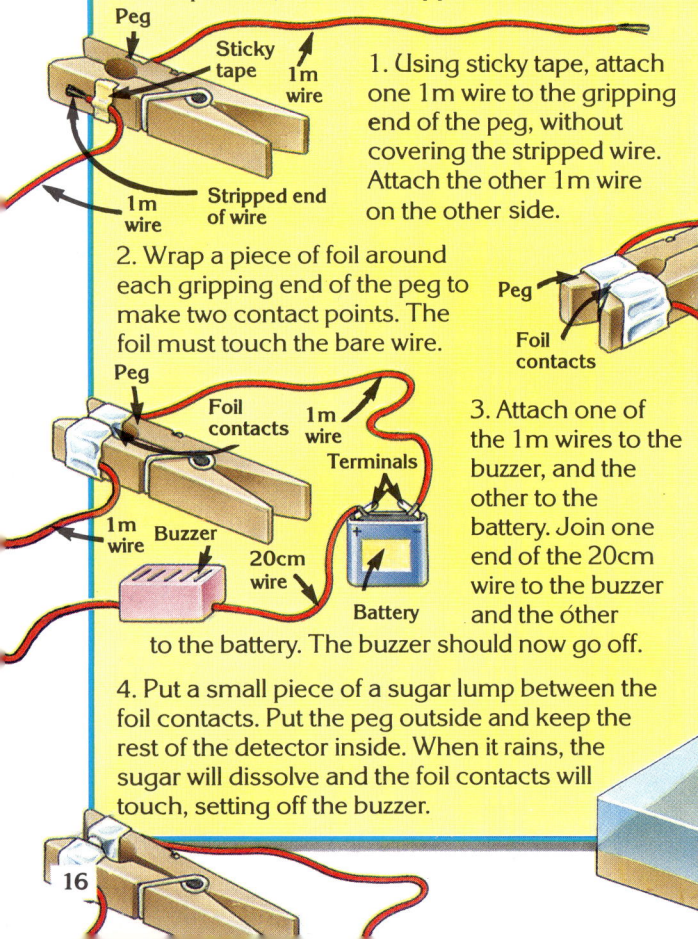

Peg
Sticky tape
1m wire
1m wire
Stripped end of wire

1. Using sticky tape, attach one 1m wire to the gripping end of the peg, without covering the stripped wire. Attach the other 1m wire on the other side.

2. Wrap a piece of foil around each gripping end of the peg to make two contact points. The foil must touch the bare wire.

Peg
Foil contacts

Peg
Foil contacts
1m wire
Terminals
1m wire
Buzzer
20cm wire
Battery

3. Attach one of the 1m wires to the buzzer, and the other to the battery. Join one end of the 20cm wire to the buzzer and the other to the battery. The buzzer should now go off.

4. Put a small piece of a sugar lump between the foil contacts. Put the peg outside and keep the rest of the detector inside. When it rains, the sugar will dissolve and the foil contacts will touch, setting off the buzzer.

## The water cycle

When water is heated by the Sun, some of it evaporates. This means it changes into water vapour, which rises and mixes with other gases in the atmosphere. When moist air rises, it cools and the vapour condenses (changes back into a liquid), forming tiny droplets which join to make clouds.

Depending on the air conditions, the water returns to the ground as rain, snow or hail. Snow forms at low temperatures, when tiny ice crystals join together.

Water falls to ground as rain, hail, sleet or snow.

Clouds rise and cool further. Water droplets get bigger.

Water soaks into soil and becomes ground water (see page 28), or runs across surface and into rivers, lakes and sea.

Water evaporates from surface of sea, rivers, lakes and land, and from plants.

Moist air rises and cools. Water vapour condenses to form clouds.

## Clouds

Clouds are found at all levels in the troposphere (see page 14). Their shape, colour and height give clues as to what kind of weather can be expected during the following hours or days. The main types of clouds are cirrus, cumulus and stratus. Not all clouds produce rain, or other forms of precipitation. If clouds move to a warmer area, the water vapour evaporates again.

Cirrus are high level clouds made from ice crystals.

Cumulus clouds may form puffy, fair weather clouds.

Stratus clouds form a thick, low level blanket of cloud, associated with light rain or drizzle.

## Thunder and lightning

Thunderstorms occur when warm, moist air rises rapidly, forming tall clouds called cumulonimbus. Thunder and lightning are caused by a build-up of different electrical charges within these clouds. Once the charge at the base of the cloud gets to a certain strength, electricity is released as lightning.

Lightning heats the air it travels through and waves of air push outwards. They travel faster than the speed of sound, creating a sonic boom (like a supersonic aeroplane as it passes). This is thunder. Lightning tends to strike a high point, such as an isolated tree or a tall building.

Cumulonimbus cloud

A flash of lightning is actually made up of a number of downward and upward strokes, all occurring within a fraction of a second.

The leader stroke zigzags towards the ground, creating a path of charged air.

The main, return stroke leaps upwards from the ground, along this path. This stroke produces the clap of thunder.

More downward and upward strokes follow.

## Hail

Hailstones are small pellets of ice, formed when currents of air lift falling raindrops back to the top of a cloud. The raindrops freeze and receive several coatings of ice as they are carried up and down in the cloud by random air currents. They finally fall as hailstones.

How hailstones are formed

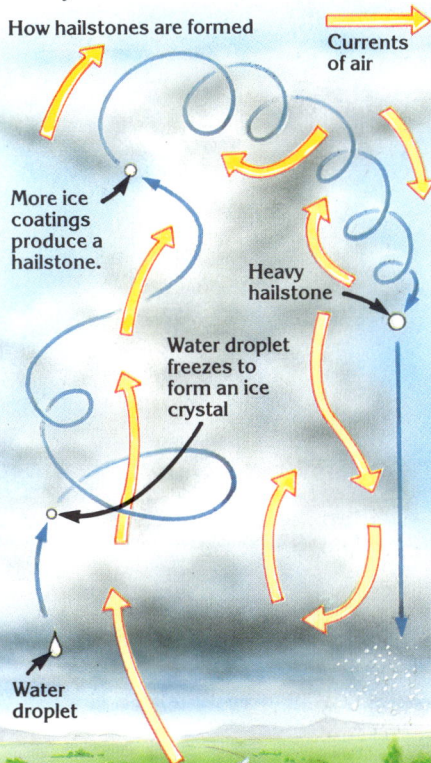

Currents of air

More ice coatings produce a hailstone.

Heavy hailstone

Water droplet freezes to form an ice crystal

Water droplet

## Weather hazards

Some types of weather may be very destructive. For instance, unusual amounts of rainfall may result in flooding or droughts. Severe droughts and famine have been experienced in Africa, when seasonal rainfall amounts were low and crops failed.

Floods caused by heavy rain often coincide with gales and high tides. Tropical cyclones (see page 8) cause severe damage, particularly at coasts.

Tornadoes are twisting whirlwinds, formed over land by hot air rising rapidly.

Tornadoes travel across the land, lifting and destroying anything in their path, including trees and cars.

# Climates

The climate of an area is the pattern of weather conditions experienced in that area over many years. One type of climate may affect a vast region or a small, local area, where it is called a microclimate.

Climates are affected by the distance from the sea, the altitude (height above sea level) and winds. The climate of an area determines the type of plants and animals found there. It also affects the lifestyle of the people.

## Energy from the Sun

Most heat reaches the Earth's surface at the equator, where the Sun is directly overhead. The poles are much colder because the heat is spread over a greater area. The amount of energy any area of the Earth's surface receives from the Sun is called its insolation. Uneven heating of the surface causes movement of air and water vapour throughout the world, forming different climates.

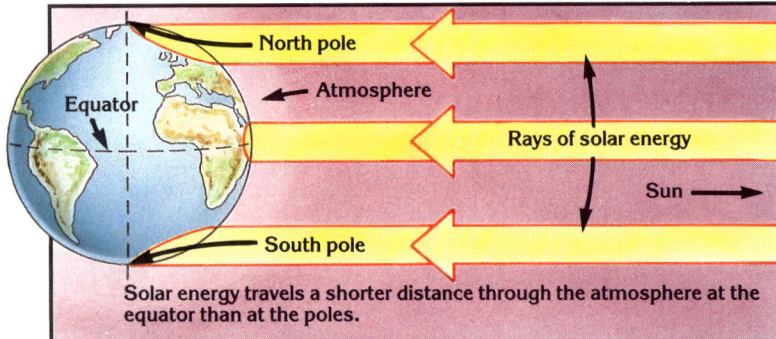

North pole

Atmosphere

Equator

Rays of solar energy

Sun

South pole

Solar energy travels a shorter distance through the atmosphere at the equator than at the poles.

## The influence of oceans and seas

Ocean currents influence the climate of any land they pass (see page 8). During the day and at night, the land and sea gain and lose heat at different rates. This makes the air above them move, forming a coastal, or maritime, climate.

The movement of air at the coast

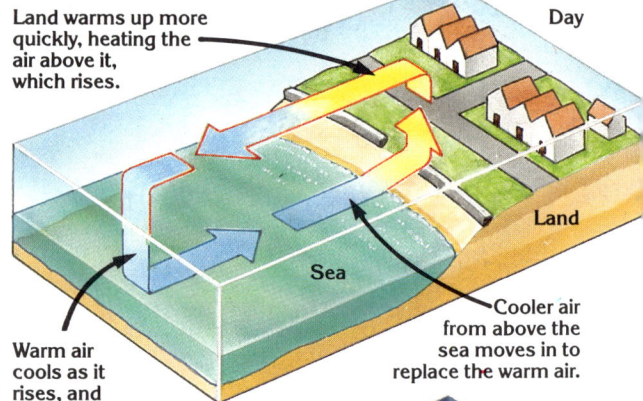

Land warms up more quickly, heating the air above it, which rises.

Day

Land

Sea

Cooler air from above the sea moves in to replace the warm air.

Warm air cools as it rises, and sinks again.

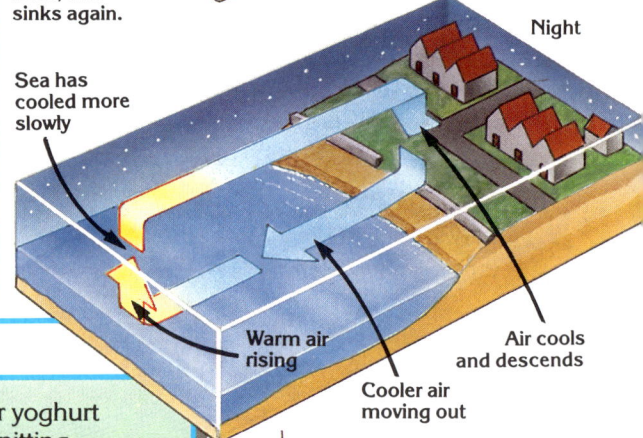

Night

Sea has cooled more slowly

Warm air rising

Cooler air moving out

Air cools and descends

## Observing wind speeds

The wind affects the climate of an area. Its speed is measured on an instrument called an anemometer. To make a model anemometer you will need 3 plastic cups or yoghurt pots of the same size, 3 knitting needles, a large cork, a long nail, 2 washers and a pole.

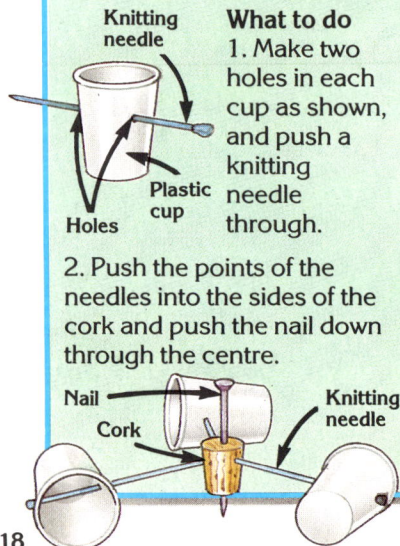

Knitting needle

Plastic cup

Holes

**What to do**
1. Make two holes in each cup as shown, and push a knitting needle through.

2. Push the points of the needles into the sides of the cork and push the nail down through the centre.

3. Place the washers on the pole, and hammer the nail down through them.

4. On different days, record the number of times the cups spin round in a set time, e.g. 15 seconds. Find out the wind speed from a weather report and make your own wind speed scale.

Loosen the nail if the cork will not turn freely.

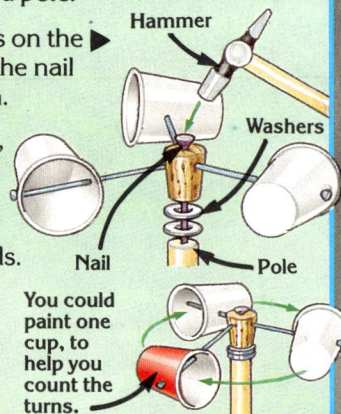

Hammer

Washers

Nail

Pole

You could paint one cup, to help you count the turns.

Nail

Cork

Knitting needle

No. of turns

Wind speed

## Urban climates

Cities tend to be warmer than the area surrounding them. This is because concrete absorbs more heat than vegetation and retains it longer, making the nights warmer.

The ground beneath a city tends to be drier, as roads and pavements stop water draining into the soil.

## Mountain climates

On a mountain, temperatures decrease with altitude, giving different climates and vegetation at different heights. Trees cannot survive on high mountain slopes because there is little soil, which is often covered with snow, and there are frequent high winds. The direction a mountain side or valley faces (its aspect) also affects the climate. One side of a mountain may receive more sunlight than the other, which is nearly always in shadow.

**Lichens**

**Coniferous forest**

**Tree line**

**Different kinds of plants grow at different heights**

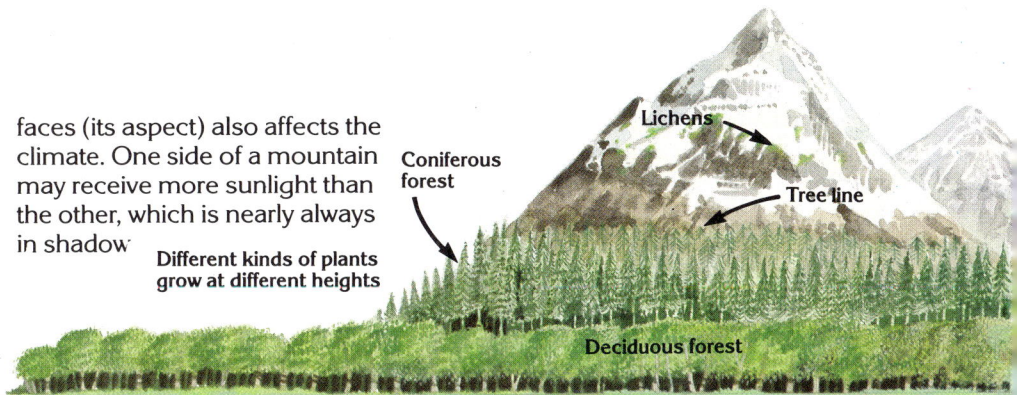

**Deciduous forest**

## Climates of the world

The different climates of the world determine the species of plants and animals found in different areas.

Climates also influence the way people live, their homes and their clothes. Where there are mountains in an area, the lower temperature high up will affect the climate and the types of living things found there.

**Major climates of the world**

### Tundra

Winter temperatures low, averaging from -30°C to -20°C in coldest months. Low rainfall. Rise in temperatures in summer months, may even reach 17°C.

Snow in winter covers low-growing plants, such as lichens.

### Polar

Extremely low temperatures with little rain or snowfall, making these icy areas frozen deserts. Animals depend on sea for food, so most wildlife found around coasts.

Animals are insulated by a layer of fat or thick fur.

### Temperate

Seasonal variation in temperature, with rainfall throughout year. Temperature range generally between -6°C and 25°C. Coastal areas greatly influenced by sea. Winds cause day-to-day weather changes.

Deciduous trees lose their leaves in autumn when temperatures fall below 10°C, the minimum temperature needed for growing.

### Tropical grasslands

Warm throughout year. Dry and wet seasons alternate, often with droughts during dry season. Temperatures between 21°C and 30°C. Scattered trees, with grasses over 1m high, which die in dry season.

Animals in the grasslands feed on trees as well as grasses.

### Deserts

Very low rainfall, less than 250mm a year. Daytime temperatures in hot deserts may exceed 38°C. Not all deserts are hot — some are cooler in winter, or even frozen (see polar climate, above). Living things have adapted to life with little water.

Tuareg herdsmen of the Sahara wear loose clothes to protect them from the Sun and sandstorms.

### Equatorial

Hot and wet all year round. High temperatures, never below 17°C. Climate provides ideal growing conditions for plants. Great variety of plant and animal species.

Cutting down and burning equatorial rain forests may be affecting world climates.

# Rocks and minerals

The Earth's crust consists of layers of rock which have been formed over millions of years. The rocks on the surface are constantly shaped and worn away by water, ice and the wind, and by movements of the Earth's crust. There are three main types of rock, called igneous, sedimentary and metamorphic rock. Their formation and composition affect the relief, or landscape, of an area. They have an economic value as they contain fuels and precious minerals, and provide materials for building.

## Minerals

All rocks are made of substances called minerals which vary in shape, size and colour. Most are made from a mixture of chemical elements, such as carbon, iron or silicon. Many rocks are made from several minerals, for example granite, which contains quartz, feldspar and mica.

Minerals may form regular, geometric shapes called crystals, for instance when molten rock solidifies or a liquid evaporates.

Diamonds are minerals of pure carbon, formed in an igneous rock called kimberlite in the upper mantle, under great heat and pressure.

## Growing a crystal

Rocks are made up of many minerals and crystals of different shapes and colours. Below is an experiment with crystals which shows how they grow in size as liquid evaporates. Copper sulphate (from a chemist) is best to use.

Copper sulphate

**Take care with copper sulphate, as it is mildly poisonous.**

1. Pour 200ml of warm water into a jar. Add some copper sulphate and stir to dissolve it. Keep on adding until no more will dissolve (it sinks to the bottom).

Warm water

Jar

2. Pour the solution into a clean jar, leaving behind the undissolved crystals in a small amount of solution. Let this evaporate, then choose a large crystal and tie some thread around it.

Crystal

3. Tie the thread around a pencil. Place this across the top of the second jar so that the crystal is suspended in the solution.

Jar — Pencil
Thread — Copper sulphate solution

4. Leave in a warm place. Your crystal will grow as the solution evaporates.

## Igneous rock

Igneous rock is formed when magma from the mantle rises, cools and solidifies. If it reaches the surface, the landform created, such as a volcano, is called an extrusive landform. If it cools inside the crust, the landform, such as a dyke or sill, is called an intrusive landform. In time, as the overlying rock is worn away, intrusive landforms may appear on the surface.

Igneous rock contains closely-packed crystals, formed as the magma cools. Large crystals are found in rocks such as granite, which forms when magma cools slowly below the surface. If it cools quickly, minute crystals are formed, making rock such as obsidian.

When a vast amount of magma rises and cools within the Earth's crust, it may form a massive intrusive landform called a batholith.

Batholiths, often made of granite, may be exposed after the Earth's surface has been eroded away.

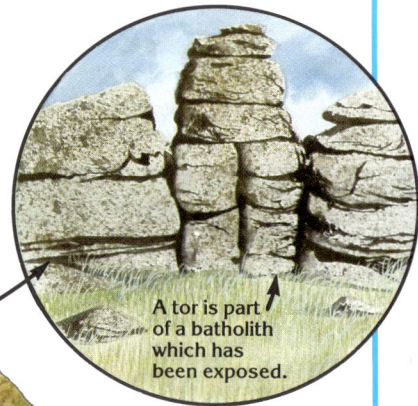

A tor is part of a batholith which has been exposed.

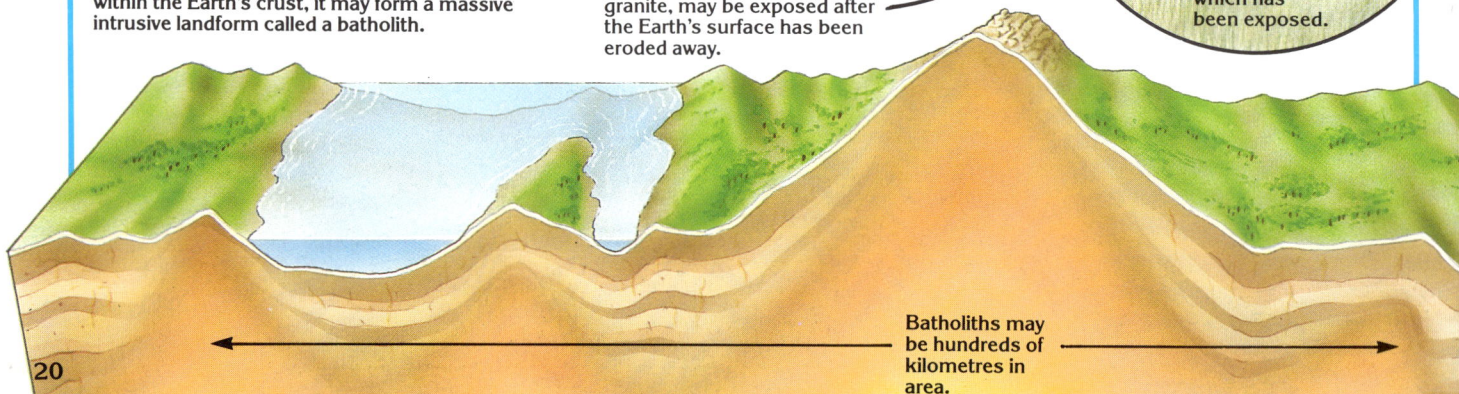

Batholiths may be hundreds of kilometres in area.

## Sedimentary rock

Sediments are materials which have collected together as a result of natural processes. For example, when a rock is worn away by water, wind or ice, the particles may be carried away and deposited elsewhere, forming a sediment.

Sedimentary rock is formed from sediments. Layers of sediment gradually build up until the bottom layers are squeezed and cemented together, forming a layer of rock called a stratum. This process often continues, producing many layers of rock.

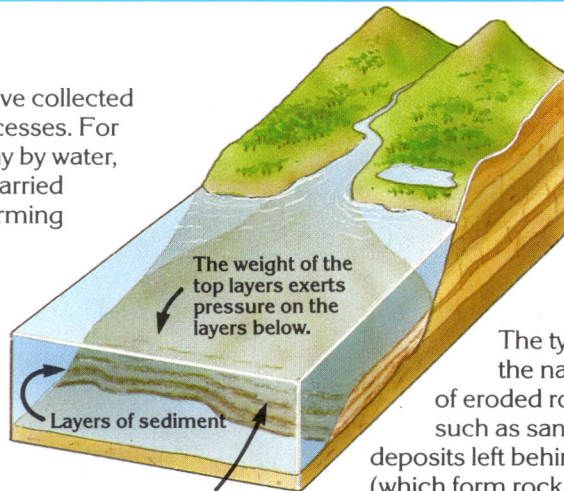

The weight of the top layers exerts pressure on the layers below.

Layers of sediment

The pressure squeezes the particles and they are cemented together, forming new rock.

Shells can be found in some limestone.

The type of rock formed depends on the nature of the sediment. Instead of eroded rock particles (which form rock such as sandstone), the sediment could be deposits left behind when water evaporated (which form rock salt). It could also be the remains of plants or animals (which form coal and limestone).

## Metamorphic rock

Metamorphic rock is formed when igneous or sedimentary rock is altered by heat or pressure, or both. It can be formed in a small area, when magma comes into contact with other rocks, or on a large scale, such as during mountain building. Some examples are slate, formed from mud and a rock called shale, and marble, formed from limestone.

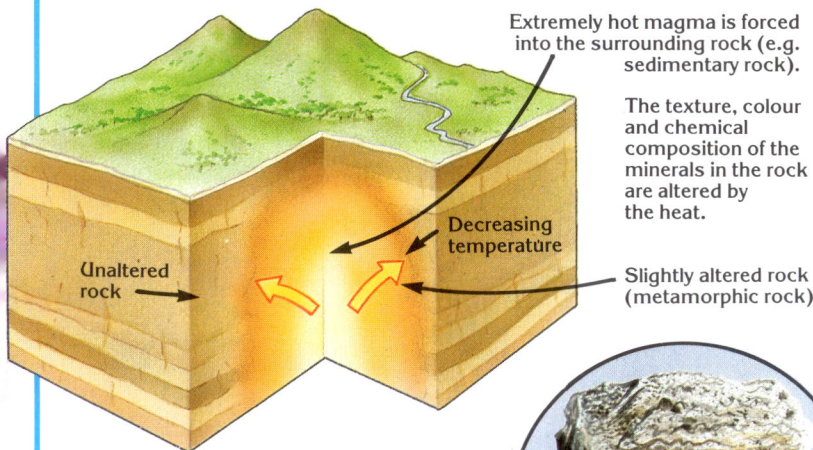

Extremely hot magma is forced into the surrounding rock (e.g. sedimentary rock).

The texture, colour and chemical composition of the minerals in the rock are altered by the heat.

Decreasing temperature

Slightly altered rock (metamorphic rock)

Unaltered rock

During the formation of mountains (see page 10), rocks are under great pressure.

The temperature of the rock may also rise due to the friction caused by movement.

Schist is a metamorphic rock formed during mountain building.

The pressure and temperature changes cause metamorphic rock to be formed over a vast area.

## The composition of rocks

The arrangement and type of minerals found in different rocks give them certain qualities, which affect the way they are worn away.

Pervious rocks, such as limestone, for example, have cracks which let water through. Porous rocks, such as sandstone, have spaces between each tiny particle, and water passes through these. These are both types of permeable rock (see page 28). Impermeable rocks do not let water pass through easily.

In the Grand Canyon, in North America, layers of sedimentary rock, such as sandstone, have been revealed as the Earth's surface has been worn away.

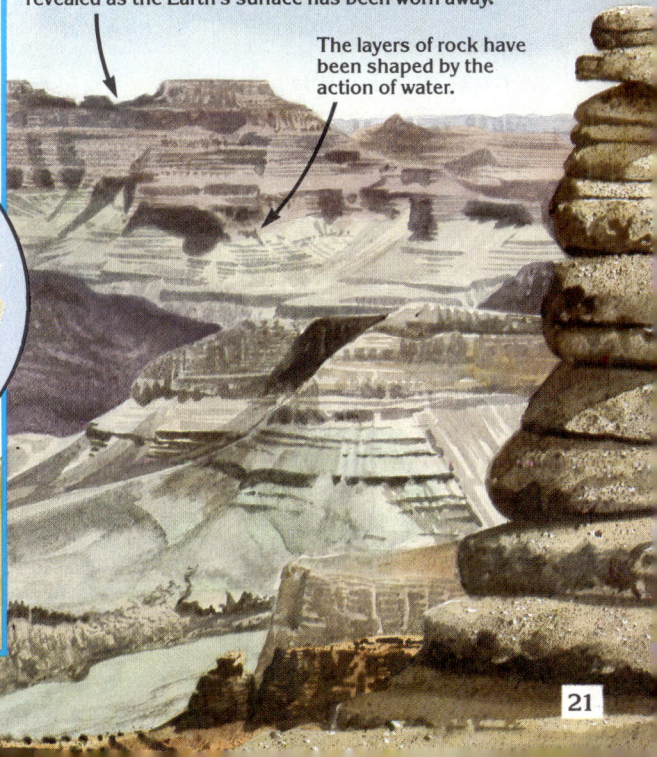

The layers of rock have been shaped by the action of water.

# The changing planet

When rock is exposed to the atmosphere, its surface is gradually broken down by various processes called weathering. There are two main types of weathering, called mechanical and chemical weathering, and most rocks are broken down by a combination of these processes. Rock material which has been weakened and broken off by weathering is called debris. It is carried away and broken down further by various forces. During this process, called erosion, the debris grinds against other rocks, breaking off more debris. Further erosion of debris may turn it into soil.

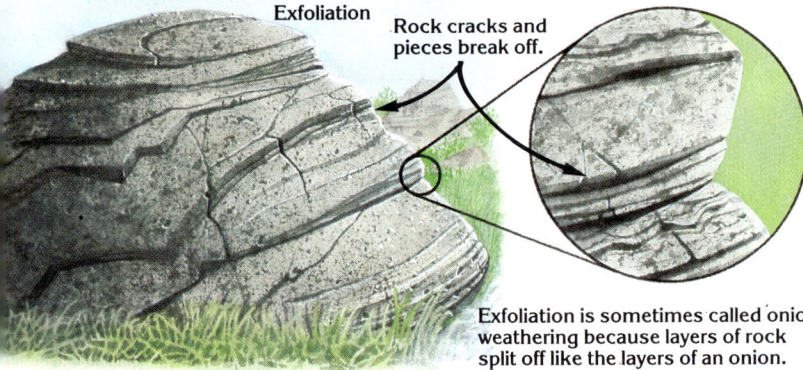

**Exfoliation**

Rock cracks and pieces break off.

Exfoliation is sometimes called onion weathering because layers of rock split off like the layers of an onion.

## Mechanical weathering

In the day, the Sun heats rock surfaces and the minerals expand. At night, temperatures fall and the minerals contract. Most rocks contain several minerals, which expand and contract at different rates, making the surface crumble and break up. This is the main type of mechanical weathering.

◄ If rocks contain only one mineral, whole areas of the surface expand and contract together and eventually peel off. This is called exfoliation.

In cold areas, rocks which contain ► cracks, or fractures, may also be broken by a process known as freeze-thaw. If water enters the cracks and freezes, it expands as it turns to ice.

The ice exerts great pressure within the rock and forces the cracks apart. If the temperature rises, the ice melts, only to freeze again if it falls. In time, pieces of rock break off.

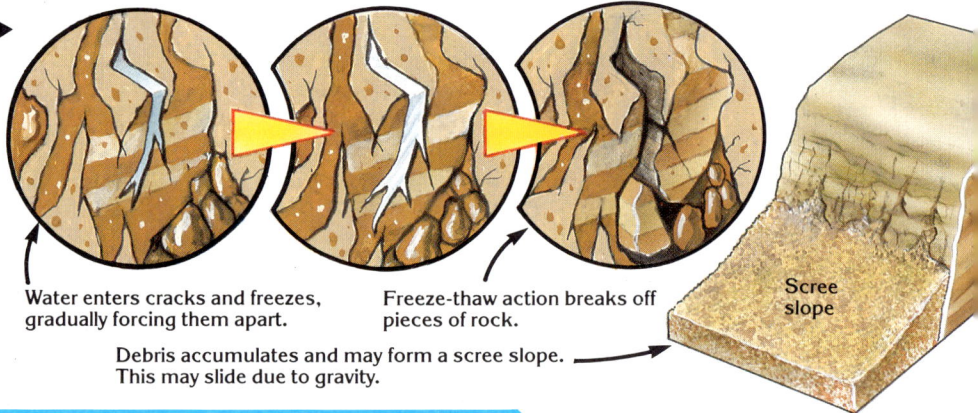

Water enters cracks and freezes, gradually forcing them apart.

Freeze-thaw action breaks off pieces of rock.

Debris accumulates and may form a scree slope. This may slide due to gravity.

Scree slope

## The effect of freezing

By freezing some clay, you can demonstrate the effects of freeze-thaw action. You will need two lumps of moist clay (one to act as a comparison), some plastic food wrap and the use of a freezer. You can buy clay from a craft shop but try using some soil from your garden as it may contain clay.

**What to do**

1. Squeeze both lumps of clay to get rid of any air bubbles and make them compact.

Squeeze each lump tightly.

Clay

2. Wrap the lumps individually in plastic food wrap. Place one lump of clay in the freezer and the other one on a window sill. Leave them there overnight.

Freezer

3. Take the clay out of the freezer and remove the plastic wrap. As the clay thaws, compare it with the lump from the window sill. The cracks in the thawed clay are due to freeze-thaw action.

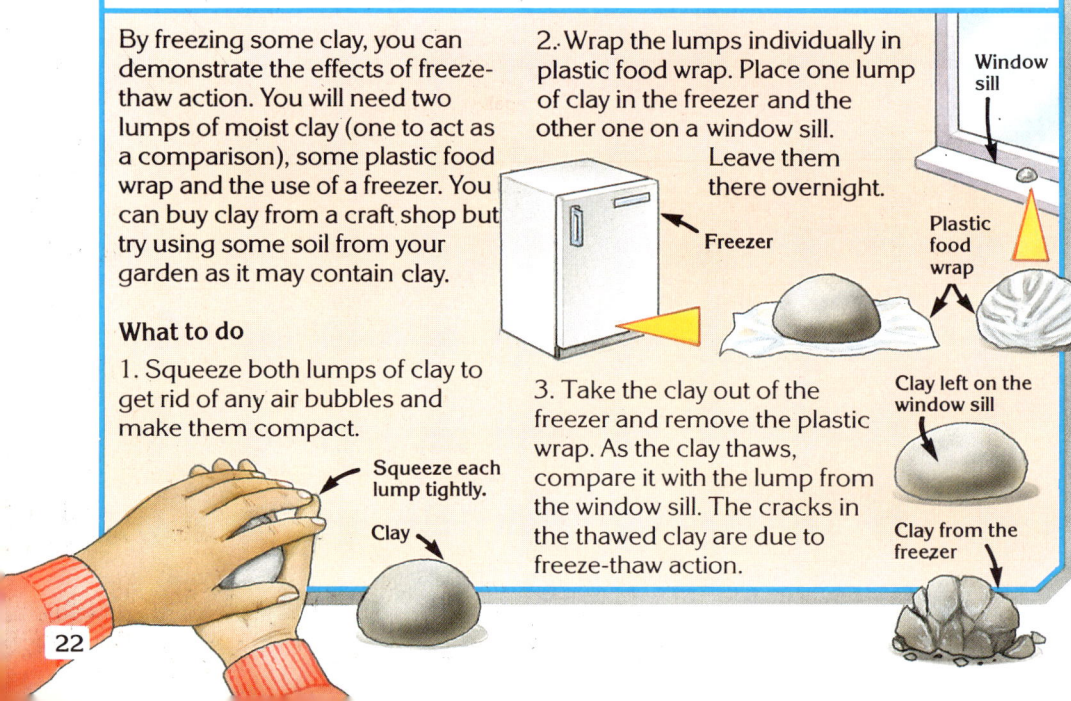

Window sill

Plastic food wrap

Clay left on the window sill

Clay from the freezer

## Chemical weathering

Chemical weathering occurs when minerals are eaten away by chemicals, such as those in rain. As it forms, rain absorbs gases from the air, making a weak acid which attacks the rock.

In rocks such as limestone, rainwater gets into cracks, making them bigger (see page 29).

Chemicals in rainwater attack and gradually eat away the rock.

## Acid rain

Acid rain is caused by air pollution. The burning of fossil fuels such as coal and oil gives off gases containing sulphur and nitrogen. These react with water droplets in the air, making the rainwater more acidic.

Acid rain breaks down the waxy coating on plant leaves and also enters the plants through their roots.

Acid rain falls on the soil and enters rivers and lakes, killing wildlife.

Acid rain makes chemical weathering worse. In cities, it is causing serious damage to old buildings and statues.

Power stations release large amounts of gases into the atmosphere.

Clouds containing acid droplets may travel great distances.

## Weathering by plants and animals

Plants and animals help to break down rocks by both mechanical and chemical weathering.

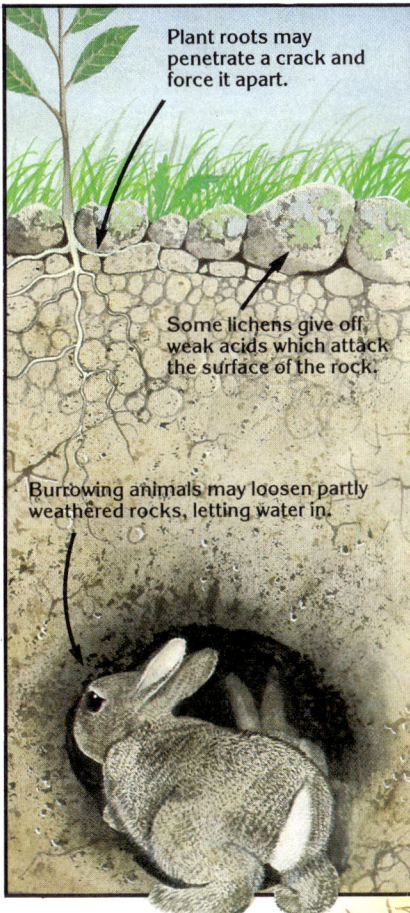

Plant roots may penetrate a crack and force it apart.

Some lichens give off weak acids which attack the surface of the rock.

Burrowing animals may loosen partly weathered rocks, letting water in.

## Erosion

Erosion occurs after fragments of rock, or debris, have been produced by weathering. Agents of erosion, such as water, ice and the wind, pick up and carry away the debris. As it is carried, it is constantly grinding against other rocks, wearing away these rocks and being worn into finer particles itself. Finally, it is deposited in a new place.

**Rivers**
Rivers carry a great deal of debris, which erodes the bed and the banks. When the river becomes too slow to carry the debris, it is deposited.

**The sea**
Waves pick up pebbles and sand and smash them against cliffs, eroding the cliffs. They also move sand and debris along the shore (see pages 30-31).

**Ice**
In cold areas, debris is frozen into glaciers. As the ice moves downhill, the debris scrapes against rocks, eroding their surface (see pages 24-25).

**The wind**
The wind picks up fine particles and blasts them against rocks, eroding the rocks. It has a particularly powerful effect in desert areas.

## Speeding up erosion

Erosion has been accelerated by man's activities. For instance, soil erosion by wind and water is a problem in many areas.

Large areas of vegetation are cleared for farming or other reasons.

The roots of the plants no longer bind together the top layers of soil (see also page 37).

The wind blows away the topsoil, leaving barren areas called dust bowls.

23

# Glaciation

During the last million years, the Earth's climate has changed several times. At certain times, it became much colder, resulting in ice ages. Areas of the surface were covered in ice, until temperatures rose again and most of the ice melted. The last main ice age was about 20,000 years ago, but some areas of the Earth's surface are still covered by thick, moving layers of ice, called glaciers.

## Where glaciers are found

The largest glaciers are ice sheets, found in Greenland and Antarctica and in areas which have very cold winters and cool summers. Other glaciers, called valley glaciers, can be found in high mountain regions, such as the Alps and the Rockies, where there is snow all year.

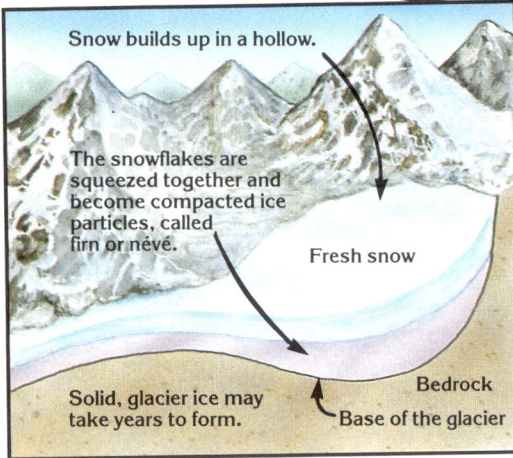

A valley glacier in Alaska

Smaller glaciers, called tributary glaciers, join the main glacier.

## Glacier ice

Glaciers are formed when snow does not melt in the summer and builds up in hollows. The pressure of the layers of snow crushes the snow crystals and turns them into compacted ice particles, like snow which has been squeezed to make a snowball.

Snow builds up in a hollow.

The snowflakes are squeezed together and become compacted ice particles, called firn or névé.

Fresh snow

Solid, glacier ice may take years to form.

Bedrock
Base of the glacier

## The moving glacier

Glaciers move because they are on sloping ground. The weight of the ice makes them move downhill, pressing on the rock beneath (bedrock). Their speed depends on the steepness of the slope, the amount of snow which falls and the thickness of the ice. Some valley glaciers flow as much 100m in a year, but in areas which are almost flat and have little snowfall, the glaciers (ice sheet glaciers) may only move a few millimetres.

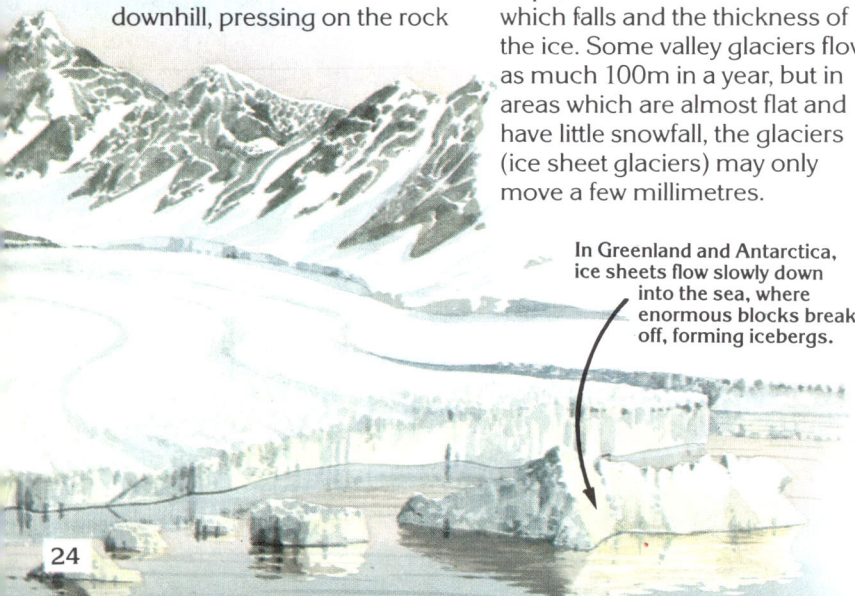

In Greenland and Antarctica, ice sheets flow slowly down into the sea, where enormous blocks break off, forming icebergs.

## Making a model glacier

As a glacier moves, friction is created as the debris grinds against the bedrock. This makes the ice move more slowly than it would do without debris. You can show this in a simple experiment, using two plastic containers (e.g. margarine tubs), some gravel or some rough stones, a piece of wood (approx. 45cm x 15cm), a cardboard box, a freezer and some water.

### What to do

1. Half-fill your containers with cold water. Add gravel or small stones to one of them, so that the bottom is covered. Top up the other container so they are filled to the same level.

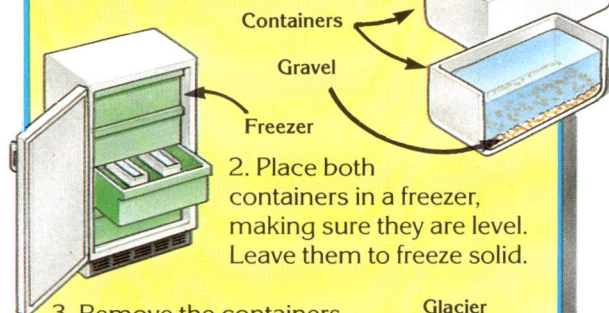

Containers

Gravel

Freezer

2. Place both containers in a freezer, making sure they are level. Leave them to freeze solid.

3. Remove the containers from the freezer and turn out your two glacier blocks. Before testing them, let them stand for ten minutes.

Glacier blocks

Ice

4. Lean the piece of wood against the box to act as your mountain slope and test both your glaciers to see which one moves more easily. You should find that your glacier with gravel moves more slowly because of friction.

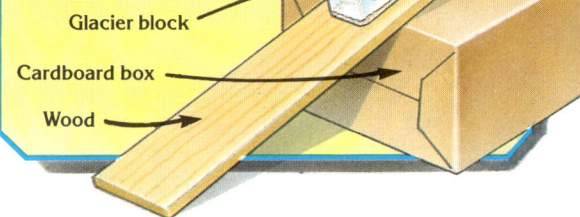

Gravel

Glacier block

Cardboard box

Wood

## Erosion by glaciers

Glaciers erode and shape the rock they pass over. Valley glaciers, which move faster than ice sheets, have a greater effect. A glacier carries a great deal of rock debris, created in many ways.

For instance, freeze-thaw action (see page 22) occurs when snow melts and then re-freezes in cracks in the rock above the glacier. This creates debris which falls down and becomes frozen into the glacier. Pieces of rock are also plucked away from the bedrock by the moving glacier.

As a glacier moves, the debris grinds against the bedrock, wearing it away. This type of erosion is called abrasion. Spurs (see page 26) are also worn away, and the valley is straightened.

**Erosion by a valley glacier**

If two cirques erode close to each other, a sharp ridge, or arête, is formed.

The ice erodes a steep-walled, saucer-shaped hollow, called a cirque, at the head of a glacier.

Crevasses (deep cracks)

Debris is carried at the sides, in the middle and beneath the glacier.

## Melting glaciers

The bottom layer of a glacier is nearly always melting. The water (meltwater) runs in channels beneath the glacier, depositing debris, called moraine. The front (snout) of a valley glacier is also constantly melting, due to higher temperatures at the bottom of the valley. Here, the meltwater forms streams which run out beyond the glacier. Normally, the snout still moves slowly forward, though, because the amount of melting ice is still less than the amount of new ice being formed at the glacier's starting point, or head.

In the warmer seasons, the ice may melt more quickly at the snout, and the glacier may retreat a short distance up the valley.

If this happens, the debris at the snout is deposited, forming a ridge called a terminal moraine. This marks the furthest point reached by the glacier.

Streams of meltwater

Snout

## Evidence of past ice ages

At the end of the last ice age, the glaciers melted away, leaving large areas of the Earth's surface shaped by their erosive action.

Glaciated valleys are U-shaped, with steep sides and a flat floor.

Erratics are large boulders which were carried by the ice and deposited far from their original place.

Drumlins are low rounded hills. It is not clear how they were formed, but it is thought they may be the result of erosion and deposition.

Long winding ridges called eskers are formed from moraine. They were deposited by water flowing below the glacier.

Some scientists are concerned that if global warming (see page 15) occurs, the world's ice sheets and glaciers may melt. This would make the sea level rise and flood coastal areas, affecting millions of people who live near the sea.

A cirque may be filled by a small lake, or tarn.

Waterfalls cascade from hanging valleys, left high on the valley side after the ice has melted.

# Rivers

Streams and rivers shape the Earth's surface by wearing away the rock they flow over and by depositing large amounts of material. The shape of a river valley changes along the upper, middle and lower stages of its course. Throughout the world, rivers are important for supplying water, transporting goods and producing energy.

## Transportation and deposition

All the material (sediment) transported by a river is called its load. The heaviest rocks and pebbles are rolled and bounced along the river bed, becoming round and smooth due to contact with each other and the river bed. This process is called attrition. Finer particles of clay and silt are carried along above the heavier ones. They are suspended in the water. Some minerals travel in solution, that is, they are dissolved.

A river deposits its load as it slows down. The largest material is deposited first, followed by the smaller particles. The fine sediment may be carried as far as the river mouth.

## The source of a river

The beginning of a river is called its source. Many rivers have their source in mountain regions where water has run across the surface from various places and flowed into one channel. A river may also begin as a spring or flow from a glacier (see pages 24-25).

How springs are formed

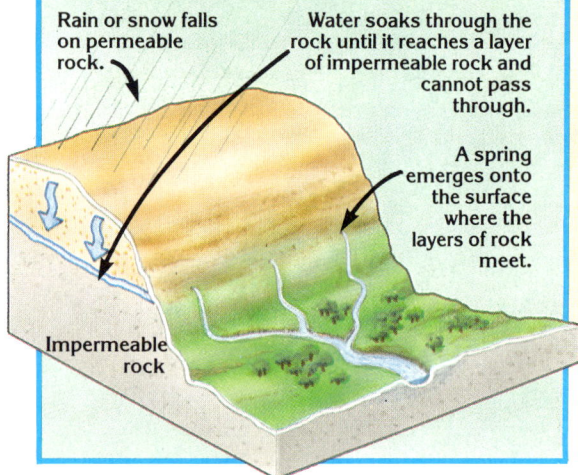

Rain or snow falls on permeable rock.

Water soaks through the rock until it reaches a layer of impermeable rock and cannot pass through.

A spring emerges onto the surface where the layers of rock meet.

Impermeable rock

## The upper stage of a river's course

The valley of a river in its upper stage tends to be V-shaped, with steep sides, formed as the fast-flowing river cuts downwards. The slope, or gradient, of the river bed is steep.

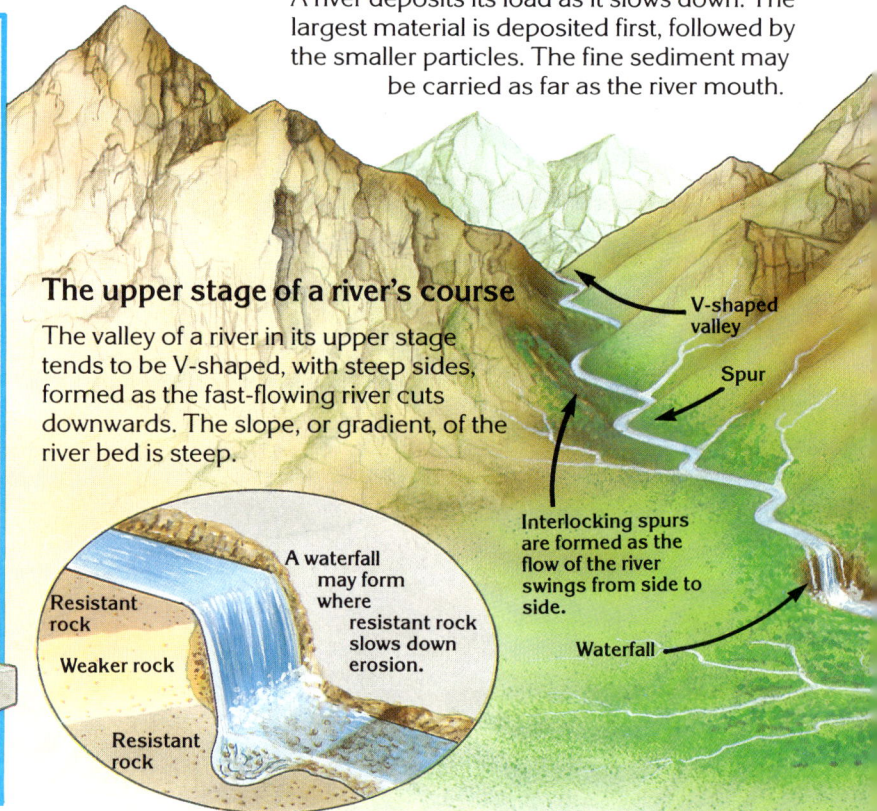

A waterfall may form where resistant rock slows down erosion.

Resistant rock

Weaker rock

Resistant rock

V-shaped valley

Spur

Interlocking spurs are formed as the flow of the river swings from side to side.

Waterfall

## Erosion by rivers

Running water erodes rock by the constant movement of the pebbles and particles of sand it carries. The amount of erosion depends on the volume and speed of the water, and the composition of the rock.

Most erosion happens early in a river's course, as the fast-flowing water carries large amounts of material. Some rock, such as sandstone, is eroded more quickly than resistant rock, such as granite.

River water loosens, lifts and carries away debris.

Rocks and pebbles roll and bounce along, wearing away and deepening the river bed.

Pebbles may be swirled around by the current, gradually forming a pothole.

Pieces of the river bed may be torn away if the force of the water is great enough. The water may also force air into cracks which weakens the rock. This is called hydraulic action (see also page 30).

River water contains chemicals from rocks and soil. It eats away the river bed and carries away the dissolved minerals.

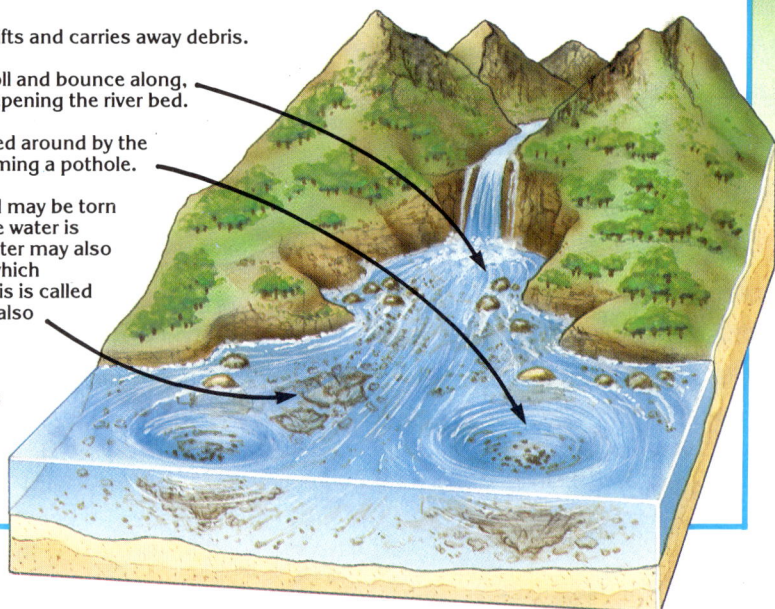

## Pollution in rivers

Many rivers around the world suffer from pollution. In many areas, chemical waste from factories, and sometimes untreated sewage, is pumped into them. Rainwater falling on fields often becomes contaminated by chemicals such as pesticides. It drains into streams and rivers, killing animal and plant life.

Birds are poisoned when they eat contaminated fish or plants from a polluted river.

## The middle stage

In the middle stage, the river's slope, or gradient, becomes more gentle and its speed begins to decrease. The valley becomes wider as the river erodes sideways.

The river begins to meander, or flow from side to side in long, looping bends.

The bends are also called meanders.

## The lower stage

The volume of water increases in the river's lower stage, as other rivers, called tributaries, join it. It slows down, as the gradient is more gentle, and meanders across the valley floor, depositing sediments. Finally, it flows into the sea or a lake.

If the river floods, the water flows out sideways onto the plain and deposits its load, which is then called alluvium. The largest sediments are deposited first, forming banks or levees, which are seen when the water recedes.

The fine sediments are deposited over a larger area, leaving fertile soil after the water drains off.

Flat valley floor (flood plain)

Delta

## Looking at sediments

A river deposits sediment by weight – the heaviest first, followed by lighter and lighter material. You can show this, using a plastic bottle (1 litre size), about 60cm of plastic tubing, some soil, water, sticky tape and a plastic funnel (or one made from card).

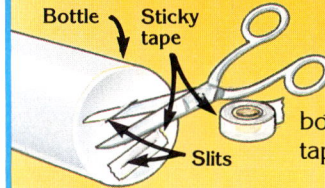

Bottle    Sticky tape

Slits

Card funnel

Soil

Plastic tubing

Container

Make sure you don't swallow any water.

Water

### What to do

1. Cut two 2cm slits in the bottom of the bottle. Stick some sticky tape over each slit.

2. Use your funnel to half-fill the bottle with soil. Then almost fill the bottle with water. Screw on the lid, shake vigorously, and leave to stand for 24 hours.

3. Unscrew the lid and place one end of the tubing into the water. Suck the water up, put your thumb over the end and bend the tube downwards, into a container. Remove your thumb and the water will drain out.

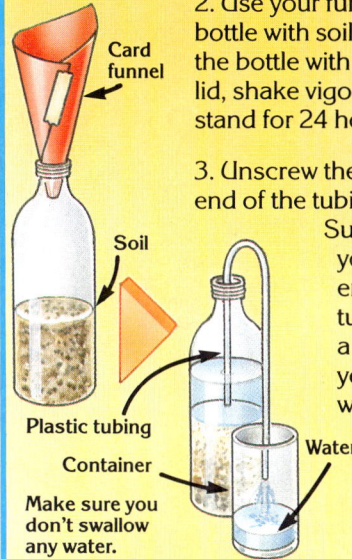

4. Pull the tape off the slits and leave for another 24 hours. This allows any remaining water to drain away. You should now see the layers of sediment. To look closely, carefully cut the bottle in half.

Bottle cut away

Layers of sediment

If the soil is very sandy, the sample will crumble. A clay soil will hold together well.

## Deltas

As a river flows into the sea, it slows down further, and any sediment it is still carrying is deposited. If the sediment is deposited faster than it is washed away by the currents and tide, it builds up an area of flat land at the mouth of the river, called a delta. The river splits up into narrower channels as it crosses the delta and finds its way to the sea. This creates a number of islands of sediment in the delta. Many people live and farm on the fertile sediments which make up delta islands. In Bangladesh, millions of people live on islands formed in the delta of the River Ganges. They grow rice and keep cattle, despite a constant risk from flooding.

On several occasions, tropical cyclones in the Ganges delta have caused severe flooding, killing millions of people.

If global warming (see page 15) increases, the Ganges islands will also be under threat from rising sea levels.

# Water under the ground

Rain falling on the Earth's surface may run into a river, evaporate back into the atmosphere, or soak into the soil. If the water soaks into the soil it may be absorbed into the layers of rock underneath, depending on their composition.

## Water in rocks

Water travels slowly through porous rock which has tiny spaces between its grains, or through pervious rock which has joints or small cracks in it. Any rock which allows water to pass through it is said to be permeable. Water enters permeable rock and moves downwards due to gravity until it reaches a layer of impermeable rock (see page 21).

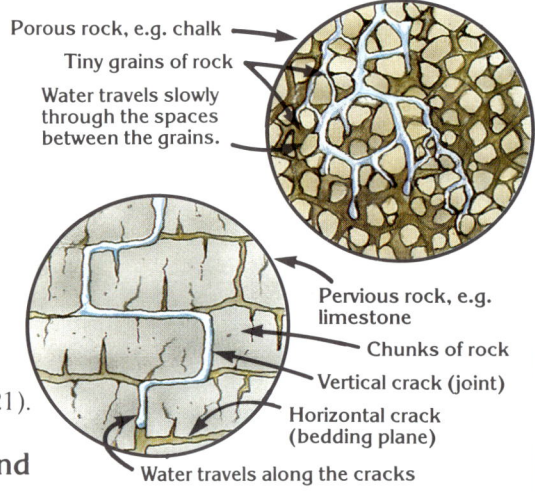

Porous rock, e.g. chalk
Tiny grains of rock
Water travels slowly through the spaces between the grains.

Pervious rock, e.g. limestone
Chunks of rock
Vertical crack (joint)
Horizontal crack (bedding plane)
Water travels along the cracks

## Water storage underground

Water which seeps down through soil and enters rock is known as ground water. It stops when it reaches an impermeable layer, and the permeable rock becomes saturated (full of water). The highest level of the water in saturated rock is called the water table.

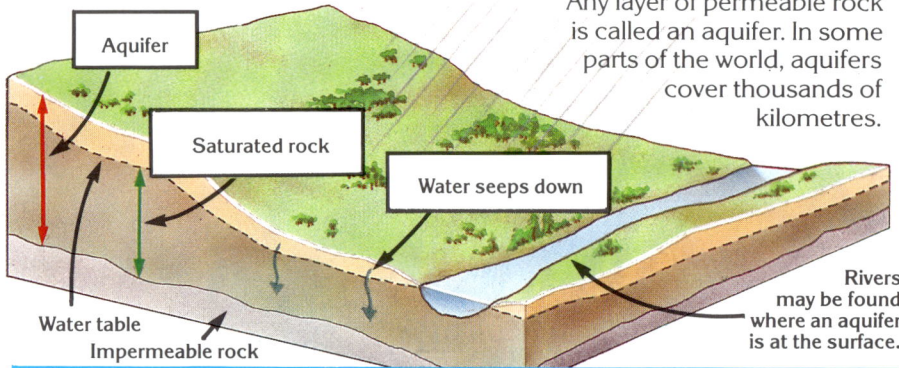

Any layer of permeable rock is called an aquifer. In some parts of the world, aquifers cover thousands of kilometres.

Aquifer
Saturated rock
Water seeps down
Water table
Impermeable rock
Rivers may be found where an aquifer is at the surface.

## Bringing ground water to the surface

If a well is dug below the level of the water table, ground water soaks into it. If the level of the water table falls, the well dries up.

Normally, water has to be pulled or pumped up from a well, but if there is enough water pressure in the aquifer, water will be pushed out of the well. This kind of well is called an artesian well.

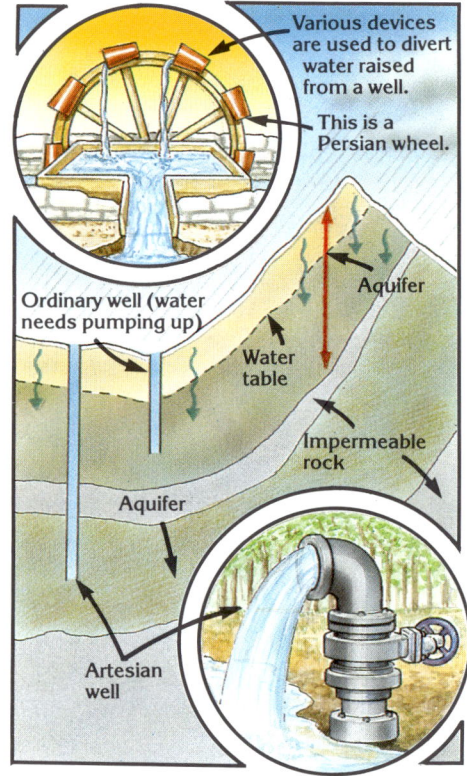

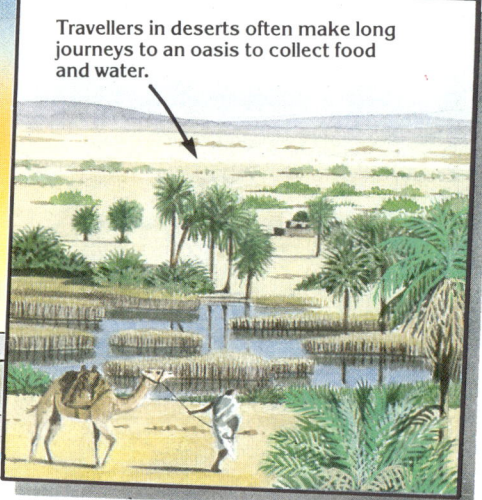

Various devices are used to divert water raised from a well.
This is a Persian wheel.
Ordinary well (water needs pumping up)
Aquifer
Water table
Impermeable rock
Aquifer
Artesian well

## Water in a desert

Rain in a desert is very scarce (see page 32), but moist areas, called oases, can be found where ground water reaches the surface. The water travels underground to the oasis, in an aquifer which is supplied with rain a long way away. Some oases may be over a thousand kilometres from the area where the rainwater entered the aquifer.

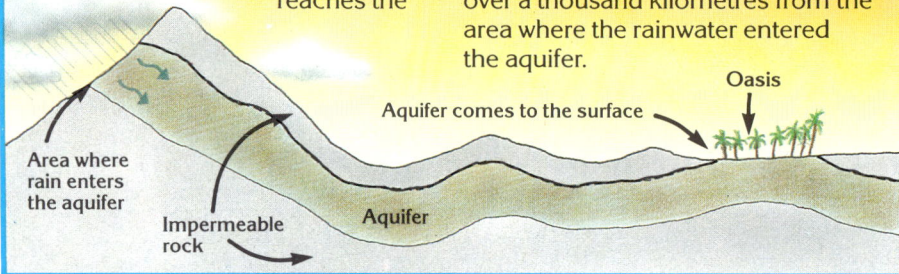

Aquifer comes to the surface
Oasis
Area where rain enters the aquifer
Impermeable rock
Aquifer

Travellers in deserts often make long journeys to an oasis to collect food and water.

# Limestone caves

Ground water, like surface water, can weather and erode rock. It is slightly acidic, having absorbed carbon dioxide both from the air and from the soil it has passed through. Limestone is particularly affected by ground water. As it passes along cracks and joints, the water dissolves the limestone, eating away at it and enlarging the cracks.

The cracks gradually widen, allowing water to flow as underground streams. The streams erode the limestone further by processes of river erosion (see pages 26-27).

The process causes areas of rock to collapse, leaving interconnected tunnels and caves within the limestone. Some water evaporates, leaving the minerals which were dissolved in it. These form features such as stalactites and stalagmites (see below).

## Testing for carbonates

Any substance containing a carbonate (a chemical substance containing carbon and oxygen) will be dissolved by an acid. Limestone contains calcium carbonate, so it is eaten away by ground water.

To test for carbonates, you will need an old eyedrop dropper or an empty ball point pen tube (stick some tape over the tiny hole in the side), some vinegar (which contains acetic acid), a dish and some substances to test, such as rocks, chalk, sea shells or old snail shells.

Shell

Pen tube

Vinegar

Dish

### What to do

1. Put a test ▶ sample in the dish. Dip the dropper or empty pen tube into the vinegar (put your thumb over the top end of the tube – this will hold the vinegar in).

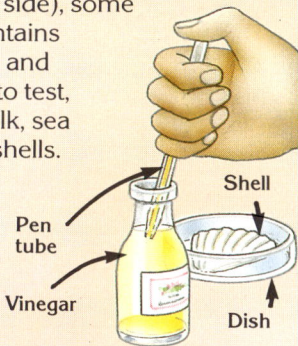

Drop of vinegar

Be careful not to let too much vinegar drip out at once.

◀ 2. Move the dropper or tube over your sample. If you are using a tube, lightly release your thumb, so the tube acts like a dropper. Let small drops of vinegar drip onto your sample.

3. Watch your sample carefully. If it contains a carbonate, it will give off fizzy bubbles of carbon dioxide.

Carbon dioxide bubbles

Fizzing shows the presence of a carbonate.

## Stalagmites and stalactites

Water is always dripping down from cracks in the roof of a cave or passage. It contains dissolved minerals, such as calcite. Each drop leaves a tiny ring of calcite on the rock as it falls. The ring grows as more drops fall, and becomes a hollow tube. If it gets blocked, water trickles down the outside of this tube and a stalactite gradually forms as it thickens.

The water which falls to the floor may evaporate, leaving a deposit of calcite which slowly grows up to form a stalagmite. Eventually a stalactite and stalagmite may meet, forming a pillar.

Chimney

### Formation of a stalactite

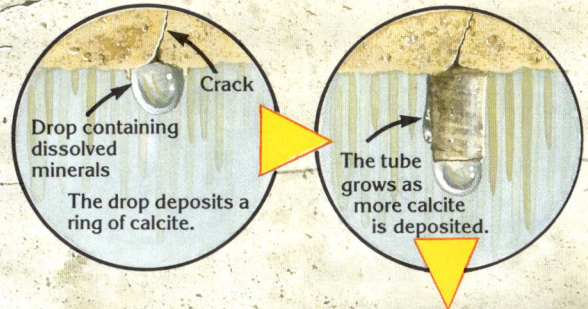

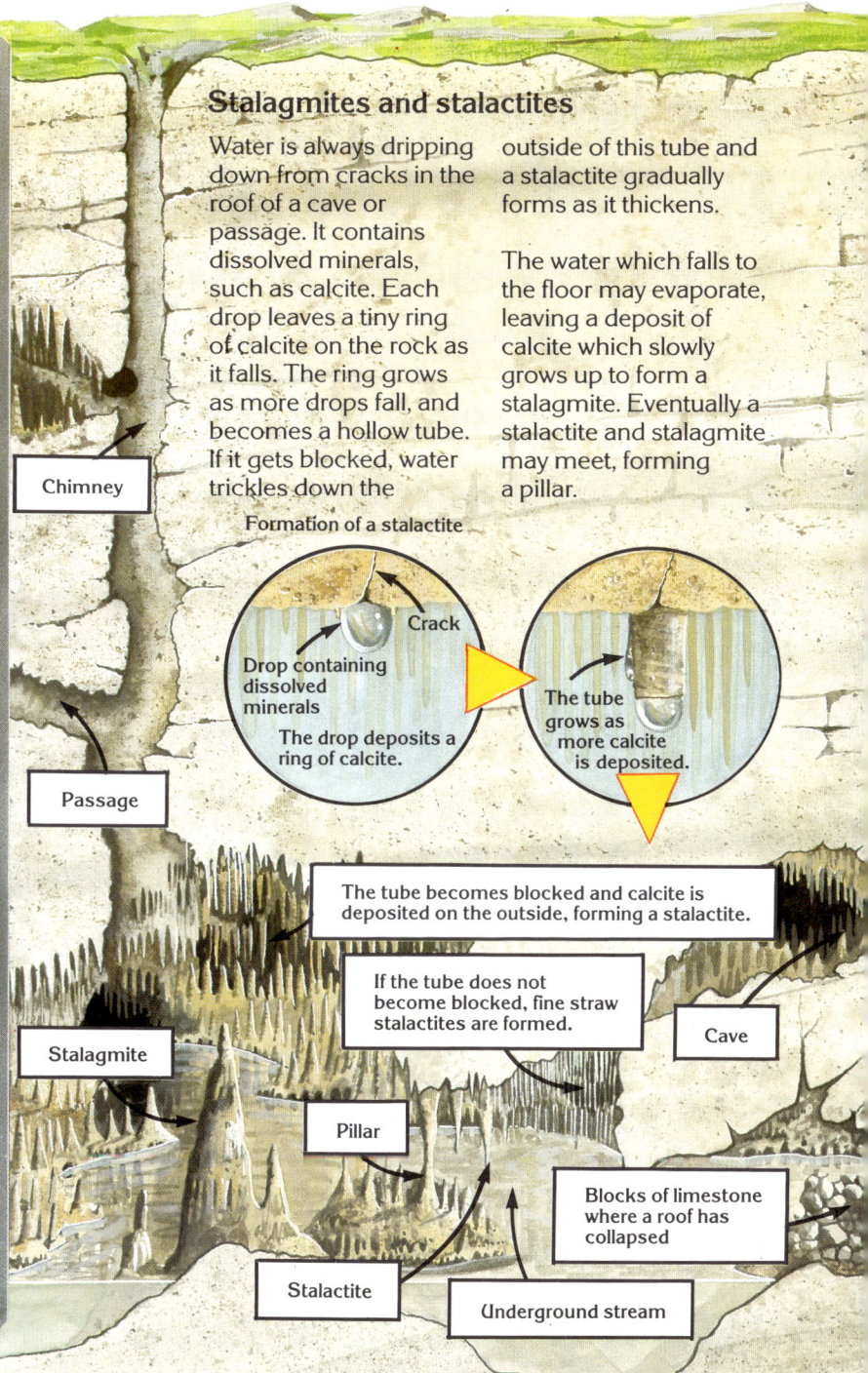

Crack

Drop containing dissolved minerals

The drop deposits a ring of calcite.

The tube grows as more calcite is deposited.

Passage

The tube becomes blocked and calcite is deposited on the outside, forming a stalactite.

If the tube does not become blocked, fine straw stalactites are formed.

Cave

Stalagmite

Pillar

Blocks of limestone where a roof has collapsed

Stalactite

Underground stream

# The work of the sea

The waves of the sea have a powerful erosive effect on shores. Some shores are rocky, with high cliffs, others combine rocks with sand, shingle (small pebbles) or large pebbles. The breaking waves smash debris against the cliffs and also move sand and pebbles along the shore. The area between the high and low tide marks shows the greatest amount of damage.

The tides are caused by the pull of the Moon's force of gravity on the Earth.

There are two low tides every day.

High tides occur between low tides.

## Longshore drift

Lines of waves usually approach a beach at an angle. This leads to a process called longshore drift. Sand and shingle are picked up, moved along the beach in a zigzag path and deposited elsewhere.

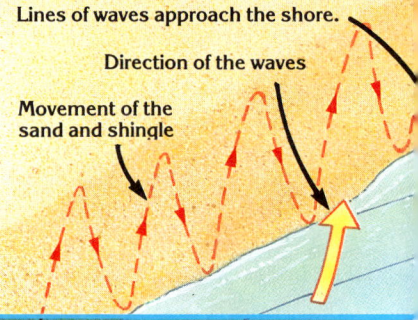

Lines of waves approach the shore.

Direction of the waves

Movement of the sand and shingle

## Waves

Most waves are caused by the wind, as it travels over the surface of the sea. The size of a wave depends on the speed of the wind, the time it has been blowing and the distance of open water it has blown across.

In the open sea, the water travels in a circular pattern, making waves.

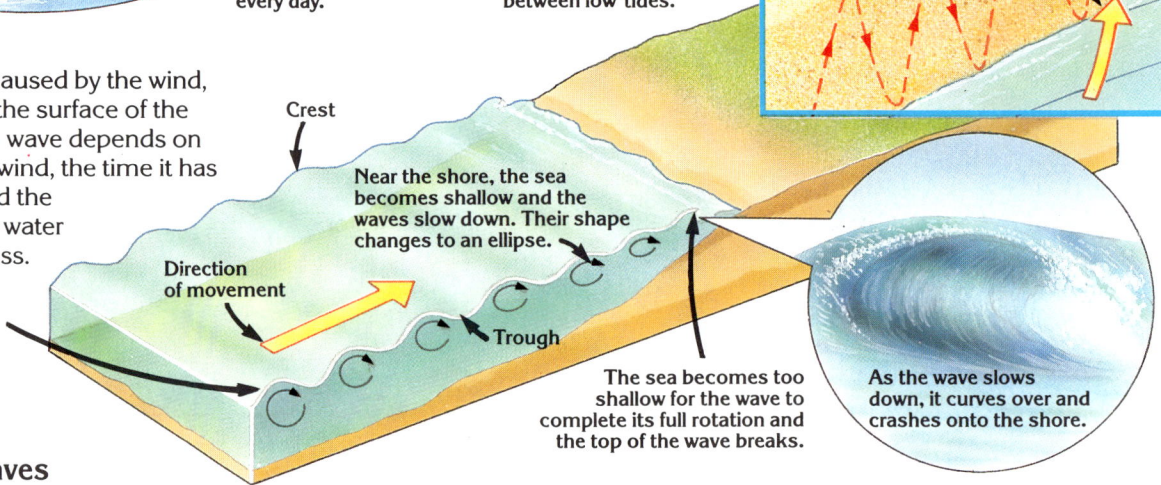

Crest

Direction of movement

Trough

Near the shore, the sea becomes shallow and the waves slow down. Their shape changes to an ellipse.

The sea becomes too shallow for the wave to complete its full rotation and the top of the wave breaks.

As the wave slows down, it curves over and crashes onto the shore.

## Erosion by waves

Waves are the main force of erosion on shores. As they approach a shore, they pick up debris from the sea floor and hurl it against the shore or cliff face. If the rock of a cliff face contains cracks, air is squeezed, or compressed, into them as the waves break. As the waves retreat, the pressure is released and the air pushes back out, shattering the rock. This is called hydraulic action. Debris is gradually broken down and rounded by the repeated action of the waves.

The continuous blasting action of the waves enlarges cracks and joints in a cliff face. eventually forming caves.

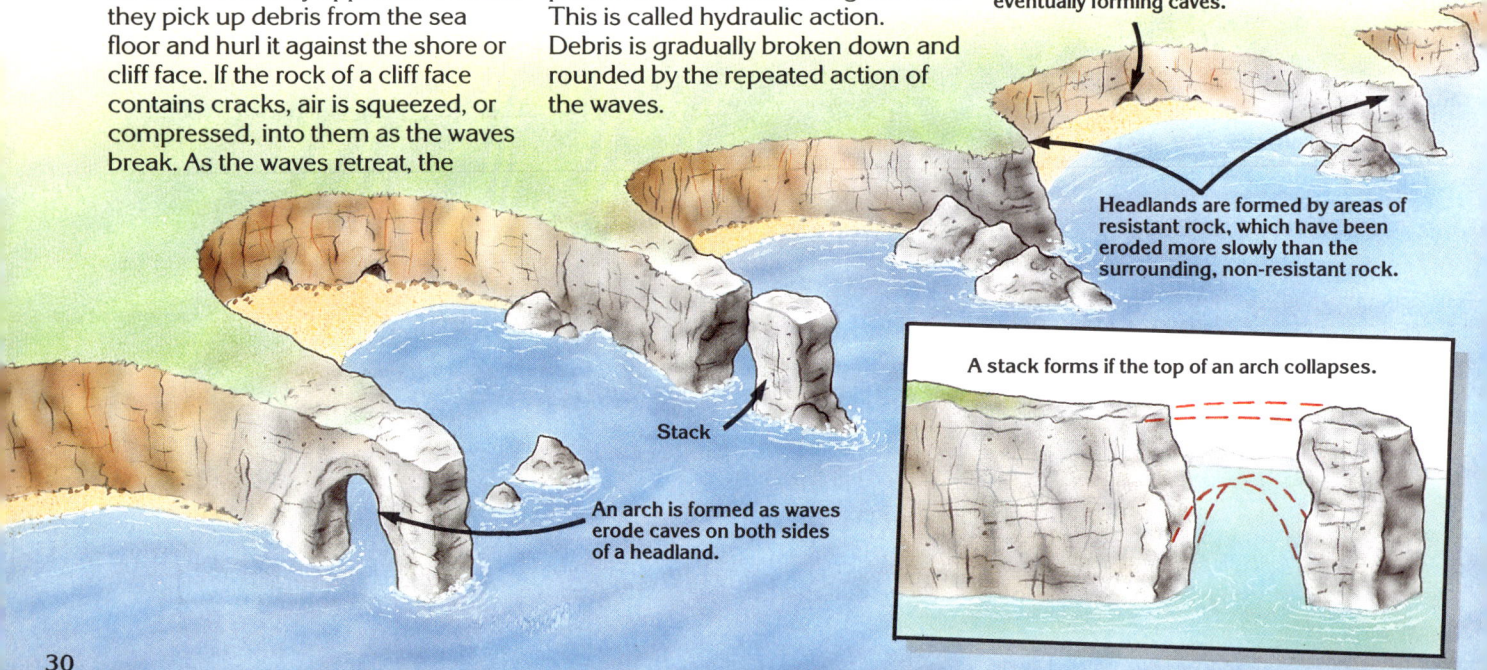

Headlands are formed by areas of resistant rock, which have been eroded more slowly than the surrounding, non-resistant rock.

A stack forms if the top of an arch collapses.

Stack

An arch is formed as waves erode caves on both sides of a headland.

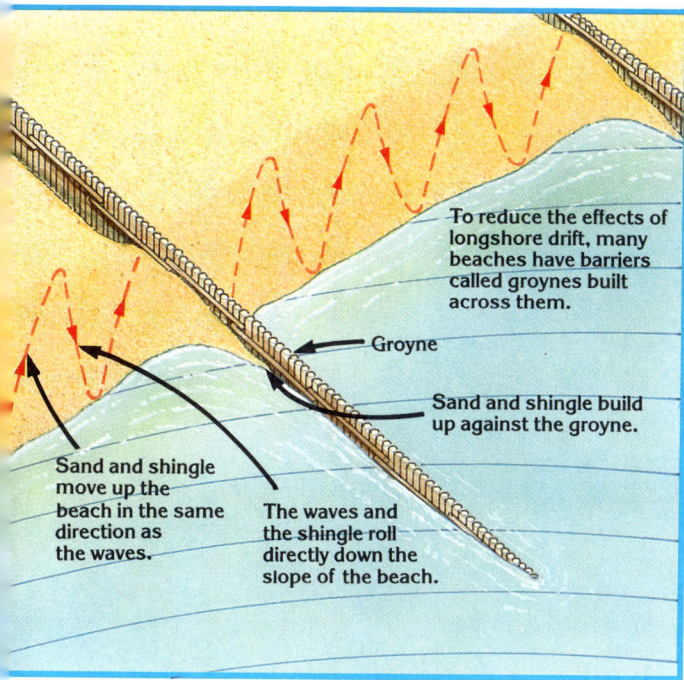

## Spits

Waves also help to build features along the shore. For instance, where the coast changes direction, or at a river mouth, longshore drift carries material straight on, off the edge of the beach. If the material is not carried away by strong currents, a ridge of sand and pebbles, called a spit, is gradually built up.

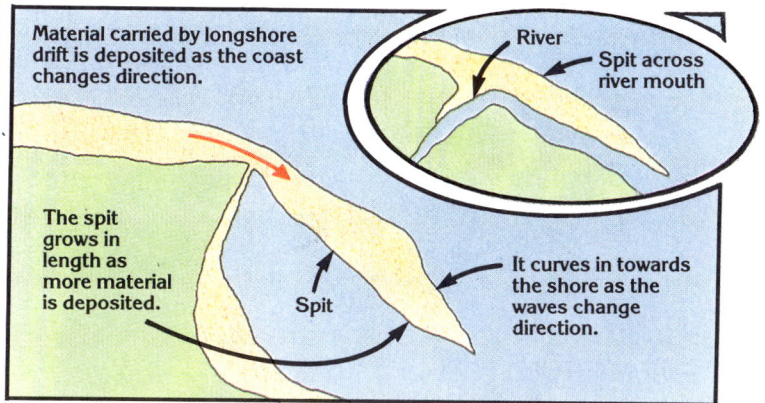

To reduce the effects of longshore drift, many beaches have barriers called groynes built across them.

Groyne

Sand and shingle build up against the groyne.

Sand and shingle move up the beach in the same direction as the waves.

The waves and the shingle roll directly down the slope of the beach.

Material carried by longshore drift is deposited as the coast changes direction.

River

Spit across river mouth

The spit grows in length as more material is deposited.

Spit

It curves in towards the shore as the waves change direction.

## Estuaries

An estuary is the tidal area where a river reaches the sea. Large areas of mud, deposited by the slow-moving river, are exposed at low tide, but covered at high tide. As the fresh water mixes with salty sea water, the salt makes clay particles in the sediment cling together. They become heavy and are deposited on the mud banks.

A river estuary at low tide

The estuary at high tide

Many species of shrimps, worms and shellfish live in the mud.

Mud banks

Some wading birds have long beaks for probing deep into the mud at low tide.

## Fresh and salt water experiment

As a river reaches the sea, any remaining sediment is deposited due to it slowing down, but also because of the action of the salt in sea water (see above). This experiment shows how salty water speeds up deposition.

1. Put equal amounts of soil into the bottom of two glasses. Fill each glass with water.

Glass
Water
Soil

2. Add two teaspoonfuls of salt to one of the glasses.

Stir both mixtures well
Teaspoon
Salt

3. Leave both glasses to stand. The salty water mixture will clear in a few minutes, leaving a layer of sediment on the bottom.

Salty water
Particles of soil remain suspended in the fresh water.
Sediment

# Deserts

Deserts are dry, barren areas where less than 25cm of rain falls each year and the wind is the main factor in shaping the landscape. Not all deserts are hot – some of the world's coldest places are deserts. Desert plants and animals have special ways of coping with the conditions.

## Where deserts are found

There are a number of reasons why some areas of the Earth's surface receive little or no rain.

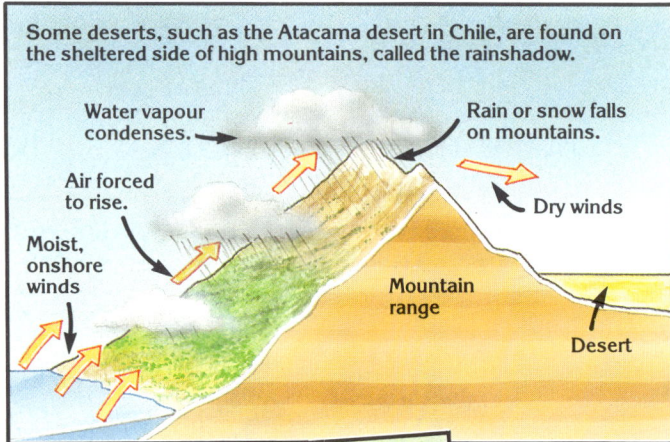

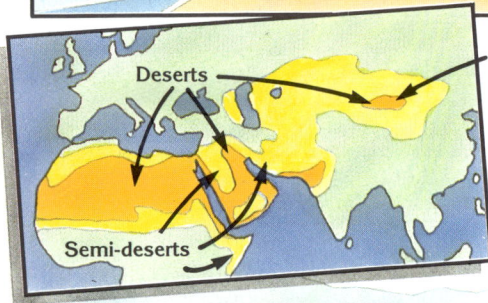

Some deserts, such as the Atacama desert in Chile, are found on the sheltered side of high mountains, called the rainshadow.

Water vapour condenses.

Air forced to rise.

Moist, onshore winds

Rain or snow falls on mountains.

Dry winds

Mountain range

Desert

Other deserts, such as the Gobi desert, are found in the interior of large continents.

Deserts

Semi-deserts

Winds lose all their moisture as they travel over land.

## Frozen deserts

Most of the snow in Antarctica and the Arctic falls at the coast, whereas areas of the interior receive very little, making them deserts. The snowfall is not very regular and most of the annual amount may fall during one blizzard. The snow has taken thousands of years to build up.

Most polar animals live near the sea, which is their food source.

Thick layers of fat or fur retain their body heat in the extreme cold.

## Hot deserts

Hot deserts have a variety of different surfaces. Only some are covered in sand. Others have stones, gravel or bare rock, or a mixture.

### Wind action

There is little to protect a desert from the action of the wind. Strong winds pick up fine surface debris and blast it against exposed rock.

Resistant rock

Layers of rock of different resistance

Direction of the prevailing wind

Most erosion takes place just above the surface, where the wind carries most debris.

Mushroom-shaped rock called a zeugen

In sandy deserts, the wind moves sand along the surface and builds ridges called dunes. The shape of a dune depends on the direction of the wind and the size of the sand grains.

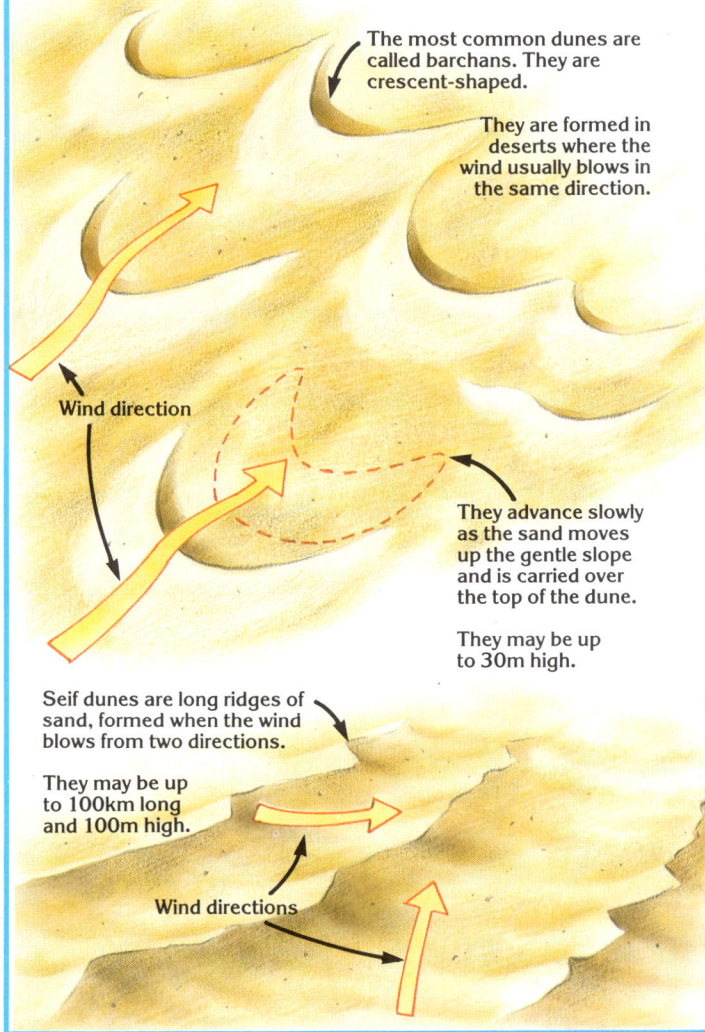

The most common dunes are called barchans. They are crescent-shaped.

They are formed in deserts where the wind usually blows in the same direction.

Wind direction

They advance slowly as the sand moves up the gentle slope and is carried over the top of the dune.

They may be up to 30m high.

Seif dunes are long ridges of sand, formed when the wind blows from two directions.

They may be up to 100km long and 100m high.

Wind directions

## Temperatures

During the day, surface temperatures in hot deserts may reach 52°C, because there are no clouds to shield the surface from the Sun. It is much cooler underground, so many animals retreat into burrows during the day. At night, temperatures fall very fast, as there are no clouds to trap the heat and prevent it being radiated into space.

The fennec fox digs a burrow in the sand, where it remains during the day.

It hunts at dusk when it is cooler.

The fox's large ears have lots of blood vessels very near the surface. As blood flows through the ears, it loses heat, which is radiated into the surrounding air. This lowers the fox's body temperature.

## Rain in deserts

Although hot deserts receive little rain, there may be occasional short periods of heavy rainfall. The water does not soak in straight away, but runs rapidly across the surface, sweeping up valley debris and carrying it along in channels called wadis.

Some desert plants produce seeds which stay buried for months or even years. After rain has fallen, they grow very quickly into plants. They flower and produce seeds, and then die off as conditions become too dry again.

When it rains, the desert is often scattered with bright flowers.

The seeds survived the dry conditions by lying dormant, or inactive, in the ground.

Many desert plants have a network of shallow roots which spread out over a wide area. The roots absorb any rain which soaks into the ground. The leaves are always very small, to minimise water evaporation from their surfaces.

Cacti

Cactus leaves are sharp spines. Their size and shape minimises evaporation and their sharpness prevents them becoming food for desert animals.

When it does rain, cacti can store up the water in their fleshy tissues.

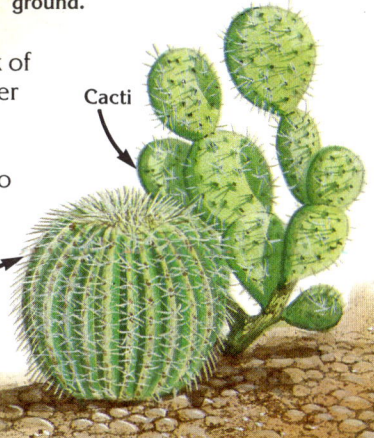

## Making a gerbilarium

Gerbils are desert animals which make popular pets. If you or a friend have gerbils, you could build a gerbilarium for them to live in.

Most pet gerbils come from the Mongolian desert, which is hot in summer and cold in winter.

Long legs allow them to cover large areas of land in search of food. They eat mainly seeds, stems and leaves.

Their long tail is used to give them balance when running and jumping.

In the desert, gerbils dig a complex system of burrows, to protect them from the very hot and cold temperatures and from predators.

Fur on the pads of their feet gives protection from the hot surface and also prevents them sinking into the sand.

Feed your gerbils on a diet of mixed seeds and occasionally fresh vegetables.

Keep your gerbils at room temperature, away from draughts and direct sunlight.

Do not disturb the gerbils in their nest.

Use a large aquarium with a tightly-fitting wire-mesh lid for good air circulation.

Put in dry peat moss, mixed with some straw, for the gerbils to burrow in.

Fix a drinking bottle inside the glass and change the water daily.

Sucker

Small leafless branch for climbing and gnawing.

Minimum 20cm

For bedding, put in clean paper for your gerbils to shred.

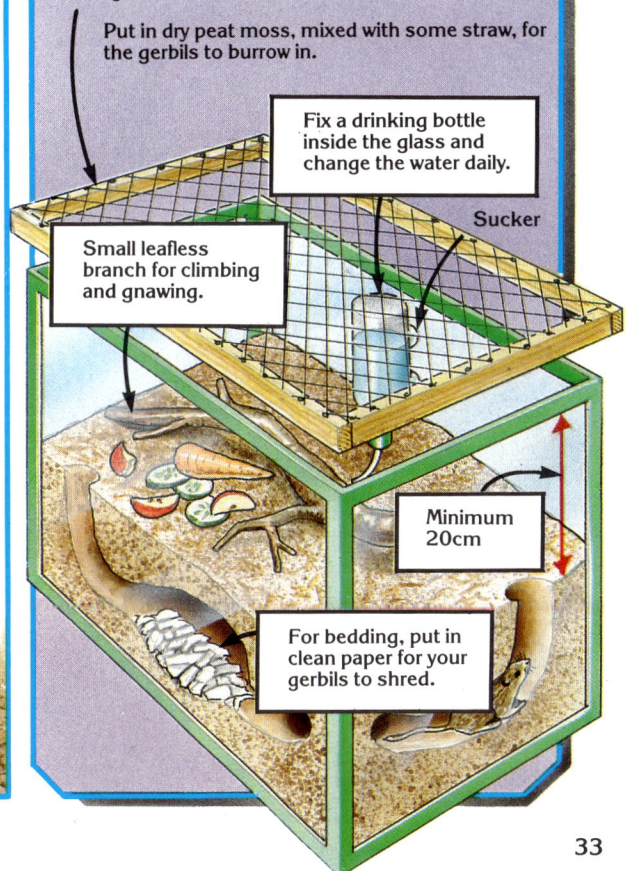

# The living world

The non-living environment (such things as the atmosphere, water, soil and rock), supports a wealth of living things. Different plants and animals, together with their environment, make up different ecosystems, such as deserts, temperate woodlands or tropical rain forests.

Everything in an ecosystem depends upon everything else for its survival, and each ecosystem depends on all the others. They combine to form the largest ecosystem, the Earth itself.

## Food chains

All plants and animals need to break down food inside them, to give them energy for living and growing. Green plants take in the Sun's energy and use it to make their own food in a process called photosynthesis. Animals cannot do this, so instead they have to eat plants or other animals.

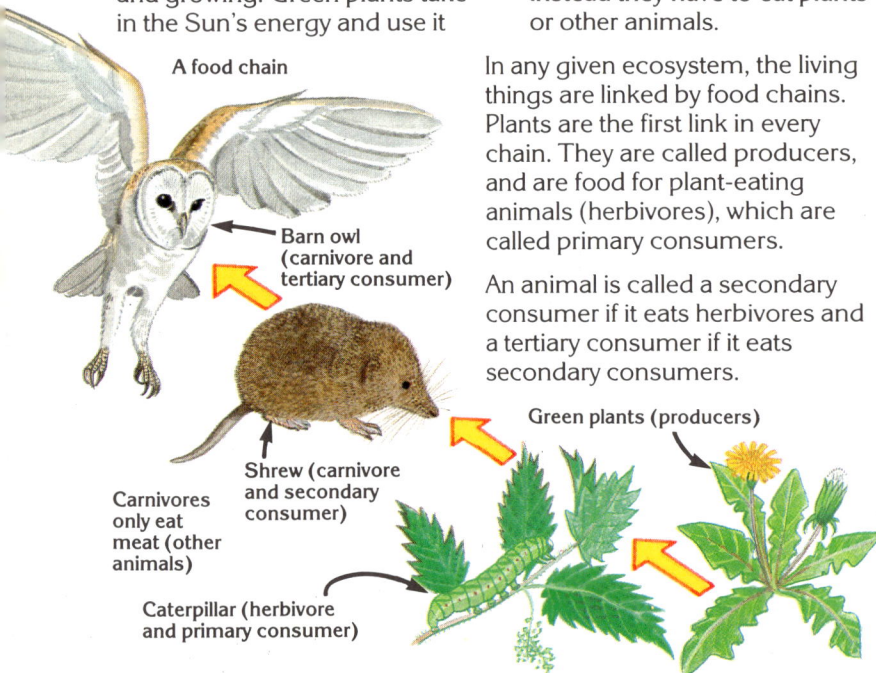

In any given ecosystem, the living things are linked by food chains. Plants are the first link in every chain. They are called producers, and are food for plant-eating animals (herbivores), which are called primary consumers.

An animal is called a secondary consumer if it eats herbivores and a tertiary consumer if it eats secondary consumers.

**A food chain**

Barn owl (carnivore and tertiary consumer)

Shrew (carnivore and secondary consumer)

Carnivores only eat meat (other animals)

Caterpillar (herbivore and primary consumer)

Green plants (producers)

## Destroying ecosystems

When part of an ecosystem is changed or destroyed, other parts may be affected. If the primary consumer is lost from a food chain, for example, the secondary and tertiary consumers may die out due to lack of food, and the producer (plants) will spread rapidly.

All over the Earth, ecosystems are being destroyed, for example as land is cleared for farming or building. The destruction of ecosystems is causing world-wide concern.

For example, rain forests contain the largest number of insect and plant species in any ecosystem. They are being cut down at an alarming rate and many thousands of species are in danger of extinction.

## Decomposers

In any food chain there are also decomposers, which feed on dead plant and animal matter. They cause it to break down, or decay (rot), producing various nutrients which enter the soil.

Bacteria, fungi and some insects are decomposers.

## Studying decomposers at work

The main decomposers are bacteria and fungi. The air is full of bacteria, and the microscopic seed-like particles of fungi, called spores. You can try an experiment which shows that they are all around you, and in what conditions they will grow.

### What to do

1. Put a slice of fresh bread on a table for a few minutes, to collect bacteria and spores. Cut it into four pieces.

2. Place one piece in each of three clear plastic bags (labelled B, C and D) and tightly seal the bags.

Fresh bread exposed to the air.

Plastic bags

3. Dry out the last piece in a hot, sunny place indoors. Place bag B in a warm room, C in a fridge and D in a freezer.

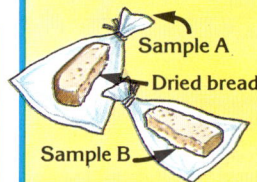

Sample A

Dried bread

Sample B

4. When the sample left out in the sun feels dry and hard, place it in bag A and place it beside sample B.

5. Observe your samples over a period of at least a week. You will find the spores grow best in moist, warm conditions.

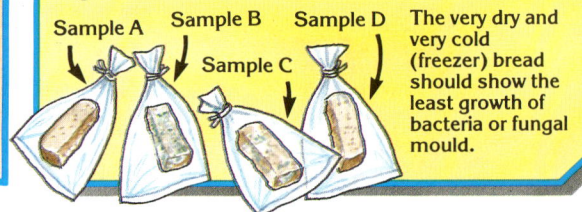

Sample A    Sample B    Sample D

Sample C

The very dry and very cold (freezer) bread should show the least growth of bacteria or fungal mould.

# Food webs

There are many different food chains in every ecosystem. They interlink because each individual species usually eats more than one kind of food. The linking food chains form complex food webs.

A rain forest food web

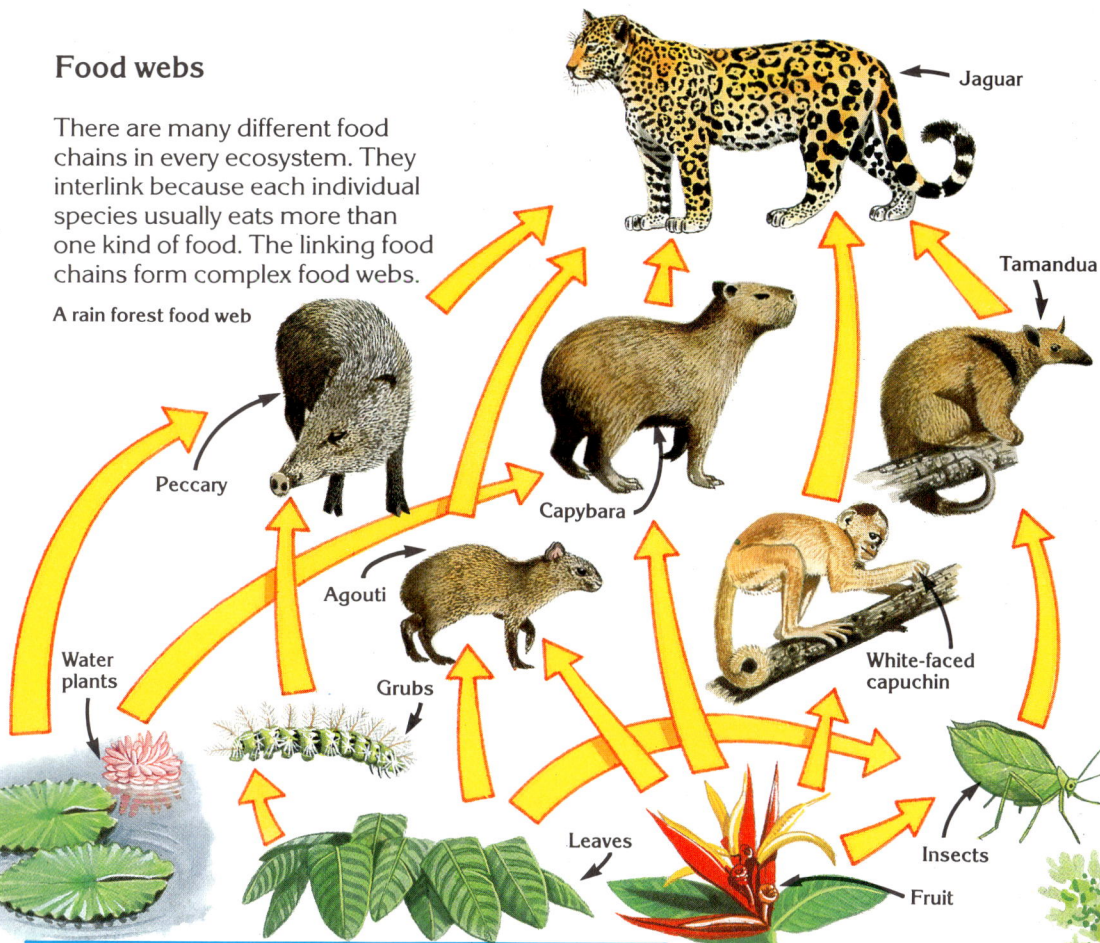

Jaguar

Tamandua

Peccary

Capybara

Agouti

Water plants

Grubs

White-faced capuchin

Leaves

Insects

Fruit

Some animals, known as omnivores, eat a mixed diet of plants and animals. They occupy different food chain levels at different times.

For instance, peccaries eat plants, so they are primary consumers in one food chain. They also eat grubs, making them secondary consumers in another food chain.

Carnivores can also occupy different food chain levels at different times.

A jaguar is a secondary consumer when it eats a capybara and a tertiary consumer when it eats a tamandua.

## Communities

The group of plant and animal species living in an ecosystem is called its community. The type of community is closely related to the type of climate, hence there are very different plants and animals living in different parts of the world (see page 19). The seas and oceans also have different climates, and hence communities, depending on such things as currents and depth.

Part of a coral reef community

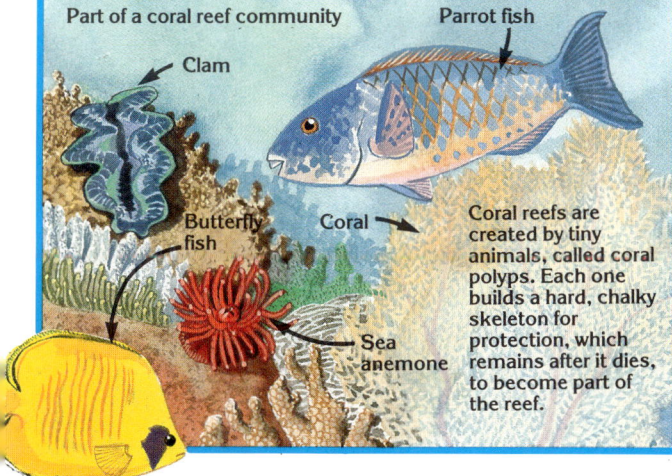

Parrot fish

Clam

Butterfly fish

Coral

Sea anemone

Coral reefs are created by tiny animals, called coral polyps. Each one builds a hard, chalky skeleton for protection, which remains after it dies, to become part of the reef.

## Niches

The role of each plant or animal in a community, for example, where it lives and what it eats, is called its niche. Many niches are similar, but no two species can occupy exactly the same niche. If they tried, competition for the same food and living space would mean that one species would die out or be driven away.

On the African grasslands, or savannah, many different species can survive because they eat different parts of the same plant.

Giraffe

Elephant

Gerenuk

Black rhinoceros

# The human population

Nowadays, there are more people living on the Earth than ever before. People create demands on the Earth and its resources, and have altered the natural environment to suit their needs.

## The effect of the landscape

Since early times, people's lives have been influenced by the landforms and natural environment of an area. People settled in permanent communities in places where they could find water, food and a safe place to live. Many communities began near rivers, springs, wells or oases, or in areas which would not flood. Fertile soils and natural resources, such as coal, also encouraged people to settle.

Castles were built on hills, cliffs or rocky outcrops which were easily defended.

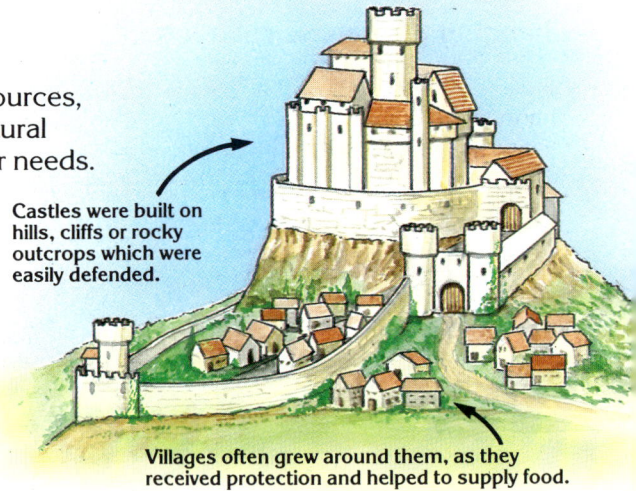

Villages often grew around them, as they received protection and helped to supply food.

## Population distribution

If all the Earth's surface was suitable to live on, there would be plenty of room for everyone. Large areas are unsuitable, however, so the world's population is unevenly distributed over the land of each continent. Few people live where the climate is too hot or too cold, the area is too mountainous or the soil is unsuitable for farming. Nowadays, most of the world's population lives in cities, towns or villages.

Some people live in areas where they have had to adapt to unsuitable landscapes or climate.

Despite steep gradients, people in many countries have settled in mountain areas.

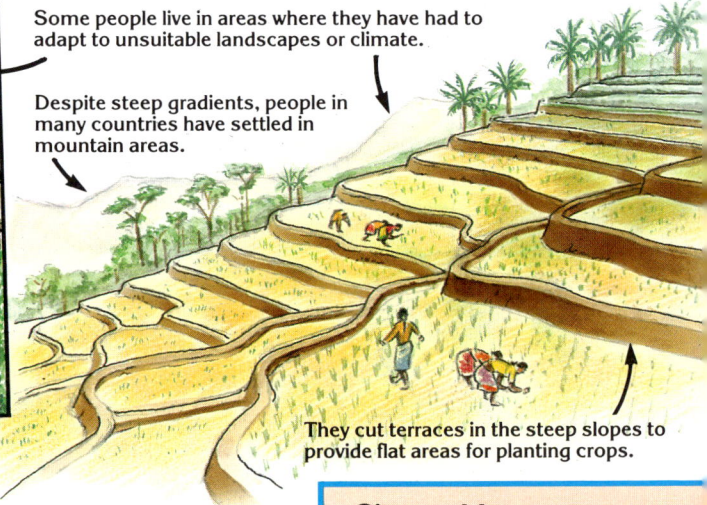

Houses in Indonesia are built on stilts to protect them from flooding during the rainy season.

They cut terraces in the steep slopes to provide flat areas for planting crops.

## A place to live

As the world's population grows, there is more demand for living space. It is estimated that the world's human population will grow to over 6 billion by the year 2000, compared to about 4 billion in 1980. In countries with large fast-growing populations, more people are being forced to live in overcrowded conditions or unsuitable places, such as on the islands in the Ganges delta (see page 27) or on boats in Hong Kong.

Hong Kong is so overcrowded that thousands of people live on boats in the harbour.

## City problems

All over the world, people ▶ move from country areas into towns and cities looking for work. This is called urban migration. It causes many problems as the populations of the cities grow rapidly. There may not be enough homes, the streets become too crowded and pollution may increase. Squatter settlements, or shanty towns, may build up on the edges of the cities.

# Changing the natural environment

Since early times, people have changed the environment for their own use, for example by clearing land for farming. When the world's population was low, this did not seriously alter ecosystems. But the demands of a growing population have caused great changes.

Natural landscapes and ecosystems have been destroyed to provide land for building cities and transport routes, and to grow more and more crops for food. Huge areas of forest have been destroyed, natural wetlands drained and dry areas watered artificially (irrigated).

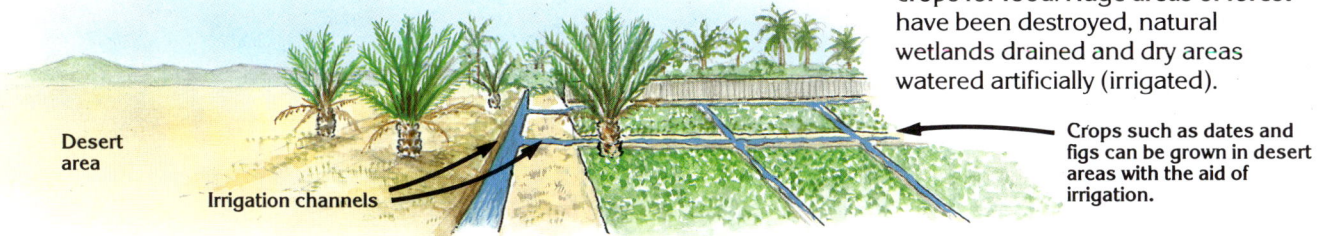

**Desert area**

**Irrigation channels**

Crops such as dates and figs can be grown in desert areas with the aid of irrigation.

These, and many other actions, have caused great problems. For instance, in many places, cleared land has lost its fertile topsoil through wind or water erosion. This is called soil erosion (see page 23). It leaves unfertile soil, on which less food can be grown. In some areas, soil erosion, combined with drought, has led to famines.

In 1985, 30 million people in Africa were threatened with starvation which was the result of a series of droughts and soil erosion.

A great deal of their land has been left infertile by over-working and soil erosion.

In shanty towns, people build makeshift homes from waste materials.

Often there is no water supply, electricity or sewage system.

## How plants prevent soil erosion

Heavy rain washes away soil if land is cleared of its natural vegetation. For an experiment which shows this, you will need two identical plastic trays, a watering can with a fine spray, some plastic food wrap, soil and turf.*

**Plastic food wrap**   **Trays**

**Holes**

### What to do

1. Cut a hole in one end of each tray. Line the trays with food wrap, cutting matching holes in the lining.

Press the turf down firmly.

2. Fill one tray with soil and pack it down firmly. Half fill the other tray with soil, and cover this with an even layer of turf.

**Soil**

3. Place both trays on a gentle slope and put a container on a level surface below each hole.

**Soil**   **Turf**

**Containers**

4. Fill the watering can with 2 litres of water and spray the turf, evenly and thoroughly. Do the same to the tray with the bare soil.

The roots help to bind the soil together, preventing it from being washed away.

**Watering can**

Water containing soil particles will drain from this box.

Less water, with no soil

*If you are unable to find some turf, you could grow a tray of cress, but leave it for 12 to 14 days, to allow the roots to bind the soil together.

37

# The Earth's energy resources

Most of the energy we use, for example in homes and industry, is taken from the Earth. For instance, wood is burnt to provide heat and light in many less-developed countries, and fossil fuels, such as coal, oil and gas, are burnt to produce electricity for use in the developed world.

When fossil fuels are used up, they cannot be renewed, or made again, in our lifetime. People are now beginning to investigate energy sources which will not run out.

## Fossil fuels

Coal, oil and natural gas are non-renewable energy resources. They were formed from the remains of plants and animals that died millions of years ago. They are taken from the Earth and used in power stations to generate electricity.

The use of fossil fuels as a major source of energy has problems. At the present rate of consumption, known oil and gas reserves could run out within the next fifty years, with coal reserves lasting for about 250 years. Also, burning fossil fuels releases gases which contribute to acid rain and the greenhouse effect.

How fossil fuels were formed

Coal comes from the remains of plants which lived in swamps.

Oil and gas were formed from the remains of microscopic marine plants and animals.

## Renewable sources

As the world's population grows and more energy is needed, many countries are developing the use of renewable energy sources – sources which will not run out, such as the Sun, wind and water. The idea is particularly popular because these are "clean" sources, and their use would not damage the environment.

## Water power

The force of moving water has been used for centuries to turn water wheels to provide power for various tasks. Nowadays, huge dams and reservoirs are built so that it can be used to generate electricity, called hydro-electricity.

## Solar power

The amount of energy which the Earth receives from the Sun is enormous. Modern technology has enabled scientists to develop ways of using this energy to produce solar power.

The world's largest solar power plant is in the Mojave desert in California.

It provides about 2,000 homes with all their energy needs.

The mirrors reflect the Sun's heat to a central boiler, containing water.

The water boils and gives off steam. This drives a turbine, linked to an electricity generator.

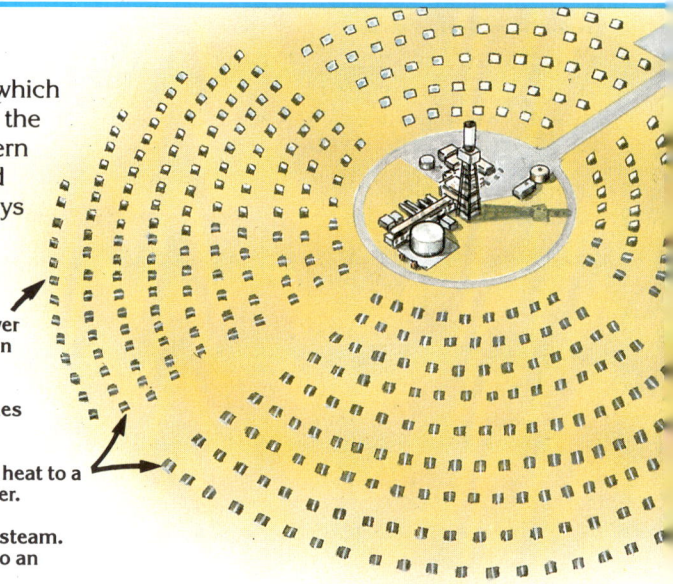

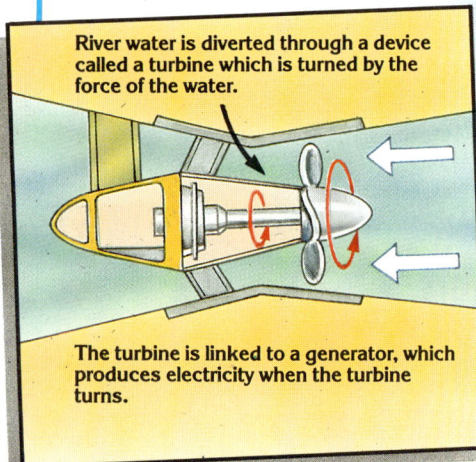

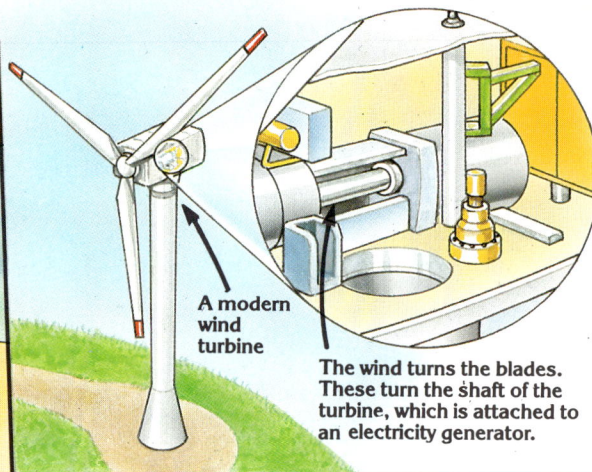

River water is diverted through a device called a turbine which is turned by the force of the water.

The turbine is linked to a generator, which produces electricity when the turbine turns.

A modern wind turbine

The wind turns the blades. These turn the shaft of the turbine, which is attached to an electricity generator.

## Wind energy

The wind has been used as a source of energy for many centuries to power sailing ships and drive machinery. Many different devices have been developed to produce electricity from the wind, or to use the wind's energy in other ways.

Layers of sand or silt covered the dead plants or animals before they could decompose completely.

Gradually the layers turned to sedimentary rock (see page 21).

The layers exerted pressure, which changed the remains to coal, oil and gas.

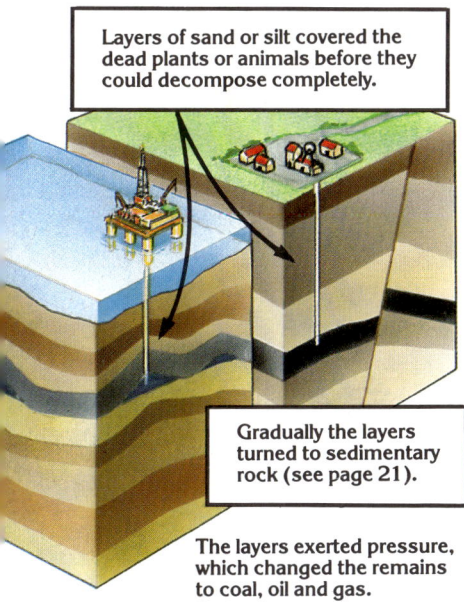

## Nuclear energy

Nuclear energy is the heat energy released when tiny particles, or atoms, are broken apart. It is used to produce electricity. Uranium, a mineral found in the Earth's crust, is the main fuel used to produce nuclear energy. Many people think nuclear energy could be the main source of power in the future, but there are many problems attached to its use.

Nuclear power stations do not produce polluting gases. But nuclear power can cause several other major environmental problems, as nuclear fuels are radioactive. This means that they give off radiation which kills living things if they are exposed to it. Its effects may be disastrous if it is released into the atmosphere or into the ground.

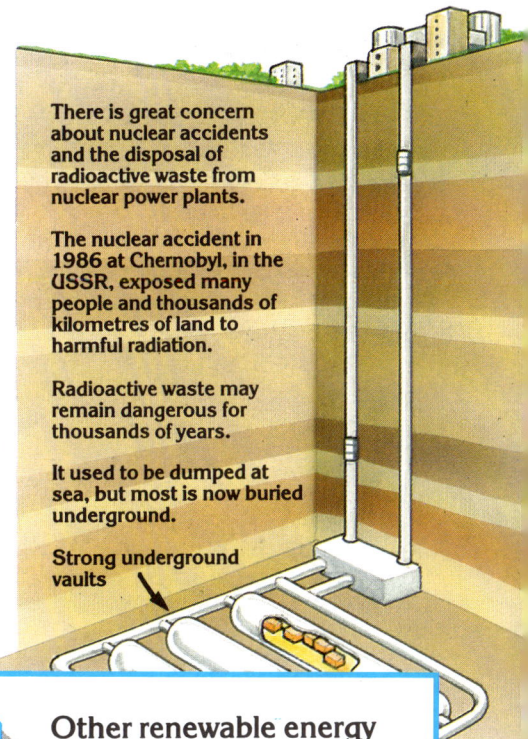

There is great concern about nuclear accidents and the disposal of radioactive waste from nuclear power plants.

The nuclear accident in 1986 at Chernobyl, in the USSR, exposed many people and thousands of kilometres of land to harmful radiation.

Radioactive waste may remain dangerous for thousands of years.

It used to be dumped at sea, but most is now buried underground.

Strong underground vaults

## Making a Savonius rotor

The Savonius rotor is a wind machine which is used by farmers in Africa and Asia to pump water for irrigation. To make your own rotor, you will need some drawing pins, a large plastic bottle, a plastic jar lid, two cotton reels, 1m length of 5mm dowel and two eyehooks.

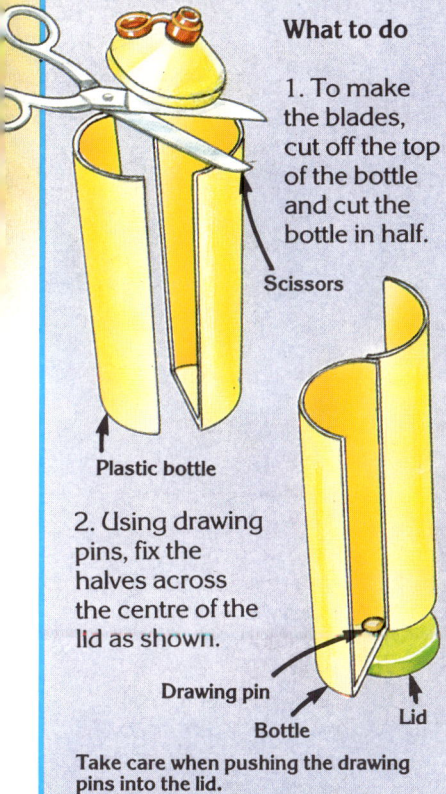

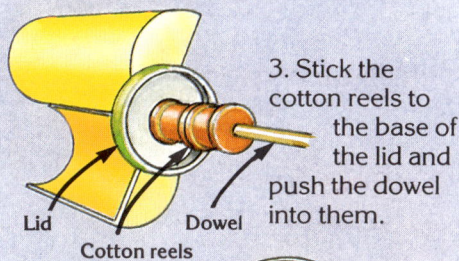

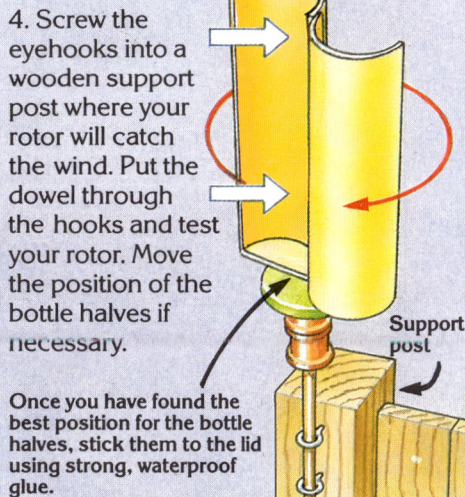

### What to do

1. To make the blades, cut off the top of the bottle and cut the bottle in half.

Scissors

Plastic bottle

2. Using drawing pins, fix the halves across the centre of the lid as shown.

Drawing pin

Bottle

Lid

Take care when pushing the drawing pins into the lid.

3. Stick the cotton reels to the base of the lid and push the dowel into them.

Lid

Dowel

Cotton reels

4. Screw the eyehooks into a wooden support post where your rotor will catch the wind. Put the dowel through the hooks and test your rotor. Move the position of the bottle halves if necessary.

Support post

Once you have found the best position for the bottle halves, stick them to the lid using strong, waterproof glue.

## Other renewable energy sources

In the future, many different natural sources of energy may be used to generate power. For instance, technology to make use of geothermal energy (heat energy from rocks within the Earth) is being developed in volcanic areas. Another source is biogas, a gas formed by rotting waste. It can be burnt to heat buildings and water.

Tidal power is already being developed.

Barrages are built across estuaries.

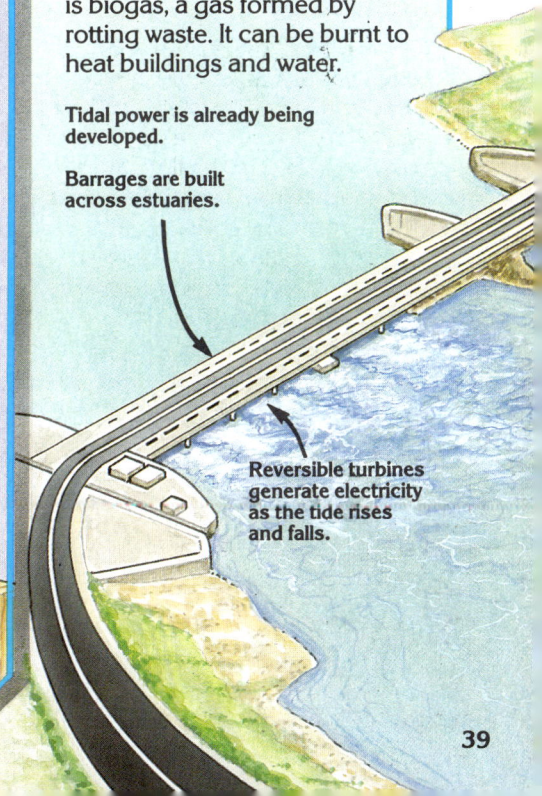

Reversible turbines generate electricity as the tide rises and falls.

# Antarctica

Antarctica is a huge, cold continent, almost twice the size of Australia. It is the only place on Earth which remains relatively unspoilt by humans.

Most of the land is covered by thick ice, though coastal areas are exposed in summer and, further inland, a number of high mountain peaks are permanently ice-free. A variety of wildlife has adapted to living in the freezing conditions.

## The frozen continent

Antarctica is the coldest and driest continent on Earth. Over 99% of it is covered by thick ice, up to five kilometres deep. The centre of the continent is a frozen desert (see page 32), where the annual snowfall averages between 3cm and 7cm and temperatures range from −50°C to −60°C. Areas near the coast are warmer, with more snow, strong winds and temperatures between −10°C and −20°C. In summer, the ice around the coast melts, revealing narrow strips of rocky shoreline, as well as the islands around the coast.

Weddell Sea

In winter, the sea round the coast freezes to form pack ice.

South pole

Transantarctic mountains

The edge of the pack ice extends about 2,000km from the coast.

Ross Sea

The pack ice reaches its furthest point in September.

## Research in Antarctica

Scientists from many countries work in research stations in Antarctica, and on the islands around its coast. They study many different aspects of the continent, such as its weather, ecosystems, geography and geology.

They also monitor changes in the world's climates, levels of air pollution and the hole in the ozone layer above Antarctica.

Records of weather conditions are made daily by instruments attached to a hydrogen-filled balloon.

They measure temperature, air pressure and humidity over 20km above Antarctica.

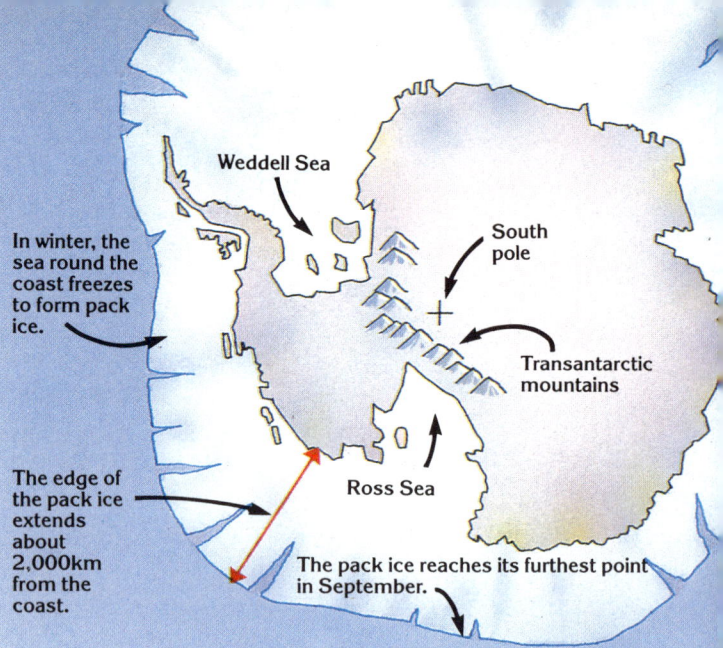

## Wildlife

The various birds and other animals which live in Antarctica need to be able to survive the freezing conditions on both the land, where they live and breed, and in the sea, which they depend upon to supply them with their food. They keep in their body heat with either a dense layer of fat, called blubber, found beneath their skin, or with very thick fur.

An Antarctic ocean food web

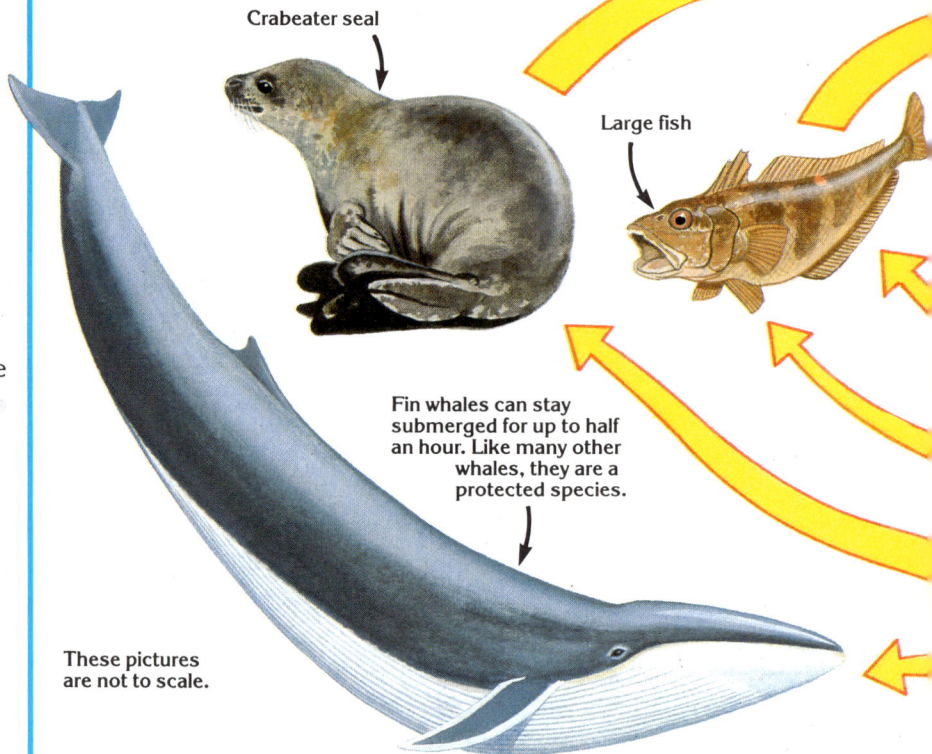

Crabeater seal

Large fish

Fin whales can stay submerged for up to half an hour. Like many other whales, they are a protected species.

These pictures are not to scale.

## The Antarctic treaty

In the past, explorers landed in Antarctica and claimed parts of it for their own country. This led to disputes about which country owned which part. In 1959, a treaty was signed by twelve nations who had decided to work together to keep Antarctica free from exploitation. They have now been joined by many other countries.

Antarctica is the only part of the world ruled by an international agreement.

The treaty has helped to protect Antarctica's wildlife.

The scientists from one country must share their discoveries with all the other countries in the treaty.

The only military personnel allowed are those helping at scientific research stations.

Scientists use snow mobiles to travel across the ice.

## Mineral exploitation

Geologists think there may be large reserves of minerals, such as coal, iron and copper, in and around Antarctica. Some countries wanted to be given permission to dig there for minerals, but the Antarctic treaty was reviewed in 1991, and any mineral exploration was prevented for fifty years.

Conservationists think that mining for minerals would endanger the animals and plants.

Airstrips and quays would be built in areas which are ice-free in summer.

These are the places where most seal, penguin and seabird colonies are found.

## Greenpeace in Antarctica

Greenpeace, the environmental group, has its own research base in Antarctica. Along with many other groups, it is concerned about the future of the continent.

Greenpeace's aim is to make Antarctica a world park, with the plants and animals protected and human activities limited and controlled. They think scientific research should continue, but they are campaigning against mineral exploration and the use of Antarctica for military purposes.

Greenpeace workers in Antarctica are constantly fighting to protect its natural ecosystems.

For instance, they have protested against the construction of an airstrip and collected rubbish left lying around a research base, which they delivered to the base commander. They are also continuing their fight against whaling.

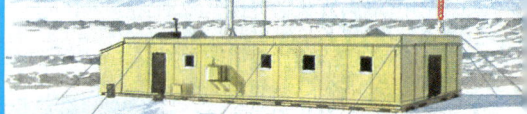

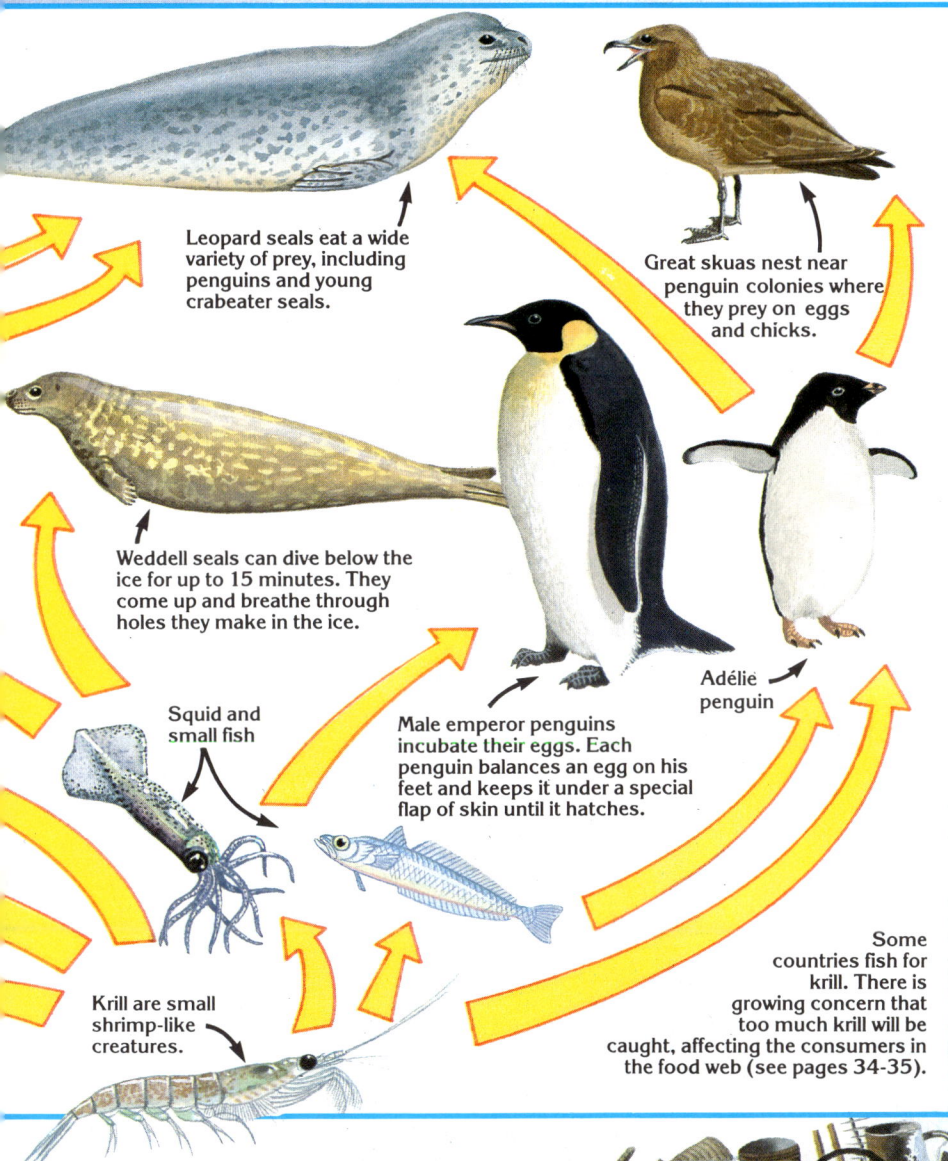

Leopard seals eat a wide variety of prey, including penguins and young crabeater seals.

Great skuas nest near penguin colonies where they prey on eggs and chicks.

Weddell seals can dive below the ice for up to 15 minutes. They come up and breathe through holes they make in the ice.

Squid and small fish

Male emperor penguins incubate their eggs. Each penguin balances an egg on his feet and keeps it under a special flap of skin until it hatches.

Adélie penguin

Krill are small shrimp-like creatures.

Some countries fish for krill. There is growing concern that too much krill will be caught, affecting the consumers in the food web (see pages 34-35).

# Controlling the future

In some ways, it is difficult to tell what will happen to the Earth in the future. Natural events and disasters, such as earthquakes, floods and hurricanes are hard to predict accurately.

There are, however, many present-day environmental problems, such as global warming, which have been caused directly by man's activities. In these cases, we are able to predict the disastrous effects of allowing these to continue. We must act together to solve them if the planet is going to be a pleasant place in the future.

## World problems

When the world's human population was much smaller, the Earth's natural resources could be exploited without affecting the environment. But now the population is growing so quickly that the demand for fuel, food and shelter is causing serious problems.

Acid rain, soil erosion, rain forest destruction and the threat of global warming are only a few of today's environmental problems. Much can be done to reduce or even solve them, but it will need the co-operation of people and governments around the world.

There are many ways in which action on a large-scale will help the environment.

For instance, if the destruction of rain forests, woodlands and marshes is stopped, many wildlife ecosystems will be preserved.

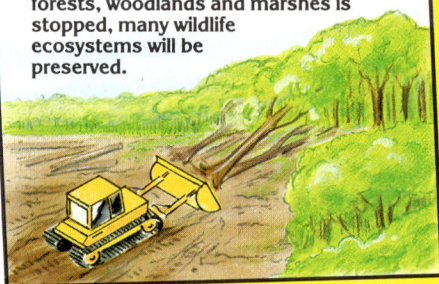

If there is a decrease in the number of motor vehicles on the roads, there will be less air pollution.

Car exhaust fumes contain many harmful gases, such as carbon monoxide and sulphur dioxide.

You can play your part in improving your environment. For instance, you could put your glass and paper waste into bottle and paper banks for recycling.

Recycling waste reduces the amount of resources taken from the Earth.

## The oceans

In the future, the oceans are likely to become a major source of food and energy, so we need to preserve ocean ecosystems and halt the damage that is being done. At the moment, enormous amounts of household and industrial waste are being dumped directly into the water. Spillages from oil tankers are also adding to the pollution.

Cleaning up the pollution is vital if the fish and other sea creatures are to survive. Without them, there will be no food from the sea in the future.

At the same time, the quantities of fish which are caught will need to be carefully controlled to protect natural ecosystems.

## Farming

As the world's population grows, so does the demand for food. Many international charities are helping to improve farming techniques in developing countries, which are often those with the fastest-growing populations. They have set up programmes to help farmers produce more food from the same area of land, to stop them destroying natural ecosystems.

Some new farmland has been created in desert border land. This land once had trees and shrubs, but turned into desert, a process called desertification, because of soil erosion (see page 37) due to overgrazing and the felling of trees, and unfavourable climate conditions, such as droughts and dry winds.

With the aid of irrigation, desert land can be reclaimed to grow crops.

The people grow crops, instead of relying on grazing animals for their food.

Irrigation in the desert has some problems. For instance, the water evaporates quickly in the heat, leaving salt deposits which make the soil too salty for some plants.

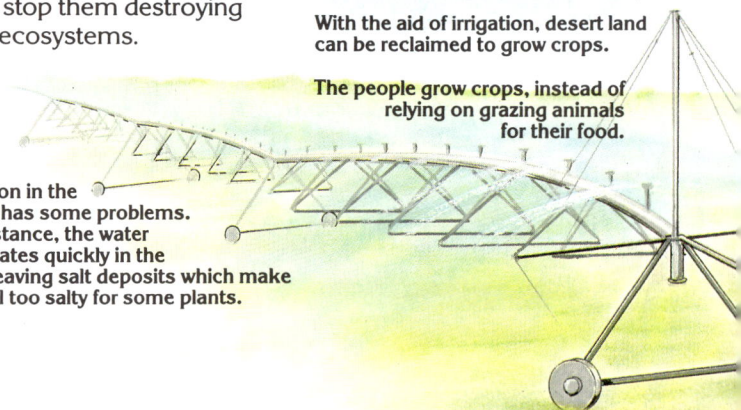

# Making a model irrigation system

In many irrigation systems, devices called Persian wheels are used to divert water. For a model wheel, you need three plastic lids, 15 lolly sticks, a plastic egg box, strong waterproof glue, a cardboard tube from a paper towel roll, three pieces of wood (20cm x 5cm x 2.5cm, 20cm x 15cm x 1cm and 10cm x 4cm x 4cm), sticky putty, two pieces of 3mm wooden dowel (20cm and 23cm), four 5mm cable clips and some foil.

Ask an adult to help you make holes in the lids and hammer in the clips.

## What to do

1. Make a hole in the centre of one of the lids, so the dowel will fit tightly. Glue 6 lolly sticks to the lid, evenly spaced, and push the 20cm dowel into the hole.

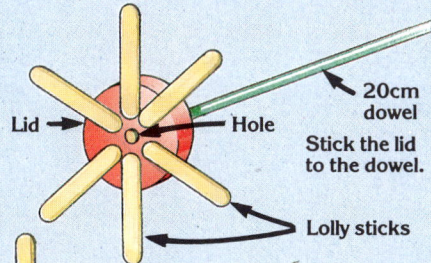

Lid — Hole
20cm dowel
Stick the lid to the dowel.
Lolly sticks

2. To make the wheel, cut up the egg box so you have six cups. Glue one cup to each stick as shown.

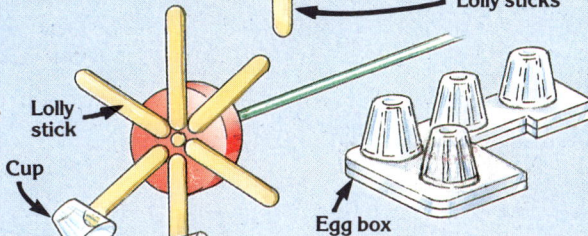

Lolly stick
Cup
Egg box

3. Cut the cardboard tube in half to make a gutter. Cover it with foil to make it waterproof.

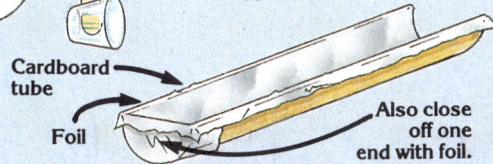

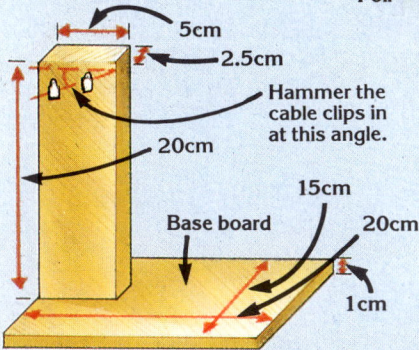

Cardboard tube
Foil
Also close off one end with foil.

5cm
2.5cm
Hammer the cable clips in at this angle.
20cm
Base board
15cm
20cm
1cm

5. Push the wheel's dowel through the cable clips. Fill a large, deep baking tray with water. Place your wheel so that when you turn the dowel it lifts some water. Using the sticky putty, stick the gutter across the rim of the tray, so that the water falls into it.

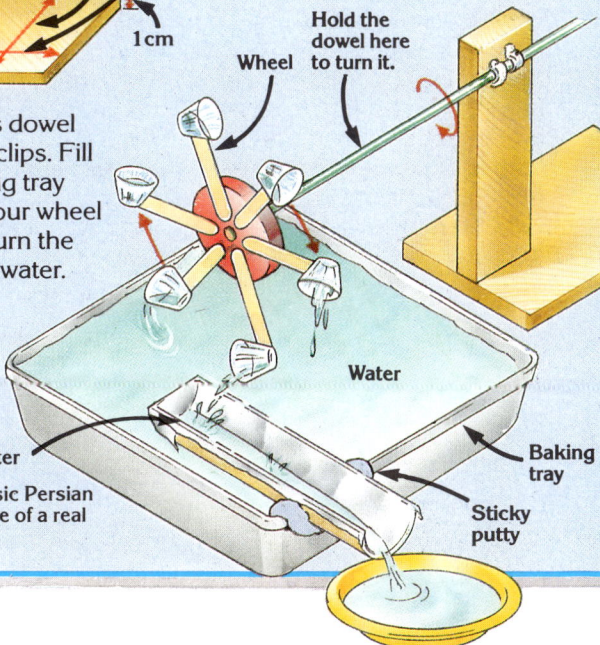

This is a model of a basic Persian wheel. There is a picture of a real one on page 28.

Wheel
Hold the dowel here to turn it.
Water
Gutter
Baking tray
Sticky putty

4. Hammer two cable clips into the larger block of wood (20cm x 5cm x 2.5cm), at an angle of approx. 45°. Stick or nail this piece to the flat piece (20cm x 15cm x 1cm).

6. In an irrigation system, a Persian wheel is usually driven by an animal. It turns a drive wheel, linked to the Persian wheel by a gearing system (gear wheel). To make such a gearing system, make two more 6-spoked wheels.

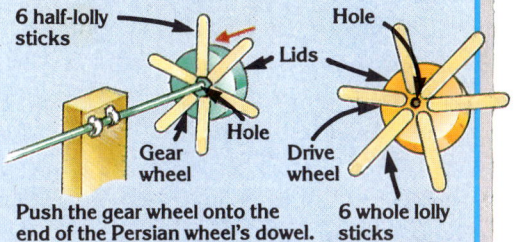

6 half-lolly sticks
Hole
Lids
Gear wheel
Hole
Drive wheel
6 whole lolly sticks

Push the gear wheel onto the end of the Persian wheel's dowel.

7. Hammer two cable clips into the last block (10cm x 4cm x 4cm) as shown. Push the 23cm piece of dowel through the clips and attach the drive wheel at the top.

Drive wheel
Cable clips
10cm
4cm
4cm

Drive wheel base

Make sure the dowel can turn, but is not too loose.

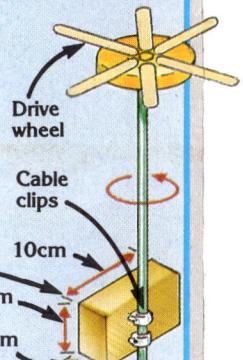

8. Position the drive wheel so that, as you turn it, the lolly sticks interconnect and turn the gear wheel (and Persian wheel). Then stick or nail the drive wheel base to the base board.

When you turn the drive wheel, the water will be lifted and flow into the gutter.

The best way to turn the drive wheel is by turning its dowel.

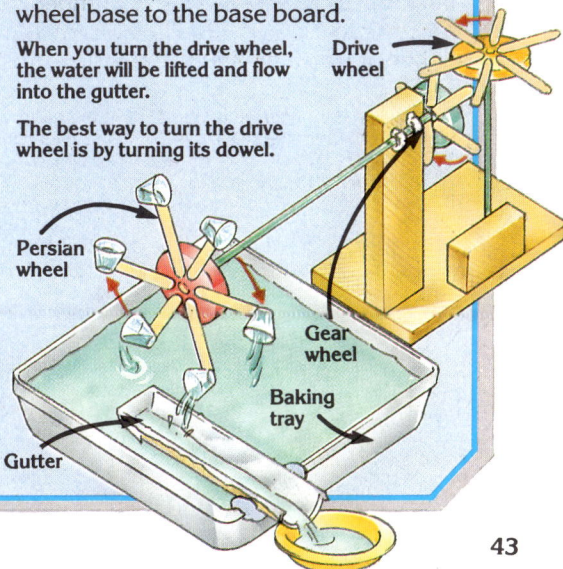

Persian wheel
Drive wheel
Gear wheel
Baking tray
Gutter

# Earth facts

The Earth is not a true sphere. It is slightly flattened at the poles. The distance around the Greenwich meridian (see below) is estimated to be 40,007km, whereas around the equator it is 40,075km.

The total area of the Earth's surface is estimated to be 510 million square kilometres. The area covered by water is approximately 361 million square kilometres.

Lines of longitude are imaginary lines which run through the north and south poles. They are used on maps and charts to measure distance in degrees east or west of the Greenwich meridian.

Lines of latitude are imaginary lines which run around the Earth, parallel to the equator. They are used on maps and charts to measure distance in degrees north or south of the equator.

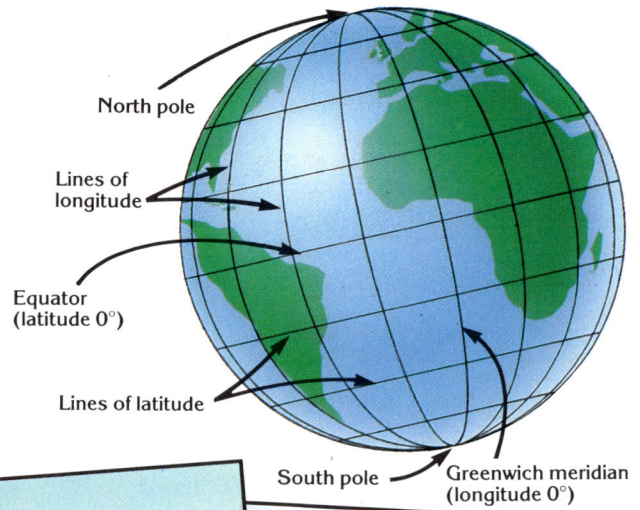

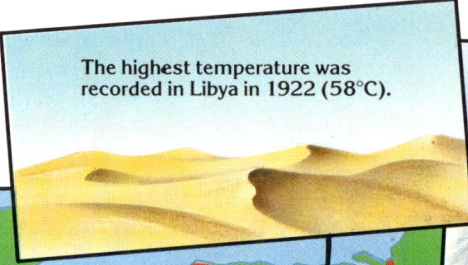

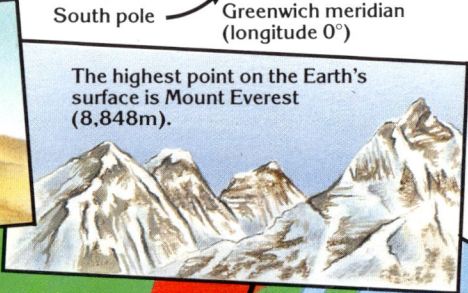

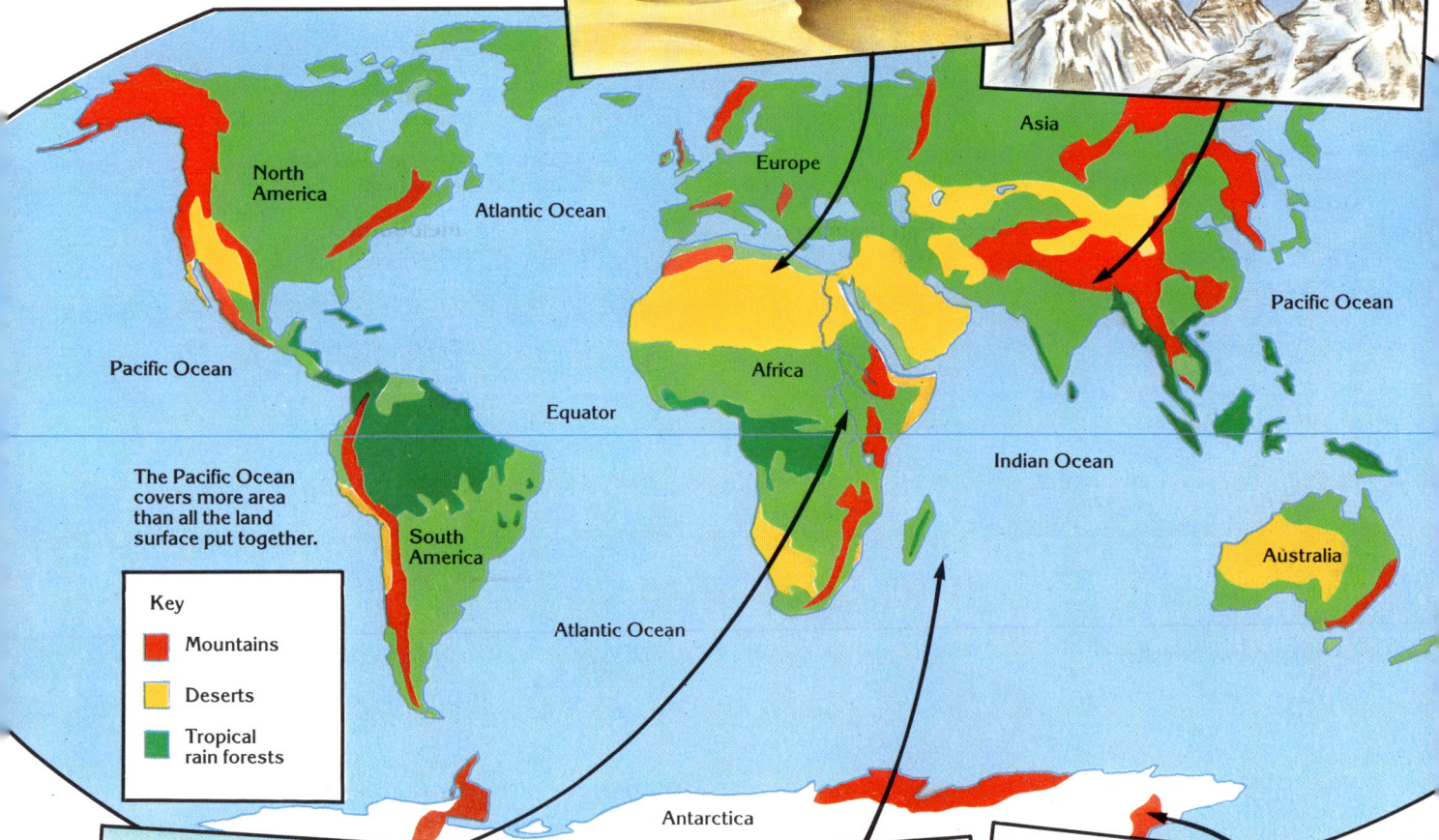

North pole

Lines of longitude

Equator (latitude 0°)

Lines of latitude

South pole

Greenwich meridian (longitude 0°)

The highest temperature was recorded in Libya in 1922 (58°C).

The highest point on the Earth's surface is Mount Everest (8,848m).

North America

Atlantic Ocean

Europe

Asia

Pacific Ocean

Africa

Equator

Indian Ocean

Pacific Ocean

South America

The Pacific Ocean covers more area than all the land surface put together.

Australia

Atlantic Ocean

## Key

- 🟥 Mountains
- 🟨 Deserts
- 🟩 Tropical rain forests

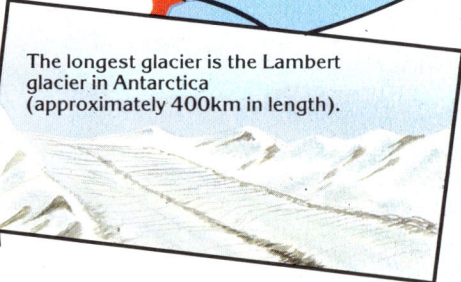

Antarctica

The longest river is the Nile in Africa (6670km).

The place with the greatest recorded rainfall in twenty-four hours is the island of Réunion (1870mm).

The longest glacier is the Lambert glacier in Antarctica (approximately 400km in length).

# Useful addresses

Below are some addresses of museums which have departments with permanent displays of rocks, fossils, wildlife etc. Your local library may be able to help you find addresses of smaller, local museums or suggest geological features in your area which you can visit. Also included are the main international addresses of some organizations concerned with the Earth and its natural environments. They may be able to provide you with further information.

## International organizations

World-Wide Fund for Nature
International,
Information Division,
Avenue Mont-Blanc,
CH-1196 Gland,
Switzerland

Friends of the Earth International,
26-28 Underwood Street,
London N1 7JQ

Greenpeace International,
Keizersgracht 176,
1016 DW Amsterdam,
The Netherlands

## United Kingdom

The Natural History Museum,
(including The Geological Museum),
Cromwell Road,
London SW7 5BD

The Royal Scottish Museum,
Chambers Street,
Edinburgh EH1 1JF

National Museum of Wales,
Cathays Park,
Cardiff CF1 3NP

Leeds City Museum,
Municipal Buildings,
Leeds,
Yorks LS1 3AA

Manchester Museum,
The University,
Oxford Road,
Manchester MI3 9PL

City Museum and Art Gallery,
Department of Natural History,
Chamberlain Square,
Birmingham B3 3DH

## United States of America

American Museum of Natural History,
Central Park West and 79th Street,
New York,
NY 10024

Denver Museum of Natural History,
City Park,
Denver,
Colorado 80205

National Museum of Natural History,
Wade Oval,
University Circle,
Cleveland,
Ohio 44106

California Academy of Sciences,
Golden Gate Park,
San Francisco,
CA 9418

Los Angeles Museum of Natural History,
900 Exposition Blvd.,
Exposition Park,
Los Angeles,
CA 90007

National Museum of Natural History,
10th Street and Constitution Ave. NW,
Washington DC 20560

## Canada

National Museum of Natural Sciences,
Victoria Memorial Museum Building,
Metcalfe and Mcleod Streets,
Ottawa,
Ontario K1A 0M8

Saskatchewan Museum of Natural History,
Wascana Park,
College Street and Albert Street,
Regina,
Saskatchewan SP4 3V7

## Australia and New Zealand

Australian Museum,
6-8 College Street,
Sydney,
New South Wales 2000

S. Australian Museum,
North Terrace,
Adelaide,
South Australia 5000

Queensland Museum,
Cultural Centre,
South Bank,
South Brisbane,
Queensland 4101

Museum of Victoria,
328 Swanston Street,
Melbourne,
Victoria 3000

The Western Australian Museum,
Francis Street,
Perth,
Western Australia 6000

National Museum,
Buckle Street,
Wellington,
New Zealand

Redpath Museum,
856 Sherbrooke Street West,
Montreal,
Quebec H3A 2K6

Royal Ontario Museum,
100 Queen's Park,
Toronto,
Ontario M5S 2C6

Provincial Museum of Alberta,
102nd Avenue,
Edmonton,
Alberta T5N 0M8

# Glossary

**Aquifer.** An area of permeable rock which is capable of holding water and allows water to travel through it.

**Astronomer.** A scientist who studies the stars, planets and other bodies which make up the Universe.

**Atmosphere.** The mixture of gases which surrounds the Earth. It has a number of layers.

**Backwash.** The movement of a wave back down a beach after it has broken (see **Swash**).

**Billion.** One USA billion = one thousand million (1,000,000,000). This is the value used throughout this book. In some other countries, e.g. the UK, one billion = one million million (1,000,000,000,000).

**Climate.** The average weather conditions experienced in an area. Climates vary greatly around the world.

**Continent.** One of the large masses of land into which the Earth's surface is divided. The world's continents are Europe, Asia, Africa, North and South America, Australia and Antarctica.

**Continental plates.** The massive interlinking pieces which form the surface layer, or crust, of the Earth. They move around in relation to each other.

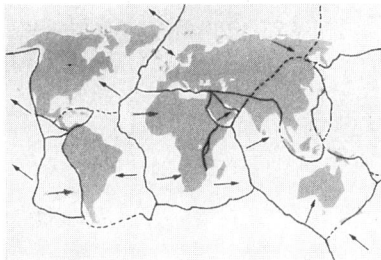

**Debris.** Fragments formed when weathering and erosion break down the surface of rocks.

**Delta.** A build-up of sand or silt, which splits up the mouth of a river into a number of channels.

**Desert.** Any area of the Earth's surface which receives less than 25cm of rain in a year.

**Desertification.** The process by which dry areas become deserts. It is a great problem at the edges of deserts where droughts have accelerated the process.

**Drought.** A long period of time with little or no rain.

**Ecosystem.** A self-contained system of living and non-living parts, consisting of plants, animals and the environment they live in.

**Environment.** Everything which surrounds a plant or animal, including the land, the atmosphere and other plants and animals.

**Erosion.** The wearing away and movement of material on the Earth's surface. The main agents of erosion are the wind, water and ice.

**Faults.** Cracks (**fractures**) which are lines of weakness in the Earth's crust and along which movement occurs.

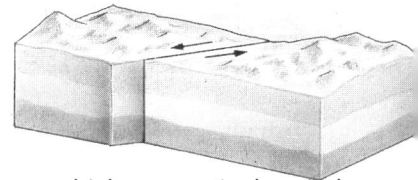

**Fetch.** The stretch of open sea which any particular wind blows across.

**Flood plain.** A flat area which extends out on both sides of a river channel. It is formed from layers of sediment, deposited when the river overflows its banks.

**Folds.** Bends in rocks, caused by movements of the Earth's crust.

**Food chain.** A chain of living organisms which are linked together by their feeding relationships. Energy is passed on through each organism in the chain.

**Fossil fuels.** Fuels such as coal, oil and natural gas, which are the remains of living matter that died millions of years ago.

**Glacier.** A mass of moving ice which travels slowly due to the force of gravity.

**Global warming.** An overall increase in world temperatures, thought to be caused by pollution in the atmosphere effectively increasing the greenhouse effect.

**Greenhouse effect.** The warming effect caused by gases in the atmosphere trapping the Sun's heat.

**Ground water.** Water which has seeped into the soil and rock below the surface of the ground.

**Humidity.** The amount of water vapour in the atmosphere.

**Hydro-electric power.** Electricity generated by using the force of moving water. Hydro-electric power is one of the most widely used forms of renewable energy.

**Ice sheet.** A vast mass of ice and snow, sometimes called an ice-cap, which covers a massive area. Ice sheets are found in the Arctic and Antarctica.

**Igneous rock.** Rock which is formed when molten rock from beneath the Earth's crust cools and hardens.

**Impermeable rock.** Rock which does not allow water to pass through it easily.

**Irrigation.** The artificial watering of an area of land in order to create fertile land on which to grow crops.

**Lava.** Magma which has flowed out onto the Earth's surface.

**Magma.** Molten (liquid) rock found beneath the Earth's surface.

**Metamorphic rock.** Rock which has been changed from one type of rock into another by great heat or pressure.

**Minerals.** Naturally-made, non-living substances with a particular chemical make-up. Rocks are composed of one or more different minerals.

**Ozone layer.** A layer of ozone gas found in the Earth's atmosphere. It absorbs some of the Sun's harmful ultra-violet rays.

**Permeable rock.** Rock which allows water to pass through it easily. The water travels through spaces between individual rock particles or cracks in the rock.

**Precipitation.** Any moisture which reaches the Earth from the atmosphere, or forms on the Earth's surface. It includes rain, snow, sleet, hail, dew and frost.

**Prey.** An animal which is killed and eaten by another animal (the **predator**).

**Renewable energy.** Energy from sources which are constantly available in the natural world, such as wind, water or the Sun.

**Sediment.** Rock debris, such as sand, mud or gravel, deposited by the wind, water or ice.

**Sedimentary rock.** Rock formed from layers of sediment which were deposited and squeezed together.

**Solar energy.** The energy contained in the Sun's rays which can be converted into electricity using a solar, or photovoltaic, cell.

**Swash.** The movement of a wave as it breaks and advances up a beach (see **Backwash**).

**Tornado.** A twisting, funnel-shaped cloud, reaching down to the ground. Tornadoes create strong, spiralling winds which may cause severe damage, e.g. to buildings and trees.

**Tropical cyclone.** A violent tropical storm in which the winds circulate around a central point, or "eye". Tropical cyclones are also known as hurricanes, typhoons or, in Australia, willy-willies.

**Tropical grasslands.** Vast open areas of grass with a few scattered trees, found in tropical regions. Grasslands are given different names in different locations. For instance, they are called savannahs in East Africa and campos or llanos in South America.

**Tsunami.** A giant wave caused by an earthquake taking place beneath the ocean. It is sometimes misleadingly called a tidal wave.

**Weathering.** The disintegration of rocks by various processes due to exposure to the weather.

# ECOLOGY

Richard Spurgeon

Edited by Corinne Stockley

Designed by Stephen Wright

Illustrated by
Kuo Kang Chen, Brin Edwards and Caroline Ewen

Scientific advisor: Dr. Margaret Rostron

# Contents

51 About this book

52 What is ecology?

54 The environment

56 Ecosystems

58 The oceans

60 Cycles in nature

62 Disturbing the cycles

64 Adaptation

66 Coniferous and deciduous forests

68 Relationships in nature

70 Population and conservation

72 Urban ecosystems

74 Tropical rainforests

76 Change in nature

78 Evolution

80 People and planet

81 Energy and the environment

82 The future

Ecology projects:

84 Building an ant observatory
Making a pond

86 Building a compost heap
Sprouting beans and seeds

87 Building a bird table
Birdwatching

88 Planting trees

90 Making recycled paper
A windowsill salad garden
Organizing your own group

92 Going further

94 Glossary

We are extremely grateful to Dr. John Rostron for all his technical and scientific assistance, to the World Wide Fund for Nature for permission to reprint their emblem on page 71 and to all the organizations listed on pages 92-93 for their co-operation. We are also grateful to Brin Edwards for natural history advice, and to Chris Oxlade for general editorial assistance and specific help with constructing and testing certain of the activities.

# About this book

Ecology is the study of all living things and how they work with each other and the world around them. This book shows how plants, animals and their environments are all linked together in one vast web, and how we ourselves are all part of this web. It explains the basic terms and ideas of ecology, using examples from the very different ecological regions of the world.

## Using the glossary

The glossary on pages 94-95 is a useful reference point. It brings together and explains all the main ecological terms used in the book.

## Useful addresses

If you want to get more involved in helping wildlife and improving the environment, or just want to find out more about what other people are doing, you can turn to pages 92-93. These have a list of addresses of leading conservation and environmental groups. Many of these organizations run activities for young people, and all of them will send you more information.

Throughout this book, there are many examples of how the things people are doing today are causing problems and disturbances in the natural world. At the same time, there are suggestions as to what can be done to help. These range from activities which will help you improve the situation in your local area, to some ideas about how the larger scale problems could be solved.

This scene shows one of the harshest of the world's environments, and some of the people and animals adapted to survive there. You can find out more about the ecology of the world's deserts on pages 64-65.

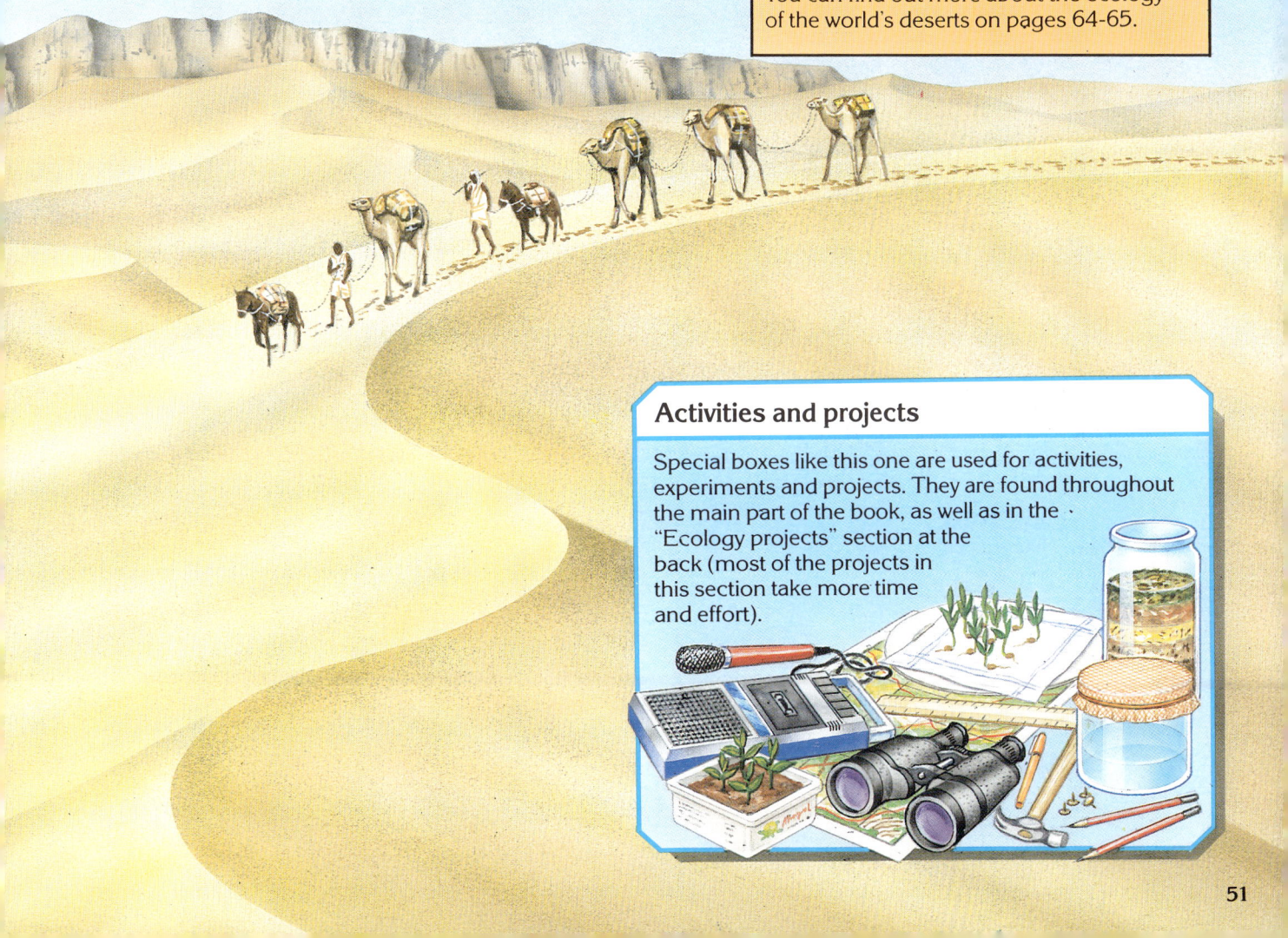

## Activities and projects

Special boxes like this one are used for activities, experiments and projects. They are found throughout the main part of the book, as well as in the "Ecology projects" section at the back (most of the projects in this section take more time and effort).

# What is ecology?

Ecology is the study of living things in their natural surroundings, or **environment**. This is everything, living and non-living, that is around them.

Your own environment is made up of all that you can see and much that you can't when you look around you. Its basic features stay very much the same, e.g. the air that you breathe, but the details are constantly changing.

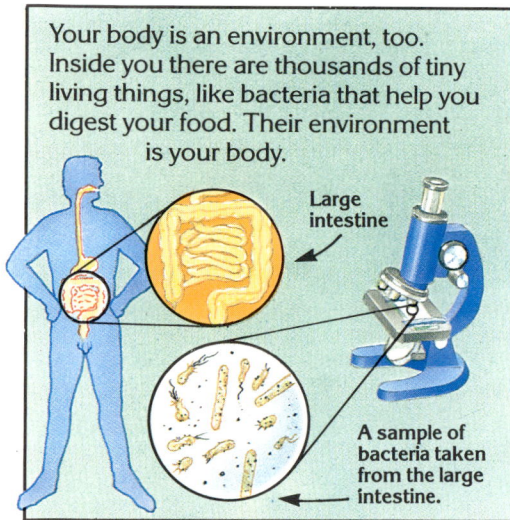

Your body is an environment, too. Inside you there are thousands of tiny living things, like bacteria that help you digest your food. Their environment is your body.

Large intestine

A sample of bacteria taken from the large intestine.

At the swimming pool

In the cinema

In the countryside

In your everyday life you live in various environments. Here are a few — there are a great many others.

On the streets of a town or city

What happens in the city will have an effect on the countryside, and vice versa.

On the beach

These different environments may not seem to be connected, but in fact they are.

At home

## Connections

Ecology investigates how plants and animals, including people, live with and affect each other and their environment.

A good starting point is yourself. Notice how you affect your own environment. Where is your food from? What happens to your rubbish? What animals and plants live around you?

Anything you do to your environment will have an effect back on you, as well as on every other living thing sharing the environment with you. The connections between all living things stretch into a vast web.

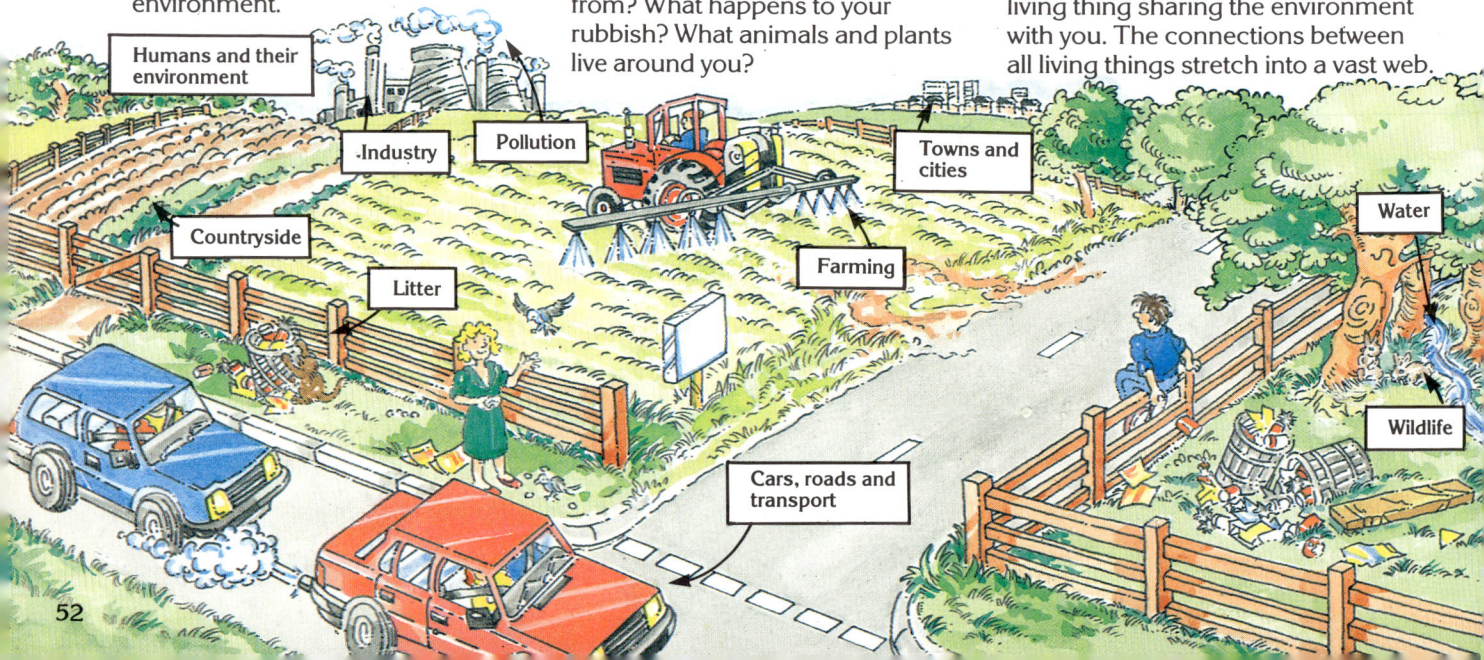

Humans and their environment

Industry

Pollution

Countryside

Litter

Towns and cities

Farming

Water

Cars, roads and transport

Wildlife

## Habitats

The natural home of a group of plants and animals is called a **habitat** and the group of plants and animals which live there is a **community**. Lift up a stone and see what lives in the habitat underneath it.

Smaller habitats are part of larger habitats. The stone may be at the side of a stream, which may be in a wood. A different, larger community lives in each larger habitat.

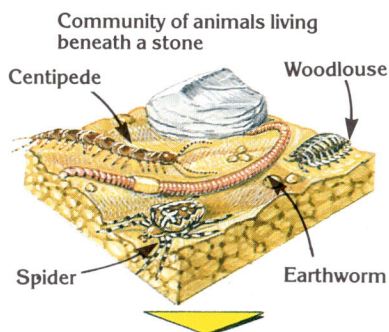

Community of animals living beneath a stone

Centipede
Woodlouse
Spider
Earthworm

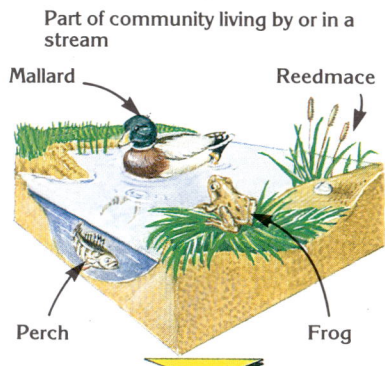

Part of community living by or in a stream

Mallard
Reedmace
Perch
Frog

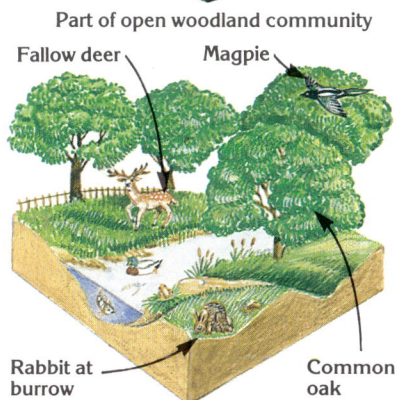

Part of open woodland community

Fallow deer
Magpie
Rabbit at burrow
Common oak

Try to find some different habitats in your area. Look everywhere – in, on, under and around. But remember to leave everything as you found it.

## A freshwater pond

A pond is a good example of a larger habitat. It is the home of a large community of different plants and animals. The pond, its community, and the non-living environment around it, make up a complete ecological unit, called an **ecosystem**. For more on ecosystems and how they work, see page 56.

Pond-dipping is a good way of studying the pond community. Gently drag a net through different areas of the pond. Make notes on what you find. Put anything interesting into a container for closer inspection (you could use a book on pond life for identification). Don't forget to put everything back into the pond when you have finished.

You can either buy a net or make your own. Get a metal coat-hanger and bend it into a circle. Stick the ends into a long piece of bamboo, or tie them to a pole, and tie an old stocking to the rim.

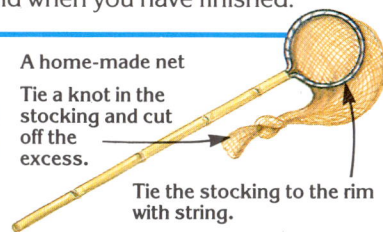

A home-made net

Tie a knot in the stocking and cut off the excess.

Tie the stocking to the rim with string.

Ponds are much less common today than they were forty years ago. Many have been filled in or have grown over. This is most unfortunate for their inhabitants. Some plants and animals only live in certain habitats. When these disappear, so do they.

## Build your own pond

You can help the wildlife in your area by building a pond. This will attract all sorts of wildlife and is not too hard to do. See pages 84-85 for instructions on how to make, stock and maintain a pond.

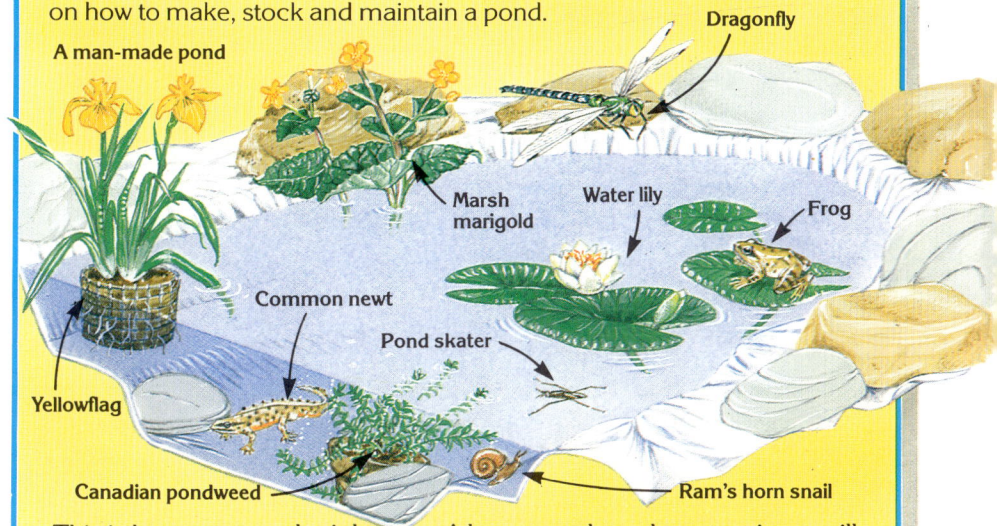

A man-made pond

Dragonfly
Marsh marigold
Water lily
Frog
Common newt
Pond skater
Yellowflag
Canadian pondweed
Ram's horn snail

This is how your pond might look when it is finished. It will take quite a bit of work and time, and must be properly looked after, but once it is established many animals will come to visit or stay and you will be able to study them whenever you want.

A home-made underwater viewer will give you a better view of pond life. Carefully cut the top and bottom off a plastic squeezy bottle. Cover one end with clear plastic wrap and attach it with a rubber band. Place it in the water and look through the open end (for safety, cover the cut edge with tape).

Underwater viewer

# The environment

As well as influencing our environment, we are constantly being influenced by it. Like all living things, we are dependent on our environment for the essentials of life.

The basis of all life on earth is the sun. Without its heat the world would be a frozen mass of lifeless rock and ice. It provides plants and animals with the energy they need to live. It generates the winds by heating the earth's land masses and the air above them, and drives the water cycle by evaporating water into the atmosphere (see page 60). It is the most vital component of the environment, without which life on earth could not exist.

## The climate

This map shows the world's six major climates. The main influences on the climate are: distance from the Equator, distance from the ocean (it is drier inland), and the height above sea level (the higher you go, the colder it gets)

The sun's energy is not evenly spread across the surface of the earth. Equatorial areas receive far more than polar areas. This imbalance creates and drives the winds around the world.

At the poles, the sun's rays pass through more atmosphere and are spread over a larger land surface than at the Equator, so it is much colder.

The interactions of warm winds and ocean currents from the tropical areas and cold winds and currents from polar regions cause climatic variations wherever they converge.

Living things are greatly affected by the conditions around them. The temperature, rainfall and other aspects of the climate in an area influence the forms, growth and behaviour of the plants and animals found there (see map on page 56).

The climate and the earth's landscape interact to create the larger environment within which life can exist. Over time, the powerful weathering effects of the climate have formed the earth's life-supporting soil.

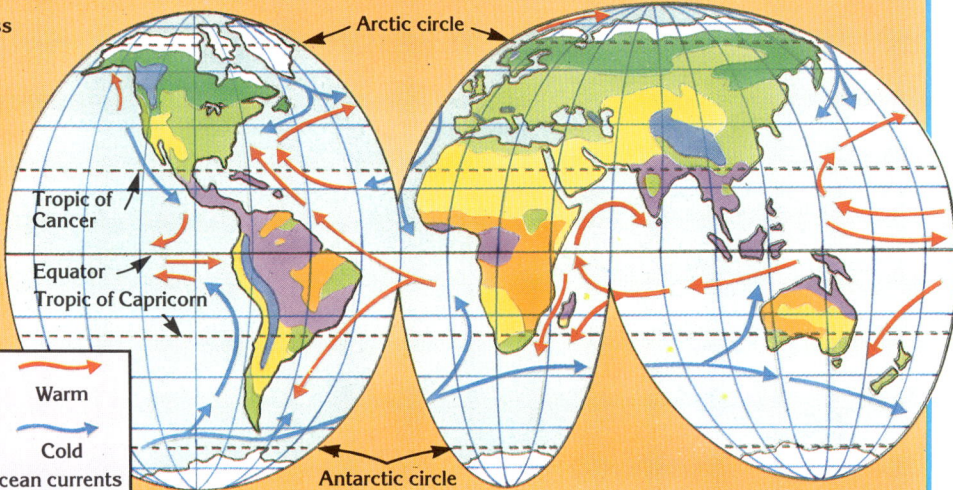

Arctic circle

Tropic of Cancer

Equator
Tropic of Capricorn

Antarctic circle

**Climate key**

- ○ Polar
- ● Mountain
- ● Cold forest
- ● Temperate
- ● Dry
- ● Equatorial
- ● Sub-equatorial

→ Warm

→ Cold

Ocean currents

## The importance of soil

The weathering effects of temperature, wind and water break down the rocks of the earth's surface to produce mineral particles which are the basis of soil. For more about the changing landscape, see page 76.

Tiny plants grow on these rock particles, die and decompose to form organic matter called **humus**. This mixture of mineral particles and organic matter is what makes up soil. Soil also contains water and air, trapped between the particles, and millions of microscopic organisms, like bacteria, as well as insects and some larger animals.

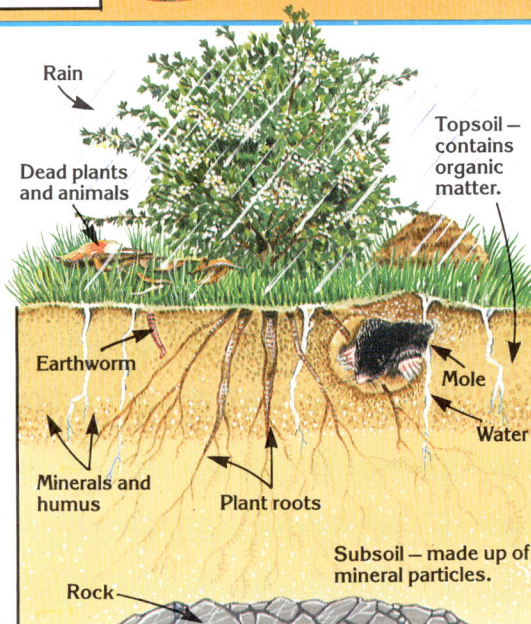

Rain

Dead plants and animals

Topsoil – contains organic matter.

Earthworm

Mole

Water

Minerals and humus

Plant roots

Subsoil – made up of mineral particles.

Rock

There are many types of soil, each with a different ratio of humus and minerals (and different types of mineral particles, formed from the breakdown of different rocks). Each type of soil supports its own range of plant species.

Soil supplies many of the essential needs of most green plants. It is the source of their water, the minerals they need to develop, and gives them a solid base in which their roots can grow.

## Soil experiments

To see what soil is made of, take a sample and shake it up in a jar of water. Let it settle for a few days, then study the different layers.

- Humus — organic matter
- Clay — mainly aluminium silicate
- Silt — mud formed from tiny pieces of rock
- Sand — mainly silica
- Gravel — larger rock particles

Now get samples of different types of soil from a variety of places. Do the same thing to each and compare the results.

To see what sort of animals are living in the soil, take a sample and put it on a piece of gauze in a funnel. Place this on a tall jar under a lamp overnight. The light and heat will force the creatures down into the jar.

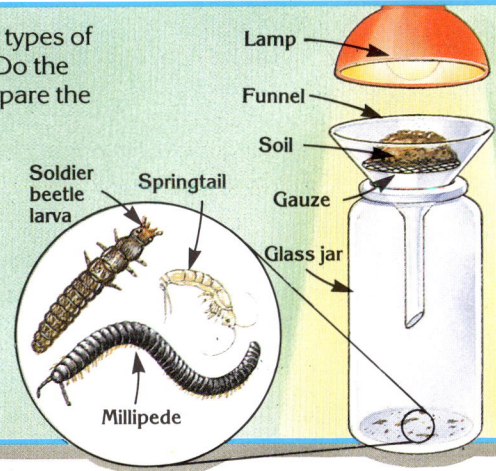

Soldier beetle larva
Springtail
Millipede

Lamp
Funnel
Soil
Gauze
Glass jar

## Soil erosion

Most of the earth's surface is covered by a layer of soil, ranging from ½ cm thick in mountainous regions to 2 m in cultivated areas. We all depend on this thin layer for our food supplies, yet everywhere it is threatened by soil erosion.

Over-grazing, poor irrigation, intensive farming and the destruction of tree cover mean that vital topsoil is left exposed, and much is being blown or washed away. If this continues, we may not have enough fertile land left to grow enough food.

In the early 1930s, farming areas in the American mid-west were devastated by soil erosion.

Lack of trees, intensive farming and large, open fields combined with a drought to create a "dust-bowl".

The topsoil turned to dust and was blown away in the winds.

## Energy for life

All living things need energy for their growth, movement and life processes. The source of this energy is the sun.

Green plants use the sun's energy to build their own food from the simpler elements around them. They are called **producers**. They use the sunlight in a process called **photosynthesis** to convert water and carbon dioxide into oxygen and carbohydrates. Some of the carbohydrates are then combined with minerals from the soil and used for growth, others form a store of food (mainly in leaves), to provide energy when needed. Animals cannot produce their own food. They depend on the food stored in plants to give them energy for life and so are called **consumers**.

Process of photosynthesis

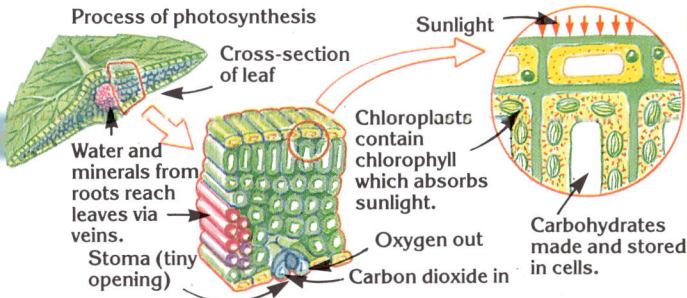

Cross-section of leaf

Water and minerals from roots reach leaves via veins.

Stoma (tiny opening)

Sunlight

Chloroplasts contain chlorophyll which absorbs sunlight.

Oxygen out

Carbon dioxide in

Carbohydrates made and stored in cells.

## Plant experiments

Put some cress seeds in two dishes lined with damp kitchen paper. Put both in a dark cupboard for one or two days, then take one out and put it by a window. After a few more days you will see how important sunlight is for healthy plant growth.

Add some food dye to the water you give the healthy cress. Study what happens. The plants draw up the water like they would from soil.

Plants move their leaves to catch the most light. Study the growth of a plant in a sunny place, then turn it round and see what happens.

Dish from cupboard

Unhealthy cress plants

Keep the paper damp all the time.

Dish from windowsill

Healthy cress plants

# Ecosystems

An ecosystem consists of a given habitat and its community. The living things within it interact with each other and their non-living (**abiotic**) environment to form an ecological unit which is largely self-contained.

Many smaller ecosystems can be found within larger ones, like a rotting tree branch, within a wood.

Biomes are the largest ecosystems into which the earth's land surface can be divided (see right). They are named after the main type of vegetation found there, and each one is home to a very large variety of plants and animals.

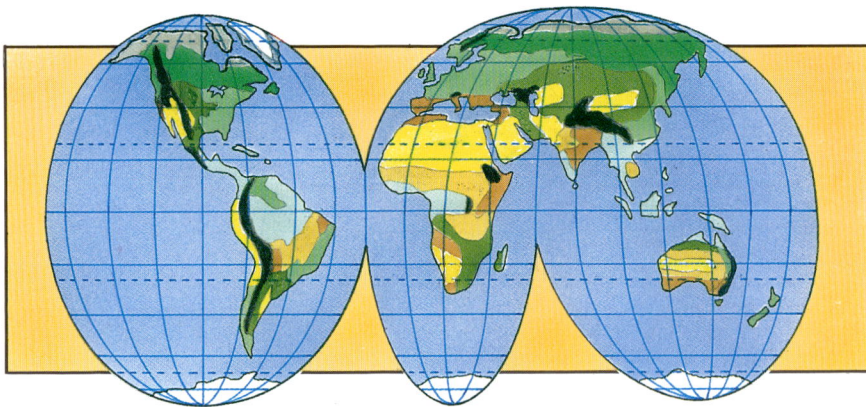

○ **Ice**

● **Mountain**

● **Maquis**. Warm, wet winters, hot, dry summers, scrubland.

○ **Tropical forest**. Hot and wet, with a great diversity of life, e.g. monkeys and exotic birds.

○ **Desert**. Extremes of temperature, little rain, scarcity of life.

● **Deciduous forest**. Warm summers, cold winters, mainly deciduous woodland (e.g. oak or beech), variety of animals.

○ **Savannah** (tropical grassland) – hot with wet winters, open plains with trees, antelopes.

● **Coniferous forest**. Cold all year, dominated by forests of conifers (e.g. spruce and pine), deer and wolves.

● **Temperate grassland**. Hot summers, cold winters, open grassy plains, buffalo.

○ **Tundra**. Very cold, windy and treeless, little animal life.

The climate of each biome (see global climate map, page 54) directly influences the different types of plant and animal that live there.

## Your local ecosystems

A good way to get to know the ecology of your local area is to make a map of the areas of interest. Get hold of a large scale map of your district and copy the main features like roads and buildings, or photocopy it. Then go out and survey the area, noting down the position of important ecosystems. Fill these in on your map and make a key to explain the symbols and colours that you use. Once you have made your map, keep your eyes open for interesting things to add.

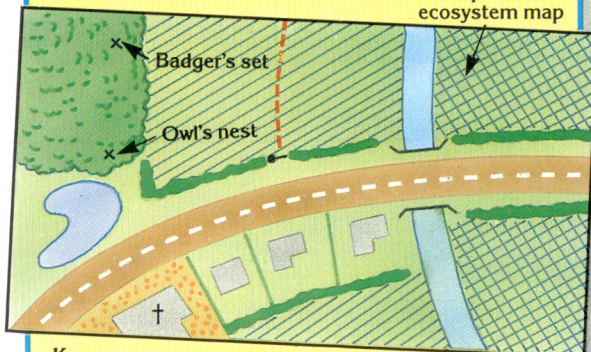

Example of an ecosystem map

Badger's set

Owl's nest

**Key**

| | | | |
|---|---|---|---|
| | Woodland | | Pond |
| | Hedgerow | | Building |
| | River or stream | | Road |
| † | Church | | Graveyard |
| | Wheat-field | | Meadow |
| | Bridge | | Gate |
| x | Point of interest | | Footpath |

## Food chains

The plants and animals in a given ecosystem are linked by their feeding relationships. The plants act as producers (see page 55), by using the sun's energy to produce food, which provides animals with the energy they need to live. The energy stored in plants as food is passed on through the community in a **food chain**. It is passed on directly to **primary consumers**, animals which eat plants, and indirectly to **secondary consumers**, animals which eat primary consumers. Other animals eat these secondary consumers and are known as **tertiary consumers**.

Each food chain also contains **decomposers**. These are bacteria, fungi and some types of insects that break down dead plant and animal matter into minerals and humus in the soil. In the process, they get their own energy for life from the food that they break down.

## Decomposers at work

Find an old log and make a study of its decay. Take notes or photographs over a period of time of the different decomposers at work. How long does it take?

A decaying log

Fungi

Lichens

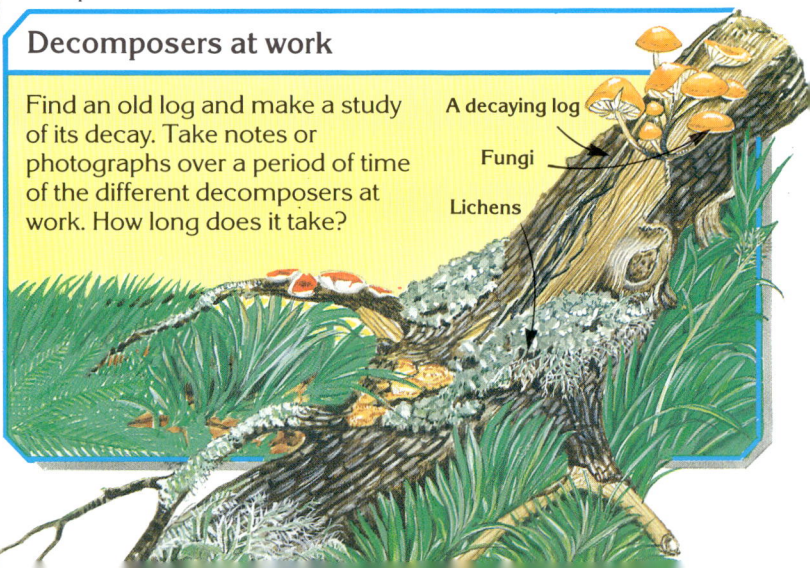

# Food webs

Each ecosystem contains many different food chains which interlink to form a more complex **food web**. This is because animals often eat a varied diet and so play different roles in a number of food chains. Patterns of feeding also link different ecosystems. Animals from one will feed off plants and animals from another. In this way, all life on earth is interlinked in one vast, continuous web.

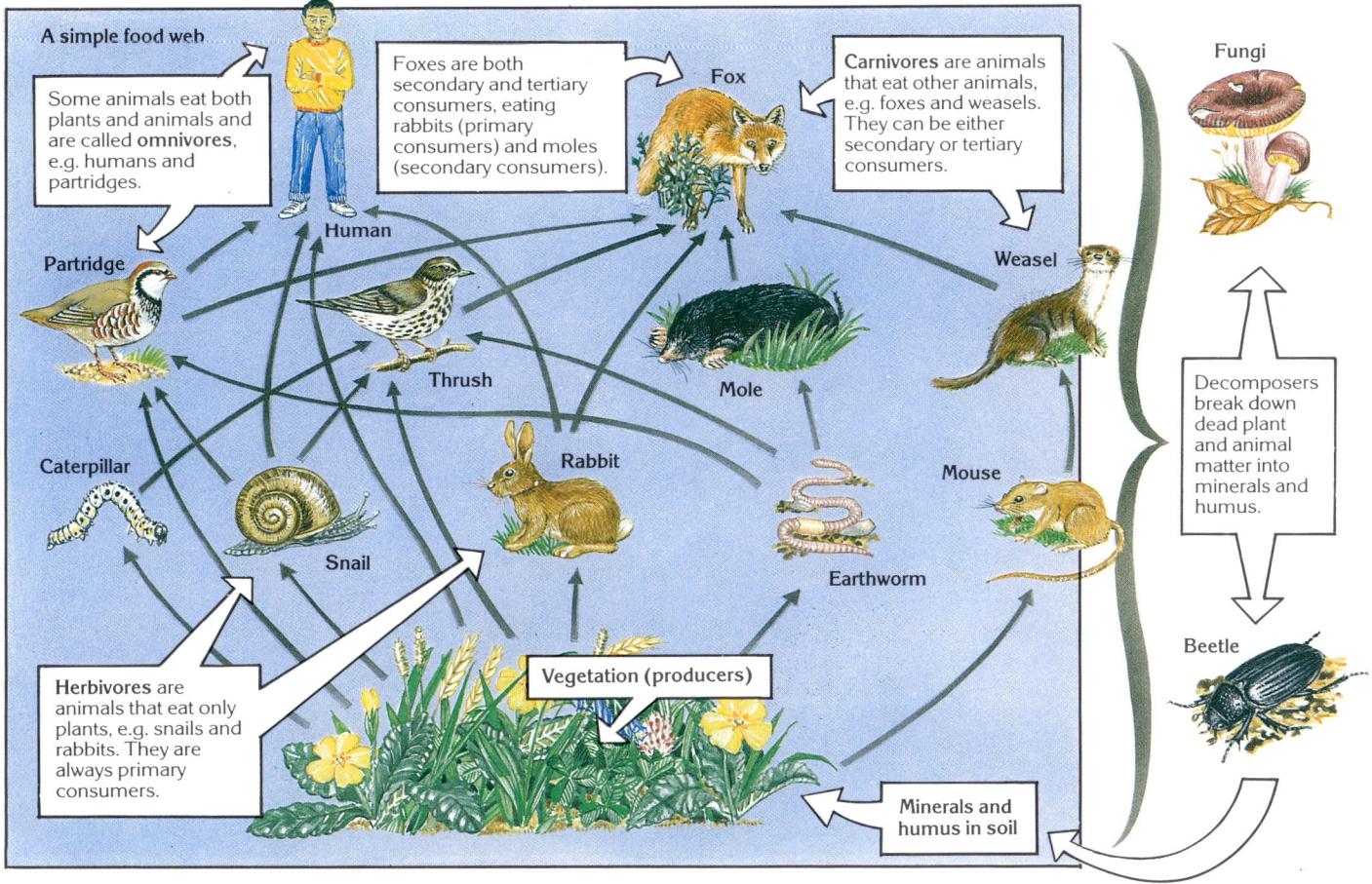

A simple food web

Some animals eat both plants and animals and are called **omnivores**, e.g. humans and partridges.

Foxes are both secondary and tertiary consumers, eating rabbits (primary consumers) and moles (secondary consumers).

**Carnivores** are animals that eat other animals, e.g. foxes and weasels. They can be either secondary or tertiary consumers.

Fungi

Human

Fox

Weasel

Partridge

Thrush

Mole

Decomposers break down dead plant and animal matter into minerals and humus.

Caterpillar

Rabbit

Mouse

Snail

Earthworm

Beetle

**Herbivores** are animals that eat only plants, e.g. snails and rabbits. They are always primary consumers.

Vegetation (producers)

Minerals and humus in soil

## Constructing a food web

To show how complicated a food web can be, you can build your own. Find some old wildlife magazines, cut out pictures of individual plants and animals, and stick them onto some card. You could also trace, copy or draw them from books. Then arrange the pictures in a food web, connecting those that eat or are eaten by each other. Make different webs for different ecosystems, e.g. your local area, an African plain or the Amazon rainforest. The more pictures you find, the more complex the web will be.

String, wool or ribbon linking pictures

## Trophic levels

Trophic levels are a way of looking at the levels in a food chain from the point of view of energy. At each level in the chain, some of the food taken in is broken down for energy and some is stored. This means that, for a given amount of food at the bottom, some is lost at each step up to a higher level, leaving less to be broken down for energy. So fewer animals can be supported at each level on that amount of food.

Pyramid of numbers (number of individuals at each level)

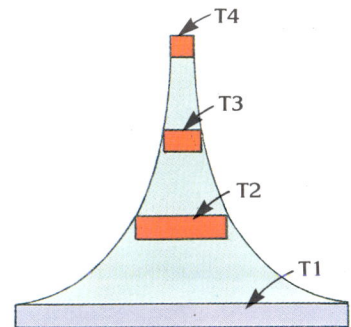

T4

T3

T2

T1

T1 – producers
T2 – primary consumers
T3 – secondary consumers
T4 – tertiary consumers

# The ocean

The oceans of the world form one vast ecosystem covering over 70% of the planet's surface. Many varied ecosystems exist within it, each with its own environment and diversity of life-forms. This vast area is little known, but it contains a wealth of resources. With more understanding and cooperation, its vast store of food, minerals and energy can be gained for the benefit of all.

These two views of the earth show the true extent of the enormous ocean ecosystem.

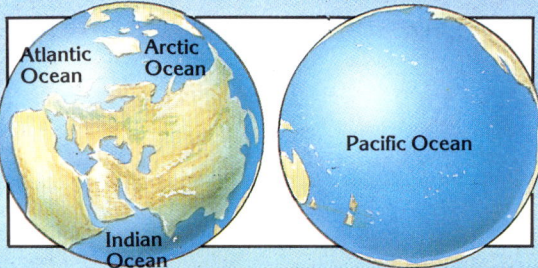

Atlantic Ocean
Arctic Ocean
Indian Ocean
Pacific Ocean

## Marine habitats

The underwater landscape is just as varied as that on land, with countless different habitats and communities. There are vast areas of sandy desert, huge mountain ranges and areas rich in plant and animal life. The most spectacular of these are the tropical coral reefs. Despite existing only in relatively small areas of the vast oceans, they support a third of all fish species.

## The marine food cycle

The ocean ecosystem has a vast and complicated food web (see page 57). From single-celled organisms to massive whales, the ocean is home to a range of plant and animal life that is just as diverse as that on land.

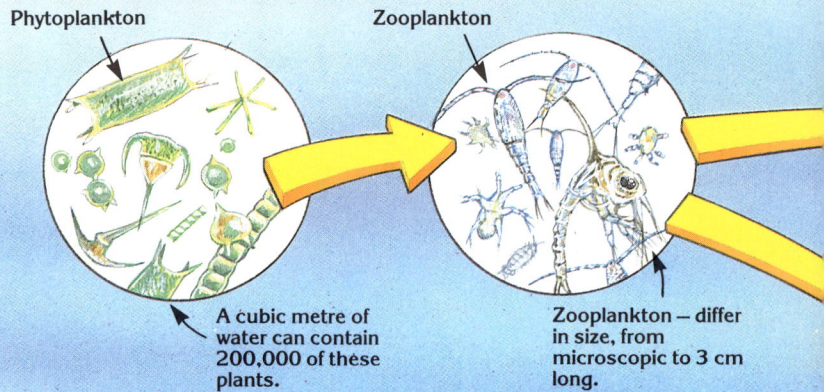

Phytoplankton

Zooplankton

A cubic metre of water can contain 200,000 of these plants.

Zooplankton – differ in size, from microscopic to 3 cm long.

Almost all of the ocean's varied plant and animal life exists in the top 100 m where sunlight can penetrate. The ocean's producers, microscopic plants called **phytoplankton**, live very close to the surface as they need the sun's energy for the process of photosynthesis. Like green plants on land, these tiny marine plants provide the basis of all life in the oceans.

Using energy absorbed from the sun, phytoplankton combine water and carbon dioxide to produce carbohydrates, the basic elements of all food webs. In the process they produce almost 70% of the world's oxygen. Phytoplankton are consumed by microscopic animals called **zooplankton**. These and other tiny creatures are eaten in turn by small fish. And so on up the food chain.

The Great Barrier Reef is one of the natural wonders of the world. Up to 170 m (500 feet) across and stretching over 2,100 km (1,260 miles) along the north-east coast of Australia, it is home to over 3,000 animal species.

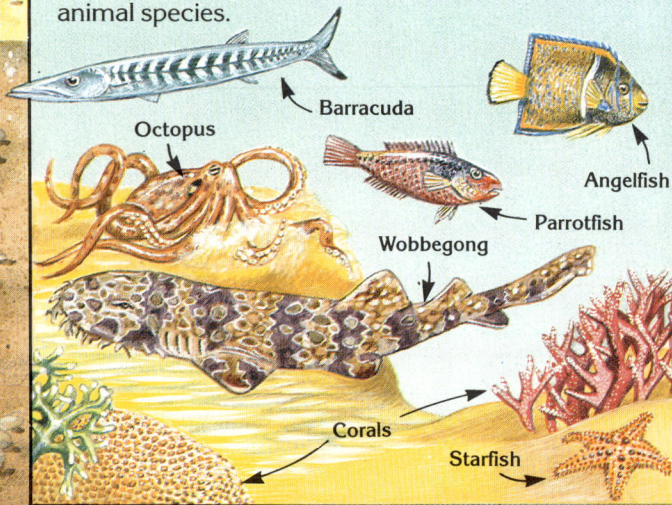

Barracuda
Octopus
Angelfish
Parrotfish
Wobbegong
Corals
Starfish

## Studying plankton

If you get the chance, study a sample of seawater under a microscope. Or study water from a pond or stream – plankton live in freshwater too. The variety of life-forms is amazing. Can you find any of these common forms of plankton?

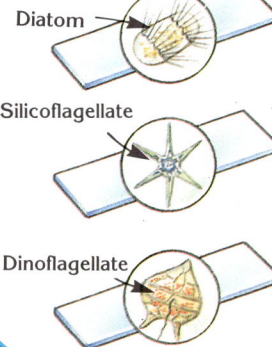

Phytoplankton:
Diatom
Silicoflagellate
Dinoflagellate

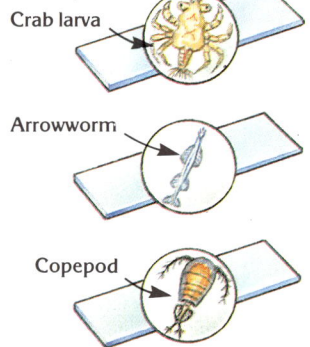

Zooplankton:
Crab larva
Arrowworm
Copepod

Seabirds

Herring

Mackerel

Anchovy

Tuna

Swordfish

Squid

The story of the battle to save the whale is told on page 93.

Right whale

Blue whale

Some of the largest creatures of the oceans actually feed on the smallest. Baleen whales, like the Blue whale which grows up to 30 m long, exist solely on a diet of zooplankton.

Sea anemone

Swimming crab

Dead matter sinks to the ocean floor where it is either eaten by bottom dwellers (in shallower areas), like crabs and sea anemones, or it decays, producing minerals. Some form new rock, the rest are circulated by currents and taken in by plants.

The average depth of the ocean is 3,700 m, though parts are much deeper. Even the darkest depths are not devoid of life, however – thousands of weird and wonderful creatures have adapted to life in near total darkness.

Angler fish – creates its own light to attract the smaller fish which it feeds on.

The oceans themselves play a vital role in the water cycle. Their huge surface area allows vast quantities of water to evaporate into the atmosphere. The water then condenses to form clouds (for more on the water cycle, see page 60).

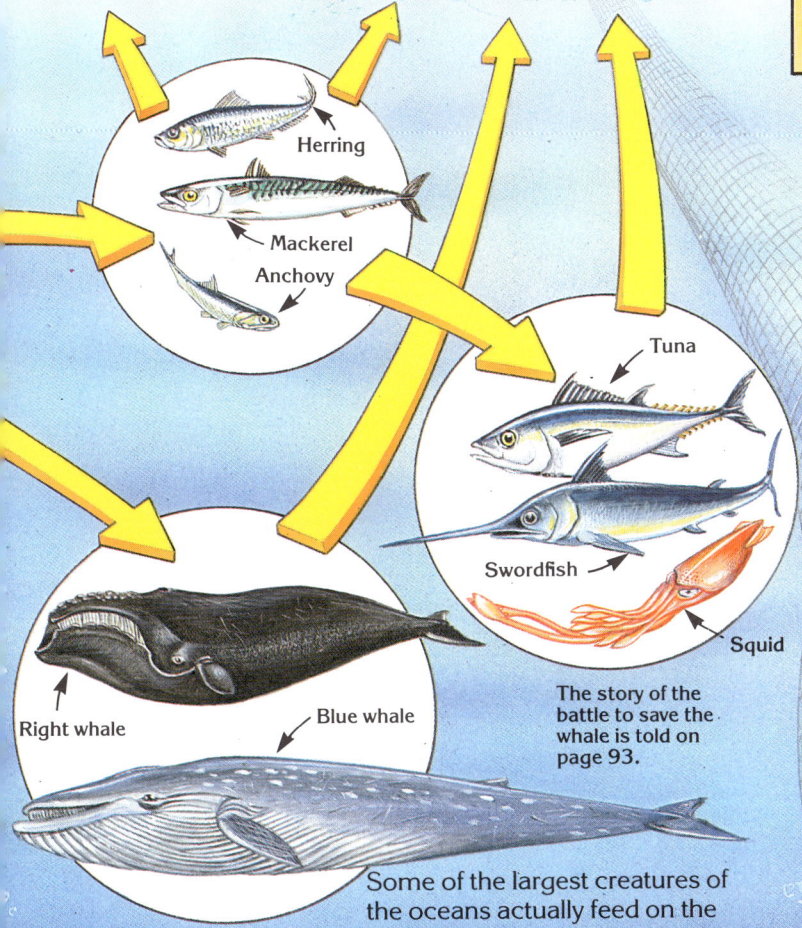

## Fishing

For thousands of years, man has harvested fish from the seas as a valuable food source. Today the global catch plays a vital part in feeding the world's growing population.

### A fish diet?

How often do you eat fish? They are very good for you: high in protein and low in fat. Find out what sorts are available in your area, and where they come from. Have any become rarer or more expensive?

Over-fishing by large modern fishing fleets now threatens the livelihoods of traditional fishermen throughout the world. This has caused stocks of many fish species to become dangerously low. It is now vital that we have more international cooperation to sustain fish harvests.

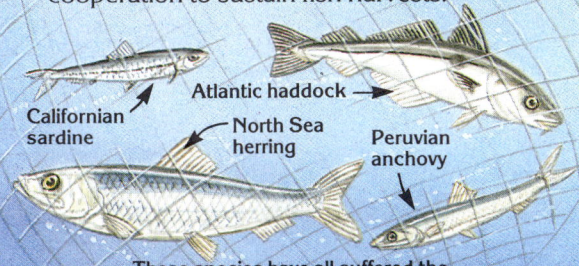

Atlantic haddock

Californian sardine

North Sea herring

Peruvian anchovy

These species have all suffered the effects of over-fishing.

## Pollution

Pollution is now a major problem in marine ecosystems. Over 80% of this comes from land-based activities, e.g. sewage and industrial waste. Conditions are worst in enclosed areas like the Mediterranean and the North Sea, where levels of pollution are now so high that wildlife and human health are threatened. Measures are finally being taken to combat this international problem, but it will be a long and difficult job.

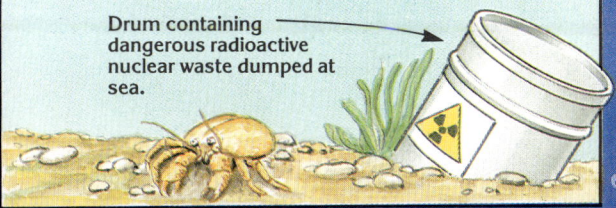

Drum containing dangerous radioactive nuclear waste dumped at sea.

# Cycles in nature

All living things can be found within a relatively thin layer on or near the surface of the earth. Apart from the sun's energy, all their needs are supplied by the small proportion of the earth's resources contained in this layer. If the water, oxygen and other elements vital for life were only used once, they would soon run out. This is why many of nature's processes work in cycles. There is a constant exchange of the elements between air, earth, water, plants and animals, and these recycling processes ensure that all living things are able to live and grow.

One of the most important elements is oxygen, which exists freely as a gas in the atmosphere (21%), and is also an essential part of both the water and carbon cycles. Carbon itself and nitrogen are also vital. Others of importance include the minerals phosphorus, sulphur and calcium, and trace elements, like iron and zinc, that are needed in smaller quantities. These are all needed to supply energy for life, and are also important in the process of growth and constant renewal of all living cells.

## The water cycle

Water is an essential of life, making up almost 75% of all living things. It is continuously recycled between sea, air and land, creating the conditions in which life can exist.

Clouds meet cold air, e.g. above mountains. Large drops of water form and fall as rain or snow.

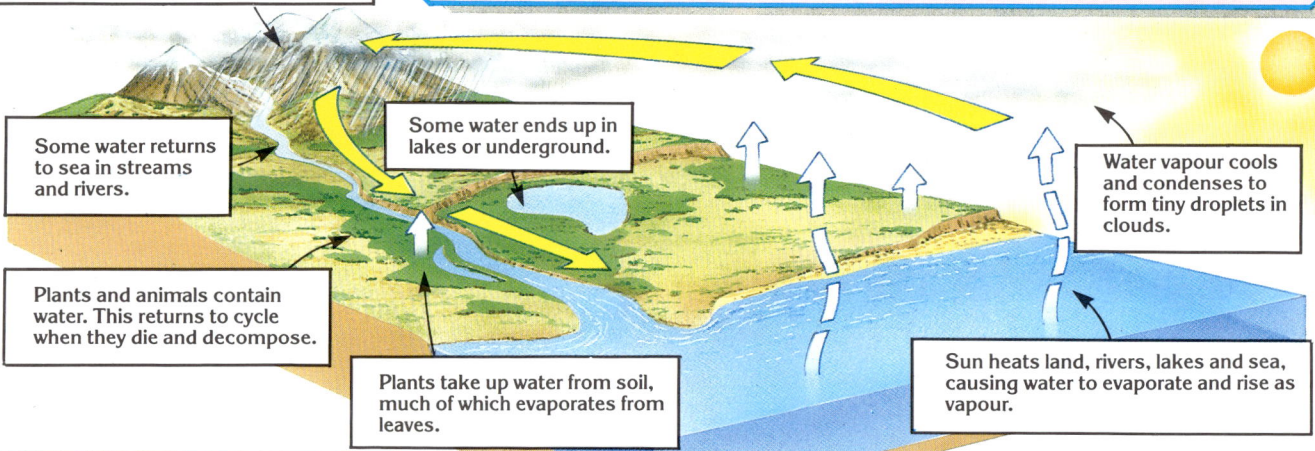

## Make your own water cycle

Using a large plastic bowl, a small container and some plastic wrap, you can make a miniature water cycle. Leave the bowl in the sun, with some water in it. The heat evaporates the water, which rises and condenses on the cool plastic to fall into the container.

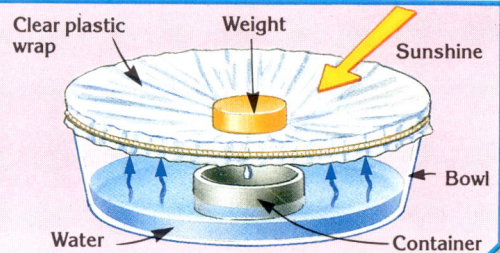

Clear plastic wrap
Weight
Sunshine
Bowl
Water
Container

Some water returns to sea in streams and rivers.

Some water ends up in lakes or underground.

Water vapour cools and condenses to form tiny droplets in clouds.

Plants and animals contain water. This returns to cycle when they die and decompose.

Plants take up water from soil, much of which evaporates from leaves.

Sun heats land, rivers, lakes and sea, causing water to evaporate and rise as vapour.

## The carbon cycle

Carbon is constantly circulating in many different forms through living things, the soil and the atmosphere.

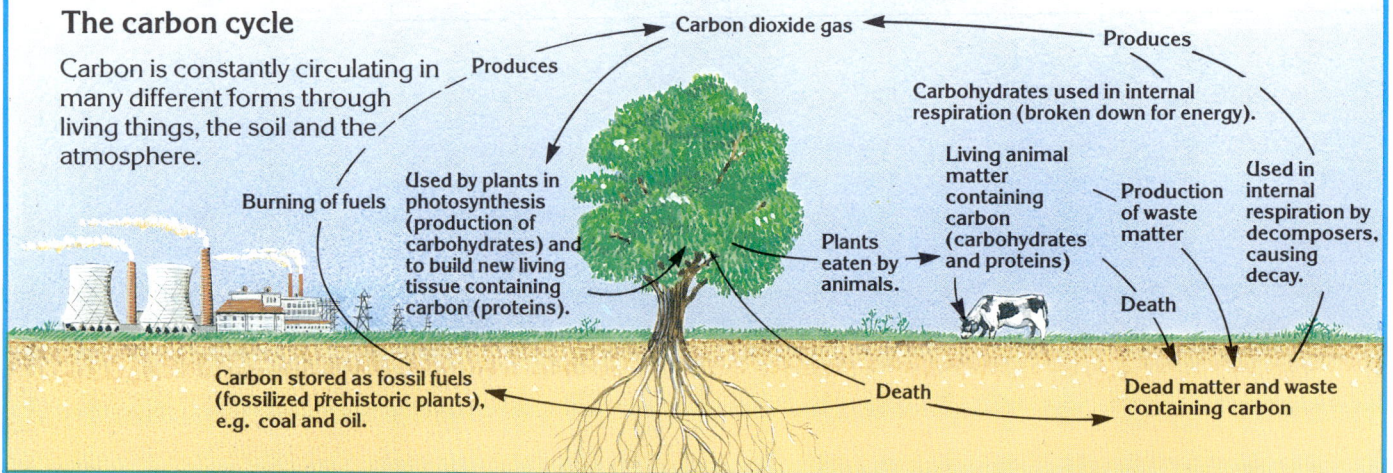

Carbon dioxide gas
Produces
Produces

Burning of fuels

Used by plants in photosynthesis (production of carbohydrates) and to build new living tissue containing carbon (proteins).

Carbohydrates used in internal respiration (broken down for energy).

Living animal matter containing carbon (carbohydrates and proteins)

Plants eaten by animals.

Production of waste matter

Used in internal respiration by decomposers, causing decay.

Death

Carbon stored as fossil fuels (fossilized prehistoric plants), e.g. coal and oil.

Death

Dead matter and waste containing carbon

## The greenhouse effect

Carbon dioxide in the atmosphere plays an important role in warming the earth by trapping the sun's heat, in what is called the greenhouse effect. Since industrialization, the burning of fossil fuels has greatly increased the amount of carbon dioxide in the atmosphere.

The future effects of this build-up on global temperatures can only be guessed at. Some experts predict that temperatures will rise, melting the polar ice packs, raising sea levels to flood coastal areas, and resulting in large-scale changes in climate and agriculture around the world.

To keep the level of carbon dioxide from rising further we must increase our use of renewable energy sources and become more energy-efficient (see page 81).

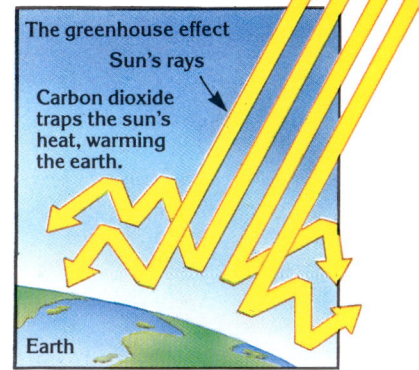

**The greenhouse effect**
Sun's rays
Carbon dioxide traps the sun's heat, warming the earth.
Earth

## The nitrogen cycle

All living things need nitrogen to build proteins for growth. The way they get this is quite complex.

Although about 78% of air is made up of the gas nitrogen, it cannot be used by plants and animals in gaseous form. It must first be converted into nitrites and then nitrates before it can be used.

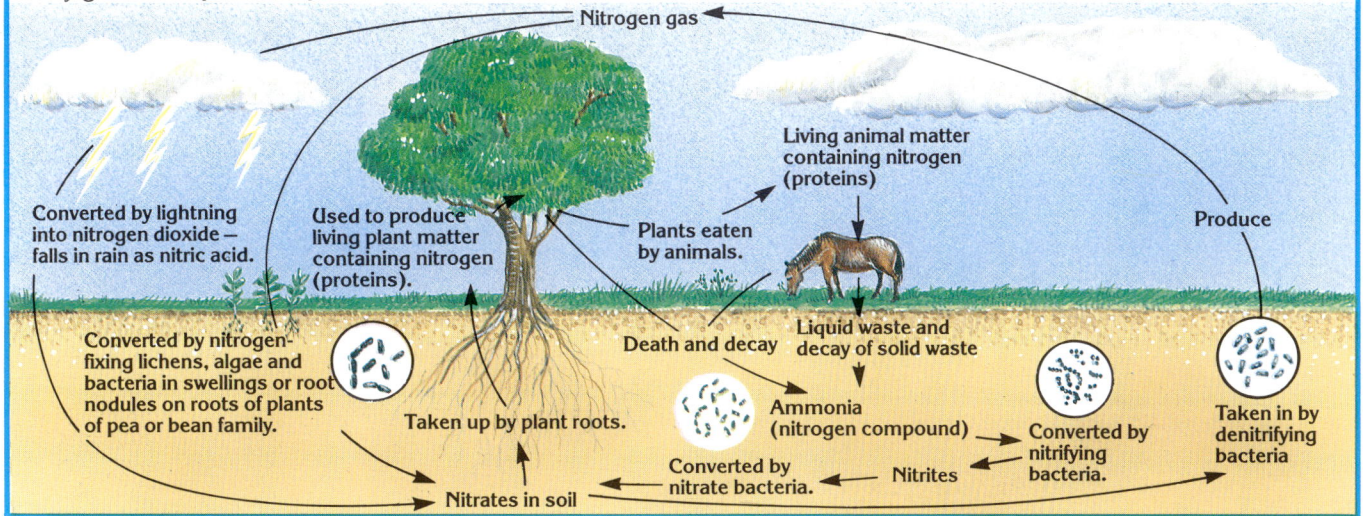

Nitrogen gas

Living animal matter containing nitrogen (proteins)

Produce

Converted by lightning into nitrogen dioxide — falls in rain as nitric acid.

Used to produce living plant matter containing nitrogen (proteins).

Plants eaten by animals.

Converted by nitrogen-fixing lichens, algae and bacteria in swellings or root nodules on roots of plants of pea or bean family.

Death and decay

Liquid waste and decay of solid waste

Taken in by denitrifying bacteria

Taken up by plant roots.

Ammonia (nitrogen compound)

Converted by nitrifying bacteria.

Converted by nitrate bacteria.

Nitrites

Nitrates in soil

## The mineral cycle

Minerals originate from the earth itself, either from the surface or from deeper down through volcanic activity. Many of these, like phosphorus and iron, are needed for the life processes of plants and animals.

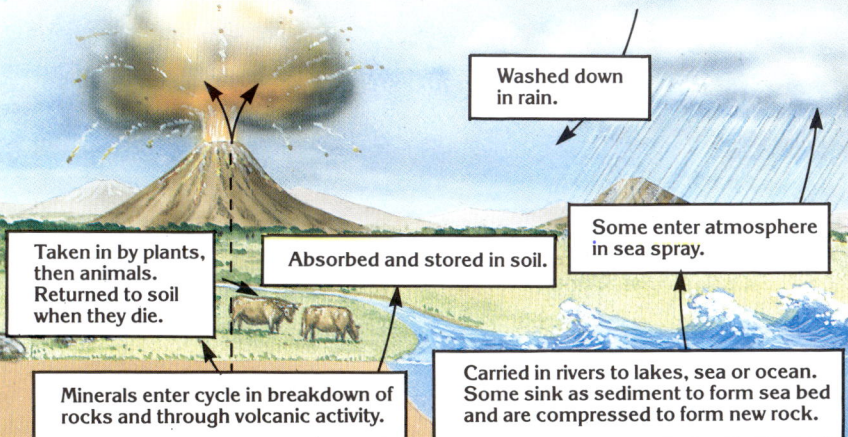

Washed down in rain.

Some enter atmosphere in sea spray.

Taken in by plants, then animals. Returned to soil when they die.

Absorbed and stored in soil.

Minerals enter cycle in breakdown of rocks and through volcanic activity.

Carried in rivers to lakes, sea or ocean. Some sink as sediment to form sea bed and are compressed to form new rock.

## The natural balance

Nature's cycles are relatively stable. Any changes that do occur take place within certain limits, so that, despite minor variations, the cycles continue and life goes on. However, man's activities are fundamentally changing the environment and disturbing these natural cycles. We are upsetting the fine balance of nature, and the results may turn out to be disastrous.

Upsetting the natural balance

# Disturbing the cycles

Nature's cycles form a balance in the natural world in which there is no waste. Everything is broken down and re-used. Man, however, is now creating an imbalance by creating waste and polluting the environment. Pollution occurs on different levels: personal, national and global.

## Pollution

Ever since people first gathered together in settlements there has been pollution. This describes everything produced by man that does not decompose (is not **biodegradable**) and so does not return into the natural cycles. It also describes our disturbance of these cycles by producing more or less of a natural substance and so upsetting the balance.

Some pollution just looks bad, whilst other forms, like some chemical and nuclear wastes, are deadly. When population was low and there was little industry, a small amount of pollution did not really matter. Nowadays, things are very different.

An early rubbish tip

A modern tip

## Recycling waste

Unlike nature, modern man produces vast amounts of waste. The average family of four in an industrialized country throws away over a tonne of rubbish a year, most of which ends up buried below ground. But how much of this actually is rubbish?

### Step 1

Study the contents of your rubbish bin to see what you are throwing away (do it outside on newspaper). Weigh the contents and separate them, putting them into different containers, e.g. glass, food waste, plastics, textiles, paper and metals.

**You should have your parents' permission (or help) before doing this.**

**Wear a pair of washing-up gloves and overalls or old clothes.**

**Never taste or inhale unknown substances.**

**Be very careful of broken glass and the sharp edges of tin cans.**

### Step 2

Now see how much can be returned into nature's cycles or recycled for human use. Here are a few examples of how this can be done – for more ideas, contact your local environmental or conservation group (see pages 92-93).

Glass. There may well be a glass-recycling scheme in your area, in which you take your bottles and jars to bottle-banks. Ask your local authority about this. Or you can invent ways of re-using jars and bottles, e.g. as containers or vases.

**Using a bottle bank**

Paper. Many charities and organizations collect bundles of old newspapers and magazines to be recycled. Contact those in your area, e.g. an old people's home, to see if you and your friends can help. To make your own recycled paper, see pages 90-91.

Aluminium cans. These can be washed, crushed (stand on them) and taken to a can recycling centre (look in the phone book). You may be paid for them. You could collect more at concerts, fairs, fetes, etc.

**Only aluminium cans can be recycled. Use a magnet to check.**

**Aluminium cans are not magnetic, other cans are.**

Organic waste. This is anything that will rot. It can be used as compost (see page 86).

### Step 3

What is left, like plastics and chemicals, cannot at the moment be recycled. Weigh this waste – the less there is the better. See if you can decrease your family's waste, e.g. by buying products with less packaging, or by always taking the same bag to the shops with you.

# Acid rain

One of the nastiest forms of pollution that we are creating today is known as acid rain. This occurs when wastes from burning fossil fuels interfere with the natural water cycle. Its effects include dying forests, lifeless lakes, damaged buildings and harm to people. We have the technology to prevent this happening, e.g. filters for power stations and catalytic converters to clean fumes from vehicle exhaust pipes. Some countries have already begun using such measures in an attempt to stop acid rain. Others have been much slower to see that action is now vital.

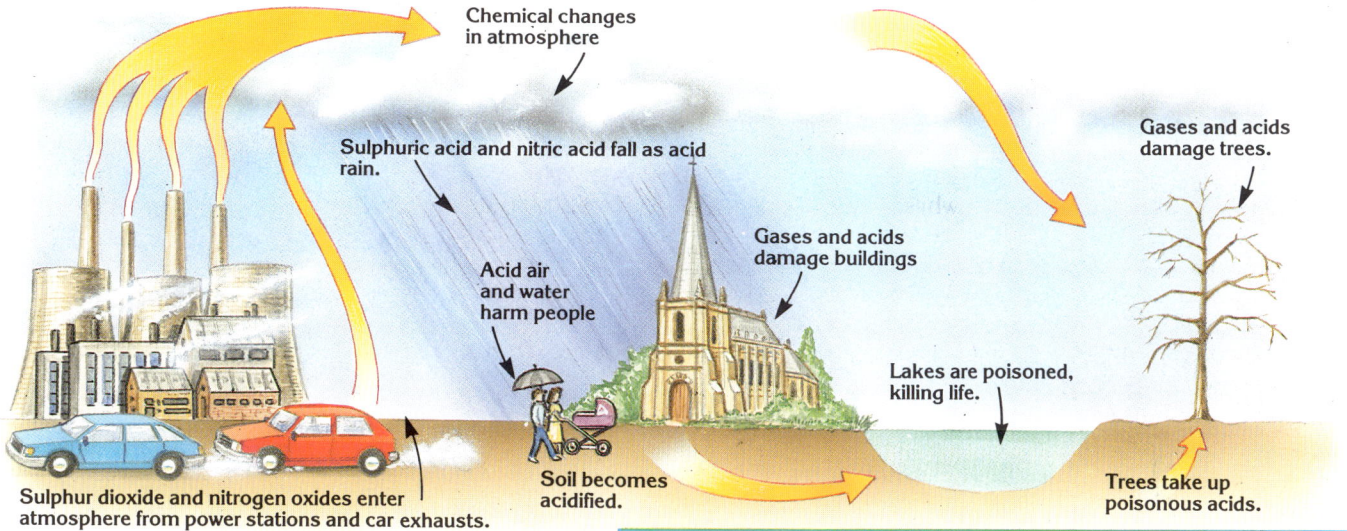

Chemical changes in atmosphere

Sulphuric acid and nitric acid fall as acid rain.

Acid air and water harm people

Gases and acids damage buildings

Gases and acids damage trees.

Lakes are poisoned, killing life.

Soil becomes acidified.

Trees take up poisonous acids.

Sulphur dioxide and nitrogen oxides enter atmosphere from power stations and car exhausts.

## Chemicals in farming

In today's intensive farming the natural nitrogen and mineral cycles are neglected. Very little natural organic waste is returned to the soil, resulting in reduced levels of minerals and humus, and lower productivity. To make up for this, farmers add chemical fertilizers to the soil. These often cause environmental and health damage, e.g. when washed into rivers and lakes, eventually ending up in drinking water.

Intensive farming in Montana, USA

Many powerful chemicals are also used to fight pests, weeds and diseases in order to keep productivity high. These pesticides, herbicides and fungicides have long-lasting and damaging effects on food webs wherever they are used. The chemicals often remain on the plants which have been sprayed, and can damage human health when these are eaten.

## Organic farming

Fuel shortages, increasing costs and environmental damage mean the long-term future of intensive farming is in doubt. We need to return to more natural farming methods, which work with nature's cycles. These methods are based on ecological principles and are known as organic farming.

Organic farming techniques, like crop rotation and the use of manure as fertilizer, are today being used successfully. They improve rather than endanger the environment by returning most organic waste to the soil, increasing humus and mineral levels and allowing nature's cycles to work.

Crop rotation. Some crops use up the nitrates in the soil and others (beans and peas) restore them (see page 61). By changing the crop grown in a field each year in a rota system, the natural cycles can be used to improve growth.

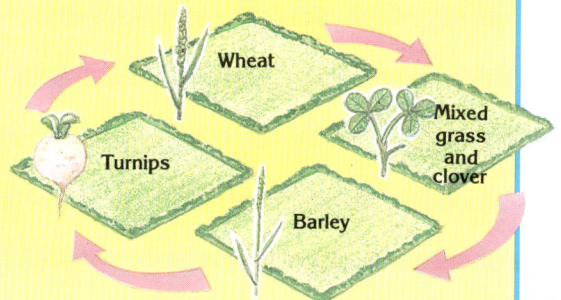

Wheat

Mixed grass and clover

Barley

Turnips

Ecologists think that these techniques should be widely adopted. Many people now prefer to eat "organic" food, knowing that it is free of chemicals and has been produced without damaging the environment.

# Adaptation

All living things must adapt to their environment if they are going to survive. Adaptation is the result of long-term interaction with the environment and has enabled life to spread to every part of the world. It includes changes in both behaviour and physical features.

## Hot deserts

Some of the best examples of adaptation occur in the world's deserts (large areas with extremely harsh environments). In hot, dry desert climates, plants and animals have developed various different survival techniques, e.g. many have physical adaptations to store water or food, or to lose heat more rapidly.

The Australian outback is the largest area of sandy desert outside the Sahara. It is made up of different types of desert, varying due to differences in climate and rock formation. The first inhabitants of the land, the Aborigines, developed a lifestyle over many thousands of years which enabled them to live in both grassland and desert. Until very recently, groups still wandered the outback, hunting and gathering food in their traditional ways.

An Australian desert

Mulga trees — they have expanded leaf stalks instead of leaves to lessen water loss by evaporation.

Marsupial mice — they avoid the day's heat in burrows and search for food at night. Their tails store fat reserves in case of food shortages.

Saltbush plants — their vast root systems collect what little water there is.

There are many other examples of adaptations to life in hot deserts. Cacti, for example, have developed spines instead of leaves to prevent water loss, and the North American jack rabbit has developed very large ears (see picture).

North American jack rabbit

The long ears contain many blood vessels near the surface, which radiate away the body's heat.

## Growing a cactus garden

A shallow clay container filled with sandy soil and decorated with some stones or wood is all you need as a basis for your cactus garden. To obtain your cacti either buy them or take cuttings from someone else's plants. To do this, break off the shoots growing at the base of the parent cactus. Let them dry for a few days before putting them in the soil. Once established, cacti need a lot of sun but very little watering or attention.

A cactus garden

Hedge cactus (Cereus)

Old man cactus (Cephalocereus)

If you dribble water onto cacti, it will roll off. Their "skin" does not allow water to be lost, so it can't get in either.

Fig cactus (Opuntia)

Golden ball (Echinocactus)

## Desertification

This is when dry, marginal land is turned into desert due to human activities like over-grazing or cutting down trees. Much of the earth's land surface is now threatened. The costs of preventing this and improving the damaged lands are low when compared to the gains in agricultural production once the lands are developed. But at present very little is being done and many traditional farmers, with little land or stock, are suffering badly.

The Sahel, Africa: early 1970s

Drought and desertification changed marginal land (land that is difficult to cultivate) into desert.

Over 100,000 people and millions of animals died.

# Icy deserts

Conditions in the freezing, icy deserts of the polar regions are just as harsh as in their hot, dry equivalents. In winter, ice and snow cover the vast continent of Antarctica and its surrounding seas, as well as the entire Arctic region (see below). But living things can still be found, adapted to life in these extreme environments.

Polar bears survive the winter by hibernating in dens hollowed out under the ice. They also have large, furry feet to act as snowshoes.

To survive the cold, all the large animals are warm-blooded, that is, able to keep their body temperature constant despite external conditions. Thick, insulating layers of fat or fur, or both, keep the heat in and the cold out.

Arctic fox — the colour of its coat changes to fit the season: pure white in winter, browny-red in summer. This is an example of camouflage (see below).

Huskies curl into balls to conserve heat and are protected by their thick coats of fur.

The native Eskimo people face the cold by smearing themselves with animal fat and wearing thick furs.

## The Arctic summer

In the brief summers much of the ice and snow melts, revealing the Arctic tundra, which, for a while, supports a great variety of plant and animal life. The plants survive the long winter either as seeds or by not freezing (many contain "anti-freeze"), and grow and produce seeds in the short summer. Hot, dry deserts, too, have short periods when life is plentiful. These occur after rain, when water brings life to dormant seeds.

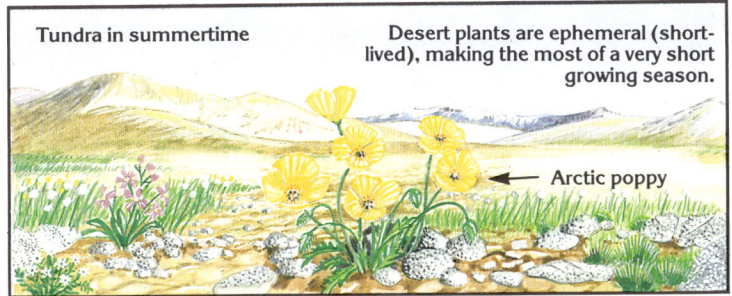

Tundra in summertime

Desert plants are ephemeral (short-lived), making the most of a very short growing season.

Arctic poppy

## Camouflage and mimicry

Camouflage is the adaptation of a plant or animal to blend in with its natural surroundings so as not to be seen. This adaptation has developed to help plants and animals hide from predators. But it is also used by predators themselves to remain unseen by unsuspecting prey. Mimicry is a camouflage technique, by which animals have adapted to look like, or mimic, something else, so as to benefit in a particular way.

Plaice — uses its dull, sandy colouration to hide from predators on the sea floor.

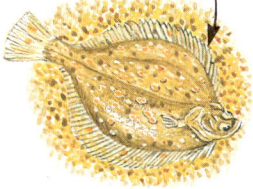

Bee-orchid — its flower looks like a bee. This attracts bees looking for a mate, which then pollinate the plant.

## A seed study

Not only do plants adapt to the environment around them, but their seeds do, too, giving them a greater chance to survive. In many cases, they are adapted for wind dispersal. Collect as many different seeds as you can find and compare the variety of shapes and sizes. Take them outside, throw them into the air and study how, and how far, they travel.

Seed adaptations

Feathery seeds, e.g. dandelion

Explosive fruits (launch seed away from plant), e.g. gorse

Helicopter seeds, e.g. maple or sycamore

Seed in edible fruit (dispersed in droppings of animal that eats it), e.g. bramble

# Coniferous and deciduous forests

Coniferous and deciduous forests are two of the three major types of forest (see also tropical rainforest, pages 74-75). Life in the two areas has developed very differently, due to the differences in climate, as the examples on these pages show.

## Man and the forests

Man's influence on the world's forests is wide-ranging. Forestry is very important to the economies of many countries, supplying wood to the paper, building and furniture industries, but it can often be ecologically damaging.

This is especially true when plantation trees of different, fast-growing species are planted to replace native trees – destroying wildlife habitats, endangering species, and ruining landscapes.

**A coniferous plantation**

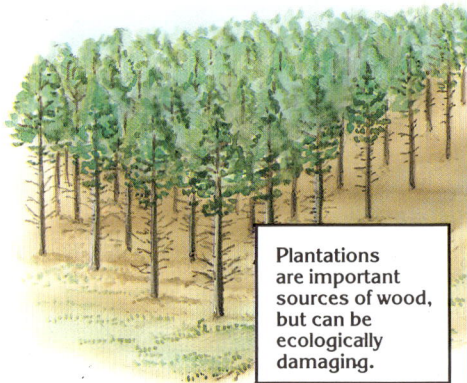

Plantations are important sources of wood, but can be ecologically damaging.

Very little of the great deciduous and mixed forests of the past survive today, due to the spread of farming and urban developments.

Man's destructive activities, like the production of acid rain (see page 63), now threaten those that remain. We must realize the dangers and act now to protect those trees. To find out how to choose, plant and care for a tree, see pages 88-89.

## Coniferous forests

Conifers are so called because their seeds are produced in cones. Vast coniferous forests of spruce, cedar, larch, pine and fir are found where conditions are cold and harsh, with brief summers and low rainfall, i.e. northern parts of America, Europe and Asia and in the world's mountainous areas. Further south, conifers exist alongside deciduous trees in mixed forests.

**A late summer scene in northern Canada**

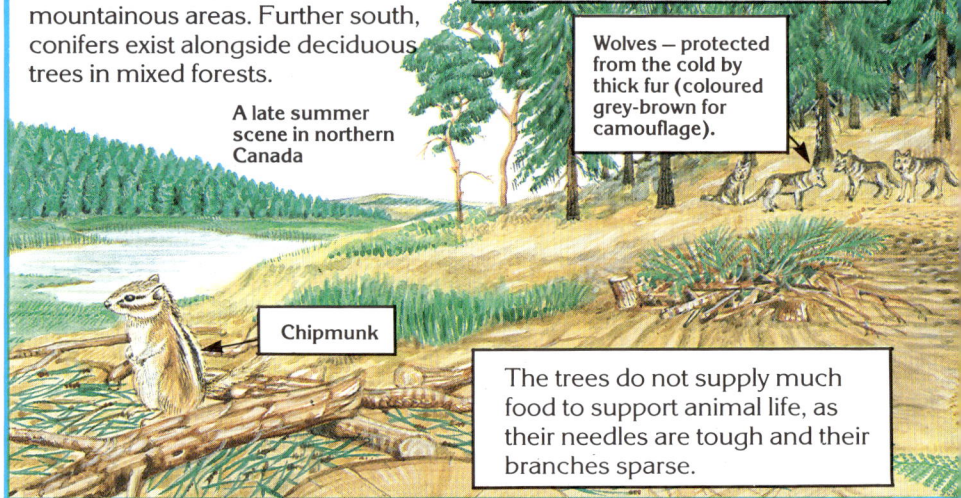

Most conifers have needles instead of leaves (their smaller surface area means less water is lost by evaporation) and the majority are evergreen (never bare of needles), so they can produce food all year round.

Wolves – protected from the cold by thick fur (coloured grey-brown for camouflage).

Chipmunk

The trees do not supply much food to support animal life, as their needles are tough and their branches sparse.

## Deciduous forests

The word deciduous describes trees that shed their leaves once a year. They are flowering plants, mainly blooming once a year in the spring. Deciduous forests are found in areas with relatively mild temperatures and plenty of rainfall throughout the year. Most of Europe, Japan, eastern Asia and the eastern USA were once covered in forests of deciduous trees, like oak, beech, maple and ash.

**A summer scene in the eastern USA**

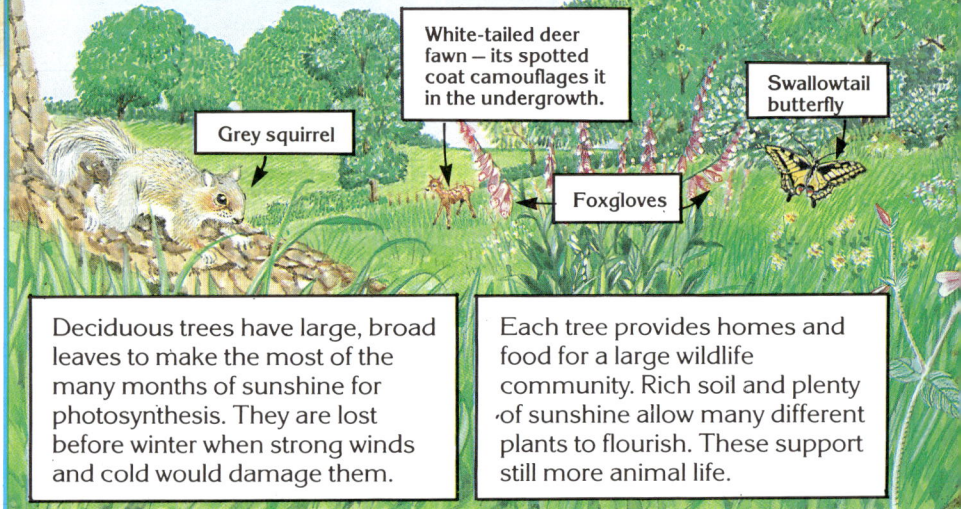

White-tailed deer fawn – its spotted coat camouflages it in the undergrowth.

Swallowtail butterfly

Grey squirrel

Foxgloves

Deciduous trees have large, broad leaves to make the most of the many months of sunshine for photosynthesis. They are lost before winter when strong winds and cold would damage them.

Each tree provides homes and food for a large wildlife community. Rich soil and plenty of sunshine allow many different plants to flourish. These support still more animal life.

Canada geese

Red crossbill — its strong beak is specially adapted to get seeds out of cones.

Douglas fir

Moose

There are few plants at ground level because of poor soil and lack of sunlight (blocked out by the conifers). This limits animal life throughout the forest.

It is too cold for most bacteria and earthworms, so decomposition of plant matter is slow, the soil remains in undisturbed layers and there is little humus. This results in less effective nitrogen and mineral cycles.

Some animals have adapted to life in the forest all year round, e.g. moose wander far to find food, and bears and chipmunks hibernate in winter, living off fat stored from summer food.

The brief warm summer sees much more activity. Insects multiply rapidly, supplying food, e.g. for birds flocking north to nest. The conifers grow fast to make the most of the extra sun.

## Identifying conifers

The shape of a conifer's needles will tell you which group of trees it belongs to. These are the major groups:

Larches: clusters of 12-20 short needles, fall in autumn.

Pines: two or more needles, joined at base.

Firs: individual needles with blunt tips.

Spruces: pointed, stiff and four-sided needles.

Cedars and junipers: small, flat, scale-shaped leaves.

Yews: flattened, leathery needles.

Acorn woodpecker — its feet and tail are adapted to allow it to grip to tree trunks.

Oak tree

Maple tree

Birch tree

Ferns and grasses

Yellow warbler

Pigmy shrew

A yearly fall of leaves and an abundance of decomposers create a soil which is rich in humus, nitrates and minerals.

Animal activity in winter is greater than in coniferous forests, but life is still more plentiful in the warm, sunny conditions of spring and summer. Plant life, insects, birds and mammals are abundant.

## Measuring tree heights

Pin a strip of paper to the tree at your height and measure this (in cm). Walk away from the tree, holding a ruler at arms length, until the strip is level with the 3 cm mark (see picture). Note where the tree-top reaches on the cm scale; divide by 3 and multiply by your height (e.g. 21 cm divided by 3, times 150 cm = 1,050 cm or 10.5 m).

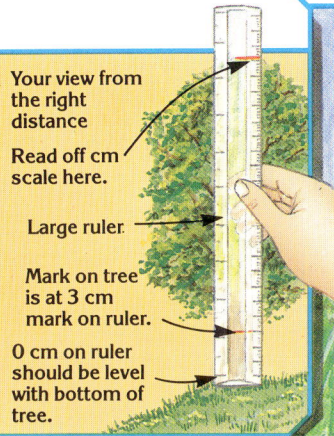

Your view from the right distance

Read off cm scale here.

Large ruler.

Mark on tree is at 3 cm mark on ruler.

0 cm on ruler should be level with bottom of tree.

In southern Europe, the south-west USA, Australia, New Zealand and southern South America, many deciduous trees have adapted to very hot, dry summers by adopting coniferous features. They are evergreen, with smaller, thicker leaves to save water.

# Relationships in nature

In the natural world, many of the relationships between living things (organisms) are to do with eating or being eaten, but there are just as many in which organisms work together, often to the advantage of those involved. There are many different ways in which this happens, some simple, others complex; some examples are given on these pages.

## Living together

Many plants and animals live with others of the same species in groups of differing sizes, with different degrees of interaction. Small numbers of animals living together are known as social groups. Larger gatherings are known as colonies.

Lions, for example, live in small social groups called prides, in which the females do the hunting as well as caring for the young. In many social groups, however, there is a more equal sharing of the work, e.g. African meerkats (small desert mammals) take turns to look after the group's offspring. The large apes come closest to our own social grouping, with the young brought up in a family framework.

A group of rare mountain gorillas — inhabitants of the upper reaches of the rainforests of Zaire.

## Colonies

Different colonial animals show different levels of social behaviour, and the degree of dependence between individuals differs greatly. Many seabirds, like gannets and penguins, only form colonies out of mutual self-interest (for safety in numbers).

A colony of cormorants

Seabird colonies can be enormous — one Peruvian island was at one point home to about 5 million cormorants.

Other creatures, however, like ants, termites and bees, live together in far more complex colonies, with groups of related individuals playing specific roles (examples are given in "keeping an ant colony", above right). They depend on each other for the smooth running and continuation of the colony.

## Keeping an ant colony

Ants are easy to keep and fascinating to watch. To see how to make an ant observatory, properly called a formicarium, like the one illustrated, turn to page 84. You can watch the ants at work within it and study their social behaviour without disturbing them too much.

**An ant observatory**

**Look for ants playing different roles: guarding the colony, finding food, tending the young, and looking after the queen.**

**Watch the ants construct a complex system of passageways and chambers.**

**Study which foods the ants prefer, by leaving them different sorts.**

**Study the different stages of their life cycle and the role of the queen.**

## Super-organisms

The word super-organism describes the closest form of colonial relationship, in which single organisms work together so closely that they effectively form a larger structure with its own, self-contained existence.

Coral is an example of this. Thousands of tiny animals called polyps combine to form a much larger coral structure. These polyps are interconnected by a network of links through which food can be shared.

Another example is the Portuguese man-of-war. This is not in fact a jellyfish, but a colony of many specialized polyps, each fulfilling a specific task. The resulting super-organism is a more effective life-form than the individual animals it is made up of.

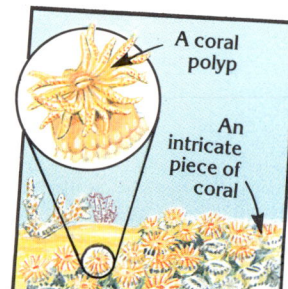

A coral polyp

An intricate piece of coral

A Portuguese man-of-war

# Symbiosis

Symbiosis describes the very close relationship between two organisms of different species that live together and gain from their interaction. One common example of this is lichen, which is found on stone and wood surfaces. The main part of a lichen's body is a fungus, within which live one or more tiny, single-celled plants called algae. Both benefit greatly from their mutual arrangement (see right).

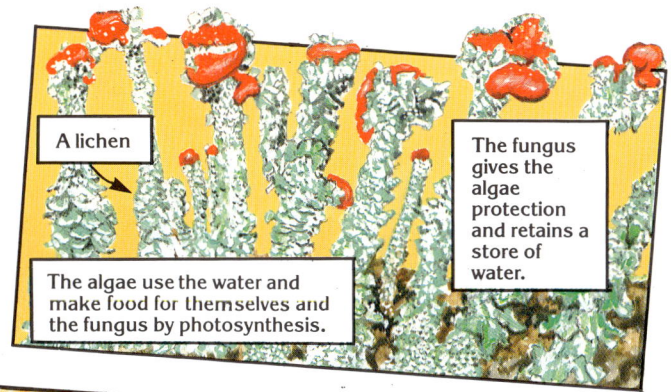

A lichen

The fungus gives the algae protection and retains a store of water.

The algae use the water and make food for themselves and the fungus by photosynthesis.

Here are two more examples of symbiosis:

In Africa ox-peckers eat insects that irritate antelope.

They also give warning of danger by flying up noisily.

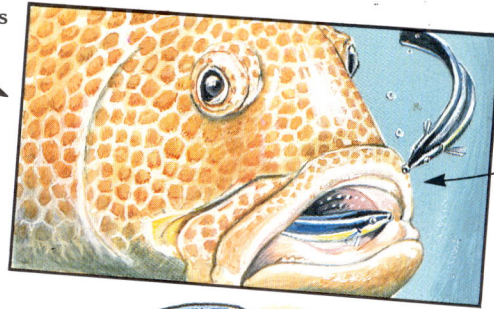

This large fish allows the smaller fish to feed on parasites that live in its mouth.

# Commensalism

Literally "eating at the same table", commensalism describes a relationship (less close than in symbiosis) between two organisms of different species in which food is involved. In most cases, one partner takes advantage of the feeding habits of another and gives little or nothing in return. The relationship between the house mouse and humans is a good example of commensalism.

The mouse takes advantage of food left around the house.

Humans gain nothing from the relationship.

# Co-operation

There are many other forms of co-operation between living things in nature, in which both participants benefit in some way, like plants needing insects for pollination and so attracting them with nectar.

# Parasites

Not all close relationships are beneficial. A parasite is a plant or animal that lives on or in another organism (the host), taking food from it whilst giving nothing or actually harming it in return. A parasite will rarely kill its host, though, as this would result in its own death, too. Lice and fleas are common parasites. Humans are often hosts to these and many others, like tapeworm and roundworm, and they also suffer from diseases, like malaria, carried by parasites.

Tapeworms up to two metres long can sometimes be found in the human intestine.

# Investigating plant galls

Plant galls are home to the larvae of various insects, which are parasitic on certain trees. The adults lay their eggs inside a leaf or bud, which reacts to this intrusion by forming a growth around them. The egg turns into the larva within the gall, later emerging as an adult insect.

Plant galls can be found on many plants and trees (especially oak, birch and willow) in spring and early summer. Go out and collect some, bringing back the leaves they are on. Place them in a jar with holes in its lid, keeping this outside, and watch for the adult insect to emerge.

Oak tree

Gall on oak leaf

Water

Adult gall wasp

Glass jar

# Population and conservation

In the natural world there is a fragile balance in plant and animal populations. There are several ways that their numbers are naturally kept in check, some of which are dealt with on this page. However, this is no longer true of the human population, the growth of which is fast destroying nature's balance, with alarming consequences for our planet.

## Population control

A relatively stable balance of numbers is maintained in the wild through competition and co-existence. Predator/prey relationships and territorial behaviour are the main means of achieving this, and these are well illustrated by the wildlife of the African savannah (see below).

## Territorial behaviour

All living things need food, shelter and living space. As a means of gaining these, many animals behave territorially – that is, they live (as individuals or as a social group) in a defined space, or territory, which is large enough to cater for their needs. This territory is defended against others of the same species, with the result that the overall population is kept down.

## The niche

The role of an animal in its community, including what it eats, where it lives and its position in the food chain is known as its ecological niche. Different species cannot live in the same niche – they compete for resources and living space until one is forced out. Sometimes it appears that two animals share the same niche, but a closer look will show that they inhabit separate, though overlapping, ones.

African buffalo – each herd keeps to a territory several kilometres wide.

Elephants feed on tall grass, whilst buffalo eat the young shoots and antelope graze on the short grass that is left – each occupies a different niche.

## Predators

Predators are animals that catch and eat other animals. They play a vital role in every ecosystem, by keeping down the population of herbivores and smaller predators on which they feed.

A pride of lions – feed on the many grazing animals, like zebra and wildebeest. Each pride has a territory of up to 8 km across.

## Feeding birds

Bird feeders or a bird table will encourage a variety of bird life into your garden or to your windowsill. Watch their different feeding preferences and techniques to work out the different niches they occupy. For details on how to make a bird table, see page 87.

Experiment with various types of food, like nuts, seeds or meat, to see what different birds prefer.

Feeding the birds throughout the winter could keep them alive.

Experiment with different feeders, like hanging bags of nuts or half a coconut, to see the birds' different feeding techniques.

## Watching predators

Try to study the predators that can be found around you. Watch the domestic cat stalking its prey – it often demonstrates the hunting techniques of its much larger African relatives. Other common predators worth studying are the birds of prey (known as raptors), like hawks and kestrels.

A kestrel watching its prey (small mammals).

Smaller birds of prey often hunt beside roads and in open country.

## The population problem

The world's human population is now over five billion and is rising rapidly (for more on the population problem, see page 80). This sheer weight of numbers, combined with the growing destruction caused by man, is putting great pressure on the world's wildlife and habitats. It is estimated that one plant or animal species becomes extinct every half an hour, whilst once common natural habitats are rapidly disappearing.

Giant panda (China)

Black rhinoceros (Africa)

Indian tiger (India and South east Asia)

Sea eagle (Europe, mainly Norway)

Medicinal leech (western and southern Europe)

These are a few of the world's many endangered species.

## Threatened habitats and wildlife

Urban expansion and the spread of intensive industry, agriculture and forestry are resulting in the destruction of important natural habitats. When these disappear, so do the many wild plants and animals that depend on them. For example, vital marine habitats, like saltmarshes and mangroves, are being polluted and destroyed at an alarming rate.

Mangrove swamp

Result of mangrove destruction

Man's greed for exotic luxuries, like fur coats and ivory jewellery, has meant that millions of animals are killed each year. As well as this, many more are caught to supply zoos, the pet trade and industrial and medical research centres. Many animals, like the cheetah and the polar bear, are now seriously endangered. This world-wide trade in wild animals is often illegal and always causes great suffering.

## The need for conservation

Protection, or conservation, of wildlife and habitats is now more important than ever. The international agreements we have at present are too often ignored. We need to protect endangered species and habitats much more carefully. But in the end, it is only by becoming more aware of how we all affect the earth's environment that we will be able to safeguard the natural world.

The giant panda is the emblem of the World Wide Fund for Nature (formerly the World Wildlife Fund).

Since 1961, they have campaigned to protect the world's habitats and wildlife.

For more on what they and other organizations are doing, see pages 92-93.

WWF

## Helping endangered wildlife

In every country of the world there are endangered plants and animals. Find out what is threatened in yours by contacting conservation or environmental groups (see pages 92-93). You could help them in their campaigns to help these species, or you could perhaps start your own group (see pages 90-91) to make local people more aware of the problems.

Another way to help these species is to protect or create the habitats that they prefer. Building a pond (see pages 53 and 84-85) and creating a pocket park (see pages 73 and 90-91) are two ways of doing this. Meadows, too, are easy to create, and are vital habitats for many

insects and rare wild flowers. If you have a garden, just leave an area of grass uncut and it will naturally develop into a meadow. If you live near a park, try to get the authorities to set aside an area as a meadow nature reserve.

A meadow reserve in a city park

# Urban ecosystems

Surprising as it may seem, large towns and cities contain a great deal of wildlife. Wherever plants and animals can find suitable conditions, including enough food, warmth and shelter, they will move in. Many have adapted their ways to life amongst people in an urban environment.

## Urban adaptations

The growth of towns and cities has produced similar urban environments all over the world. In different places, different animals have adapted to fill similar niches. For instance, the brush-tailed opossum, the raccoon and the red fox play the same kind of role in urban environments on their different continents. All originally lived in open woodland, but they adapted to farmland and urban areas when these took its place.

The brush-tailed opossum and the raccoon often live in the roof spaces of suburban houses, whilst the fox makes its den in parks and areas of wasteland. All three often scavenge in dustbins for scraps of food. Their ability to adapt to different habitats and their varied diet have enabled them to live successfully in man-made environments.

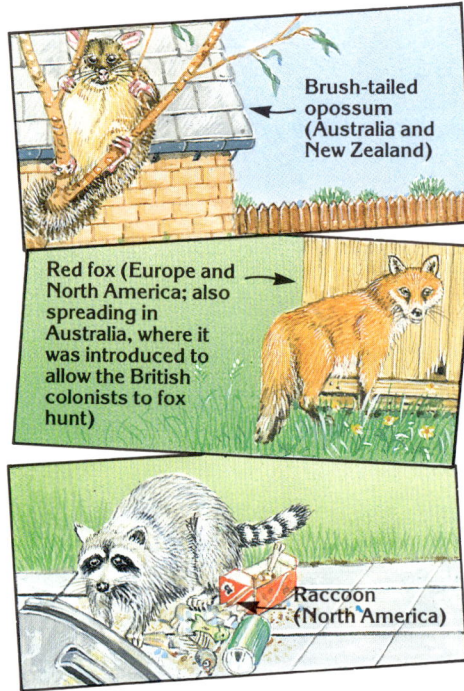

Brush-tailed opossum (Australia and New Zealand)

Red fox (Europe and North America; also spreading in Australia, where it was introduced to allow the British colonists to fox hunt)

Raccoon (North America)

One bird that is found only in man-made environments is the house sparrow. Originally feeding on grain, its diet is now far more varied. This, and its ability to nest on houses and other buildings, enables it to thrive in towns and cities.

House sparrow – spread across the world in the wake of the European colonizers.

Now common in Europe, North and South America, South Africa, Australia and New Zealand.

## Succession

Wherever there is an area of abandoned land, it will not be long before nature moves in. Over a period of time, a variety of plants and animals will replace each other in a process called **succession**. Mosses and grasses will usually be the first arrivals, followed by flowering plants. These attract insects, which bring birds and other wild animals. If the land is left long enough, larger plants and trees will grow. See page 76 for more about succession.

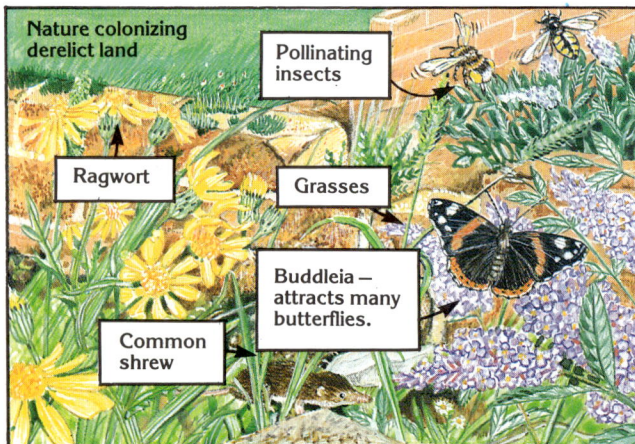

Nature colonizing derelict land

Pollinating insects

Ragwort

Grasses

Buddleia – attracts many butterflies.

Common shrew

## City safari

You do not have to be in a tropical jungle or on an African plain to go on safari – a wildlife expedition around town can be just as rewarding. Study the plants and animals in those areas of your town or city that are slightly off the beaten track: wasteland, cemeteries, the wilder parts of the park and the riverbanks and canals. All you need for a satisfying safari is good observation, and perhaps a little patience. You could take your friends and make it a full-scale expedition.

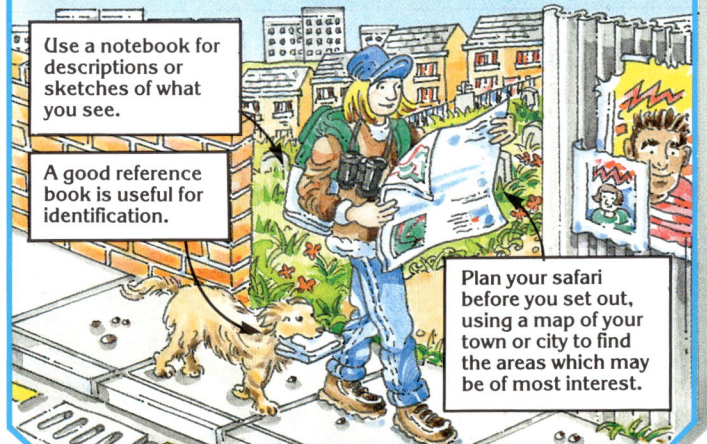

Use a notebook for descriptions or sketches of what you see.

A good reference book is useful for identification.

Plan your safari before you set out, using a map of your town or city to find the areas which may be of most interest.

## Transport and pollution

Pollution from the ever-growing volume of vehicle exhaust is making life more and more unpleasant in many of the world's major cities. The air contains many harmful gases like ozone, which is formed when nitrogen oxides from the exhaust react in sunlight with oxygen. Ozone, carbon monoxide, hydrocarbons and lead and dust particles all endanger the health of the cities' people and wildlife.

The removal of lead from petrol and the use of devices known as three-way catalytic converters to control exhaust fumes are two ways of lessening the problem. A long term solution, however, will only come from radical changes in

In Tokyo, Japan, special electronic signs show the levels of noise and air pollution.

transport policy and city planning. A greater emphasis on improved rail systems and public transport, combined with methods of "traffic calming", will help achieve this.

An example of "traffic calming"

The aim is to create a better sense of community, safer roads and a pleasanter environment.

Bends, bollards and road humps keep vehicle speed down.

Pedestrians and cyclists are better catered for, with wider pavements and cycle paths.

The streets are made more attractive with trees, flowerbeds and benches.

## A lichen pollution test

Plants called lichens are sensitive to air pollution, especially the air's acidity (see acid rain, page 63), so you can use their presence or absence as a guide to how clean your air is. Shrubby and leafy lichens only survive in clean air. In the most polluted areas there are none at all. Look for them on walls, stones and trees, and use this scale to rate the air quality.

Polluted

No lichens (possibly green algae)

Grey-green crusty lichen (tombstones)

Orange crusty lichen (tombstones)

Leafy lichen (walls and trees)

Shrubby lichen (trees)

Clean

## Creating a pocket park

Creating a miniature nature reserve, or pocket park, on derelict ground or wasteland is quite a task and probably calls for a team effort. The aim is to create a complete ecosystem in miniature, with perhaps a pond, areas of grassland and trees and bushes, in the heart of a town or city. It will provide pleasure for all the local people, and attract native wildlife back to the area.

There may already be a project in action in your area — ask at your local library or community centre, or contact your local conservation or environmental group. You could probably join in and help. If not, you could search for a suitable site in your area (like a piece of wasteland) and start your own project with a group of friends (for more about this, see pages 90-91).

Why not see if your school (or one in your area) has some spare land for a pocket park.

Try to get friends, teachers and adults interested in helping you.

# Tropical rainforests

Great rainforests stretch around the Equator, covering large parts of Central and South America, Central Africa, South-east Asia and northern Australasia. These forests are the most complex ecosystems in the world and contain a wealth of resources. Despite their importance, though, they are being destroyed at an alarming rate.

Rainforests grow in areas where rainfall and temperatures are both high and constant. Over millions of years they have developed into the earth's richest wildlife habitats. They cover less than 10% of the planet's land surface, but they contain between 50% and 70% of all plant and animal species. The greatest of all the forests is Amazonia in Brazil, featured on these pages.

Harpy eagle

Emerald tree boa

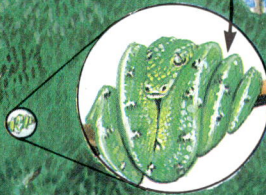

Toucan — its large, strong beak helps it pick fruit from a distance and also frightens predators.

Woolly monkey

## Build your own rainforest

Using a large fish-tank, you can (almost) re-create the rainforest environment in miniature. Place a layer of gravel and charcoal at the bottom, covered with a few centimetres of rich compost. Shape the ground with small stones under the compost. Dampen the compost and add a variety of exotic plants. With a glass top and kept in a warm, well-lit spot, out of the sun, the plants should flourish.

The air is moist, and water is continually recycled between compost, plant, air and tank. Add a little water every few months.

A variety of exotic plants — available from plant or flower shops.

Small flowering plants, like orchids, add colour.

Delicate ferns

Don't plant them too close together, as they need room to grow.

Native Indian, hunting with blow-pipe. Brazil's Indian population has fallen from 5 million to 200,000 over the past 400 years.

Many of the largest trees have developed buttresses for support, as their roots are very shallow.

## Layering

All rain forests have a similar structure, with five main layers, each with its own specific plant and animal life. These layers often merge together, or sometimes one or more are absent.

**Emergent layer** — made up of a few of the tallest trees which rise 10 to 15 m above the mass of greenery below. From here, Harpy eagles and other birds of prey watch alertly for the animals on which they feed.

**Canopy** — 30 to 40 m above the ground, and some 10 m thick, this is a continuous green roof formed by the interlinking leaves and branches of the tree tops. Most of the forest's many plants and animals are found here, taking advantage of the abundant sunshine.

**Understorey** — made up of the tops of smaller trees that receive less light, like palms, and of younger trees struggling to reach upwards. Much sparser than the canopy, it has its own community of plant and animal life.

**Shrub layer** — consisting of shrubs and small trees, this layer depends on sunlight penetrating the upper layers. If none reaches here, both this and the herb layer will be sparse.

When a gap appears in the canopy, sunlight reaches the lower regions, causing the shrub and herb layers to grow rapidly.

**Herb layer** — ferns and herbs making up a layer of undergrowth. Elusive ground dwellers, like the tapir, live down here, along with many insects.

Plants known as epiphytes grow on other plants without harming them. They are abundant in the canopy.

Arrow-poison frog — its bright colouration warns others that it is extremely poisonous. The Indians use its poison on their hunting arrows.

Hummingbird

Ocelot

Common iguana

Climbing plants, like llianas, stretch from the forest floor to the canopy.

It is estimated that one square kilometre of forest is destroyed every two and a half minutes — over one million acres per week.

The forest floor is covered by several centimetres of fallen leaves. Here, organic matter is rapidly recycled by the decomposers, and minerals are transferred directly to shallow plant roots. This process is so efficient that the lower layer of soil has little mineral content and most of the forest's mineral wealth is stored in the vegetation.

When the forest is cleared and burned, the minerals stored in vegetation are turned to ashes. The root systems are destroyed, allowing rain to wash away the ashes and topsoil. The remaining soil soon becomes infertile, turning areas once rich in life into wasteland. It takes centuries for the forest to return, if ever.

## People of the forest

The rainforest is home to many native peoples, who live in harmony with its environment. Their knowledge of the forest is very important to us, if we are to understand its workings and resources. But every day these people are being forced from their own lands with no regard to their wishes or basic human rights. Both they and their knowledge are being destroyed, along with the forests in which they live.

## The importance of rainforests

Tropical rainforests play a vital role in regulating the world's climate, through their position in the oxygen, carbon and water cycles. They are the most important source of raw materials for new medicines and are a vital source of new foods (at least 1,650 rainforest plants could be used as vegetables).

We have hardly started to tap the rainforests' vast resources. However, this must be done in a sustainable way, that is, we must find a balance between making good use of the forest resources, like timber, rubber and nuts, and conserving the forests themselves.

Tapping rubber in the rain forest

## Destruction of the rainforests

Almost 50% of the world's rainforests have already been destroyed, and the destruction continues. The underlying causes of this are the growing populations, poverty and unequal land distribution in countries with rainforests. This is made worse by the rich nations' demand for timber, and large, badly-planned aid programmes. A long-term solution will only be found when these underlying causes are properly dealt with.

The result of forest clearance

# Change in nature

Everything around us is constantly changing, from microscopic living cells to the landscapes in which we live. Some changes are rapid, others take millions of years. On these pages are examples of different sorts of change, both natural and man-made.

## The changing landscape

For billions of years, great natural forces, like the earth's movement, volcanic activity, erosion and the rising and falling of oceans, have been reshaping the face of the earth and its environments. They are still doing so, but so slowly that it is hardly noticeable.

The features of Monument Valley (western USA) have been carved by erosion over millions of years.

More short-term changes in the natural world are known as **succession**. This is when a series of different plants and animals replace each other over a period of time until a **climax community** is formed. This is a community which will survive virtually unchanged if there are no disturbances in the climate, e.g. the tropical rainforests.

Succession resulting in a climax community.

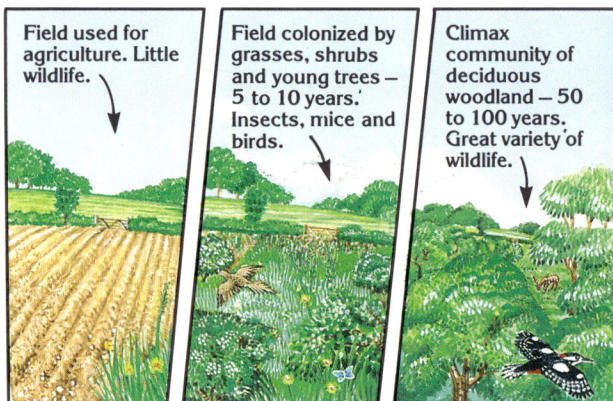

Field used for agriculture. Little wildlife.

Field colonized by grasses, shrubs and young trees — 5 to 10 years. Insects, mice and birds.

Climax community of deciduous woodland — 50 to 100 years. Great variety of wildlife.

The changes made by man to the earth's natural conditions can be seen all around us. In many places, farming, industry and urban developments have changed natural landscapes into man-made environments such as fields, towns and cities. Much of this has taken place over centuries, but increasing populations and industrialization in recent times have caused a dramatic increase in both the scale and intensity of these changes.

## Changes in climate

The climate in different regions of the world changes throughout the year, according to the season. This is because the earth's axis is tilted whilst it travels around the sun. In tropical areas, with temperatures constant all year round, the amount of rainfall determines the season — dry or rainy. Further north and south, the climatic changes are much greater (especially in temperature), and there are four main seasons — winter, spring, summer and autumn.

The earth revolves around the sun at an angle, with its axis 23° off-centre.

The angle of the sun's rays creates the difference in climate.

Summer in London will be winter in Sydney.

## Photographing seasonal change

If you can get hold of a camera, try to take a series of photographs of the same natural scene over a period of time (perhaps the first day of each month for a year). The changes you will catch on film are fascinating. You could use them for a display, showing the variety of seasonal change.

The same scene in winter and summer

There are also more long-term climatic changes, which dramatically affect the earth's environment. Over the last 900,000 years there have been roughly ten major cold periods (ice-ages), with warmer weather between them. At present, it seems that we are in one of these warmer periods.

This graph shows the changes in global temperatures over a span of 900,000 years.

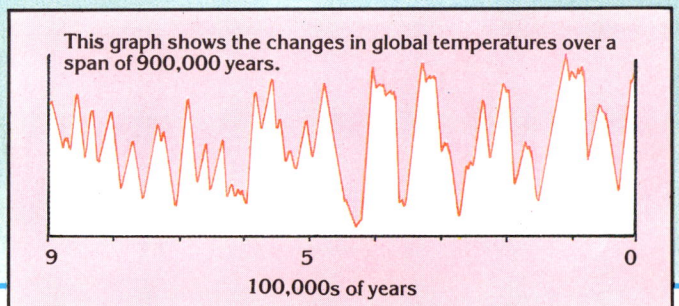

100,000s of years

Natural climatic changes take place gradually over thousands of years and so are no great threat to us at present. Of far greater importance is the danger that our large-scale industrial activity is changing the earth's climate. These changes will happen much more quickly and could well be much more dramatic. The greenhouse effect (see page 61), smoke and dust clouds blocking out sunlight, and the destruction of the ozone layer are all real threats.

## Destruction of the ozone layer

High up in the atmosphere, a layer of ozone protects the earth from the sun's deadly ultra-violet rays, which cause skin cancer.

It seems that chemical compounds known as chlorofluorocarbons (CFCs), used in some aerosol cans and in making polystyrene and refrigerators, are gradually destroying this vital layer.

Some international action has already been taken to slow down the manufacture of CFCs, but many scientists want much more to be done.

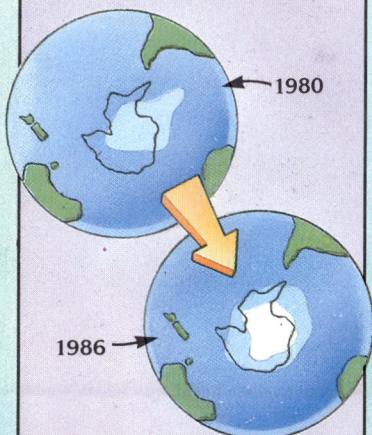

1980

1986

These two pictures show the alarming growth of the hole in the ozone layer above Antarctica.

## Changes in living things

Everything in the living world is changing. Cells in all living things are constantly breaking down and being replaced by new ones. Individual plants and animals are produced, grow, reproduce and die – to be replaced by new generations. There are also great changes in life cycles and behaviour patterns whilst they live.

The seasonal differences in climates result in many changes in living things. Many animals adapt their life cycles to the changes in temperature and availability of food. Some **migrate** to other areas, often hundreds of miles away, where conditions are more suitable for feeding or breeding, or both.

The Arctic tern breeds in the summer on the shores of the Arctic ocean, then flies 20,000 km to the Antarctic to feed during its summer.

It travels over 40,000 km each year.

Many plants have adapted to seasonal changes by adjusting the times at which they produce flowers and seeds. Herbaceous perennials, for instance, die back at the end of each year, and leave just their underground stem and roots to survive the winter. Annuals survive the cold months as seeds. They flower and produce more seeds in the warmer months, dying off before winter.

Other animals, like snakes and hedgehogs, avoid the worst seasonal conditions by **hibernation**. They spend the winter months in a deep sleep, in which their body functions shut down to a minimum. Fat stored from summer feeding provides the little energy they need. **Aestivation** is like hibernation, except that it takes place where animals (like the African lungfish) need to survive very hot temperatures and drought conditions.

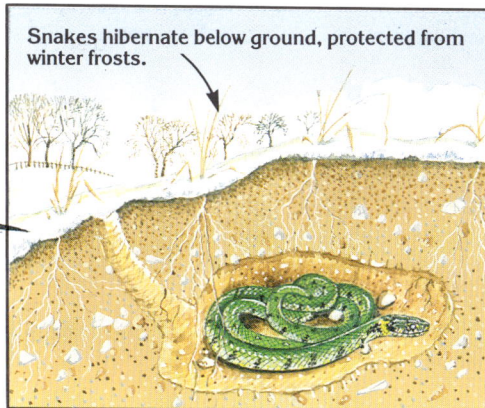

Snakes hibernate below ground, protected from winter frosts.

Daffodils are herbaceous perennials

Poppies are annuals

## Watching butterfly metamorphosis

One of the most astonishing changes in the life cycles of living things is that from a caterpillar into a butterfly or moth, in a process called **metamorphosis**. To watch this, first build a container as shown in the diagram. Then find some caterpillars, placing them inside the box with a plentiful supply of the plant on which they are feeding (make sure this never runs out). At some point the caterpillars will transform themselves into pupae, from which the adult butterflies or moths will emerge. These should be let go as soon as possible.

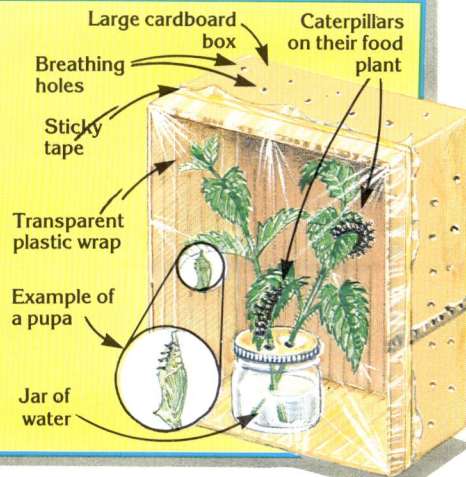

Large cardboard box

Caterpillars on their food plant

Breathing holes

Sticky tape

Transparent plastic wrap

Example of a pupa

Jar of water

# Evolution

Living things have been changing and developing ever since life started around 3.5 billion years ago. This process of long-term change is known as evolution. By studying this and its link with changes in the environment, ecologists have learnt a lot about the planet's workings. They have also seen how vital the links are between living things and their environment.

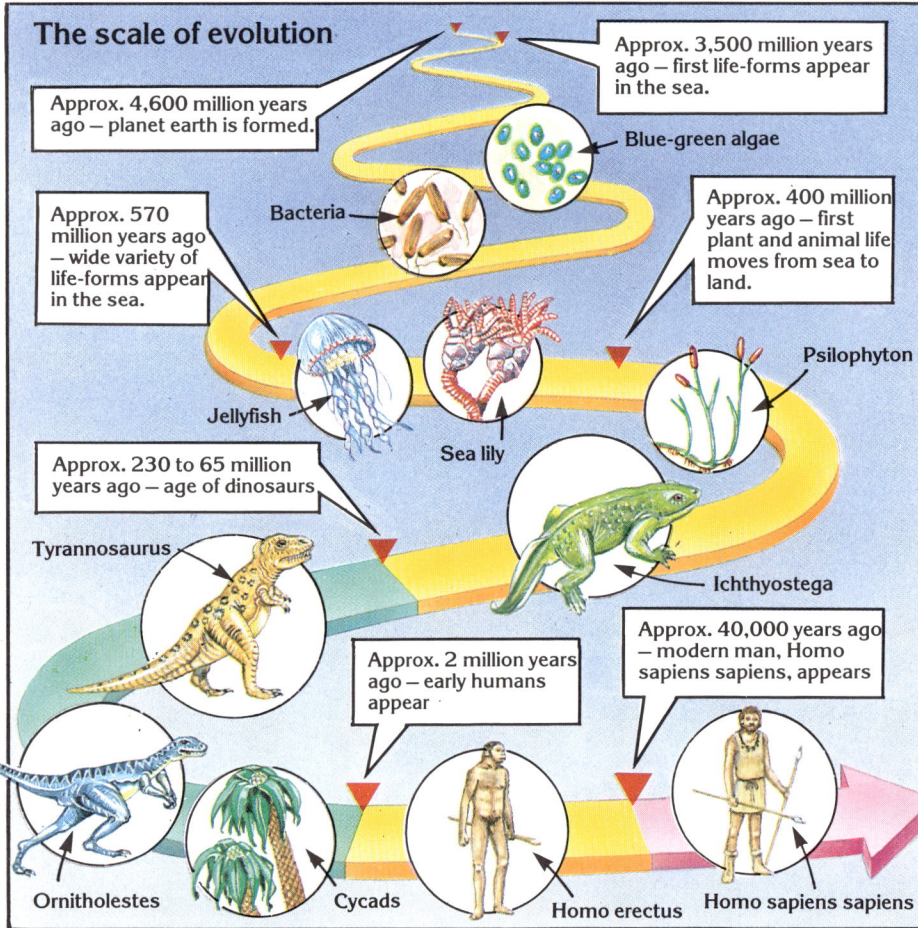

## The scale of evolution

Approx. 4,600 million years ago – planet earth is formed.

Approx. 3,500 million years ago – first life-forms appear in the sea.

Blue-green algae

Bacteria

Approx. 570 million years ago – wide variety of life-forms appear in the sea.

Approx. 400 million years ago – first plant and animal life moves from sea to land.

Jellyfish

Sea lily

Psilophyton

Approx. 230 to 65 million years ago – age of dinosaurs

Tyrannosaurus

Ichthyostega

Approx. 40,000 years ago – modern man, Homo sapiens sapiens, appears

Approx. 2 million years ago – early humans appear

Ornitholestes

Cycads

Homo erectus

Homo sapiens sapiens

The development of a human embryo in the mother's womb can be seen as evidence of the process of evolution. In the nine-month period of pregnancy, it undergoes a complicated process of development, starting off as a single cell and finally being born as a complex human.

These changes mirror those that took place over billions of years, in which life evolved from tiny, single-celled organisms into the complex structures of today. At one point, the human embryo even develops tiny gill slits, showing the connection to our distant relatives of the fish world.

The development of a human embryo

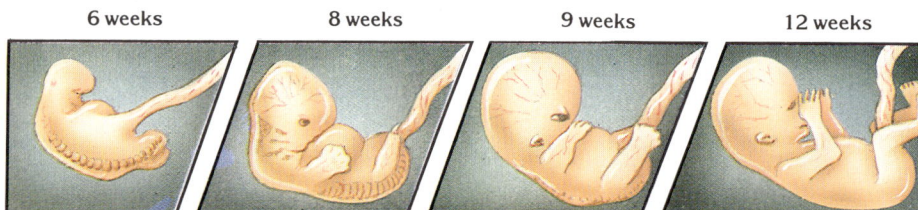

6 weeks     8 weeks     9 weeks     12 weeks

## Fossils — a key to evolution

A fossil is the remains or the imprint of a plant or animal that has somehow been preserved in rock. Sometimes this happens when the shell or bone of an animal turns to mineral and thus its shape is preserved. Or the shape of the plant or animal is left imprinted in the rock, once its actual body has decayed away. The study of fossils, known as palaeontology, is one of the main ways we can find out about life in the distant past and how it has evolved.

Because they are found in specific layers of rock that can be aged, scientists can tell how old the fossils are.

By comparing fossils of different periods, we can see how life evolved.

Sometimes whole dinosaur skeletons are found fossilized.

Tools

Fossilized bones

A fossil hunter, or palaeontologist

## Fossil hunting

Fossils are commonly found where sandstone, limestone or slate are exposed, though they are found elsewhere, too. All you need is a hammer and chisel and something to keep your samples in. Be observant when looking for fossils, as it is often very hard to spot the signs. Look for anything that seems out of place – different shapes, colours and types of rock. Use the hammer and chisel to break up lumps of rock to look inside. If you are successful, you could start your own fossil collection.

Here are some examples of what you may find:

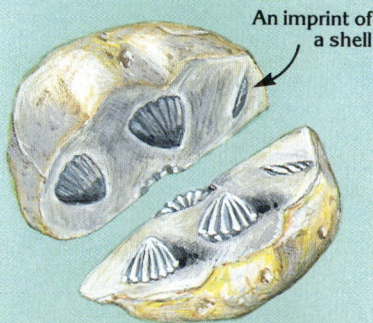

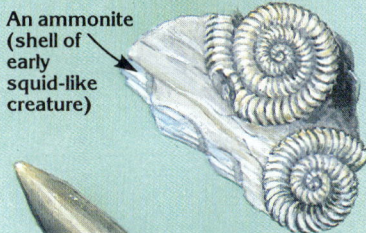

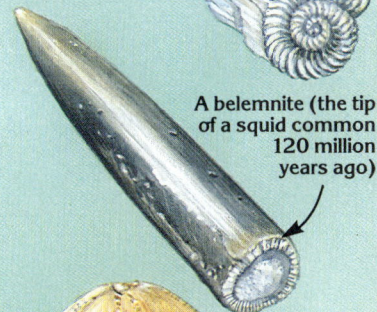

An imprint of a shell

An ammonite (shell of early squid-like creature)

A belemnite (the tip of a squid common 120 million years ago)

A sea urchin fossil

## Darwinism

There are many different ideas about how the evolutionary process works. For the last 150 years, the theories of Charles Darwin have been accepted by most people as the best explanation. These depend on the idea of natural selection, or "survival of the fittest", to explain how living things have evolved into so many complex forms.

The natural selection theory states that the plants and animals that adapt best to their environment survive.

These then pass on their adaptations, which can include slight changes in physical structure, to the next generation.

In this way, living things can gradually change, or evolve, over long periods of time.

For example, smog in 19th century Britain made survival easier for dark coloured peppered moths rather than silver ones, so more passed on their characteristics and their numbers increased.

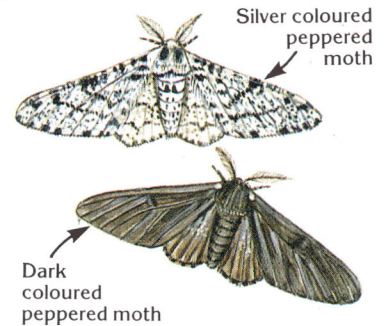

Silver coloured peppered moth

Dark coloured peppered moth

## Beyond Darwinism

Some modern scientists think there are many things about evolution that Darwinism fails to explain adequately. They see natural selection as only one part of a much more complex process. Some think that evolution from simple cells into complex organisms shows that living things have an in-built tendency to organize their body structures and functions in ever more complicated ways. Whatever the truth, we are still a long way from fully understanding evolution.

## The living planet

The earth itself has been changing over billions of years, too. In fact, life and the planet have constantly been evolving together, each affecting the other's development. For example, it was the early blue-green algae that, over millions of years, created the oxygen in the atmosphere, without which more complex life-forms would not have developed. Some scientists argue that the whole planet and its atmosphere works like a living organism. The idea of a "living" planet is known as the Gaia hypothesis, after the Greek Goddess of the Earth.

The planet earth seen from space – one vast living organism?

## Man's responsibility

We now have the ability to create our own environments, and thus to control, to an extent, our future evolution. We also control the future of the earth and all that it supports. However, we are only just beginning to realize what a huge responsibility this is. There are many choices to be made and there is much to be done – some of our options are discussed in the following four pages.

# People and planet

The human population is increasing at such a rate that both the environment and the balance of nature are threatened. This is one of the world's most urgent problems. But there are no simple answers, because it is the result of wide-ranging social, economic and political conditions which are all interconnected and which must be dealt with as a whole.

## Population growth

It took thousands of years for the world's population to reach 1 billion*, sometime in the 1830s, but only another 100 years for the 2 billion mark to be reached in the 1930s. By 1975 the population had reached 4 billion and 12 years later it had grown by another billion, reaching 5 billion towards the end of 1987. It is thought that it will finally level out at about 10 billion towards the end of the next century.

This graph shows the growth, and predicted growth, of the world's population.

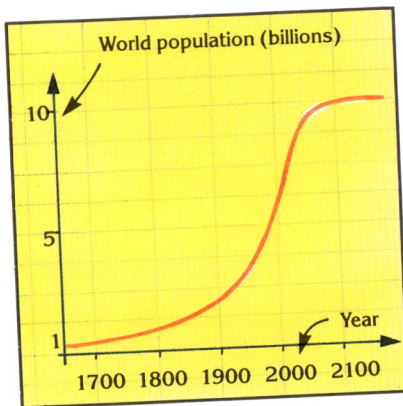

World population (billions)

Most of this growth is taking place in the world's poorest countries, where the birth rate is greater than the death rate.

## Population and resources

The earth has enough resources to support its population of 5 billion and more. But at present this is not happening. Millions of people in the poor world are living in hunger and poverty. The population problem is not so much "too many people" or "not enough land", as not managing to properly feed and support the growing populations.

Population problems do not necessarily come from a shortage of land:

Holland has a high population density but no problem, because it can afford to feed its population. India and Brazil have more land per person, but have a problem because they are poor.

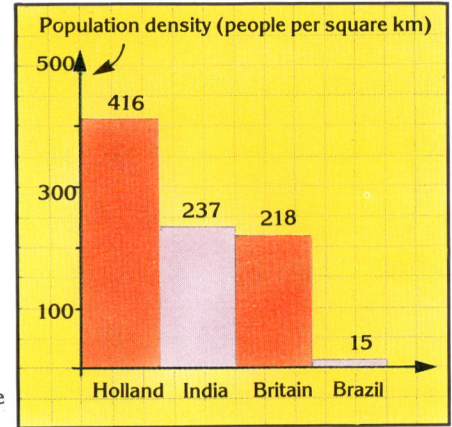

Population density (people per square km)

| Holland | India | Britain | Brazil |
|---|---|---|---|
| 416 | 237 | 218 | 15 |

A major part of the problem is the unequal sharing of the earth's resources between the rich and poor nations, and between the rich and poor people within those nations. The average American born today, for example, will use 40 times as much of the earth's resources (e.g. food, fossil fuels, metals, etc.) as their equivalent in a poor African country. One cause of this is the unfair system of international trade, in which poor nations are forced to compete with each other to produce and export crops (like coffee) more and more cheaply, to the benefit of the rich nations.

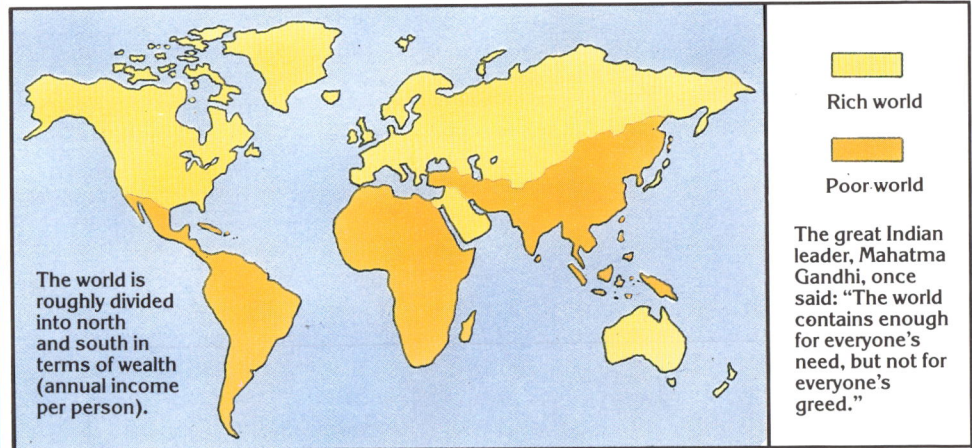

The world is roughly divided into north and south in terms of wealth (annual income per person).

Rich world

Poor world

The great Indian leader, Mahatma Gandhi, once said: "The world contains enough for everyone's need, but not for everyone's greed."

## Population and the environment

Many of the world's major ecological threats, like desertification (page 64) and rainforest destruction (page 75), are not necessarily caused by growing populations. The international economy, controlled by the wealthy nations, is also partly to blame. Many poor farmers are pushed off the best land, which is then used to grow export crops for the rich countries. They are forced to use poorer land or clear forest to produce the food they need to survive. To stop the environmental damage that this causes, there need to be changes in both national and international economic policies. The rich nations are the ones who can influence these policies, and so they control the future of the poor nations and their environments.

* These figures are based on the American billion, i.e. 1,000,000,000 (in other countries, e.g. Britain, one billion = 1,000,000,000,000).

# Energy and the environment

Energy is vital for many of our basic needs, like cooking, heating and transport. Its production has a big influence on the environment we live in, so we must choose carefully the sources of energy that are to be used in the future. The choices that we make now will determine what the society and environment of tomorrow will be like.

## Today's energy

The wealthy nations depend mainly on fossil fuels (coal, oil and gas) to provide their energy. They also produce some by nuclear power (using radioactive uranium) and some by hydro-electric power (using falling water). But the methods used are now seriously damaging the environment, e.g. the burning of fossil fuels causes acid rain and the greenhouse effect, and nuclear power produces long-term radioactive pollution and waste (and the danger of accidents).

In poorer countries the main source of domestic energy is wood (oil is used for industrial and transport purposes). This, too, has resulted in major environmental problems, with widespread deforestation (cutting down of trees) and soil erosion.

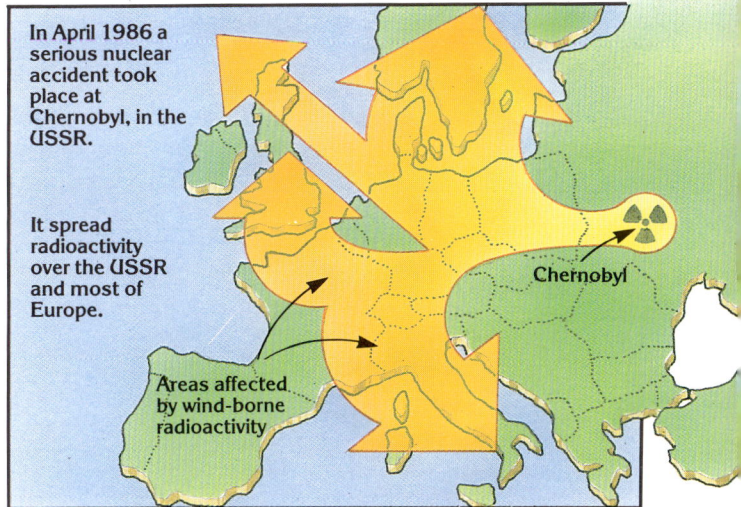

In April 1986 a serious nuclear accident took place at Chernobyl, in the USSR.

It spread radioactivity over the USSR and most of Europe.

Chernobyl

Areas affected by wind-borne radioactivity

## Renewable energy

Safer and cleaner forms of energy production are now being introduced in many countries. These are known as renewable energy sources, as they will not run out, like fossil fuels eventually will. They are now being used successfully in different areas of the world and promise plenty of energy in the future, with far less risk to the environment. Below and to the right are some examples.

● Solar power can be active (the use of solar panels to produce electricity) or passive (using more glass in buildings to trap the sun's heat) and has great potential, even in less sunny climates like those of northern Europe.

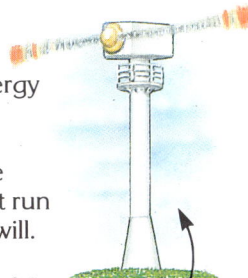

Wind power generator in Scotland.

● Wind power is now being used for large-scale electricity production. It is especially useful for supplying remote communities and small-scale users.

● The use of specially planted, fast-growing plants and trees could supply local fuel needs.

● Burning industrial waste and urban refuse in smaller, more efficient combined heat and power (CHP) stations produces energy as well as solving the refuse problem.

Other sources include converting wave and tide energy into electricity, and the tapping of geothermal energy (the heat of the earth's core). There are some environmental problems with the use of some of these sources on a large scale, but these are minor when compared to the problems and limits of fossil fuels and the dangers of more nuclear accidents.

Glass buildings make use of the sun's heat.

## Energy efficiency

One way of lessening our use of fossil and nuclear fuels is to use energy more efficiently, so that less is actually needed. This can be done on a national scale – by saving energy used in industry and transport. But it can also be done at the level of the individual. Your actions, too, will make a difference. Here are some ideas:

Insulate your hot-water tank and pipes (as in the picture) — your water will heat up quicker and stay hot longer.

Don't waste electricity, e.g. turn off lights when not in use, have a shower or all-over wash instead of a bath (it uses less heated water).

Draughtproof your doors and windows — this is simple to do and very effective.

Help your parents insulate the loft (if you have one) — this can save up to 20% of your energy bill.

# The future

We are now finding ourselves faced with choices about the sort of environment that we want to live in. The main choice is whether to start working with nature, by understanding and working with its natural cycles, or to carry on working against it. The future of all the people in the world, and of the world itself, depends on the choices that we make today.

## Solving the environmental crisis

Today, man's pressure on the natural world is causing a worldwide environmental crisis. Below are some of the main problems that we now face, along with some actions that we could take to improve the situation.

### Soil erosion

Soil erosion occurs when the vital topsoil is removed in the wind and rain.

– reforestation (the planting of trees) – trees and hedgerows act as wind-breaks and their roots bind the soil.

– organic farming – organic matter retains water longer and binds the soil better, preventing it drying up and blowing away.

– smaller fields – the smaller the field, the more protected the soil will be.

### Rainforest destruction

– reforms in land ownership in rainforest countries – to take the pressure off rainforest land.

– control of ranching and logging in rainforest areas, by lessening the rich world's demand for meat and tropical hardwoods.

– sustainable methods for using the forest's resources (methods that work with the natural cycles, and so can go on continuously), e.g. rubber-tapping.

### Acid rain and other pollution

– pollution filters on power stations and motor vehicles.

– renewable energy sources.

– alternatives to artificial chemicals in farming.

– an end to pollution from industrial and nuclear sources.

### Desertification

Desertification takes place when poor, arid land is over-used and turns to desert.

– less dependency on export crops in the poor world (these are grown on the best land, forcing poor people onto the more sparse land which soon turns to desert).

– appropriate irrigation techniques.

– more tree-planting schemes.

### Destruction of habitats and wildlife

– more and larger wildlife parks in towns and countryside.

– stricter international controls and safeguards to protect natural habitats and prevent the killing and trading of wild animals.

### Ozone depletion

The protective ozone layer in the atmosphere is in danger of being destroyed.

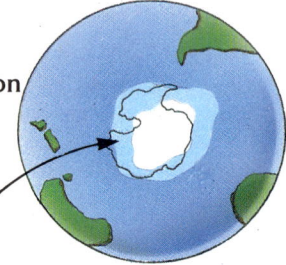

– a complete ban on the production and use of chlorofluorocarbons (as soon as it is practically possible).

### The greenhouse effect

– renewable energy sources.

– a halt to the destruction of the rainforest (these act as 'sinks', taking carbon dioxide from the air and using it up in photosynthesis).

– lower levels of energy use and wastage.

### The wasting of our natural resources

– recycling of essential minerals.

– emphasis on building things to last and repairing them (rather than just throwing them away).

– better schemes to encourage us to change our wasteful lifestyles.

## Practical action

All the suggested actions on the previous page must happen worldwide if they are to be successful. This demands much more international cooperation, especially between rich and poor nations. The trouble is that politicians tend to be more concerned with gaining support in their own countries in the short-term, than with the long-term future of the world and its people.

Many people believe that even all these actions will not be enough, and that we must all make very great changes in the way we live. They are working towards this in what is known as the green movement (see Green politics, on page 93). This used to be called the ecology movement.

At the moment it is mainly charity organizations, like Oxfam, that are successfully helping the world's poor to help themselves.

They give small-scale aid to communities, solving their problems without destroying local ways and traditions.

They use appropriate technology that the users can work and maintain, like this wind-powered pump in Africa.

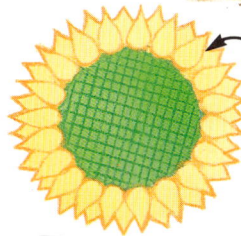

The sunflower is one of the images used in the green movement. It represents regrowth (of a more ecologically-sound society).

The problems are worldwide, but we can all do something to help. Every small change you make to your life will mean that the overall situation improves. This book shows you some ways you can help – if you want to do more, contact the groups listed on pages 92-93.

## Genetic engineering

One major problem that we are now facing is the control of genetic engineering. This is when scientists use living organisms (or parts of them) to change or create other life forms. They often experiment with genes, the parts of cells holding the genetic "code" that determines the characteristics of an organism.

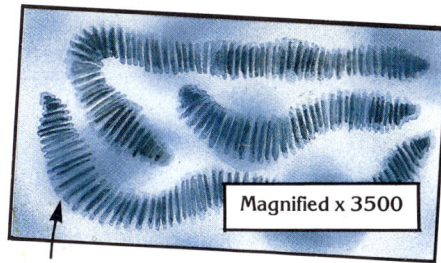

Magnified x 3500

By changing the information stored in the genes of an organism, scientists alter the characteristics of the new generation it produces.

Genetic experiments show how modern technology can be both a promise and a threat. For instance, some micro-organisms have been engineered to kill caterpillar pests, but some people feel that these organisms could seriously threaten the balance of nature. We need much stricter controls on such experiments than are now in use.

## Antarctica – a test case

Antarctica is a continent almost untouched by the activities of man. However, many of the rich nations are now showing a keen interest in it, as it may hold huge reserves of oil and minerals. Other, poorer countries are also demanding a share. Environmental groups, like Greenpeace, believe it should be held in trust for the future as a world park. What happens to Antarctica is a test of our ability to cooperate now, in the interests of future generations.

Antarctica has a land surface greater than that of the USA and Mexico combined.

As a world park, Antarctica would be open to all for scientific research and protected from destruction.

Any oil pollution would seriously endanger the fragile ecosystem. The low temperature would drastically slow the breakdown of oil.

## The holistic view

It is now very important that we learn to respect the natural world, not just because it supplies our basic needs (like food, water and air), but because it has a right to exist on its own merits. When we see that we are a part of this natural world, and not separate and above it, we begin to see the importance of protecting the great variety of living things it is made up of.

The holistic view looks at the natural world as an interconnected whole – the web of life – rather than a collection of many different parts. If we destroy separate strands of this web, we will end up destroying the web itself. If we do that, then we destroy ourselves.

# Ecology projects

On the next few pages are some larger-scale projects that you could do, either alone or with friends, parents or teachers. They are all enjoyable and will help you learn more about ecology.

## Building an ant observatory

For an introduction to keeping an ant colony, see page 68. Here you can find out how to make a formicarium, or observatory, to keep the ants in.

**What you will need:**

3 pieces of wood (30 cm long, 4 cm wide and over 2 cm deep)

2 pieces of perspex or plastic (30 cm by 34 cm)

Some strong glue (for use on plastic and wood)

6 thin nails (4 cm long) and a hammer

A piece of old stocking and a strong elastic band

Some garden soil, sand and leaf litter

A colony of ants

### What to do

Take the 3 pieces of wood and, using the glue and nails, fasten them together in a U-shape as shown.

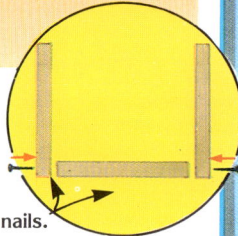

**Take care when using hammer and nails.**

Wait until the glue dries. Then take one piece of plastic and, putting glue around the outside of the wooden frame, stick the two together. Turn it round and do the same with the second piece of plastic on the other side.

Leave this to dry for a day or two. Now fill it with alternating layers of sand and soil (so the tunnels and chambers will show), topping it off with a thin layer of leaf litter.

Leave a 10 cm gap at the top, to allow the ants some space. You could put in some twigs and leaves, too.

Collect the ants (try under large stones), using a soft brush and a jar – try to include the much larger queen ant. Empty them into their new home.

Give them some water (a moist lump of cotton wool), and some sugar, apple or other food-scraps. Secure the stocking or tea-towel around the top with the elastic band. Now watch the ants work.

## Making a pond

One way to improve your environment and help local wildlife is to build a pond. To see what it might look like when completed, turn to page 53.

**What you will need:**

A spade

A very large sheet of plastic

Some large stones and some hay or straw

Old carpet or rags

Pond plants (grown in baskets) and pond weed

Plenty of water (rainwater is best)

A bucket of water, weeds and mud from another pond

### Positioning

If you have a garden, putting in a pond will add interest. If you don't, you could try to find some land nearby, like school grounds or parkland, and get permission to build a pond there.

Keep the pond away from trees if you can, as falling leaves can be a big problem in autumn.

It is best to place the pond near some sort of cover, like a flower bed, hedge or rockery, as this will give frogs and toads some sort of protection.

### Digging the pond

When making your own pond, you are free to design its shape.

Dig a hole at least 2 m across and 0.5 m deep.

The sides should be gently sloping, with shelves at different levels.

Remove all the stones that stick out of the bottom and sides, and cover the bottom with old carpet or rags (this will stop anything puncturing the plastic).

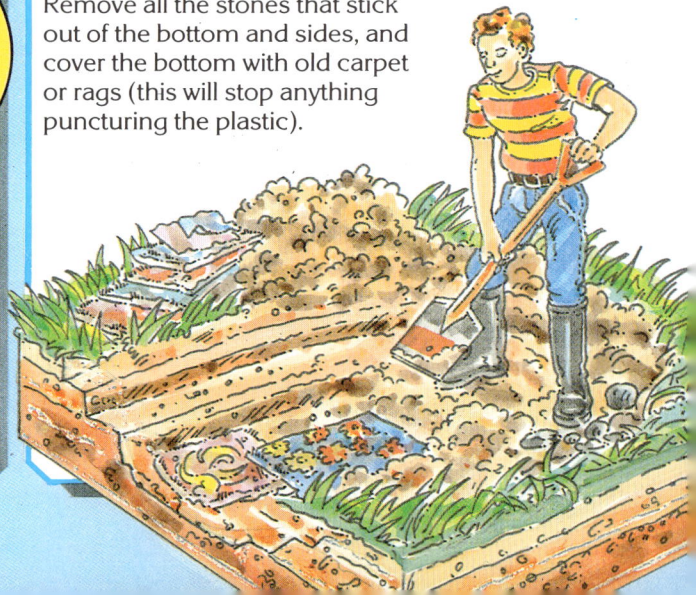

## Laying the plastic

Wash the plastic sheet thoroughly (to get rid of any chemicals still on it). Then lay it in the hole. Don't worry if it doesn't fit the contours exactly – the weight of the water will help.

Secure the sheet with large stones around the edge of the pond. You could use paving stones for this.

Place a 10 cm layer of soil over the bottom of the pond (using some of the earth that you have just dug up). This will give plants a good base to grow from.

Add some hay or straw at the bottom to encourage scavengers and decomposers.

You could place a dead tree branch sticking out of the water, to give birds somewhere to perch.

## Filling the pond

Using a hosepipe or buckets, fill the pond with water. Don't fill it right up to the top – leave 5 to 10 cm – or else it will overflow when it rains.

Add your bucket of water, weed and mud from another pond. This will be full of animals, plants and seeds and will help life establish itself in your pond much more quickly.

Place your plants in the pond. These should be indigenous (plants that grow naturally in your local area). To make it easier to arrange them, you should keep them in their in baskets. Use small stones to attach pond weed to the bottom.

Let the mud and soil in the water settle.

Place some larger stones on the bottom for shelter, and also near the edges to help animals get in and out.

## Keeping the pond

If the pond gets too murky, put in plenty of pond-snails. These clean the water by feeding on the tiny algae that can make it dirty.

A few leaves blown into the pond will be beneficial. They will decompose on the bottom, releasing minerals. But try to keep the pond free of too many, especially in autumn, as they will cause problems.

Larger animals, like toads, frogs and newts, will find their own way to your pond after a while. Keep an eye out for them, but be patient.

Unless you want an ornamental fish pond, don't add fish to your pond (especially if it is quite small). They are greedy predators and will eat the smaller pond life.

You may need to top up the water level in dry periods, as some water will evaporate.

# Ecology projects

## Building a compost heap

If you have a garden and enjoy gardening, a compost heap is a useful addition. Most soils will benefit from added compost, as it returns vital minerals that are used up in plant growth, and it is more natural than adding chemicals.

### What you will need:

Organic waste from the kitchen (tea leaves, potato peelings, left-over food, etc. – but not meat scraps)

Organic matter from the garden (like cut grass, leaves and weeds)

A nitrogen "activator" (speeds up decay), like manure

Some soil

Plenty of water

Some planks (of the same length) and 4 wooden posts

A hammer and nails

A piece of old carpet or plastic sheeting

### What to do

The first thing to do is to box in the site:

Find a spot for the heap – about a square metre in size.

Firmly plant four corner posts. Use planks for the walls. Include gaps for ventilation.

You could use bricks, too. Make sure that it's stable and has ventilation gaps.

The bottom layer should be twigs and sticks. Then add alternating layers of garden waste, kitchen waste, compost "activator" and soil. ▶

Keep the layers moist by adding water, and pack them down firmly.

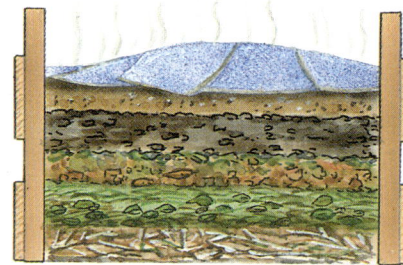

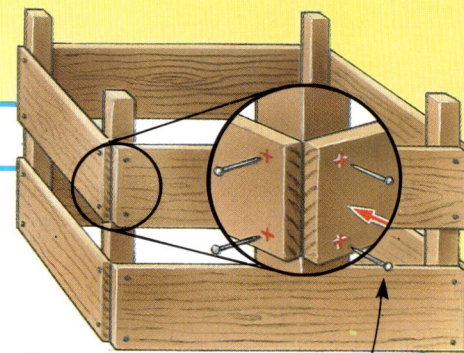

Take care when using a hammer and nails. Keep the nail straight and tap gently to begin with. Finish by hammering firmly.

◀ When the heap is about 1.5 m high, lay the old carpet or plastic sheeting over the top – this keeps in the heat.

Leave it for 5 to 6 months, keeping it damp throughout this time. You could start a second heap in the meantime.

Decomposers will break down the organic matter in the heap, creating a mineral-rich compost. This can then be added to your vegetable patch, flower bed or any other soil, and will help your plants to grow.

## Sprouting beans and seeds to eat

Making bean and seed sprouts is easy, fun and supplies cheap and healthy food (they are a good source of vitamin C).

### What you will need:

Some large plastic containers

Some beans or seeds from a shop, e.g. mung beans, cress, chickpeas or alfalfa seeds

Some pieces of muslin or old tea-towels

Some strong elastic bands

### What to do

Clean out your plastic container – you could use a large yoghurt carton, or cut the top off a large plastic soft-drinks bottle and use the main body. Put in the beans or seeds, cover them in water and leave them to soak overnight.

Attach the muslin or tea-towel over the top with the elastic band and strain out the water. Leave the container and its contents in a warm, dark place overnight. The next day, take it out, wash the beans or seeds in water, drain them and put them back again. Do this each day and check their progress.

After 3 to 4 days, they should be ready to eat. Wash them and add them to a salad or use them as a sandwich filler – they are delicious and very nutritious.

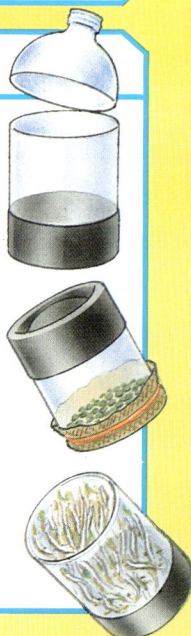

## Building a bird-table

Building a bird table and providing a regular supply of food will encourage birds to your garden, and help to keep them alive in the long winter months. For more information on feeding birds, see page 70.

### What you will need:

A strong wooden post about 1.5 m long

A piece of wood 40 cm square and 1 cm thick

A hammer, nails and 4 strips of wood 36 cm long

### What to do

◄ One end of the post must be shaped to a point, to go into the ground more easily. Get an adult to help you do this, or buy one with a pointed end.

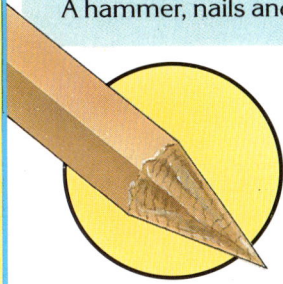

Carefully nail or tack the ► 4 strips of wood to the outside edge of the table-top, as shown here. These will stop the food from blowing away.

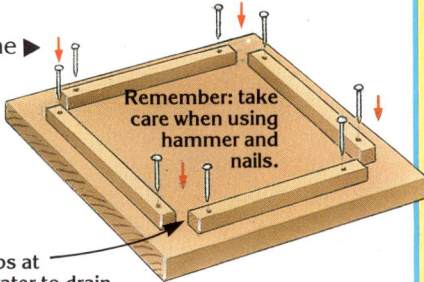

**Remember: take care when using hammer and nails.**

**There should be small gaps at each corner to allow rainwater to drain.**

◄ Nail the table-top to the top of the post (you could first drill small holes in the table-top for the nails, to prevent the wood splitting).

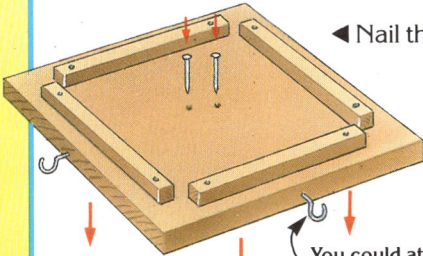

**You could attach hooks from the sides to hang bags of nuts or other feeders.**

Position the table where you can see it, but also where the birds can see cats when they approach.

◄ You could add a bird bath, too. Just fill an old baking tin or tray with a little water, and put it on the bird table. The birds will always enjoy a good bath.

One point to remember is that you should not really feed the birds in spring and summer, as there will be plenty of their natural food available. This is better for the young and growing birds than bread and kitchen scraps.

## Birdwatching

Birdwatching is an interesting and enjoyable activity in both city and country, and can become a life-long passion. Try it and see.

### What you will need:

A pair of binoculars are useful – of the many sizes, the 8 × 30 mm ones are light and powerful enough for most purposes.

A notebook, pen and coloured pencils – for notes and drawings of what you see.

A small tape-recorder – for recording either bird song or a commentary of what you see.

A reference book to identify what you see.

### Some helpful hints

The best time to see bird activity is just before dawn, though dusk is a good time, too. Midday is when there is least activity.

Birds are more active in the breeding season (spring and early summer) than in the nesting season (mid-summer onwards). Some are more active again in autumn as they prepare to migrate.

When stalking: keep quiet, move carefully and slowly, use cover and camouflage, and concentrate on the birds.

When observing: find some cover, get comfortable, keep still and quiet, and be patient.

Much of this advice is useful when watching other wildlife, too.

# Ecology projects

## Planting trees

On these pages you can learn how to choose, plant and maintain your own tree or trees. In doing so, you will improve the local environment and help wildlife by providing a vital habitat. Before you start, however, it is important you realize how much time and effort is involved. As well as the actual planting of the tree, there will also be several years of care before it can be left to itself.

**What you will need:**

A young tree (sapling) or trees

If you are growing trees from seed, you will also need: flower pots (or plastic containers with holes in the bottom), compost and a selection of tree seeds or seedlings.

A garden spade and fork

A strong wooden stake, about 1.5 m long (only necessary if the sapling is over 1 m high)

Wooden posts and protective wire fencing.

An adjustable rubber tie (from a gardening store)

Some mulch (wet straw, leaves, etc.) or peat

## Planning your planting

To be successful, tree-planting must be carefully planned before anything is actually done. Several things need to be taken into account:

### Where?
In your garden, your street, the school grounds, the local park or green, almost anywhere in fact. However, you will need permission from the relevant authority or landowner, unless it is your land. Make sure that nobody living nearby will object.

### What sort of tree?
It is important to choose indigenous trees (those that are native to your area), as these will be better suited to the conditions and wildlife there. If you are planting near to buildings, roads or underground pipes, you should plant trees that don't grow too high. Their shorter roots are less likely to cause damage.

### Will you need help?
Tree-planting is much easier if done by two or more people, though it can be done alone. If you are planting a lot of trees, or planting in public areas, it is best to get people from the local community involved. They can help by both planting the trees and looking after them afterwards. For advice, contact your local conservation group, council or gardening centre.

## Choosing your tree

The most satisfying way to raise saplings is to grow them from seed yourself, although this also takes the most time. Collect different types of freshly-fallen seeds in autumn and winter. Sow them in pots filled with moist compost, and wait for the spring. Some (like oak and beech) may germinate straight away, whilst others (like ash) won't germinate until a year later.

An acorn (seed) from an oak tree (native to Europe, Asia and North America) ▶

A beech nut and husk (native to Europe, though common in Asia and North America) ◀

A capsule (containing seeds) from a eucalyptus tree (native to Australia) ▶

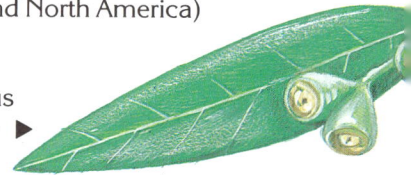

The other option is to buy the young trees ready-grown from a local nursery or garden centre. This can be quite expensive, though it will give more immediate results.

These are points to look for when choosing a sapling:

Well-balanced branches

Strong straight stem

Plentiful, undamaged roots (these should be kept damp)

The smaller the sapling, the easier it will be to transport and the quicker it will grow.

Take care when transporting. Trees can die of "shock".

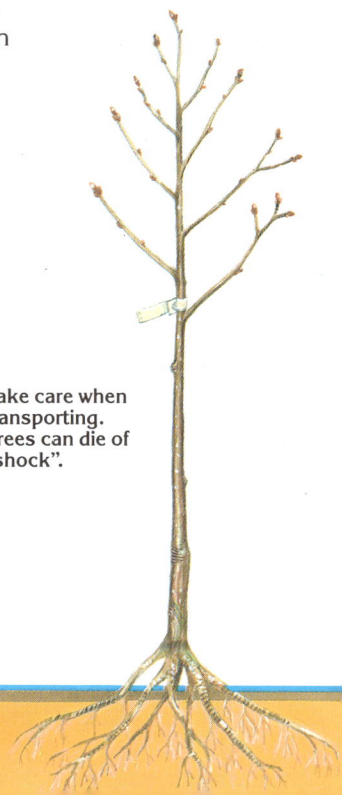

## How to plant your tree

When growing from seed, you should plant the young tree outside once it has reached 10 to 12 cm (see picture). It will need a lot of protection for quite some time, so should be planted in a sheltered, protected spot.

Dig a hole the size of your pot, loosening the soil at the bottom (to help drainage). Remove the sapling and compost from the pot, put it in the hole, and keep it well watered.

It might be necessary to protect it with a fence (as shown).

When planting a larger sapling, you will need to prepare the hole more thoroughly (see picture). Though if it is under 1 m high, you won't need the supporting stake.

Dig a hole the width of the roots and deep enough for the tree to sit in it up to its collar (where root and stem meet).

Break up the soil at the bottom of the hole with the fork.

Drive the stake (if needed) firmly into the ground, to about 30 cm below the bottom of the hole.

Soak the roots well, and place the tree carefully in the hole. Shovel in some soil, shaking the sapling carefully to allow soil to get under and between the roots.

Firm gently with your foot. Add more soil and tread it down more heavily. Continue until the hole is filled and the soil is firmly trodden down.

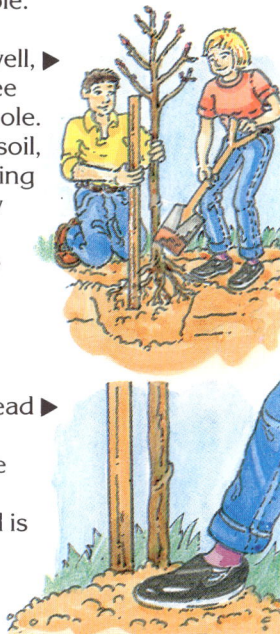

The collar

Attach the tree to the stake with the rubber tie, and water the area well. Spread a layer of mulch or peat around the base of the tree (this prevents weeds from growing and also stops the soil drying up).

If there is any danger of damage (e.g. mowing-machines or grazing animals), put up a fence around the tree.

## Looking after your tree

For the first few years, the tree will need some care and attention.

If you are planting on public land, get the local community interested, as they could help in maintaining and protecting the trees.

Make sure the tree is watered, especially in dry periods.

Keep the ground at its base as free of plants and grass as you can (they compete for water and minerals), but avoid chemical weedkillers.

Adjust the rubber tie and repair the stake and fencing when necessary.

It is important to remember, when choosing, planting and maintaining trees, that they should be treated carefully. Trees are complex living organisms and are easily damaged and killed. If well planted and maintained, they will give people pleasure, as well as providing food and shelter for wildlife.

A mature common oak

A mature beech tree

A mature eucalyptus tree

# Ecology projects

## Making recycled paper

### What you will need:

- Old newspaper
- Wire mesh (from a garden centre or hardware store)
- Some absorbent cloths
- 2 buckets or bowls
- Wooden spoon or liquidizer
- Powder paint (to make coloured paper)
- Plastic bag
- Weights, e.g. heavy books

### What to do

Soak some old newspaper in a bucket overnight. The next day, drain off the extra water. Using the liquidizer (with permission if necessary) or your wooden spoon, mash up the paper and water into a pulp (and clean the liquidizer afterwards). Mix in the paint if you want coloured paper.

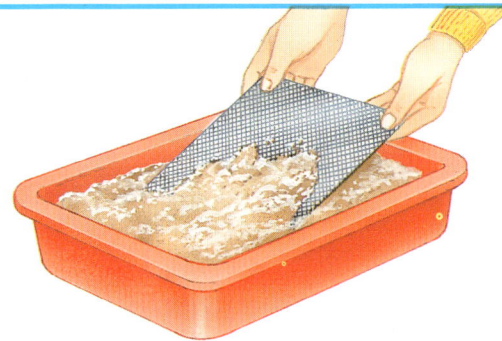

Put the pulp into another bowl and add an equal volume of water. Mix these together. Slide the wire mesh into the mixture, lifting it out covered in pulp.

## A windowsill salad garden

### What you will need:

- Plastic margarine tubs
- Peat-based seed compost
- Some seeds (e.g. radish, parsley, spring onion, mint, etc.)

### What to do

Fill the tubs with compost to within 1 cm of the rim, and firm this down. Plant the seeds under 1 cm of compost and water them. Place them on a windowsill in the kitchen, and water them once or twice a week. Herbs like mint or parsley can be used to flavour cooking (cut off small pieces with scissors when needed), and the radishes or spring onions can be pulled up and used in salads. You could then start growing other herbs (like basil, sage and thyme) or perhaps lettuce or a miniature tomato plant.

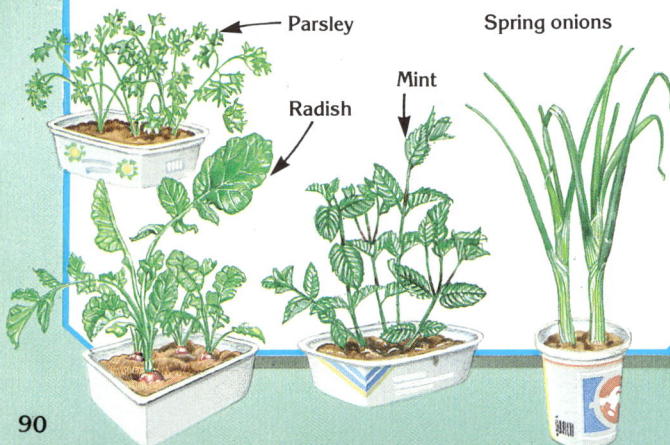

Parsley

Spring onions

Mint

Radish

## Organizing your own group

If there is something you feel particularly strongly about (like cleaning up the litter in your area), you could try setting up a group to do something about it. The example here shows how you might create a pocket park on a piece of wasteland (see also page 73).

First, talk to your friends and see if they want to join in and help. Then try putting up notices or posters at school or in the library, telling people about what you want to do and how to contact you.

Prepare for your first meeting by noting down points for discussion, and ideas for action. It might be useful to invite an expert to give a talk or offer advice.

At the meeting, choose who is the chairperson (to make sure the meetings run smoothly), the secretary (to record decisions and inform members of future events) and the treasurer (to be in charge of money and accounts). You should also cover the first steps to take:

1. Find out who the land belongs to (ask your local authority), so you can get permission for your project.

2. Raise some money for things you may need to buy, e.g. seeds and shrubs. You could do odd jobs, or organize a raffle or sponsored walk.

3. Find out what help is available from the local authority or conservation group, and see what garden tools you can borrow.

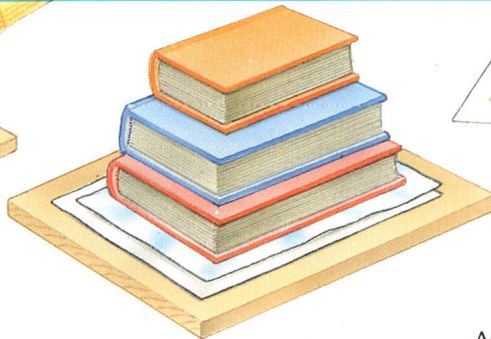

Lay a cloth on a clean, flat surface. Place the mesh (with the pulp side down) quickly and carefully onto the cloth. Press it down hard, then peel off, leaving the pulp on the cloth. Put another cloth on top and press down firmly.

Repeat these steps with your remaining pulp and cloths. When this is done, place the plastic bag on the top and weight the pile down.

After several hours (when the pulp has turned to paper), gently peel the paper off the cloths. Leave the pieces on some newspaper or kitchen towel until completely dry. The paper should now be ready for use.

Decide what each group member should do, and set a date for the next meeting.

Try to interest other people in what you are doing – get group members to write to the local papers, or put up notices or posters in libraries, schools and community or youth centres. Show how your work will improve the local environment and help its wildlife.

**This is a poster about a canal clearing project. Try designing a poster about a pocket park.**

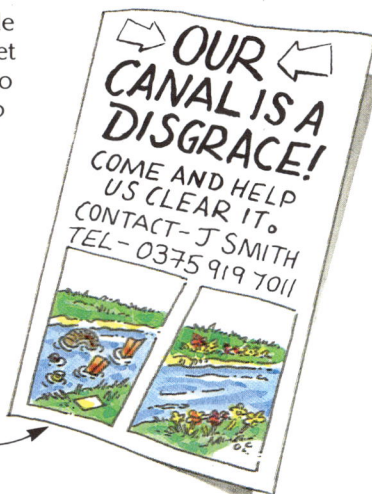

OUR CANAL IS A DISGRACE!
COME AND HELP US CLEAR IT.
CONTACT- J SMITH
TEL- 0375 919 7011

You should have regular progress meetings until you are ready to start work on the site. Plan the layout, including perhaps a pond (see pages 84-85), some meadow (page 71) and plenty of trees (pages 88-89). Also, arrange to get rid of any large pieces of rubbish from the site (contact your local authority).

### Working on your pocket park

1. Clear the ground of all rubbish, bricks and rubble.

2. If there is no topsoil, you can order it from a garden centre. Mix it in with the soil already on the site.

3. After preparing the soil (digging it up, especially where it is compacted, and perhaps adding topsoil), plant plenty of seeds from different types of grass and wild flowers.

4. Make sure that you only use indigenous (native) plants, as these will support far more wildlife.

After everything is planted, you should keep working at the site – it will need to be maintained for quite some time (e.g. keeping it free of rubbish and protecting the young plants). All this hard work will certainly be worthwhile, once the park is set up.

If you want to get involved but don't fancy setting up your own group, you could join an environmental or conservation group. Many have their own local groups which organize activities, and they are always interested in new members (see addresses overleaf).

# Going further

Below are some addresses of environmental, conservation and Third world development groups from around the world. Some are campaign groups (spreading information and influencing public, business and government actions), whilst others are involved in conservation work (like creating, maintaining and improving natural sites). Most have local groups which you can join.

## International organizations

**Friends of the Earth (FOE)** – campaigns for protection of wildlife and habitats, and improvement of the environment at local, national and international levels. Youth section called Earth Action.

366 Smith Street, Collingwood VIC 3066, Australia

53 Queen Street, Room 16, Ottawa, ONT K1P 5CS, Canada

26-28 Underwood Street, London N1 7JQ, England

PO Box 39-065, Auckland West, New Zealand

530 7th Street SE, Washington DC 20003, USA

---

**World-Wide Fund for Nature (WWF)** (formerly World Wildlife Fund) – campaigns to protect wildlife and habitats throughout the world. Uses education to show the importance of the world's natural resources.

Level 17, St Martin's Tower, 31 Market Street, GPO Box 528, Sydney NSW 2001, Australia

35 Taraniki Street, PO Box 6237, Wellington, New Zealand

60 St Clair Avenue East, Suite 201, Toronto, ONT M4T 1N5, Canada

Panda House, Weyside Park, Godalming, Surrey GU7 1XR, England

1250 24th Street NW, Washington DC 20037, USA

---

**Intermediate Technology** – works on long-term development in poor countries, using technology appropriate to the needs of the rural poor. Aims to help people to become more self-reliant.

103-105 Southampton Row, London WC1B 4HH, England

777 United Nations Plaza, New York NY 10017, USA

## Finding a local group

One way to find a local group is to check in your local telephone directory, under the heading "charities". Another method is to ask at your local library for information on local groups. But the best way to find out is to write to the organization's central office (some addresses are given below) and ask them whether there is an active group in your area.

**Greenpeace** – uses peaceful but direct action to defend the environment. Campaigns to: save the whales (see opposite), oppose nuclear power and weapons, stop acid rain and protect Antarctica.

134 Broadway, 4th Floor, Broadway, NSW 2007, Australia

Nagel House, 5th Floor, Courthouse Lane, Auckland, New Zealand

427 Bloor Street West, Toronto, ONT M5S 1X7, Canada

30-31 Islington Green, London N1 8XE, England

1611 Connecticut Avenue NW, Washington DC 20009, USA

---

**Oxfam** – involved in practical, long-term improvement of agriculture, health-care and social conditions in poor countries, as well as giving vital short-term emergency aid where and when it is needed most.

Community Aid Abroad, 156 George Street, Fitzroy, VIC 3065, Australia

251 Laurier Avenue West, Suite 301, Ottawa, ONT K1P 5J6, Canada

274 Banbury Road, Oxford OX2 7DZ, England

115 Broadway, Boston, MASS 02116, USA

---

**Survival International** – campaigns to protect surviving native peoples and the environments in which they live. Publicizes the risks to native peoples, and campaigns for their basic human rights around the world.

310 Edgware Road, London W2 1DY, England

2121 Decatur Place NW, Washington DC 20008, USA

## National organizations

These organizations cover a variety of areas, including the environment, conservation and the Third World. Many will have local groups that you can join. If you are interested in further action, write to any of the addresses given here (including a stamp for return postage) and ask for information.

### Australia

Australian Conservation Foundation, GPO Box 1875, Canberra, ACT 2601

Centre for Appropriate Technology, PO Box 795, Alice Springs, Northern Territory 5750

Rainforest Information Centre, PO Box 368, Lismore, NSW 2480

Total Environment Centre, 18 Argyle Street, Sydney, NSW 2000

The Wilderness Society, PO Box 188, Civic Square, Canberra, ACT 2608

### New Zealand

Environmental Council, PO Box 10-382, Wellington

Nature Conservation Council, PO Box 12-200, Wellington

Royal Forest and Bird Protection Society, PO Box 631, Wellington

Tree Society, 41 Masterton Road, Rothesay Bay, Auckland 10

## Canada

Canadian Nature Federation,
453 Sussex Drive, Ottawa, ONT K1N 6Z4

Ecology Action Centre,
1657 Barrington Street, Suite 520, Halifax,
Nova Scotia, B3J 2A1

Energy Probe / Probe International,
100 College Street, Toronto, ONT M5G IL5

Forests for Tomorrow,
355 Lesmill Road, Don Mills, ONT M3B 2W8

Sea Shepherd Conservation Society,
PO Box 48446, Vancouver BC V7X 1AZ

Society Promoting Environmental
Conservation,
2150 Maple Street, Vancouver BC V6J 3T3

Young Naturalist Foundation,
56 The Esplanade, Suite 306,
Toronto, ONT M5E 1A7

## United Kingdom

British Trust for Conservation
Volunteers (BTCV),
36 St. Mary's Street, Wallingford,
Oxfordshire OX10 OEU

The Living Earth,
86 Colston Street,
Bristol BS1 5BB

Men of the Trees, Turns Hill Road,
Crawley Down, Crawley,
West Sussex RH10 4HL

The National Trust, PO Box 12,
Westbury, Wiltshire BA13 4NA

Royal Society for the Protection of
Birds (RSPB),
The Lodge, Sandy, Bedfordshire SG19 2DL

Scottish Conservation Projects,
70 Main Street, Doune, Perthshire FK16 6BW

WATCH, 22 The Green,
Nettleham, Lincoln LN2 2NR

## United States

Defenders of Wildlife,
1244 19th Street NW,
Washington DC 20036

Food First,
1885 Mission Street,
San Francisco, CA 94103

National Audubon Society,
950 3rd Avenue,
New York NY 10022

Rainforest Action Network,
466 Green Street, Suite 300,
San Francisco CA 94133

Sierra Club,
330 Pennsylvania Avenue NW,
Washington DC 20005

The Wilderness Society,
1400 Eye Street NW,
Washington DC 20005

## Greenpeace — saving the whales

One of the most famous campaigns by an environmental group was that of Greenpeace, when they attracted the attention of the world to the fate of whales in the 1970's. Some species, including the humpback, blue, fin and sperm whales, had been hunted to the edge of extinction, and whaling was still going on unchecked. Greenpeace activists confronted the whalers, preventing them from harpooning the whales. Their actions were captured on film, and shown to millions around the world on television news or in the papers.

The media coverage given to these actions resulted in growing public pressure to ban whaling. This, in turn, led to the 1982 decision of the International Whaling Commission (IWC) to ban commercial whaling for five years from 1985. However some countries have continued whaling since then, though on a smaller scale. Greenpeace are continuing their campaign against these whaling nations. They believe that after 50 million years of peaceful existence in the oceans, whales have earned the right to survive in peace.

By getting their inflatable craft between the whale and the harpoonist, the activists save the whale from a painful death.

## Green politics

Many people believe that we must all make major changes in the way we live our lives if we are going to save the planet and ourselves from a harsh and difficult future. This view is put forward by "green" political parties all over the world, many of which are represented in their national parliaments. The West German green party (die Grünen), for example, increased their number of seats from 27 to 42 (out of 520) in the 1987 elections.

The green parties claim to offer an alternative to the usual political choices of the left, the centre or the right. They propose such things as a fairer sharing of the world's resources between rich and poor nations, and have far-sighted plans for the rebuilding of a new and better society. They believe that all governments should place people, the environment and the quality of life at the top of their list of priorities when making policy decisions.

# Glossary

**Acid rain**. Rain and snow containing toxic chemicals which enter the atmosphere as industrial and vehicle **pollution**. It kills many living things, especially trees and freshwater plants and animals, and causes damage to buildings and people's health.

**Adaptation**. The process by which living things adjust to their environment, also any attributes they have developed to this end (e.g. a cactus spine is a leaf adaptation – with a small surface to conserve water).

**Appropriate technology**. Tools, machinery and methods that are suitable for use and maintenance by the people that use them (e.g. hand tools rather than tractors in areas where oil and spare parts cannot be obtained).

**Biome**. One of the large **ecosystems** into which the earth's land surface can be divided. Each is the **climax community** of a region with a particular **climate**.

**Camouflage**. The use of colour or patterns by a plant or animal to merge into its surroundings, or disguise itself as another plant or animal (**mimicry**).

**CFC s (Chlorofluorocarbons)**. Chlorine-based compounds, used mainly in aerosols, refrigerator coolants and polystyrene, which are thought to be responsible for the slow destruction of the **ozone layer**.

**Climate**. Large-scale weather conditions (e.g. temperature, wind and humidity) that are characteristic of a certain region.

**Climax community**. A **community** that remains virtually unchanged, as long as there are no climatic or environmental changes (see also **Succession**).

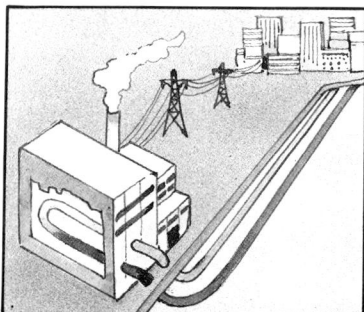

**Combined heat and power stations (CHP s)**. Particularly energy-efficient power stations, built in urban areas. They use the hot water produced by electricity generation to heat local houses, schools, etc.

**Community**. The plants and animals within a certain **habitat**.

**Consumers**. Organisms that feed on other organisms.

**Crop rotation**. A farming method in which different, specially-chosen crops are grown in one field each year over a four or five year cycle. It helps to control pests and avoid the depletion of minerals in the soil.

**Decomposers**. Organisms that live by breaking down dead bodies, releasing the minerals they contain.

**Deforestation**. Clearing trees for fuel or timber, or for farmland or new settlement land.

**Desertification**. The process by which **marginal land** (traditionally used for grazing by peasant peoples) is transformed into useless desert by overgrazing or other over-intensive farming methods, or by a **climate** change.

**Ecosystem**. A virtually self-contained system, consisting of a **community** of plants and animals in a given **habitat**, together with their environment.

**Evolution**. The long-term process of change in organisms, often occurring over millions of years.

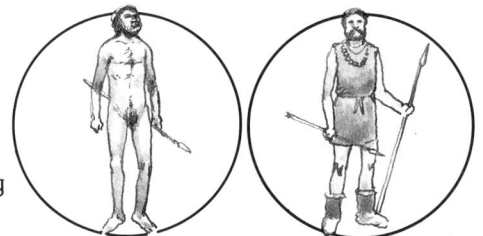

**Extinction**. The dying out of a species of living thing, and hence its complete disappearance from the earth.

**Food chain**. A chain of organisms, linked together because each is food for the next in line. Energy passes from one level (**trophic level**) to the next. All the food chains in an **ecosystem** are connected together in a complex **food web**.

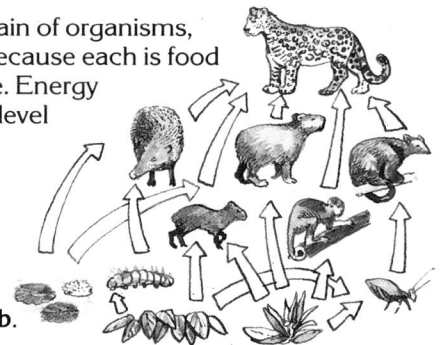

**Genetic engineering**. Altering genes to create organisms that are useful to man. Genes carry information about an organism's basic characteristics.

**Greenhouse effect**. The trapping of the Sun's heat by atmospheric gases, causing the warming of the atmosphere. People's output of an increasing amount of these gases (mainly carbon dioxide) threatens to increase world temperatures more and more.

**Habitat**. A specific area, small or large, that is inhabited by a particular **community** of plants and animals.

**Intensive farming**. Farming by modern methods to maximize output, e.g. using artificial fertilizers, insecticides and other chemicals, and growing the same crop in the same field each year. These methods harm the soil and hence the natural cycles of the land.

**Irrigation**. The watering of land, mainly by using channels or ditches. Bad irrigation methods can make land infertile, e.g. by bringing up too much salt to the topsoil.

**Marginal land**. Land that is only just good enough for agriculture or grazing animals.

**Natural selection**. The theory of evolutionary processes first expounded by Charles Darwin. It suggests that those individual organisms within a species which have the best **adaptations** to their environment are the most likely to survive long enough to breed, hence these adaptations become established in later generations, and the species as a whole gradually "improves".

**Niche**. The position filled by a particular organism within its **ecosystem**, including its activities, such as feeding, and its relationships with other organisms.

**Organic**. Anything which is or was part of an organism (contains the element carbon).

**Organic farming**. Farming methods that work with nature's cycles, e.g. using **organic** animal waste (dung) as fertilizer, natural pest control, and **crop rotation**.

**Ozone layer**. A layer of the atmosphere containing ozone gas. This gas blocks out the sun's harmful ultra-violet rays, but man-made gases may be destroying it.

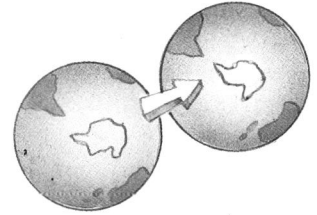

**Photosynthesis**. The means by which plants use the sun's energy to build their food (carbohydrates) from water and carbon dioxide.

**Pollution**. The contamination of an area, and its natural cycles, with unnatural substances or an excess of natural ones, and the consequent damage caused.

**Producers**. All green plants, which make food from simple materials by **photosynthesis**. They are the basis of all **food chains**.

**Renewable energy**. Energy from constant, natural sources, such as the sun, wind and waves.

**Soil erosion**. The process by which vital topsoil is lost (mainly blown away by wind or washed away by rain), having been loosened due to such things as **intensive farming**, **deforestation** and poor methods of **irrigation**. The land becomes barren.

**Succession**. The series of natural, progressive changes in an area, as one **community** replaces another, until a **climax community** is created.

**Sustainable development**. The use of methods of development that do not interfere with natural cycles or damage the ecological balance of an area (also sustainable forestry, farming, etc.)

**Territory**. An area occupied by one or more organisms and defended against incursion or attack by other other organisms (especially of the same species).

**Trophic levels**. Different layers of a **food chain**, each containing organisms which get their food and energy from similar sources.

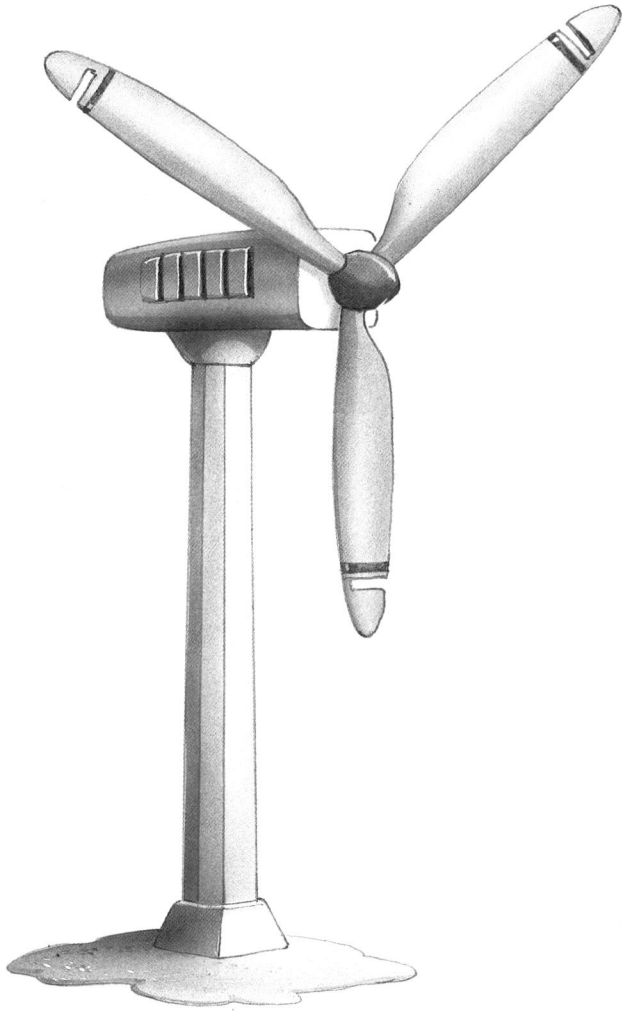

# ENERGY & POWER

Richard Spurgeon and Mike Flood

Edited by Corinne Stockley

Designed by Stephen Wright

Illustrated by Kuo Kang Chen and Joseph McEwan

Additional designs by Christopher Gillingwater

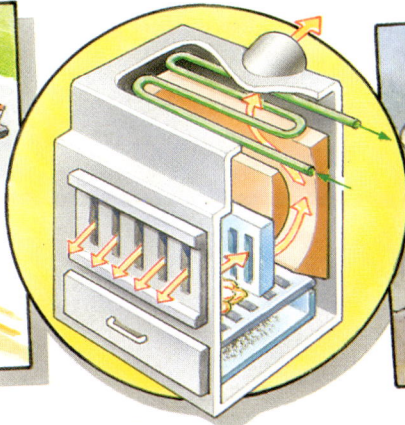

# Contents

99   About this book
100   What is energy?
102   Energy changes
104   Stored energy
106   Movement energy
108   Electricity
110   Energy and the earth
112   The coal industry
114   Oil and gas
116   Nuclear power
118   The electricity industry
120   Making an electromagnet
121   Renewable energy/Solar energy
123   More solar projects
124   Energy from plants
126   Wind energy
128   Energy from water
130   Energy efficiency
132   Efficiency in industry
133   Efficiency in transport
134   Energy in the future
136   World energy facts
140   The economics of energy
141   Further information
142   Glossary

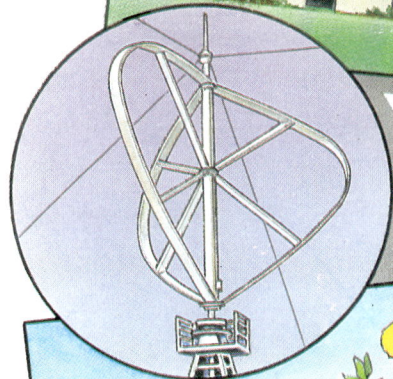

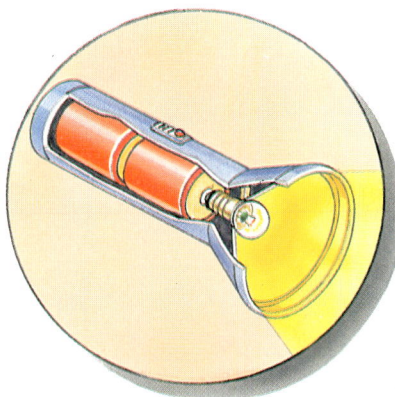

We are grateful to "Green Teacher", Machynlleth, Powys, Wales, for permission to use adaptations of material previously published by themselves (projects on pages 121, 123, 126 and 129).

The figures on pages 136-139 are based on those given in the BP Statistical Review of World Energy (July 1989), produced by the British Petroleum Company plc, Britannic House, Moor Lane, London EC2Y 9BU,

England, and the World Population Data Sheet, produced by Population Concern, 231 Tottenham Court Road, London W1P 9AE, England. We are grateful for permission to use these statistics.

# About this book

Energy is vital to the world and all the people who live in it. This book explains all about energy and how it is related to power. It looks at all the different forms of energy and how we use them in our daily lives.

There are sections on both traditional sources of energy, such as coal and oil, and also renewable sources, such as the sun and the wind. The book also looks at problems linked with producing energy, for example, the damage caused to the environment by burning fossil fuels, and the unbalanced use of energy around the world. It also examines ways in which we can secure enough energy for the future.

## Using the glossary

The glossary on pages 142-143 is a useful point of reference. It explains all the more complex terms in the book, as well as introducing some new related words.

## Useful addresses

On page 141, there is a list of some of the groups, associations and other organizations you could write to if you want to learn more about energy and power. They will be able to provide you with written material which you can use for projects, and also possibly other addresses you could write to.

## Activities and projects

Special boxes like this one are found throughout the main section of the book. They are used for simple activities and experiments which will help you to understand the scientific ideas and principles behind the production and use of energy. All these activities have clear instructions and are easy to do. They all use basic materials.

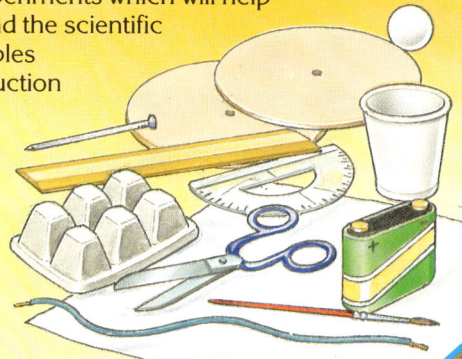

This scene shows a hydro-electric power station with its enormous dam. It makes use of moving water to turn turbines and produce electricity. The movement energy turns into electrical energy. For more about hydro-electricity, see pages 128-129.

# What is energy?

Everything that changes or moves has some form of energy. People depend on energy in many ways – it is what makes things happen. It is used all around us, in transport, in industry and in the home. On these pages, you can find out much more about what energy is and how it behaves.

Below are a few examples of different forms of energy being produced or used. For more about them, see pages 102-109.

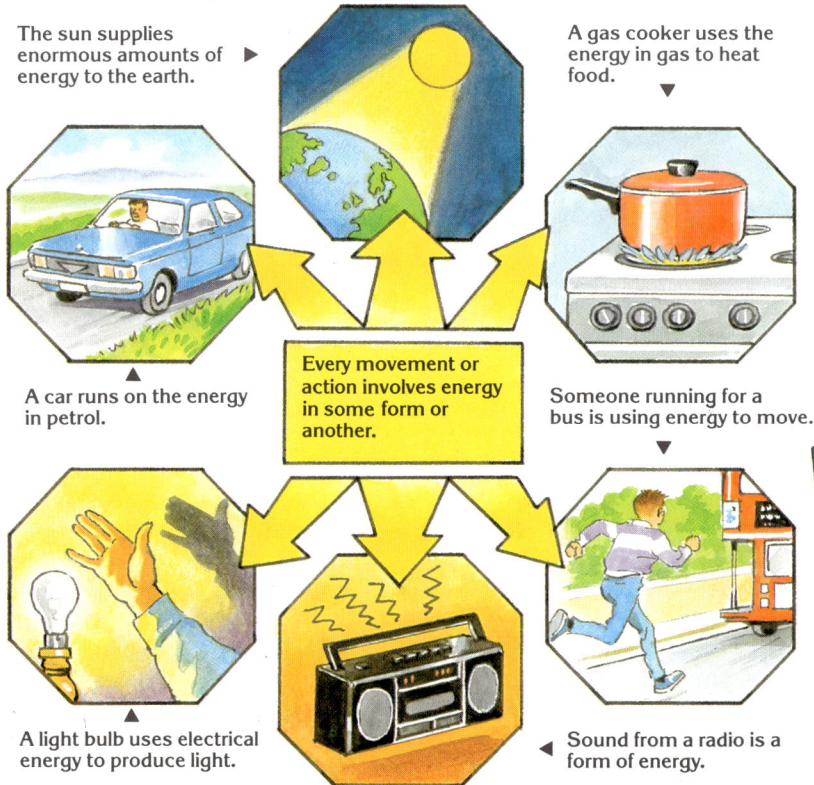

The sun supplies enormous amounts of energy to the earth.

A gas cooker uses the energy in gas to heat food.

A car runs on the energy in petrol.

Every movement or action involves energy in some form or another.

Someone running for a bus is using energy to move.

A light bulb uses electrical energy to produce light.

Sound from a radio is a form of energy.

## Stored energy

Energy makes things move or change. The energy in moving things is called kinetic energy. But energy can also be stored in many different things and in a number of different ways. For example, there is a lot of energy stored in things such as wood and coal, and also in food. This energy is locked up in the chemical make-up of the substance, and can only be released when this chemical make-up changes. It is called chemical energy.

Stored energy is released when wood is burnt.

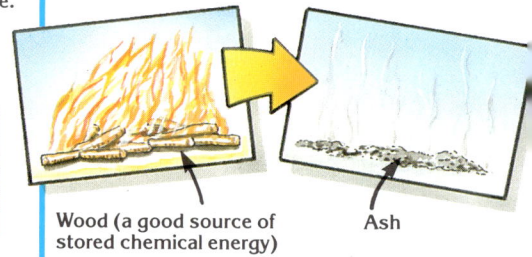

Wood (a good source of stored chemical energy)

Ash

Burning the wood changes its chemical make-up, releasing some of its chemical energy as heat energy (for more about energy changes, see pages 102-103).

People depend on stored energy. Without energy from our food, we could do nothing, not even breathe. Without fuels like wood, coal or gas, most people could not cook or keep warm, industries would not work, and cars, trains and aeroplanes would not move.

Energy is also stored in coiled-up springs and stretched elastic bands. In this form it is called strain energy. For more about this, see page 105.

The coiled spring at the base of the toy has stored energy (strain energy).

When the spring expands, the energy is released as kinetic (movement) energy.

## Energy and your body

At this moment, you are using energy in many different ways. You are using light to read this book and heat to keep warm. You are also using energy to stay alive. Without the energy you get from the food you eat, your body would not be able to work. Actions like breathing and the pumping of blood around your body depend on energy.

Your food supplies your body with the energy it needs to do things.

Running

Walking

Talking

## Measuring energy

Energy is normally measured in very small units called joules (J). A thousand joules is a kilojoule (kJ). An ordinary-sized apple (100g), for example, contains 150kJ. The same weight of milk chocolate will provide over 15 times as much energy

(2,335kJ). Eating too much high-energy food, like chocolate, may lead to health problems. Try to find out how much energy there is in the food you eat. Often the number of kilojoules that a type of food contains is written on the tin, box or wrapper.

Each 100kJ you eat will allow you to:

walk quickly for 5 minutes

cycle for 3 minutes

jog for 2 minutes

sleep for half an hour

## Power

Heat from the coal boiled water to make steam, which powered the engine.

Coal was burnt in the fire-box of the steam engine.

The terms "power" and "energy" are often confused. In the scientific world, the word "power" means only one thing, that is, the rate (how fast) energy is produced or used. Machines are used

to turn one form of energy into a different form (for more about energy changes, see pages 102-103). For example, an old-style steam engine turned the chemical energy in coal into movement.

The more energy a machine uses in a certain period of time, the more powerful it is, and the more energy it can provide. A two-bar electric heater is twice as powerful as a single-bar heater. Over the same period of time, it will provide twice as much energy.

The power of a single-bar fire is equivalent to that of seven strong people working very hard.

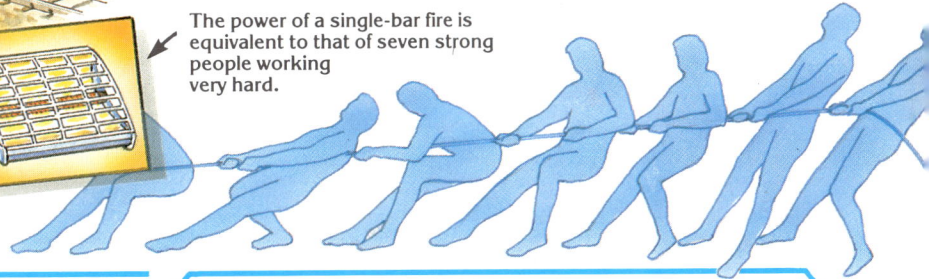

## Measuring power

Power is measured in units called watts (W). A thousand watts make up a kilowatt (kW). Power is the measurement of energy used up in a certain time. One watt is equal to one joule per second. For instance, a 60 watt light bulb uses 60 joules (J) of energy each second (s).

Some appliances are used for longer periods than others. An electric iron is used on average for 20 minutes a day, whereas a television might be on for five hours. The energy used (J) equals the power of the appliance (W), times the number of seconds it is used for (s).

$$1W = 1 J/s$$

$$J = W \times s$$

Below are the power ratings of some household appliances.

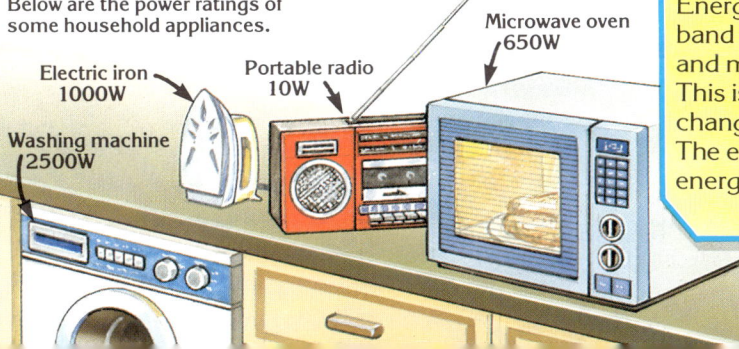

Electric iron 1000W

Portable radio 10W

Microwave oven 650W

Washing machine 2500W

## A matchbox paddle-boat

You can make a tiny paddle-boat with two used matches, two empty matchboxes and a small, thin elastic band.

Place the two matches into the sides of one empty matchbox, pointing slightly downwards. Attach the elastic band loosely between the matches.

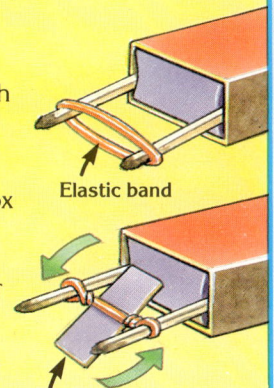

Elastic band

Cut one end off the other matchbox tray, slide it into the elastic band and twist it, so that it winds up the elastic band. Place it in some water and watch it go.

Energy stored in the twisted elastic band is released to turn the paddle and make the boat move forward. This is an example of an energy change (see pages 102-103). The energy changes from strain energy to moving, or kinetic, energy.

You may have to trim the paddle so it can spin all the way round.

# Energy changes

Energy exists in many different forms – the main ones are shown here. When something happens, energy is always involved. One form of energy changes into one or more other forms. For example, a battery, when connected up, changes chemical energy into electrical energy (see below).

## Forms of energy

Kinetic energy (movement energy – see page 106) ▶

Potential energy (see page 105) ▶

◀ Electrical energy (see page 108)

Heat (or thermal) energy (see pages 106-107) ◀

Chemical energy (stored in things such as fuel and food – see pages 100 and 104) ▶

Sound energy (see page 107) ▶

◀ Electromagnetic energy (e.g. light energy and X-rays – see page 109)

Nuclear energy (stored inside the nuclei of atoms – see page 105) ◀

## Conservation of energy

When you use one form of energy, it changes into one or more other forms. The total amount of energy at the start is the same as the total amount of energy after the change. You cannot create energy or destroy it. This is known as the Law of Conservation of Energy.

The chemical energy stored in the torch batteries changes to electrical energy in the wires.

The bulb changes the electrical energy to light energy (as well as heat energy).

Chemical energy

Heat energy

Light energy

The total amount of energy remains the same.

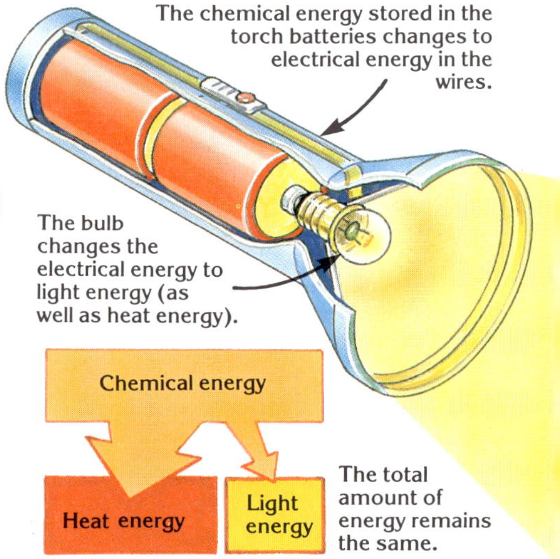

## A funnel record player

Old-fashioned record players show an example of a simple energy change. The loudspeakers on these record players were much less complicated than those of today. You can make something similar using a paper funnel and a needle. You will also need an old, unwanted record and the use of a turntable.

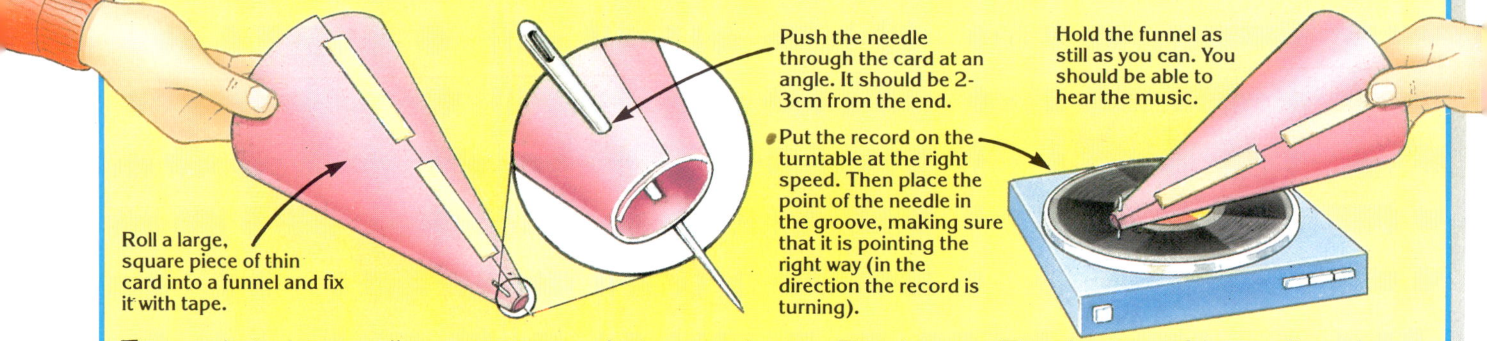

Push the needle through the card at an angle. It should be 2-3cm from the end.

Hold the funnel as still as you can. You should be able to hear the music.

Roll a large, square piece of thin card into a funnel and fix it with tape.

Put the record on the turntable at the right speed. Then place the point of the needle in the groove, making sure that it is pointing the right way (in the direction the record is turning).

Tiny marks in the record's groove make the needle vibrate as it passes over them. The needle passes on the vibrations to the air inside the funnel, producing sound waves. The shape of the funnel concentrates these waves so the sound can be heard more clearly.

The vibrations of the needle make the paper funnel vibrate (kinetic energy), which creates wave patterns in the air (sound energy).

# Energy efficiency

The Law of Conservation of Energy states that energy cannot be created or destroyed. However, when energy changes from one form to another, some energy is "lost", that is, it is changed into other forms of energy that may not be wanted.

A light bulb turns electrical energy into light energy. However, a lot of energy is "lost" as heat energy, which is probably not needed.

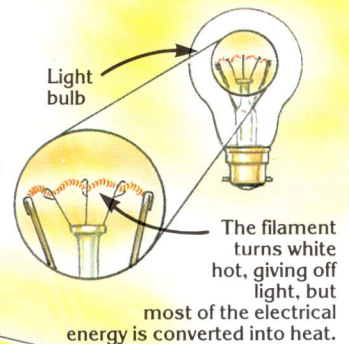

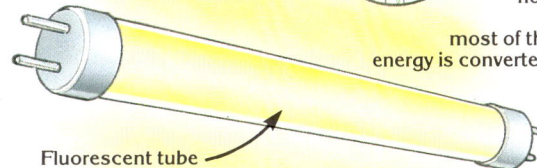

Light bulb

The filament turns white hot, giving off light, but most of the electrical energy is converted into heat.

Fluorescent tube

## Energy chains

Energy chains are an easy way to show how energy can change from one form to another, perhaps several times. They can also show how energy is "lost" along the chain. Because of this energy "loss", the amount of useful energy passed on along the chain gets less and less. An example of an energy chain is given below.

Nuclear reactions inside the sun release enormous amounts of energy, some of which travels across space in the form of light (see pages 109 and 110).

Plants use some of the sun's light energy to make their own food (containing chemical energy) which is stored in the plant. Some energy is also used by the plant for its own growth.

When people eat plants, they create their own store of chemical energy. Some of this is used to keep their bodies working, for example, for breathing and moving (kinetic energy). Some is "lost" as body heat.

The kinetic energy used in winding up an alarm clock changes into strain energy in the spring of the clock. Some energy is "lost", due to friction in the moving parts of the clock.

When the alarm goes off, the strain energy changes into mechanical energy (in the hammer). The vibration of the bells produces sound energy. Some energy is "lost", due to friction.

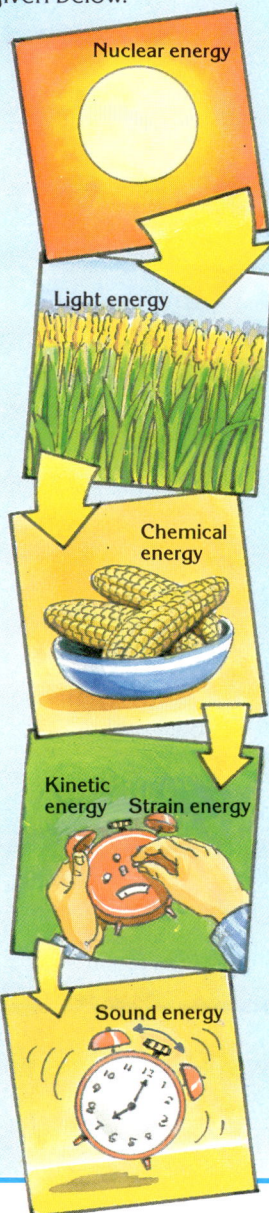

Nuclear energy

Light energy

Chemical energy

Kinetic energy    Strain energy

Sound energy

Machines and appliances are described as efficient if they change most of their energy into the useful form of energy that is needed. For example, fluorescent tube lights are more efficient than normal light bulbs, because they turn more of the electrical energy into light and "waste" less as heat. For more about energy efficiency, see pages 130-133.

Friction is another cause of energy "loss". It is the resistance between two objects when they come into contact with each other, or the resistance between a moving object and the air moving past it.

Friction changes kinetic (movement) energy into heat and sound energy. For example, a car moving on flat ground with its engine off will gradually slow down and stop due to friction.

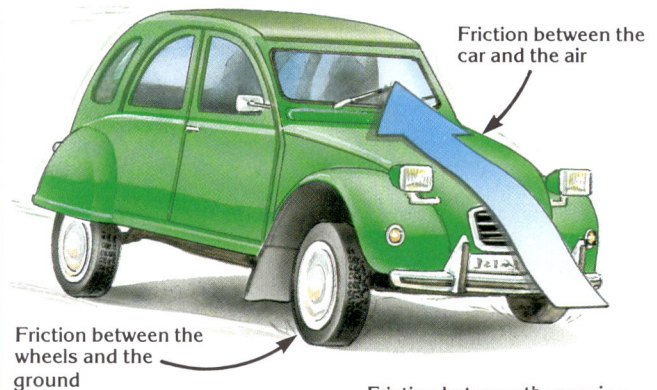

Friction between the car and the air

Friction between the wheels and the ground

A small amount of energy is "lost" as sound (the noise that the car makes).

Energy is "lost" as heat (in all the places that there is friction).

Friction between the moving parts of the car

The less friction there is, the less energy is "lost" and the more efficient the car is (the further it will go on a certain amount of petrol).

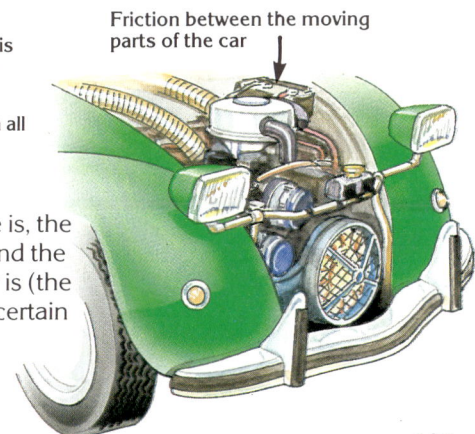

# Stored energy

The forms of energy on these two pages are all types of stored energy, that is, they are all "hidden", or latent, energy. Under certain conditions, they can all change into other forms of energy (for more about energy changes, see pages 102-103).

## Atomic structure

Everything around you is made up of "building blocks" called atoms, which are far too small for the eye to see. In most everyday things there are billions of atoms, yet atoms themselves are made up of much smaller things (subatomic particles) called protons, neutrons and electrons.

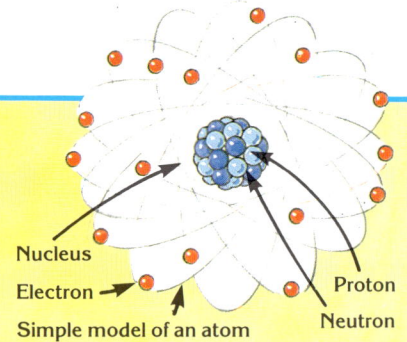

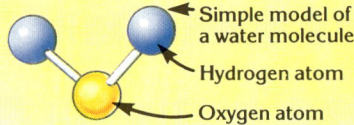

Nucleus

Electron

Simple model of an atom

Proton

Neutron

Simple model of a water molecule

Hydrogen atom

Oxygen atom

A molecule is a group of atoms joined (bonded) together. For example, a water molecule is made of two hydrogen atoms and one oxygen atom. Atoms and molecules are important in stored energy.

## Chemical energy

Chemical energy is the energy stored in the chemical make-up of certain substances. It is stored in the bonds between the atoms in their molecules. When these bonds are broken (for example, when a substance burns), some of this energy is released as heat and light.

For example, every methane molecule in natural gas is made up of one carbon atom and four hydrogen atoms. When the gas is burnt in air, the methane molecules break apart. The stored energy is released as light and heat energy. The carbon and hydrogen atoms combine with oxygen in the air to form water and carbon dioxide.

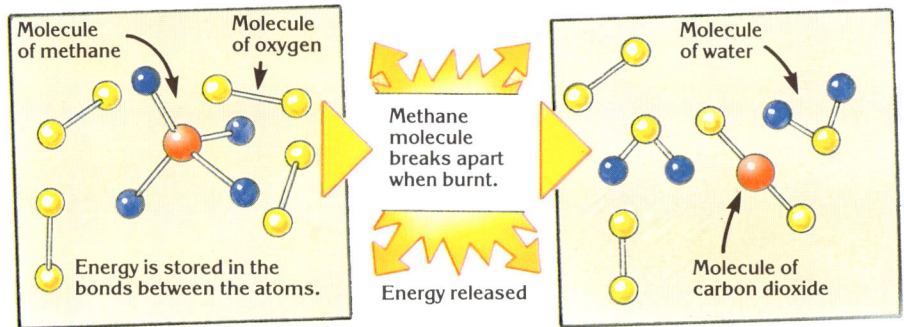

Molecule of methane

Molecule of oxygen

Energy is stored in the bonds between the atoms.

Methane molecule breaks apart when burnt.

Energy released

Molecule of water

Molecule of carbon dioxide

## Fuels

A fuel is something that can release heat energy. Some common examples of fuels are wood, coal, oil and gas. Fuels are used in the home and, in much greater amounts, in power stations (see pages 118-119). The food we eat is also a kind of fuel – it is "burnt up" inside our bodies to give us energy.

Common types of fuel

Oil

Wood

Coal

Wood, coal and oil have more complex chemical structures than natural gas, but they burn in a similar way, producing carbon dioxide and water vapour. They also produce more waste products because they are impure (they contain other substances as well as carbon and hydrogen). Coal, for example, produces ash and gases such as sulphur dioxide due to minerals it contains.

Because of their different chemical structures, a certain amount of one fuel will give off more heat than the same amount of another. A certain amount of natural gas gives off more heat than the same amount of oil, and oil gives off more heat than coal.

Power stations using coal and oil produce a lot of pollution.

Sulphur dioxide

Nitrogen oxides

Carbon dioxide

The waste gases they release into the air are partly to blame for environmental problems such as acid rain and the greenhouse effect (see page 113).

Water vapour

## Make your own battery

A battery is a store of chemical energy. The stored energy turns into electrical energy when the battery is used. Inside the casing, different chemicals are stored which react together to create an electrical current.

You can make your own battery using some very basic things. You need one copper-coated and one zinc-coated (galvanized) nail, some thin, insulated wire (about 50cm), a compass and a container of salty water or watered-down vinegar.

To measure the small electric current that you will produce, you need to coil the wire as many times as you can around the compass, to make a simple meter (you should be able to make more coils than are shown here). Leave some wire at each end.

Attach the compass to a flat surface, making sure the pointer is lined up with the coiled wire.

Strip the insulation from the ends of the wire. Ask someone if you are not sure how to do this.

Tape

Bare ends of the wire

Twist and tape the bare ends round the two nails.

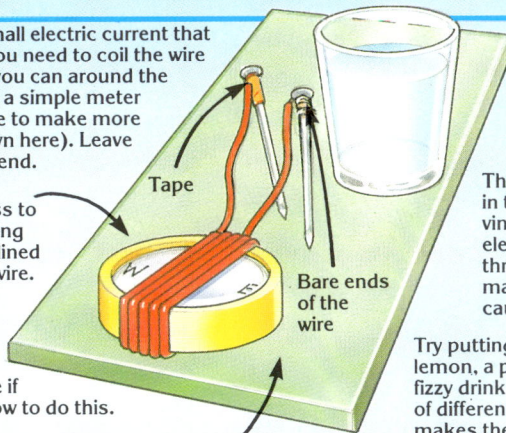

Put the nails into the container with the salty water or vinegar.

Watch out for movement in the compass needle. This shows if any electrical energy is being produced.

The reaction which takes place in the chemicals (salt or vinegar) in solution releases electrical energy. This flows through the wire, creating a magnetic field which causes the needle to move.

Try putting the nails into a lemon, a potato, a glass of fizzy drink — in fact, try lots of different things. Which makes the best home-made battery?

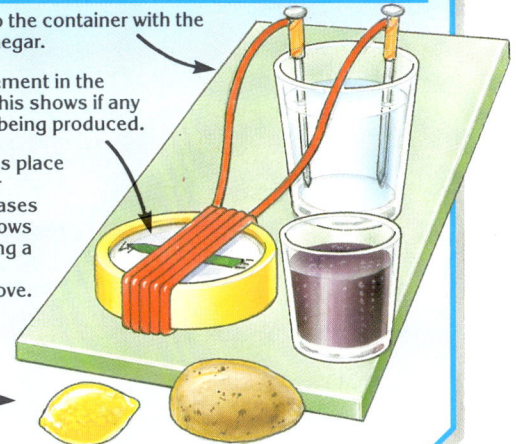

## Strain energy

Strain energy is another form of stored energy (see also page 100). It results from stretching or compressing an object, and is the energy an object has because it is "trying" to return to its original shape.

When you wind up a clockwork watch, you are storing strain energy in its spring.

The energy in the stretched (or compressed) spring is slowly released as kinetic (movement) energy to move the wheels and cogs of the watch.

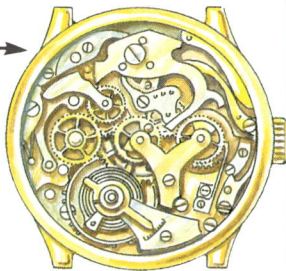

## Nuclear energy

Nuclear energy is another kind of stored energy. It comes from the energy that holds together the tiny particles (protons and neutrons) in the nucleus of an atom. There are two ways of releasing this energy: fission and fusion.

### Fission

Nucleus of heavy atom (uranium or plutonium) breaks apart, releasing enormous amounts of energy.

This happens inside a nuclear reactor at a nuclear power station, and when a fission, or atom ("A"), bomb explodes.

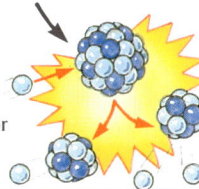

### Fusion

Small nuclei (e.g. those of deuterium and tritium) fuse (join) together, releasing vast amounts of energy.

This is happening all the time in the sun. It also happens when the most powerful nuclear weapon, a fusion, or hydrogen ("H"), bomb explodes.

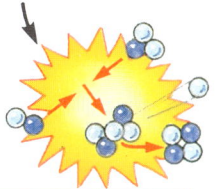

## Potential energy

Potential energy is the energy that an object has because of its position in some kind of force field, such as a gravitational or magnetic field. The example below shows a set of events involving two different forms of potential energy, one caused by gravity, the other caused by a magnet.

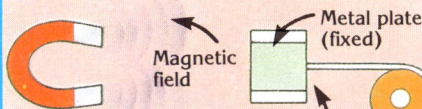

Metal plate (fixed)

Magnetic field

The metal plate has magnetic potential energy. If it were not fixed in position, it would move towards the magnet.

The weight has some gravitational potential energy, because it is in a raised position in the earth's gravitational field. Without the string, it would fall.

When the plate is detached and free to move, it is drawn towards the magnet by the magnetic field. It does a job of work against the earth's gravitational field by lifting the string and weight.

The weight now has more gravitational potential energy (it is higher up).

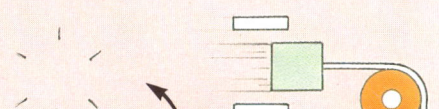

When the magnet is taken away, the gravitational potential energy of the weight turns into kinetic (movement) energy as it falls back down.

For more about gravitational potential energy and kinetic energy, see page 106.

# Movement energy

The energy contained in any moving object is called kinetic energy (also known as movement or motion energy). Many forms of energy are based in some way on kinetic energy. The main ones are described on these two pages.

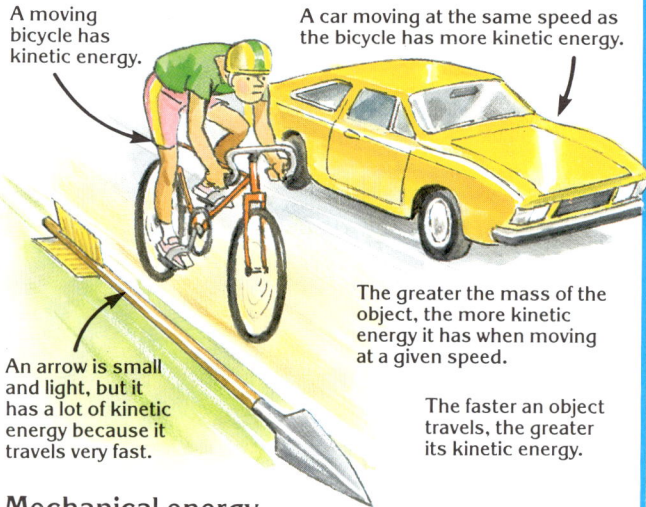

A moving bicycle has kinetic energy.

A car moving at the same speed as the bicycle has more kinetic energy.

An arrow is small and light, but it has a lot of kinetic energy because it travels very fast.

The greater the mass of the object, the more kinetic energy it has when moving at a given speed.

The faster an object travels, the greater its kinetic energy.

## Mechanical energy

Mechanical energy is a term that is used to describe several different types of energy. For example, it covers both kinetic energy and gravitational potential energy, and the combination of the two (see below).

A rock balanced on the edge of a cliff has gravitational potential energy because of its position (see page 105). It is capable of doing work.

If it is attached by a rope to an object, using a pulley system, the rock will lift the object some distance when it is pushed over the edge.

When this happens, the rock's gravitational potential energy will change into kinetic energy and the rock's speed will increase:

As it begins to fall, it has mainly potential energy, and a small amount of kinetic energy.

Lower down, more of the gravitational potential energy has changed into kinetic energy, as the rock has speeded up on its way down.

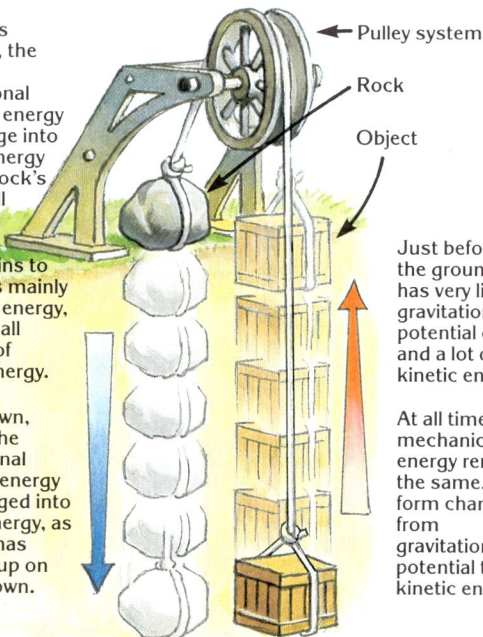

← Pulley system

Rock

Object

Just before it hits the ground, it has very little gravitational potential energy and a lot of kinetic energy.

At all times, its mechanical energy remains the same, but its form changes from gravitational potential to kinetic energy.

## Heat energy

Heat energy is closely connected to kinetic energy, as it is the energy which causes the atoms and molecules of a substance to vibrate (move about). When a substance is heated, its atoms or molecules begin to vibrate more vigorously. When it cools down, its atoms or molecules vibrate more slowly. Heat energy flows from hot objects to cold ones and continues to flow until they are the same temperature.

## Heat and temperature

Temperature can be thought of as a measure of the vibration of the atoms or molecules of a substance. However, the amount of vibration caused by a certain amount of heat is different for each substance. If you add equal amounts of heat to identical amounts of two different substances, they will end up with different temperatures. Different substances are said to have different thermal capacities.

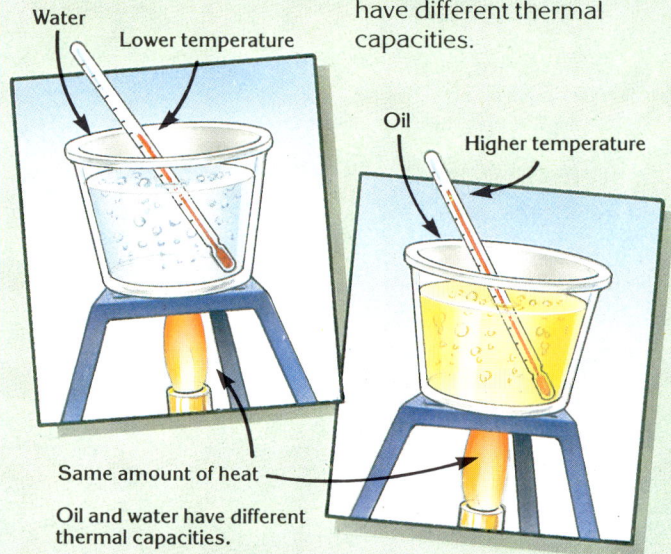

Water

Lower temperature

Oil

Higher temperature

Same amount of heat

Oil and water have different thermal capacities.

Temperature is the measure of how hot something is, and is usually measured in degrees Celsius (°C). The amount of heat energy an object can possess is related to its temperature, but also to other factors, such as its size and density.

A red-hot needle has a high temperature, but does not have much heat energy. If it is dropped into a bowl of cold water, there is very little change in the water's temperature, because the needle is so small. A larger object of the same temperature would heat up the water more, because it possesses more heat energy.

Heat energy is measured in joules (J). It takes 4.2J to raise the temperature of 1g of water by 1°C. To heat 10g of water from room temperature (16°C) to boiling point (100°C) takes 3,528J.

Conduction is a way in which heat energy travels in solids and liquids. Heat spreads when the vibration of one atom or molecule is passed on to the next. Some materials, such as iron and copper, allow heat to flow through them easily and are called conductors (they conduct heat well). Others, such as wood and expanded polystyrene, do not allow an easy flow, and are called insulators (they are bad conductors).

Metals such as copper are often used for making pots and pans, as they are good conductors of heat. The heat from the plate reaches the food quickly.

Wooden handles and spoons are insulators. They stop the heat reaching your hands.

Convection is another way in which heat energy can be transferred. When the atoms or molecules of a liquid or gas are heated, they gain more energy and so move more quickly and further apart. The heated liquid or gas expands and becomes less dense. It is lighter, so moves upwards, away from the heat source. The colder, more dense liquid or gas moves down.

The convection currents created by a heater

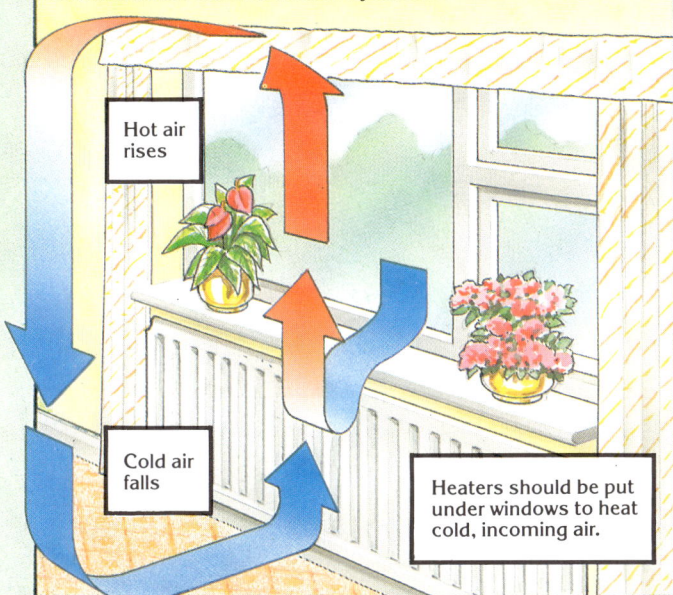

Hot air rises

Cold air falls

Heaters should be put under windows to heat cold, incoming air.

Radiation is a third way in which heat energy can be transferred. The heat energy travels in the form of electromagnetic waves, mainly infra-red radiation (see page 109). Radiation does not depend on the movement of atoms or molecules, so this energy is the only form of energy that can travel across a vacuum (for example, through space).

## A heat-sensitive spiral

A card spiral can be used to show the convection currents of air above a heat source. The energy in the moving air makes the spiral turn.

Cut out a large circle from thin card, and draw a line in the shape of a spiral. The gaps between the lines should be about 1cm wide. You could decorate the spiral with a brightly coloured design.

Carefully make a tiny hole in the centre. Push a long piece of cotton through and tie a knot underneath.

Cut along the spiral with some sharp scissors (be careful how you use these).

Hang the spiral over a heater and watch what happens.

Convection currents are almost invisible, but you can sometimes see them (as a "shaky" effect in the air) above a very hot fire, or above the ground on a very hot day.

## The mechanical equivalent of heat

In the 1840's, the scientist Joule worked out the connection between heat and mechanical energy. Using a machine like the one shown here, he measured how much mechanical energy (in the falling weights) was needed to raise the temperature of the water by a certain amount (by stirring it).

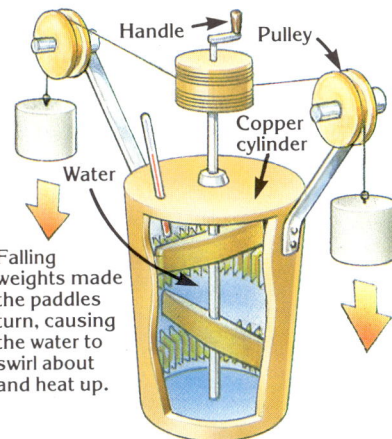

Handle
Pulley
Copper cylinder
Water
Falling weights made the paddles turn, causing the water to swirl about and heat up.

## Sound energy

Some opera singers can shatter a glass with the sound of their voice. This shows that sound is a form of energy (because it can do a job of work).

The sound of the singer's voice sets off a wave which travels through the air.

The sound wave moves as particles in the air knock into each other, passing on the energy. These particles have kinetic energy.

The glass resonates with the energy of the sound (the molecules in the glass vibrate at the same rate as the molecules in the air), causing it to crack.

# Electricity

We use electricity, or electrical energy, all the time in our daily lives (for more about how it is produced, see pages 118-119). It powers many different appliances, such as irons and cookers, and it can also give us heat and light by making metal wires glow, for example in electric fires or the filaments of light bulbs. The way electricity behaves is connected with the behaviour of the tiny particles called electrons which form part of atoms (see page 104).

## Static electricity

Static electricity is the electricity "held" in an object which has an electrical charge. An object has an electrical charge if its atoms have more or fewer electrons than atoms of the same substance would normally have. Most objects have no charge because their atoms have the normal number of electrons. But if they gain or lose electrons, they become charged, and can then attract or repel other objects.

If you rub a balloon against your clothing, you can make it stick to the wall or ceiling.

This is because the rubber in the balloon becomes charged with static electricity, and is attracted to the wall.

An electrical charge builds up in the base of a cloud.

The flash of lightning is a very powerful electrical spark.

Lightning is a result of static electricity. Water molecules in a cloud rub together with air molecules, creating an electrical charge in the base of the cloud. This is attracted to the earth and the charge (electrons) is released as a flash of lightning.

## Current electricity

You can think of an electric current as a flow of electrons. It is measured in amperes, or amps (A). The electrons flow because a force acts on them (an electromotive force, or emf). This force is measured in volts (V).

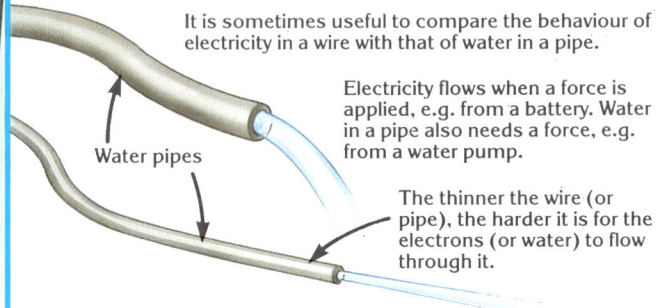

It is sometimes useful to compare the behaviour of electricity in a wire with that of water in a pipe.

Water pipes

Electricity flows when a force is applied, e.g. from a battery. Water in a pipe also needs a force, e.g. from a water pump.

The thinner the wire (or pipe), the harder it is for the electrons (or water) to flow through it.

Electricity travels most easily through metals, such as copper and iron. These are called conductors. It can also pass through water or, if the force is powerful enough, through air as a spark (as in lightning). Some things, such as plastic and rubber, slow down the electrical flow, and are called insulators.

Copper is the metal most often used in electrical wires.

The wires are covered in plastic, which insulates them, making them safe to touch.

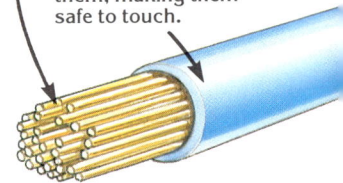

The amount of power (the rate of flow of electricity) is related to the size of the current and the electromotive force. If an emf of one volt causes a current of one amp to flow through a wire, it will produce one watt of power.

$$W = V \times A$$

W = power in watts

V = electromotive force in volts

A = current in amps

## Storing electricity

It is very expensive and difficult to store electricity as electricity. Instead, it is almost always changed into another form of energy for storage. For example, batteries are used to store electricity (as chemical energy – see page 105). Another way is to use the electricity to drive a device called a flywheel. The energy is "stored" as mechanical energy.

The current makes the flywheel turn very quickly, turning electricity into mechanical energy.

Some of the energy stored in the flywheel can be turned back into electricity using a generator.

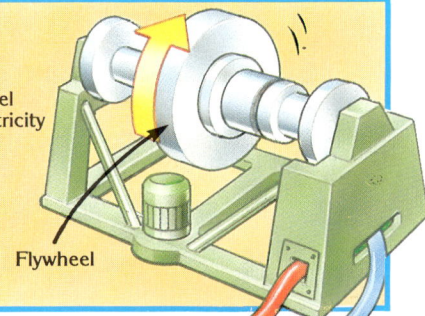

Flywheel

# Electromagnetic energy

Electromagnetic energy can be thought of as a combination of electricity and magnetism (magnetic energy). It travels in the form of regular wave patterns. The electromagnetic spectrum is the range of the different, related forms of electromagnetic energy. These have different wavelengths and frequencies (see right and below).

The wavelength is the distance over which the wave pattern repeats itself.

The frequency is the number of waves that occur in one second. It is the number of wavelengths per second.

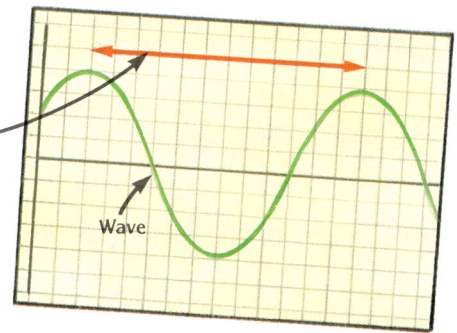

Wave

## The electromagnetic spectrum

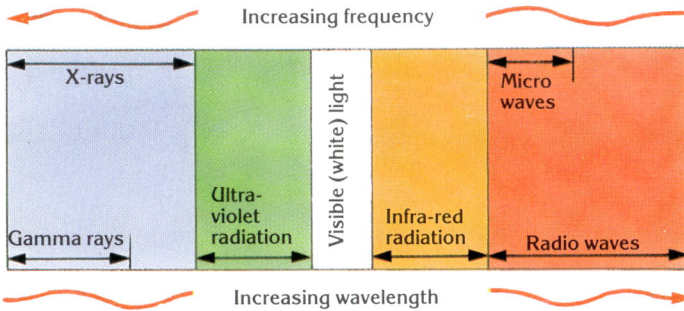

Increasing frequency

X-rays

Gamma rays

Ultra-violet radiation

Visible (white) light

Infra-red radiation

Micro waves

Radio waves

Increasing wavelength

Without the different kinds of electromagnetic energy from the sun (ultra-violet radiation, visible light and infra-red radiation), there would be no life on earth. The sun provides us with light and heat, as well as supplying plants, the basis of life on earth, with the energy they need to grow (see pages 110-111).

The other forms of electromagnetic energy are very useful, too. For example, radio waves are used to communicate over long and short distances. Microwaves are a particular kind of radio wave, and are used in radar (RAdio Detection And Ranging). They are also used in microwave ovens to cook food.

## Splitting the spectrum

Visible (white) light is made up of light of different wavelengths (seen as colours). These make up a smaller spectrum within the electromagnetic spectrum. The colours of this spectrum can be seen by passing light through a glass prism. You can simulate this effect with some clear plastic rulers.

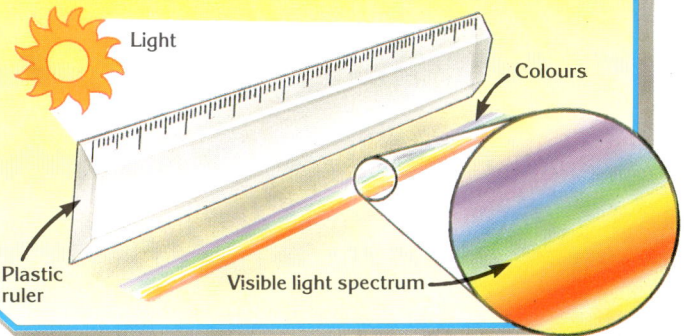

Light

Colours

Plastic ruler

Visible light spectrum

Radar works out the position of an object by sending out microwaves and timing how long it takes for them to come back after being reflected off the object.

Infra-red radiation can be used to make thermal images. These are similar to photographs, but show up areas with different temperatures.

Thermal image of heat loss from a house

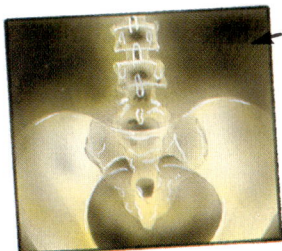

X-ray image

X-rays are used to show breaks and fractures in bones. The rays pass more easily through flesh than through bone, and record an image of the bone on special photographic plates.

## The quality of energy

Some forms of energy are more useful than others – they can be used to do a large number of things, and do them more efficiently. These more useful forms of energy are said to be of a higher quality. For example, electricity is a much higher quality form of energy than low temperature heat energy. It can be used for many more things, such as powering appliances and producing light.

High quality forms of energy can be changed into other forms of energy (for example, electricity into heat) very efficiently, that is, without losing much energy in the process. But changing low or medium quality energy into high quality energy is very inefficient and wasteful (see below and right).

Power stations turn hot steam (a medium quality energy) into electricity (a high quality energy).

This is very inefficient — two-thirds of the energy is lost as heat.

In this case, heat is lost in water vapour.

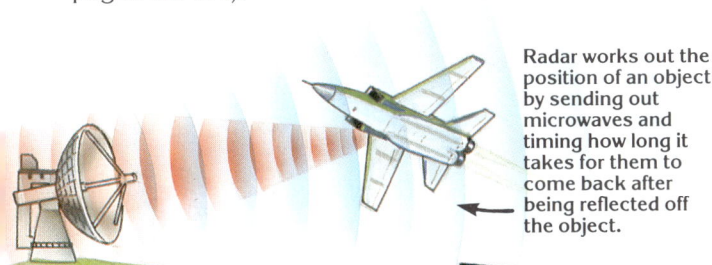

# Energy and the earth

The sun produces tremendous amounts of energy, which streams into space in all directions. Some of this energy is captured by the earth. It is what makes life possible on our planet – without it, the earth would be a frozen mass of ice and rock, and no living thing would survive.

The sun's energy reaches the earth in the form of electromagnetic energy (see page 109), the only form of energy that can travel across space. Most of this energy reaches the earth as infra-red and ultra-violet radiation, and visible light. The many uses of this solar energy are described on pages 121-123.

The amount of energy the earth receives from the sun is the equivalent of the energy supplied by over 100 million large power stations.

The sun produces 400 million million million million watts of power.

The sun is over 145 million kilometres away, and its mass is one third of a million times greater than that of the earth.

Nuclear fusion (see page 105) takes place in the core of the sun, where the temperature can reach 14,000,000°C. This releases vast amounts of energy.

## Energy in water

Water covers 70% of the earth's surface, and is vital to all living things. It is continuously circulating, in the water cycle, between the surface and the atmosphere, driven by the sun's energy. There is a lot of energy contained in the movement of water. This has been used for hundreds of years, for example in water mills. Today, it is widely used to produce electricity in hydro-electric power stations (for more about this, see pages 128-129).

### The water cycle

Heat from the sun makes water evaporate from the surface of the land and sea, forming water vapour.

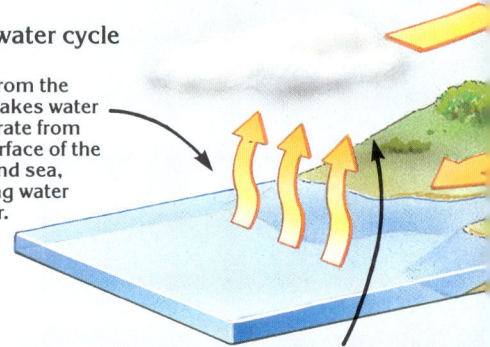

As the air rises, it cools. The water vapour begins to condense (become liquid again), forming masses of small droplets (clouds).

## Energy in the wind

More of the sun's energy falls at the equator than at the poles, so the equatorial regions are much hotter. As it is heated, the air in these regions expands and rises, and colder, denser air rushes in. These air movements cause winds all over the world and influence weather patterns.

Patterns of air movements or winds ▶

The same amount of the sun's energy is spread over a larger area at the poles than at the equator.

Heated air rises (up to 13km above the surface), flows north and south, cools and sinks.

Some air flows back to the equator, some flows to the polar areas.

Cold air flows away from the polar regions.

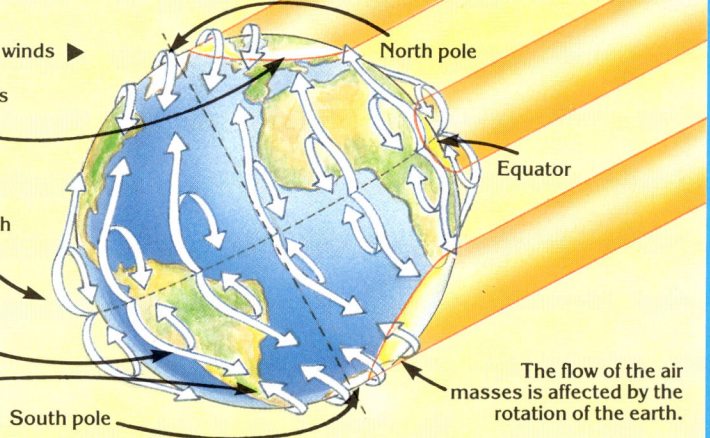

North pole

Equator

The flow of the air masses is affected by the rotation of the earth.

South pole

Blades

Windmills have been used for centuries to capture the energy in the wind.

Shaft

Gear wheels, turned by the revolving shaft

Millstones – corn is ground between them, making flour.

The energy of the wind has been used by people for hundreds of years, for example to sail boats, pump water and grind corn. It is now used more and more to produce electricity. For more about wind power, see pages 126-127.

Wherever the wind blows over water, some of its energy goes into creating waves. So these, too, are indirectly produced by the energy of the sun. The energy in waves is one example of the energy in water (see above and right).

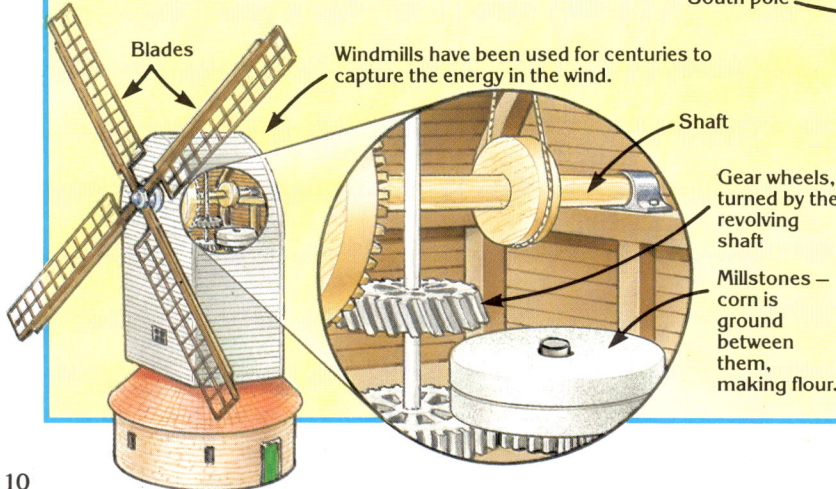

As the clouds cool further, the water droplets get bigger. Finally, they fall as rain or snow.

Moving water in rivers has a lot of kinetic energy.

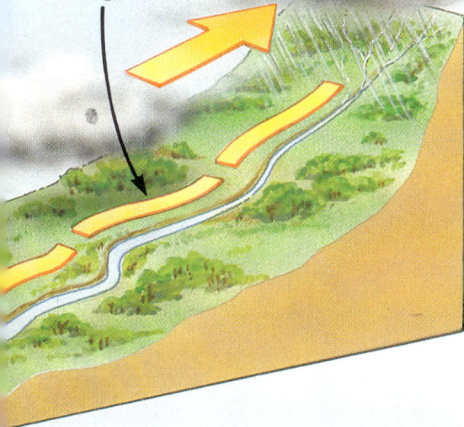

The energy of moving water in rivers is used in hydro-electric power stations. Another type of energy in water is wave energy. You can find out more on page 128 about how this could be used to produce electricity. It may also be possible in the future to produce energy by using the temperature difference between the top and lower layers of water in the oceans (see page 129).

The constant rising and falling of the tides is now also being used to produce electricity. For more about this, see page 128.

Tides are caused by the pull of the moon's gravity and the spinning of the earth.

These create two bulges in the water of the oceans, with troughs (low points) in between.

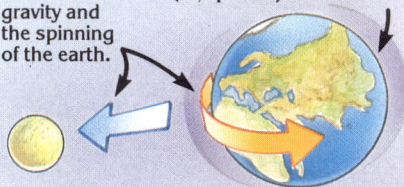

As these bulges and troughs travel around the earth once a day, they raise and lower the levels of the seas and oceans, creating high and low tides.

The effects of the tides are very slight in mid-ocean, but they are very noticeable on the shores, and especially obvious in bays and river estuaries.

## Energy in plants

All green plants take in the sun's energy, as part of a process called photosynthesis, in order to make their own food. This is stored as chemical energy, and used ("burnt") to give the plants energy to grow.

If plants are burnt, the stored chemical energy can be turned into useful heat energy. Fast-growing trees and other plants can provide a great deal of energy in this way (see page 125).

The sun's energy is changed into chemical energy stored in the plant.

When the plant is eaten by an animal, this chemical energy is stored in the animal's body, and then used to keep it alive.

Coal, oil and gas are known as fossil fuels because they are the remains of plants and animals that lived millions of years ago. They are vast stores of chemical energy. Without them, our modern way of life would not be possible. For more about them, see pages 112-115.

### The formation of coal (a fossil fuel)

Plants grew millions of years ago. In swamps, they sank to the bottom when they died and did not rot (as there was no air).

Over millions of years, other layers formed on top.

Plant matter turned to coal under pressure.

This is now brought up and used as fuel.

## Energy in the earth

The earth itself is a store of an enormous amount of heat energy. This can be seen in volcanic activity, when molten rock (so hot it has become liquid) is pushed up through the earth's crust.

For many years, people in countries such as Iceland, Japan and New Zealand have used steam and hot water coming up from the earth to provide them with heating. These energy sources are now used on a larger scale (see page 129).

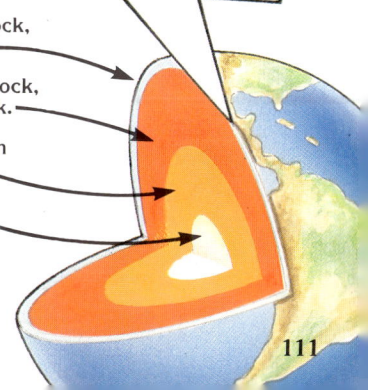

Active volcano

Molten rock, called lava

The layers of the earth (see below) get hotter going down. The inner core is thought to have a temperature of about 3,700°C.

Crust – a thin layer of solid rock, between 6 and 30km thick.

Mantle – a thick layer of hot rock, partly molten, 2,800km thick.

Outer core – a layer of molten metal, 2,240km thick.

Inner core – thought to be a ball of solid metal, 2,440km thick.

# The coal industry

Coal is a fossil fuel, formed from plant matter that grew millions of years ago. It is burnt to supply heat energy and, indirectly, electricity (see pages 118-119). Coal is found in many parts of the world, but most is found in the northern half (mainly in China, the old USSR, Europe and North America – see page 139).

About 20% of the world's energy comes from coal, and its use is increasing. There are enough reserves to make it an important source of energy for another 200-300 years, but the way we use it at present causes serious environmental problems.

## Modern coal mines

There are three main types of coal mine – shaft mines (underground, connected to the surface by vertical shafts), drift mines (underground, connected to the surface by sloping tunnels) and open cast mines (on the surface).

Modern shaft coal mine

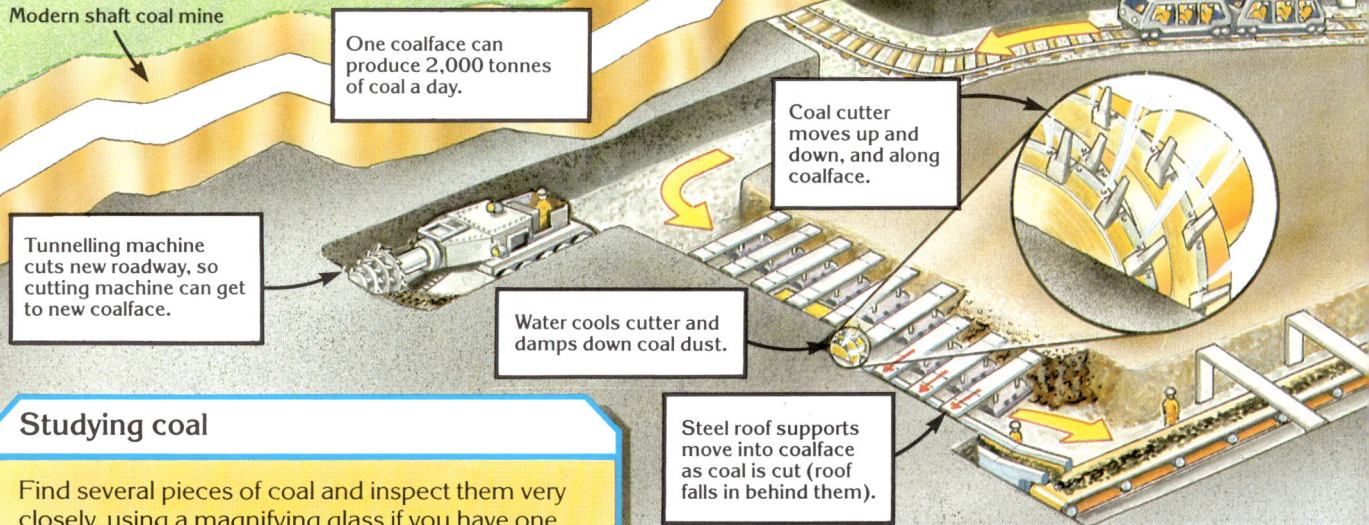

One coalface can produce 2,000 tonnes of coal a day.

Tunnelling machine cuts new roadway, so cutting machine can get to new coalface.

Water cools cutter and damps down coal dust.

## The history of coal mining

Coal has been dug out and used for thousands of years. The first real mines (called bell pits because of their shape) were dug in Great Britain in the 12th century.

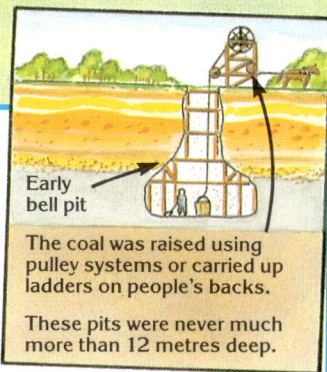

Early bell pit

The coal was raised using pulley systems or carried up ladders on people's backs.

These pits were never much more than 12 metres deep.

As the demand for coal grew, so did the depth and size of coal mines. This led to advances in mining technology, as problems such as cave-ins and flooding had to be overcome. During the Industrial Revolution in Europe in the 1800's, mining methods improved and more coal was produced.

Coalfaces are often several hundred metres below the surface.

Underground train system carries workers around mine.

Coal cutter moves up and down, and along coalface.

Steel roof supports move into coalface as coal is cut (roof falls in behind them).

## Studying coal

Find several pieces of coal and inspect them very closely, using a magnifying glass if you have one. Break a piece in half and look inside. You will find that some types of coal break more easily than others, and you should be able to spot evidence of the plants the coal was formed from.

Split piece of coal

You might find tiny, whole fossilized plants.

There are different types of coal, some soft, others hard. They all contain different amounts of impurities (other substances, such as metal ores or sulphur).

## Using coal

Coal is used throughout the world to produce energy. Many power stations burn coal to produce electricity – the heat from the burning coal turns water into steam to drive the turbines (see pages 118-119). Many industries, such as the steel industry, burn coal to heat their furnaces. They also burn other coal-based fuels, such as coke. Coal and coke are also burnt in some homes to provide heat and hot water.

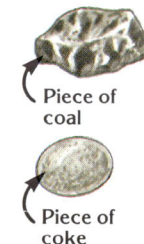

Piece of coal

Piece of coke

Coke is made by heating coal to high temperatures without air.

Surface buildings, e.g. winding towers for lifts, preparation plant (where coal is washed and sorted) and power house.

Rail and road links for transporting coal. It may be carried further by ship.

Shaft with lifts for workers and equipment.

Usually, more than one coalface is worked at the same time.

Conveyor belt transports coal to bunker. Skips of coal loaded from here.

Permanent steel roof supports

Cut coal collected on conveyor belt, and moved away from coalface.

Shaft with lifts bringing skips of coal (up to 10 tonnes) to surface.

Coal can also be used to make other products, such as tar and industrial chemicals, though the chemicals (which are used to make products such as plastics) are now mostly produced from oil and gas.

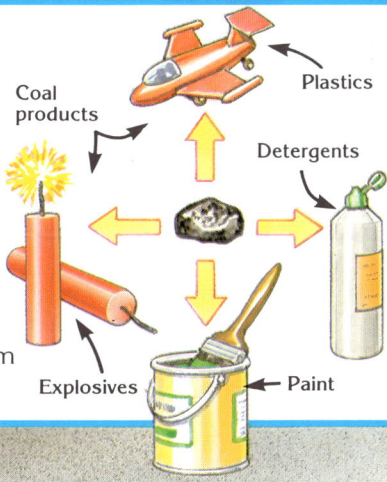

Coal products

Plastics

Detergents

Explosives

Paint

# Fossil fuels and the environment

The burning of fossil fuels, in power stations and motor vehicles, is causing great damage to the environment. It releases gases into the atmosphere which are partly to blame for the two major problems known as acid rain and the greenhouse effect.

## Acid rain

Acid rain is a very damaging mixture of polluting chemicals in rain and snow, produced as a result of burning fossil fuels.

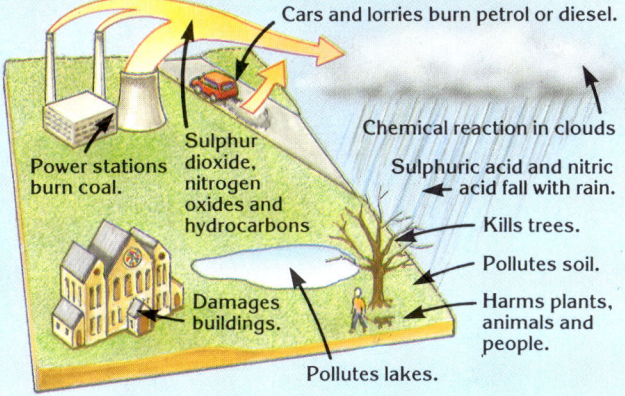

Cars and lorries burn petrol or diesel.

Chemical reaction in clouds

Power stations burn coal.

Sulphur dioxide, nitrogen oxides and hydrocarbons

Sulphuric acid and nitric acid fall with rain.

Kills trees.

Pollutes soil.

Harms plants, animals and people.

Damages buildings.

Pollutes lakes.

## The greenhouse effect

The greenhouse effect, also known as global warming, is the gradual warming up of the earth, due to the build-up of certain gases in the atmosphere. Its effects may take another 30 or more years to become obvious, but it may cause polar ice to melt, making the seas rise and flood low areas. It may also alter the world's climates, forcing major changes in farming patterns.

Chlorofluorocarbons (CFCs) produced by industry

Methane produced in nature.

Carbon dioxide released by burning fossil fuels, and burning down tropical rainforests.

These gases let in the sun's short-wave radiation, but stop the earth's long-wave radiation from leaving. This means heat is trapped, as in a greenhouse.

It is very important that we take action quickly to stop this damage. Acid rain can be prevented by using new anti-pollution technology in power stations. Many countries are now doing this, but others say they cannot afford the expensive devices needed.

The greenhouse effect is much harder to solve. Part of the answer is to stop burning so much fossil fuel. This can be done by becoming more energy-efficient (see pages 130-133), and by making more use of renewable energy and, possibly, nuclear power.

# Oil and gas

Over 60% of the energy used in the world comes from oil and natural gas, so these substances have a vital role in the world's economy. Oil is the main fuel for transport, and both oil and gas are burnt to produce heat or used to produce other useful substances, such as plastics. The largest underground oil reserves are found in the Middle East. The largest gas reserves are in the USSR.

## How oil and gas were formed

Oil and gas were formed from the remains of plants and animals that once lived in the sea. Over millions of years, these remains were buried under mud and rock, under great pressure and at high temperatures. This gradually changed them into oil and gas.

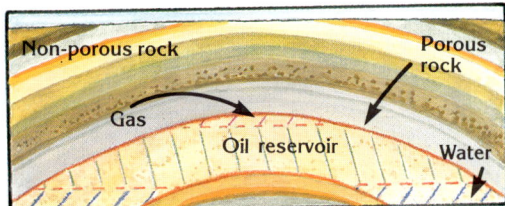

Non-porous rock  Porous rock  Gas  Oil reservoir  Water

Some oil and gas makes its way to the earth's surface and escapes.

Large amounts of oil and gas are trapped below ground in certain areas of rock, forming reservoirs.

Some reservoirs contain only gas.

An oil reservoir is a volume of rock which has spaces in it that are filled with oil. Rock with spaces in it, such as sandstone, is called porous rock. You can imagine a sandstone reservoir as a huge container of marbles, with oil in the spaces between them.

## Recovering oil and gas

Geologists work out where there may be oil and gas by studying the rock structure. If oil is discovered, production wells are drilled to bring it up to the surface. Gas and water are then taken out, and it is pumped through pipelines to a refinery.

Large oil refinery

At the refinery, oil is broken down into many different forms (see main picture, right).

Oil is transported to and from refineries by pipeline or in large ships called oil tankers.

Oil rig in the North sea

The gas which is brought up is cleaned and treated. Firstly, water and other liquids are removed from it. It is then usually separated and used in various ways (see page 115). If it is to be transported, it may be turned into a liquid (by chilling).

As the oil fields on land are used up, more and more areas under the sea are being drilled for oil.

Rigs at sea have to survive the battering of powerful winds and waves.

About 20% of today's oil is produced from offshore platforms.

## Refining and using oil

The crude oil (petroleum) that flows from a well is very thick. Before it can be used, it has to be cleaned and broken down into the different usable forms of oil, in a process called refining.

The different forms are separated in tall columns called fractionating columns. Each form of oil, called a fraction, is a mixture of hydrocarbons (substances made from just carbon and hydrogen). They range from "heavy" fractions (with large molecules) to "light" fractions.

The distillation of oil is the first stage of refining. Follow the process up from the bottom.

Fractionating column

The fractions are piped away to separate storage areas.

The separate forms of oil (fractions) turn back to liquid at different temperatures, and are caught in trays at different levels.

As the vapour passes up the column, it cools.

Gases (methane, butane and propane)

110°C

Gasoline

180°C

Kerosene

260°C

Diesel oils

340°C

Furnace

Crude oil is heated to 400°C and turns to vapour.

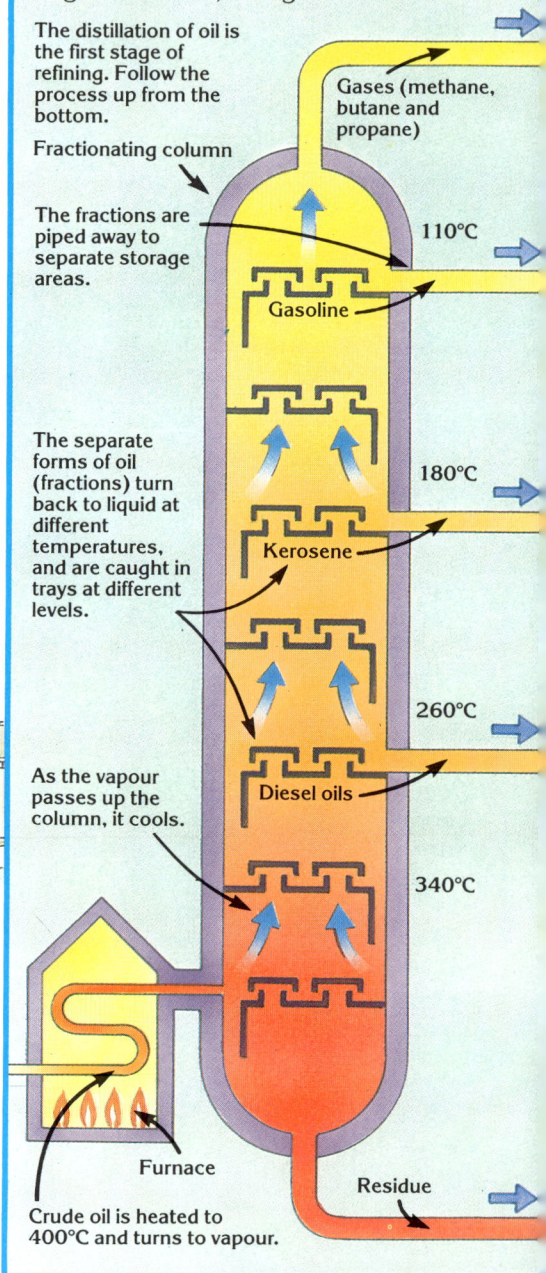

Residue

Oil is a useful source of energy for several reasons. As a liquid, it can be stored and moved easily. It is easy to burn and has a high energy density (it has a lot of energy packed into a small volume). The different forms of oil are used in many different ways. The most important of these is transport.

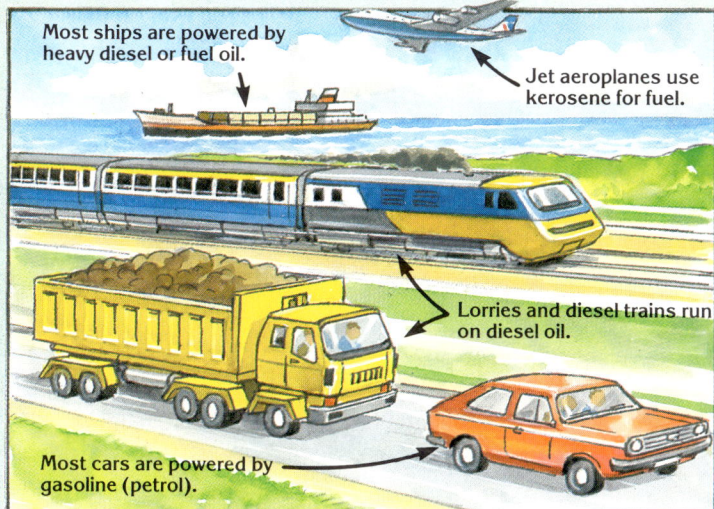

Most ships are powered by heavy diesel or fuel oil.

Jet aeroplanes use kerosene for fuel.

Lorries and diesel trains run on diesel oil.

Most cars are powered by gasoline (petrol).

Heavier oils are burnt in the home for heat, and very heavy ones are used in power stations to produce electricity. Other forms of oil are converted into products like chemicals, plastics, and weedkillers.

## Oil spills

Oil spills from tankers or oil rigs can cause a lot of damage to the environment. For example, the Exxon Valdez spill in Alaska, in March 1989, created an oil slick of around 2,400 square kilometres, causing damage that may take ten years or more to clear up. There are a number of techniques used to control this sort of damage. Try them yourself, on a smaller scale, by creating your own oil spill. Tip a small amount of vegetable cooking oil into a bowl, sink or bath of water.

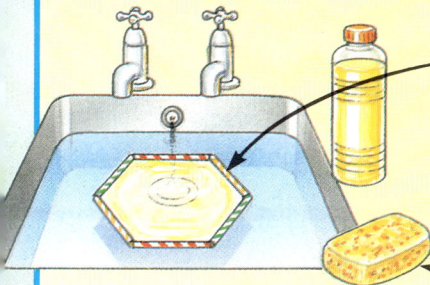

Try to work out the most effective way of controlling or breaking up the spill. Use drops of washing-up liquid to break it up, or drinking straws connected with string, which make floating barriers to contain its spread.

Is it possible to mop up the spill using a sponge or kitchen paper?

Notice how oil sticks to your fingers. It kills seabirds by sticking their feathers together, so that they can no longer keep warm, fly or float.

## The uses of gas

Natural gas is made up of a number of very light hydrocarbons, and is a clean fuel, containing no sulphur (one of the main causes of acid rain). After being cleaned and treated, it is usually separated into the different hydrocarbons.

The gas which is piped into the gas mains and delivered to houses and factories is made up almost entirely of methane, the hydrocarbon which is present in the largest amounts. The other hydrocarbons are used in other ways (see below).

Natural gas consists of methane, ethane, propane and butane (all hydrocarbons).

85-95% of natural gas is methane.

Molecule of methane

Carbon atom

Hydrogen atom

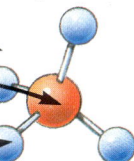

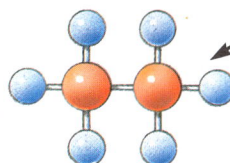

Methane is used for heating and cooking. It is also used to make ammonia (for making fertilizers) and methanol (for making plastics).

Molecule of ethane

Ethane is used in the chemicals industry (e.g. for making plastics).

Molecule of propane

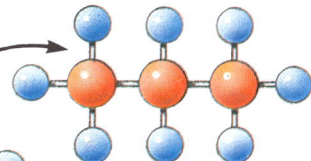

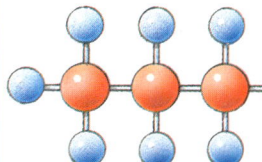

Molecule of butane

Butane and propane are compressed into a liquid known as liquefied petroleum gas (LPG). This is used as a bottled gas (for cooking and heating), to make other chemicals, and as a transport fuel.

A different type of gas, called town gas, can be produced from coal. It is also possible to produce a lot of methane from household rubbish. So even when the reserves of natural gas run out, there will still be ways of producing gas.

When rubbish is buried below ground, it rots, giving off methane gas.

Landfill gas site

At a landfill gas site, this gas is collected and used (burnt) to provide heat, e.g. for generating electricity. For more about energy from rubbish, see pages 124-125.

115

# Nuclear power

There are about 350 nuclear power stations around the world. They supply almost 20% of the world's electricity. Some of the countries which get an important part of their electricity from nuclear energy are the USA, the USSR, Canada, France, Japan, the UK and West Germany. Scientists once dreamed of a nuclear future with electricity that was "too cheap to meter", but nuclear power has not yet lived up to this, and there are many problems still to be overcome.

## Types of nuclear reactor

There are several different types of nuclear reactor, all using nuclear fission (for more about this, see page 105). The most widely used is the pressurized water reactor (PWR), first built in the USA in 1957. The fast-breeder reactor (FBR) is a different sort of fission reactor that actually "breeds" its own fuel (it produces more fuel as a result of its nuclear reactions). But fast-breeders are proving very difficult to develop.

Scientists are also working on ways of controlling nuclear fusion (see page 105) with a view to developing fusion reactors. However, this research still has a very long way to go.

## Inside a reactor

In a pressurized water reactor, heat is produced by nuclear fission in the core. The heat creates steam to drive the turbine generators which produce electricity (for more about this, see pages 118-119).

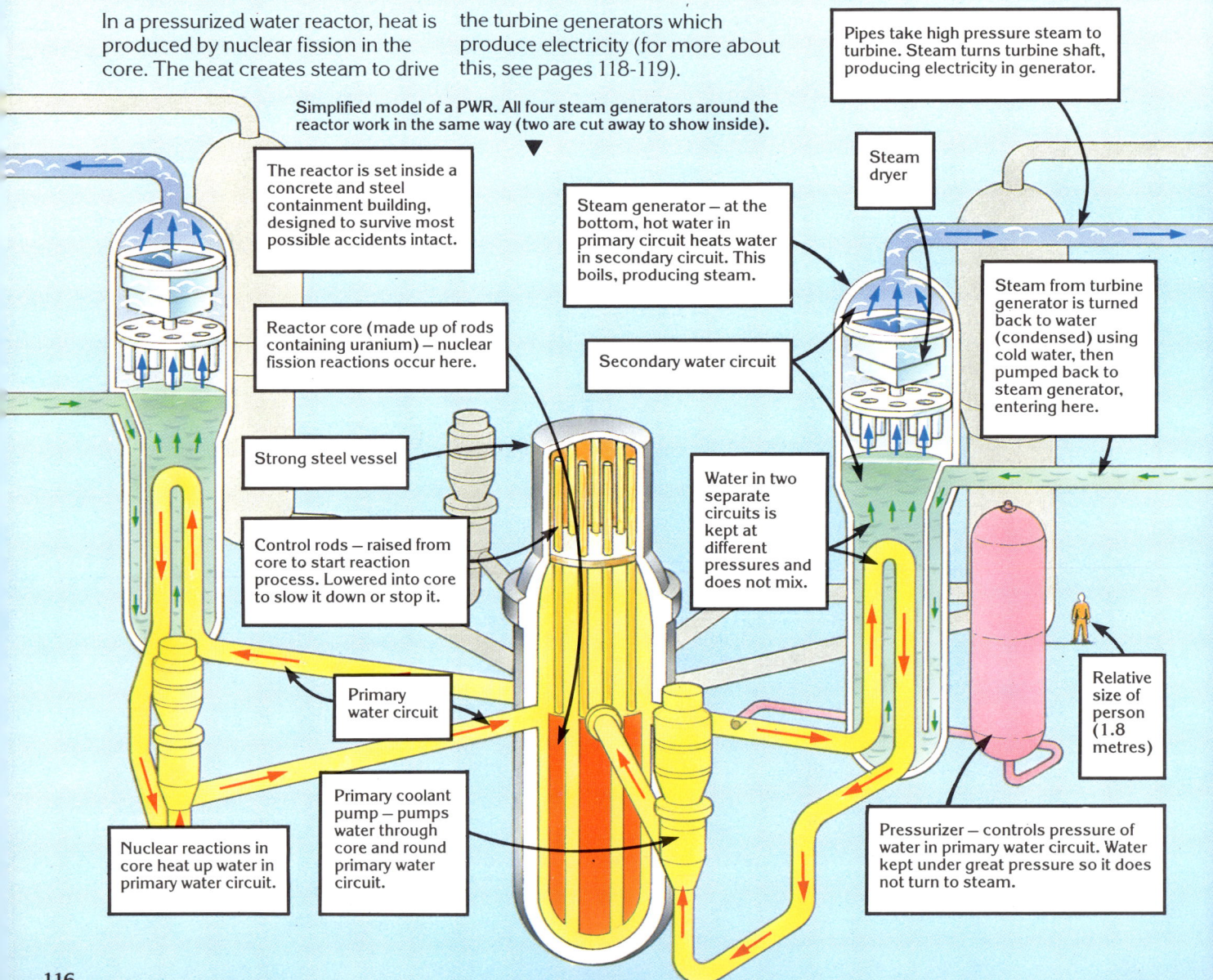

Simplified model of a PWR. All four steam generators around the reactor work in the same way (two are cut away to show inside).

Pipes take high pressure steam to turbine. Steam turns turbine shaft, producing electricity in generator.

The reactor is set inside a concrete and steel containment building, designed to survive most possible accidents intact.

Steam generator — at the bottom, hot water in primary circuit heats water in secondary circuit. This boils, producing steam.

Steam dryer

Steam from turbine generator is turned back to water (condensed) using cold water, then pumped back to steam generator, entering here.

Reactor core (made up of rods containing uranium) — nuclear fission reactions occur here.

Secondary water circuit

Strong steel vessel

Water in two separate circuits is kept at different pressures and does not mix.

Control rods — raised from core to start reaction process. Lowered into core to slow it down or stop it.

Primary water circuit

Relative size of person (1.8 metres)

Nuclear reactions in core heat up water in primary water circuit.

Primary coolant pump — pumps water through core and round primary water circuit.

Pressurizer — controls pressure of water in primary water circuit. Water kept under great pressure so it does not turn to steam.

## Nuclear fuel

Uranium is the main nuclear fuel. It is mined in places throughout the world, such as North and South America, India, Africa, Australia and the USSR.

Mined uranium is first purified, and then often "enriched" by adding more uranium atoms of one special type. This type is far more likely to undergo nuclear fission than the other type, which makes up most of the ore. The enriched uranium is made into pellets, which are put together to form rods (see page 116).

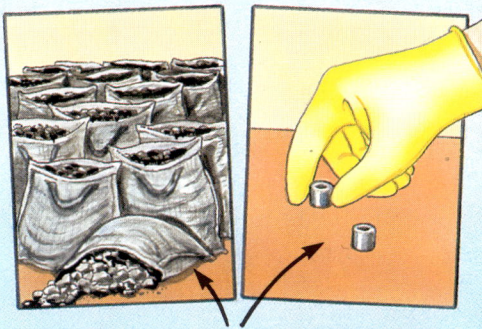

Two pellets of nuclear fuel for use in a PWR are equivalent to 2½ tonnes of coal.

This is enough to produce all the electricity one person in the UK uses in a year.

## Radioactivity

Some substances, like uranium and plutonium, are radioactive. This means they are unstable and give off particles or rays, known as radiation.

There are three main types of radiation – alpha, beta and gamma. Each has different characteristics, but all can cause damage, especially cancer, in humans. Neutron radiation is another kind of radiation, found in the core of nuclear reactors.

This sign warns of the presence of radioactive substances.

Nuclear power workers must wear or carry meters which show if they have been exposed to too much radiation.

## Problems

Power stations using coal and oil are a major source of environmental problems such as acid rain and the greenhouse effect. Although nuclear power is a "cleaner" way of producing power in this sense, it also has its own set of problems. These must be solved before we increase our use of nuclear power.

### Radioactive waste

The large amounts of radioactive waste created by the nuclear process cannot be destroyed. Some of it is so dangerous that it must be isolated for hundreds of thousands of years.

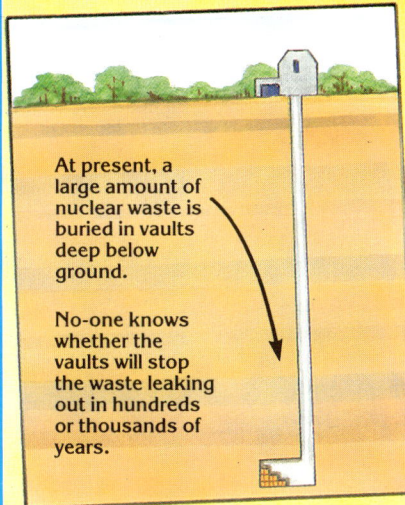

At present, a large amount of nuclear waste is buried in vaults deep below ground.

No-one knows whether the vaults will stop the waste leaking out in hundreds or thousands of years.

### Cost

Nuclear power stations are relatively cheap to run, but expensive to build, and there are many hidden costs – such as the costs of research and dealing with nuclear waste.

### Accidents

The consequences of a nuclear accident can be many times more serious than those of accidents which occur in other power industries. The nuclear accident in 1986 at Chernobyl, in the USSR, showed this very clearly. It killed 30 people and exposed thousands more to radiation. It also contaminated millions of square kilometres of land.

The damage at Chernobyl could have been even worse if there had been a meltdown.

In a meltdown, the core melts due to the intense heat.

The radioactive material then burns through the containment building into the ground, through the rock, and into the underground water system.

## Make up your own mind

You can get hold of a lot of information about nuclear power, and be able to compare the arguments for and against, by writing to electricity and nuclear energy organizations, and to anti-nuclear campaign groups. You could try organizing the arguments in a pamphlet or on a wallchart, and then hold a discussion at school or your local youth centre.

# The electricity industry

Electricity is very important to our modern way of living. It is hard to imagine life without it. Electricity is mostly produced in power stations, using large generators. These are usually powered by steam, which is produced by burning fossil fuels or from the heat of nuclear reactions. Some smaller generators, though, are driven by diesel engines, and others by water and wind power.

## Generators

A generator is a machine which produces electricity from mechanical energy. The simplest type (for example, a bicycle dynamo) uses the mechanical energy (for example, of the moving bicycle) to turn a magnet inside a fixed coil of wire. Because of the relationship between magnetism and electricity, this produces electricity in the wire.

In a power station generator, the magnet used is a powerful electromagnet. It is turned inside a fixed coil of wire by a piece of machinery called a turbine, which is turned by jets of steam. The whole generator produces very large amounts of electricity. The electromagnet itself is supplied with a current to make it work (see page 119).

Many out-of-the-way communities, not connected to a grid system (see page 119), depend on small generators for their electricity. These use diesel engines, instead of steam, to turn the turbine shaft. Places such as hospitals also have back-up diesel generators, in case something stops their supply of electricity from the grid system.

Energy from the sun, wind, waves, tides and flowing water can also be used to produce electricity. These are called renewable energy sources (see pages 121-129).

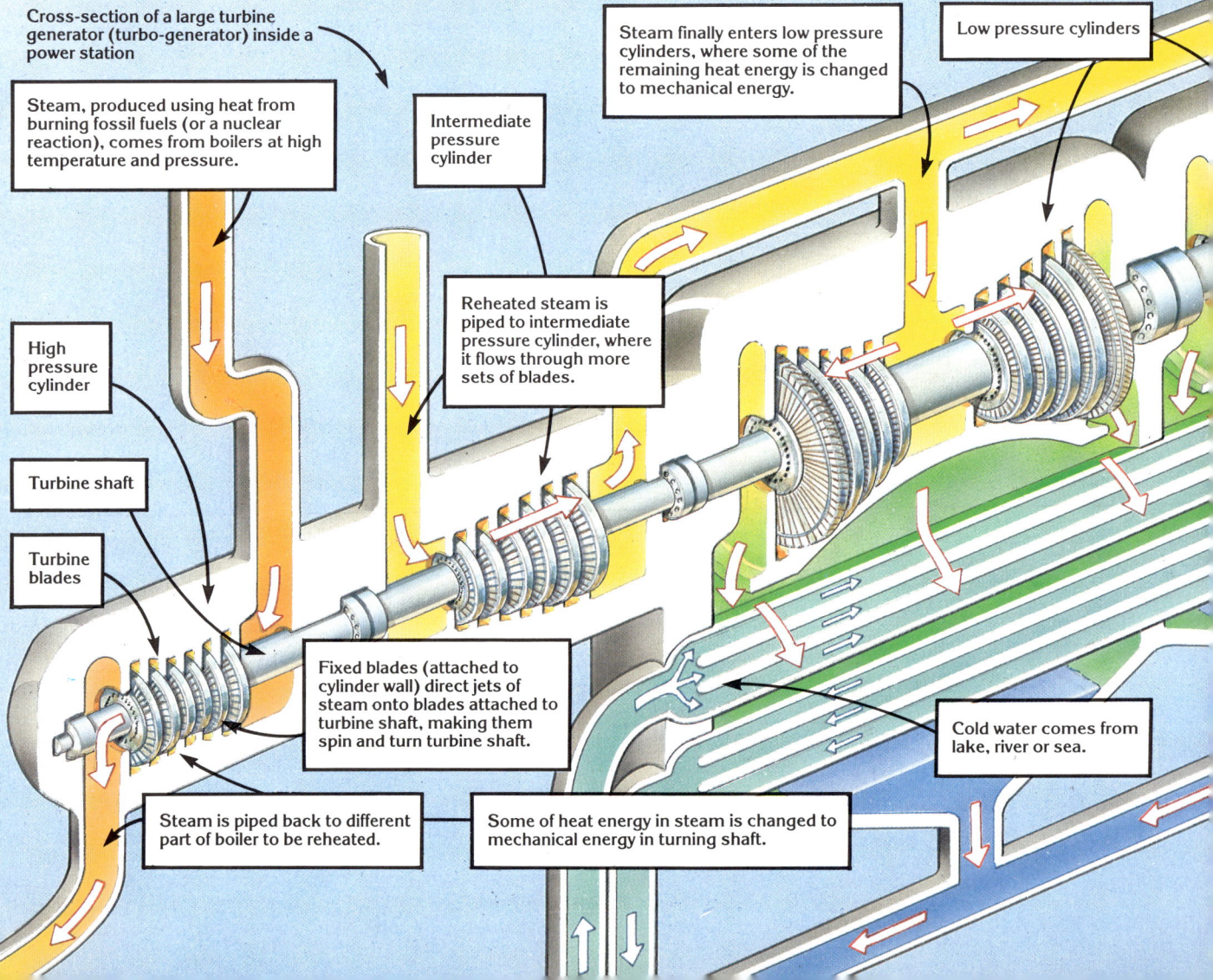

Cross-section of a large turbine generator (turbo-generator) inside a power station

Steam, produced using heat from burning fossil fuels (or a nuclear reaction), comes from boilers at high temperature and pressure.

Intermediate pressure cylinder

Steam finally enters low pressure cylinders, where some of the remaining heat energy is changed to mechanical energy.

Low pressure cylinders

Reheated steam is piped to intermediate pressure cylinder, where it flows through more sets of blades.

High pressure cylinder

Turbine shaft

Turbine blades

Fixed blades (attached to cylinder wall) direct jets of steam onto blades attached to turbine shaft, making them spin and turn turbine shaft.

Cold water comes from lake, river or sea.

Steam is piped back to different part of boiler to be reheated.

Some of heat energy in steam is changed to mechanical energy in turning shaft.

## Electromagnets

An electromagnet is a magnet made by coiling a piece of wire around a piece of a certain type of material, such as iron. The magnet can be "switched on" (producing a magnetic field) by putting an electric current through the wire. On page 120, you can see how to make your own electromagnet.

Small electromagnets are used in electric bells.

When the switch is pressed (closed), the circuit is completed. The electromagnet is turned on and the metal arm is attracted.

The hammer strikes the bell.

The movement of the arm breaks the circuit, switching off the magnet (the arm goes back).

If the switch is still being pressed, the magnet goes on again (the process is repeated).

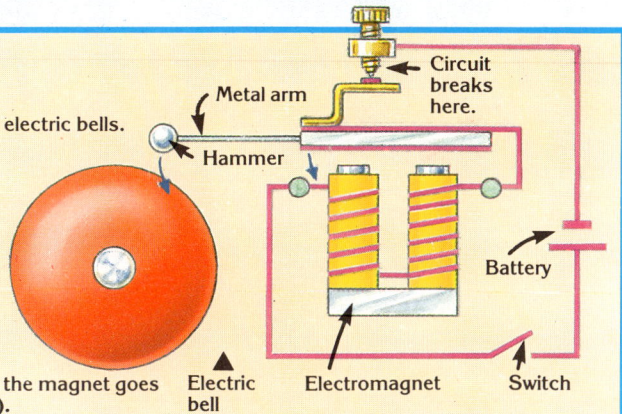

Circuit breaks here.

Metal arm

Hammer

Battery

Electric bell

Electromagnet

Switch

---

Turbine shaft rotates very rapidly (about 3,000 times a minute).

Turbine shaft is linked directly to electromagnet (rotor) which turns inside fixed coil of wire (stator), producing electricity.

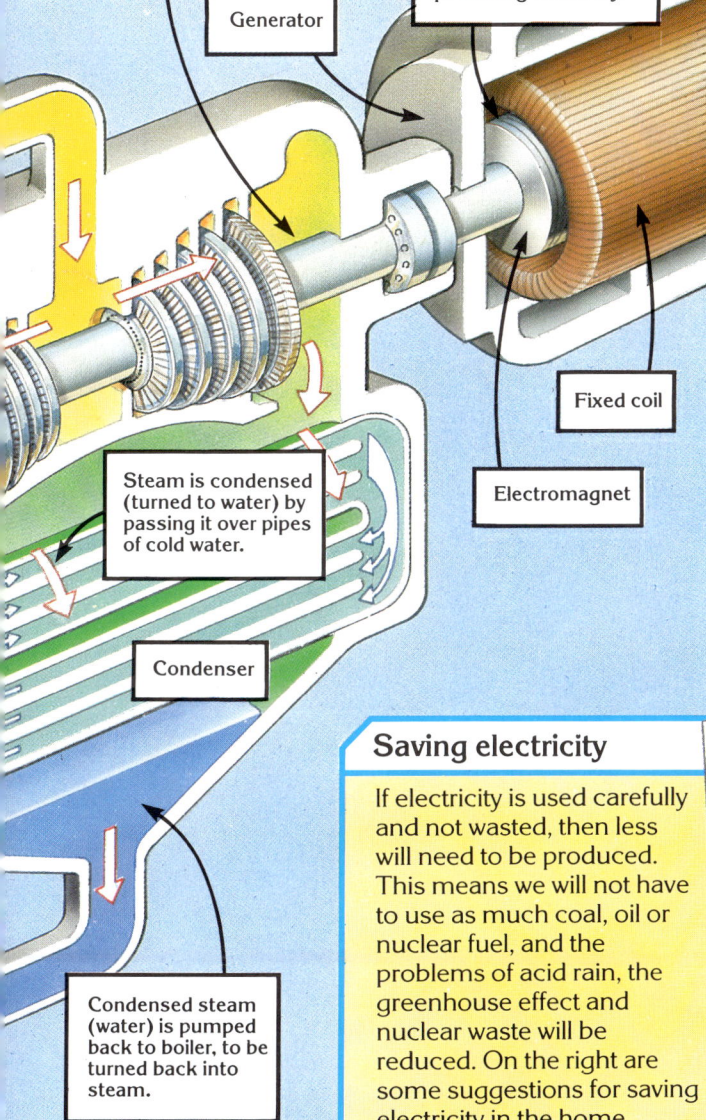

Generator

Fixed coil

Electromagnet

Steam is condensed (turned to water) by passing it over pipes of cold water.

Condenser

Condensed steam (water) is pumped back to boiler, to be turned back into steam.

## The grid system

Electricity produced in power stations is fed into a network of cables known as a grid. This links the power stations together and carries the electricity to where it is needed – places such as homes, offices and factories. Devices called transformers are used to increase the voltage of the electricity fed into the grid system, and decrease it at the other end (people's homes and places of work). The voltage is the measure of the force that drives the current through the wires. You can think of it as the amount of pressure "pushing" the electricity through the wires.

It is easier, and cheaper, to transmit electricity at high voltage, because less electricity is "lost" through heating the cables. However, it would not be safe to use very high

Electricity cables are usually suspended from pylons or buried underground, because they carry very dangerous high voltage electricity.

Transformers at power stations increase the voltage from 25,000V to 400,000V.

High voltage electricity cables are made of aluminium (a good conductor).

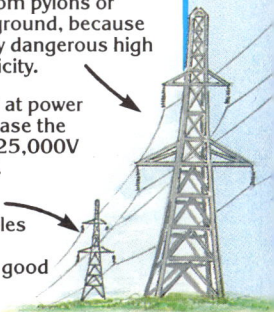

voltage in the home, so it has to be stepped down to a much lower level. Different countries use different household voltage levels (usually 110V or 240V).

## Saving electricity

If electricity is used carefully and not wasted, then less will need to be produced. This means we will not have to use as much coal, oil or nuclear fuel, and the problems of acid rain, the greenhouse effect and nuclear waste will be reduced. On the right are some suggestions for saving electricity in the home.

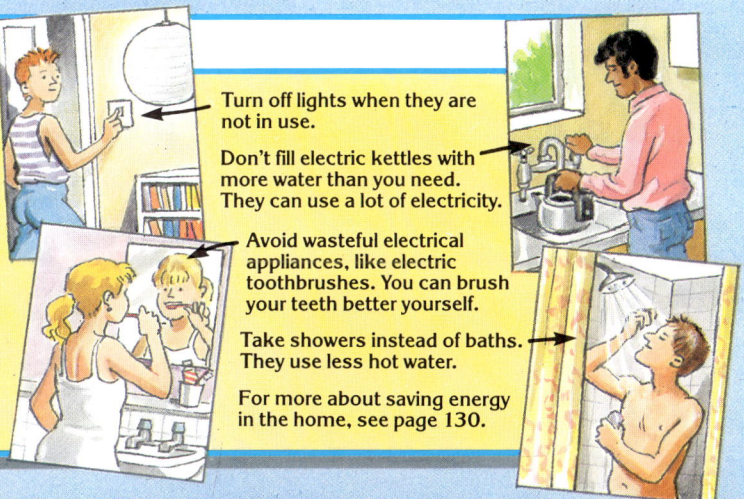

Turn off lights when they are not in use.

Don't fill electric kettles with more water than you need. They can use a lot of electricity.

Avoid wasteful electrical appliances, like electric toothbrushes. You can brush your teeth better yourself.

Take showers instead of baths. They use less hot water.

For more about saving energy in the home, see page 130.

# Making an electromagnet

Electromagnets are introduced on page 119. They are used in power station generators, but have many other uses, too, such as lifting old cars in scrap metal yards. Below you can find out how to make your own electromagnet and switch system.

## What to do

Strip 2cm of the insulating plastic coating from both ends of the two wires, using a pair of scissors or a pair of pliers.

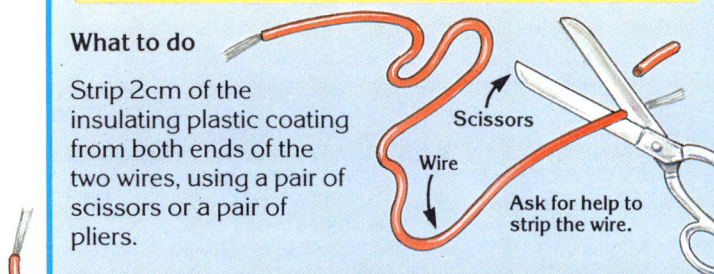

Scissors

Wire

Ask for help to strip the wire.

50cm of wire left at the start

Bolt

Always wind in the same direction.

Longer wire (1.5m)

Leaving 50cm free on one end of the longer wire, wind it tightly onto the bolt. When you get to the end, wind the wire back on top of the first coil. Make several more layers, ending up with the wire back at the start.

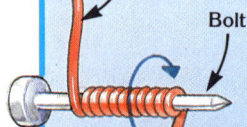

The more coils you can get onto the bolt, the more powerful the electromagnet will be.

Leave about 30cm free and tape the wire in place.

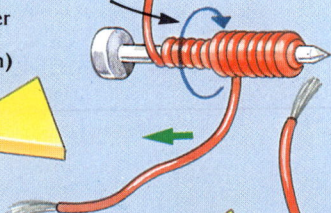

When an electric current is passed through the wire, the combined wire and bolt will become an electromagnet.

Tape

30cm of wire

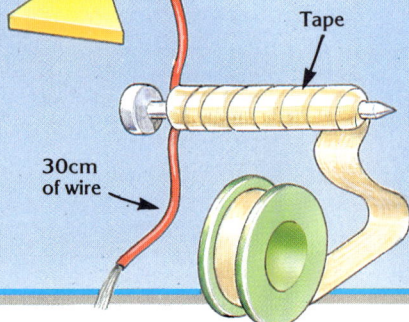

To make the switch, first twist the bare end of the 30cm wire from the electromagnet around the point of a drawing pin. Push this, through a paper clip, into the wooden block or piece of board. Then twist one of the bare ends of the second piece of wire (the unused 50cm piece) around the point of the second drawing pin. Stick this into the block of wood 3cm from the other pin and tape the wires down.

Attach the two remaining loose ends of wire to the two terminals of the battery.

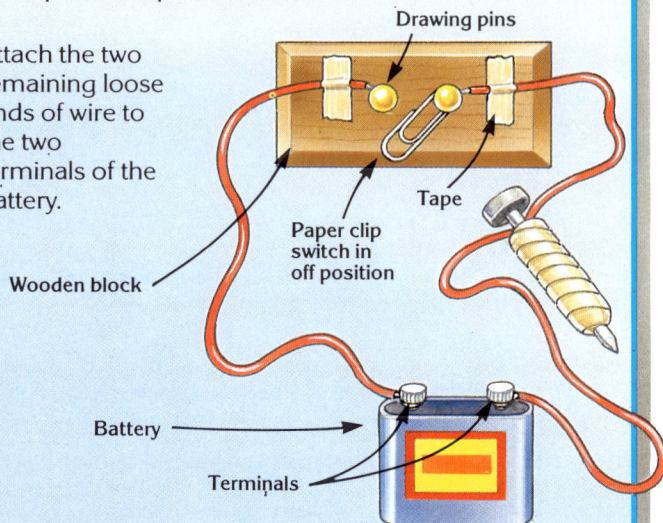

Drawing pins

Tape

Paper clip switch in off position

Wooden block

Battery

Terminals

## Using your magnet

Your magnet should now work when you complete the electrical circuit by closing the switch. This allows current to flow through the wire. To close the switch, swivel the paper clip so that it touches the second drawing pin.

The magnet should now pick up the paper clips or iron filings. Experiment with other things to see what else it will attract.

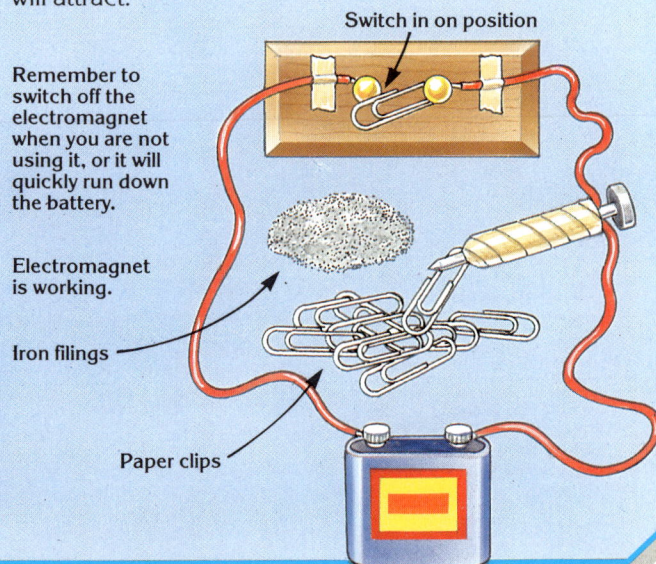

Remember to switch off the electromagnet when you are not using it, or it will quickly run down the battery.

Switch in on position

Electromagnet is working.

Iron filings

Paper clips

# Renewable energy

Renewable energy sources (also known just as "renewables") are those that will not run out. They are constantly renewed in the world's natural cycles (see pages 110-111) and are likely to play an increasingly important part in providing our energy in the future. The renewables include the sun, winds, waves, tides, rivers and plant matter. On the following pages (121 to 129) you can find out more about these different energy sources.

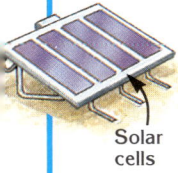

Solar cells

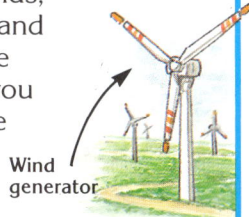

Wind generator

Renewable sources will be able to provide a great deal of energy, whilst causing far less damage to the environment than nuclear or fossil fuel sources. They do not produce as much waste or pollution, and do not contribute as much to major problems such as the greenhouse effect.

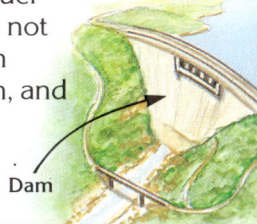

Tidal barrage

Dam

# Solar energy

The sun provides the earth with enormous amounts of energy, some of which can be used for heating purposes and to produce electricity. This is known as solar energy, and is one of the main types of renewable energy. Some people believe that solar energy will be the main source of our energy in the long-term future.

## Passive solar heating

The sun gives some heat to almost all buildings through their walls and windows. This is known as passive solar heating. The amount of solar energy used in this way can be increased by designing buildings with special features. The ancient Greeks were aware of this over 2,500 years ago.

The ancient Greeks used thick walls for their houses to absorb the sun's heat in the day, keeping the insides cool.

At night, heat stored in the walls kept the houses warm.

These basic ideas have been adapted and improved to increase the amount of useful energy supplied free by the sun. Modern houses, offices and other buildings designed with passive solar features need less heating, and save a lot of money in bills.

This house in Milton Keynes, England shows some passive solar features.

The house is positioned so that large windows on the south side make the most of the sunshine. They have long, heavy curtains to keep out the cold at night.

The house is well insulated (with the methods shown on page 130) to keep the warmth in.

# Passive solar experiment

This experiment shows how the sun's heat can be used to heat the inside of a house, and how having a window facing the sun can increase the amount of heat captured. It shows the effects of passive solar heating.

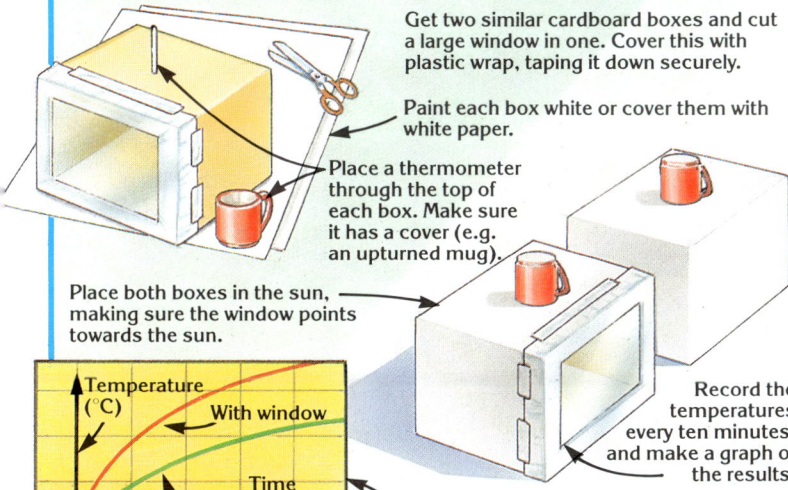

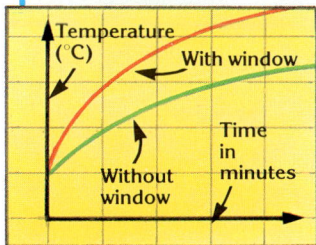

Get two similar cardboard boxes and cut a large window in one. Cover this with plastic wrap, taping it down securely.

Paint each box white or cover them with white paper.

Place a thermometer through the top of each box. Make sure it has a cover (e.g. an upturned mug).

Place both boxes in the sun, making sure the window points towards the sun.

Record the temperatures every ten minutes, and make a graph of the results.

Temperature (°C)

With window

Without window

Time in minutes

You should find that the box with the window becomes hotter more quickly.

## Active solar heating

Active solar heating systems "collect" heat in one area, and then move this heat (using a device such as a pump or a fan) to another area. They are usually used to provide hot water, but can also be used to produce high temperatures for generating electricity.

Active solar heating is more effective in sunny countries. For example, in Israel it produces 90% of the hot water used in houses. The most common solar water heater is the flat plate collector (also called a solar panel).

This form of water heating was first used in the USA in the 1890s. Scientists have since improved on the basic design, by using special glass (to reflect less radiation), different surfaces (to absorb heat better) and vacuum tubes (to lessen heat loss).

Flat plate collector

The colour black absorbs most of the sun's radiation, and so heats up quickly. White, however, reflects this radiation, and so keeps much cooler.

Blackened metal plate (behind the glass) absorbs the sun's heat.

The heat from the plate is passed on to water running through pipes welded to the plate.

The glass cover and insulation material prevent the heat from escaping.

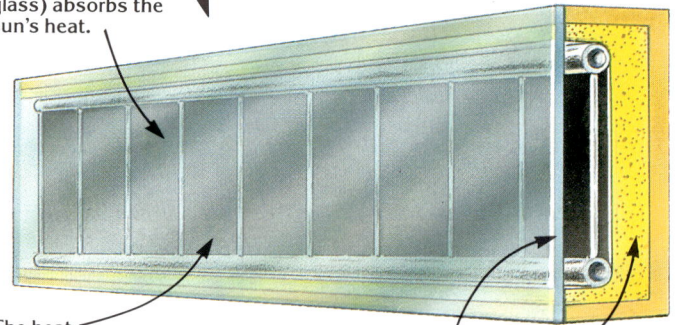

### Making a solar water heater

It is easy to make a simple solar water heater. All you need is a long black hosepipe. On a sunny day, coil this up so that as much of the pipe as possible is in the sunshine (as shown below).

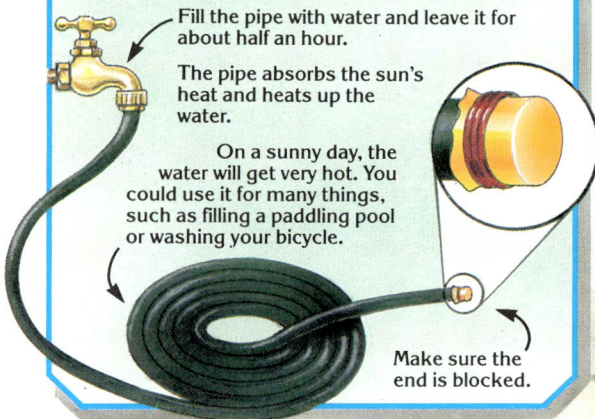

Fill the pipe with water and leave it for about half an hour.

The pipe absorbs the sun's heat and heats up the water.

On a sunny day, the water will get very hot. You could use it for many things, such as filling a paddling pool or washing your bicycle.

Make sure the end is blocked.

Some solar collectors produce very high temperatures, which are used in industry and research, and for generating electricity. Temperatures of up to 3,000 °C can be produced by combining flat mirrors and parabolic (curved) reflectors to concentrate and focus the sun's rays onto a very small area.

Solar furnace at Odeillo, in France

The 42m diameter parabolic reflector is made of hundreds of small mirrors, and is built onto the back of the research institute.

60 flat mirrors concentrate the sun's rays onto the reflector, which focuses them onto a small receiver.

Receiver

The heat is used in research experiments in the institute building.

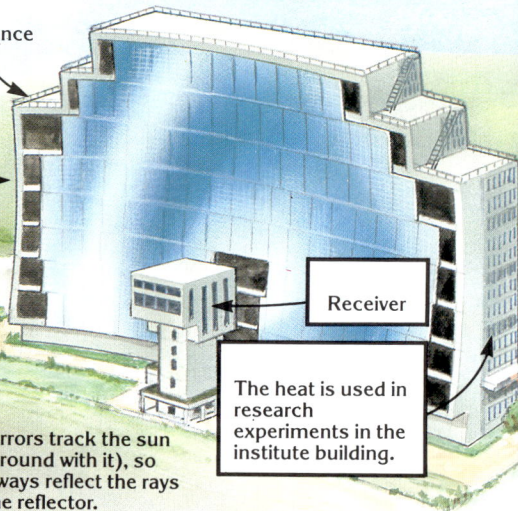

The mirrors track the sun (move round with it), so they always reflect the rays onto the reflector.

## Solar cells

A solar (or photovoltaic) cell turns the energy in sunlight directly into electricity. The most common type is made from silicon, the main ingredient of sand. Solar cells were first developed in the 1950s for use on satellites, but were extremely expensive to produce.

A lot of research into new materials and techniques has gone into the design of modern solar cells. They are now much cheaper and more efficient, and are beginning to be produced in much greater numbers. They are already used quite widely, and for a number of different purposes.

Solar cells

Pump

Solar cells powering a water pump in Mali, West Africa.

Solar cells can produce electricity even when the sun is behind clouds.

A solar powered calculator includes a solar cell.

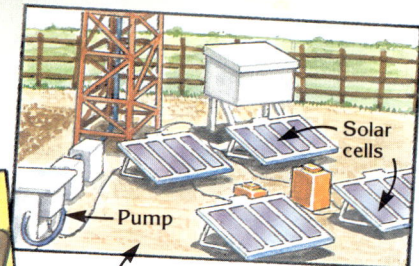

# More solar projects

Below are two more projects which show how the sun's energy can be put to work.

## Making a solar oven

The heat of the sun can be used in a simple solar oven to bake food. The instructions here describe how to make one of these ovens. After trying it out, you could also try to invent a larger oven, using the same idea, to bake larger pieces of food.

### What you will need

2 polystyrene cups
A large plastic pot, such as a "family size" yogurt or salad pot
Some newspaper
A sheet of black paper
A large sheet of paper or card
Plastic food wrap
Aluminium baking foil
Some food (e.g. sliced carrot or apple)
Sticky tape

### What to do

Line one of the cups with black paper, and place the food inside it. Tightly cover the top with plastic wrap.

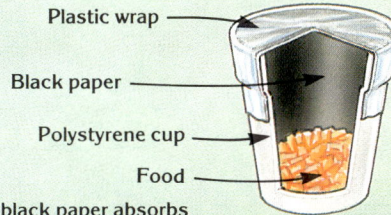

Plastic wrap
Black paper
Polystyrene cup
Food

The black paper absorbs the sun's heat and the plastic wrap prevents any hot air escaping.

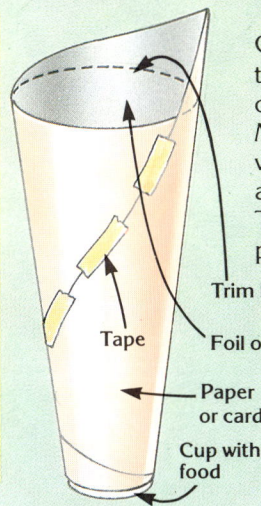

Cover one side of the sheet of paper or card with the foil. Make a cone by wrapping this sheet around the cup. Trim it and tape it in place.

Trim here
Tape
Foil on the inside
Paper or card
Cup with food

The foil reflects the sunlight and the cone shape directs it onto the food.

Place the cup and cone inside the other cup, and then place it all in the large pot, packing it with crumpled newspaper or tissue paper (this will insulate the solar oven).

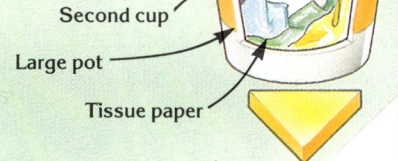

Second cup
Large pot
Tissue paper

Place your solar oven in the sunshine, angled towards the sun, and leave it until the food is cooked. The time this takes will depend on how hot the sun is, but apple or carrot will take about half an hour in bright sunshine.

You may have to move the pot as the sun moves round.

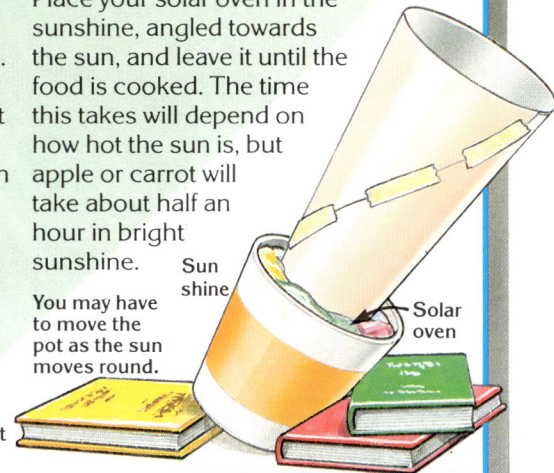

Sun shine
Solar oven

## Making a solar still

Solar stills are used in the sunnier parts of the world to get pure water from impure water. You can make a simple version at home, but you will need a very sunny day for it to work properly.

### What you will need

Large plastic bowl
Smaller bowl (e.g. a soup bowl)
Plastic food wrap
Small weight (e.g. a heavy coin)
Sticky tape

### What to do

Pour 2cm of salty water into the large plastic bowl and place the small bowl in the centre. Cover the top of the large bowl with plastic wrap, fixing it with sticky tape around the sides. Put the weight in the centre of the plastic wrap, so that it pulls it down in the centre.

Place the still outside in the hot sunshine. The water should turn to vapour (evaporate), and then turn back to water (condense) as it cools on the underside of the plastic wrap. The pure water should run down the inside of the wrap, and then drip into the small bowl. To help it condense, you could pour a little cold water on the top (to keep it cool).

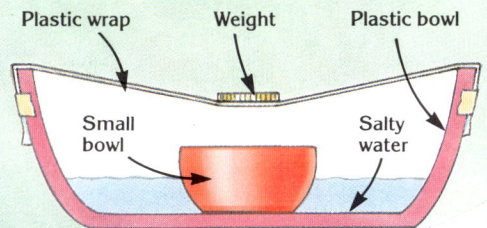

Plastic wrap
Weight
Plastic bowl
Small bowl
Salty water

This whole process is known as distillation.

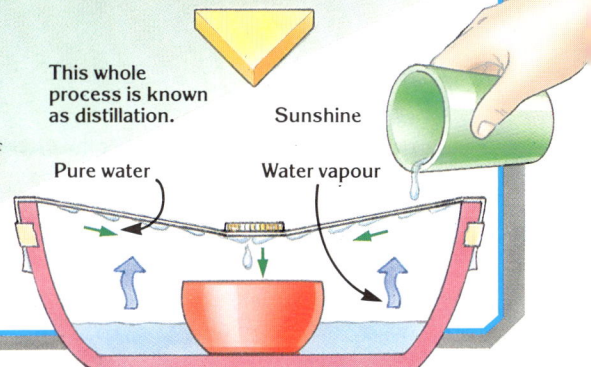

Sunshine
Pure water
Water vapour

# Energy from plants

Plants are the beginning of most of the energy chains on earth. They capture the sun's energy as they grow (see page 103), and animals eat them to create their own store of energy. Living or dead plant or animal matter (organic matter) is called biomass, and the energy it contains can be released and used in many different ways. It is all energy from plants, since the energy in usable animal matter, such as dung, comes indirectly from plants.

## Biomass in poor nations

Over two billion people, almost half the world's population, depend on biomass to supply the energy they need for cooking, heating and light. Many of the poorer nations of Africa, Asia and South America get 80% or more of their energy from wood. Another important source of fuel for their fires and stoves is animal dung, which is burnt when wood is scarce or too expensive.

Wood, dung or charcoal is burnt on stoves and open fires that are very inefficient.

A typical three-stone fire, commonly used for cooking in Africa, Asia and South America.

Unfortunately, the burning of wood and dung creates serious problems. The demand for wood has resulted in deforestation. This is when so many trees are cut down that the soil erodes away and the climate begins to change. Dung would normally rot and return important chemicals to the soil, so when it is burnt, less of these chemicals are returned to the soil, which means less food will grow.

Tree-planting, or reforestation, is part of the solution to these problems.

Trees provide a source of energy, shade from the heat, and food for people and animals.

Trees also protect the soil by sheltering it from the wind and rain, and binding it together with their roots.

Charcoal is also widely used in poor countries. It is made by burning wood in a confined space (kiln) with very little oxygen. It is a very useful fuel, which burns at a high temperature with a clean flame and very little smoke. It is easy to carry and use, and is used for heating and cooking in homes in many large cities.

## Biomass in wealthy nations

Some of the world's richer countries, like Canada, Sweden and Finland, have large forests and use a lot of wood to supply energy for homes and industries. In most of the other rich countries, though, wood is used mainly for building, and energy is supplied by other fuels. However, these countries are now beginning to recognize the potential in getting more of their energy from biomass.

## Refuse

Household and commercial refuse (rubbish) is a major potential source of energy. A lot of it is actually biomass, like paper, food scraps and wood. It can be burnt in special power stations, to produce heat and/or electricity. For example, 20% of the space and water heating in the Swedish city of Malmö comes from burning refuse.

A refuse-burning power station. Trucks deliver refuse, which is burnt on a grate, producing hot gases. The heat from these boils water in a boiler, producing steam which is used to drive turbine generators (as in other power stations – see pages 118-119).

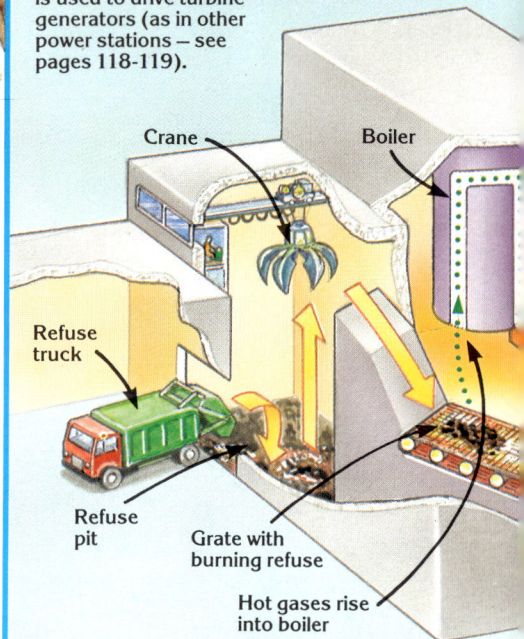

Crane

Boiler

Refuse truck

Refuse pit

Grate with burning refuse

Hot gases rise into boiler

## Using old newspapers

Old newspapers can be collected for recycling. Find out if there is a paper collection scheme in your area (contact your local environmental or conservation group). If not, you could turn your old newspapers into a useful fuel source. All you need is the newspapers and some thin wire.

Roll up the newspaper as tightly as you can, so it is about the same shape as a log of wood. Use the wire to tie it up securely. These newspaper logs can be burnt in the same way as logs of wood.

Refuse can also be used to produce energy in other ways. When buried beneath the ground, it rots and produces gases. These gases have been a major nuisance, but they are now being used, particularly in the USA and parts of Europe. They are piped off and burnt for heating or to generate electricity.

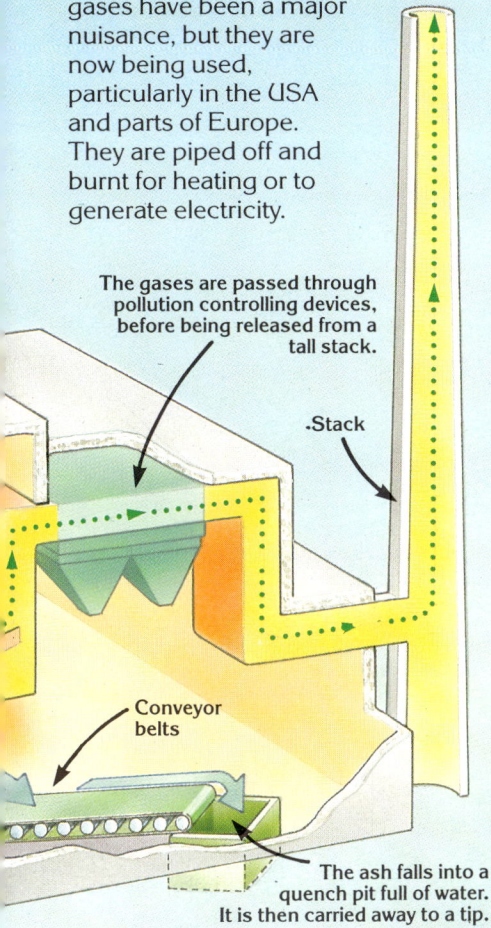

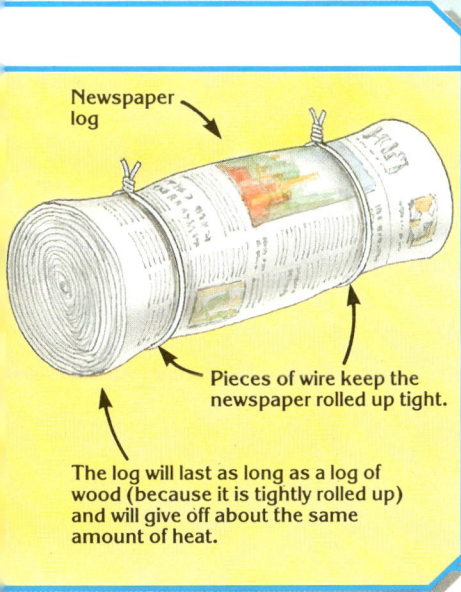

The gases are passed through pollution controlling devices, before being released from a tall stack.

Stack

Conveyor belts

The ash falls into a quench pit full of water. It is then carried away to a tip.

Newspaper log

Pieces of wire keep the newspaper rolled up tight.

The log will last as long as a log of wood (because it is tightly rolled up) and will give off about the same amount of heat.

## Waste digesters

Sewage and waste from farms and industries are being used more and more to produce "biogas". The waste rots in containers called digesters, producing the gas. This can be burnt to heat buildings and water.

This makes good use of the waste products, and reduces the pollution they would otherwise cause. Digesters are becoming more common, for example on large farms.

Waste digester on a farm

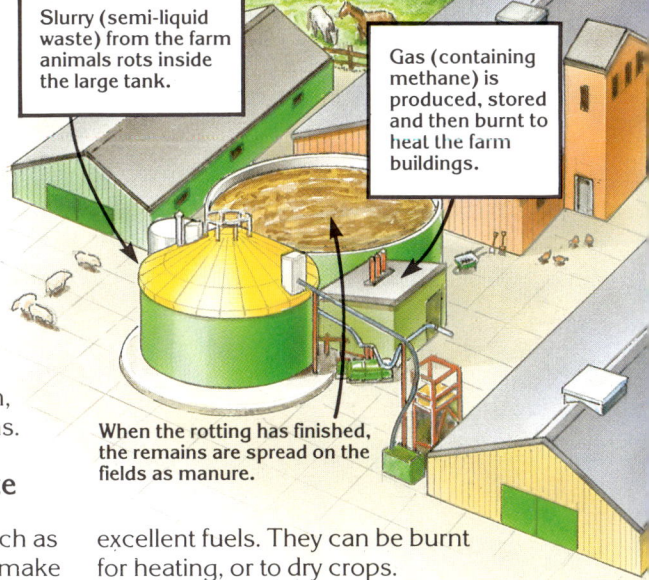

Slurry (semi-liquid waste) from the farm animals rots inside the large tank.

Gas (containing methane) is produced, stored and then burnt to heat the farm buildings.

When the rotting has finished, the remains are spread on the fields as manure.

## Straw and wood waste

Straw and wood waste, such as sawdust and wood chips, make excellent fuels. They can be burnt for heating, or to dry crops.

Small straw-fired boiler

The burning straw heats up water, which is piped around the farm buildings.

Many farms, and some small country industries and estates, such as Woburn Abbey in England, are now using straw-fired furnaces to supply some of their energy for heating. The cost of setting up a system along these lines is soon made up in savings, as the source of this energy is freely available. The straw is burnt in a furnace, which heats water in a boiler. This is then piped to where it is needed.

Enough heat is produced to keep several buildings warm.

## Growing fuels

Some fast-growing plants (such as some types of tree) are now being grown on spare farmland, specifically to be cut down and used as a source of energy. These "forest farms" provide an extra source of income for the farmers. One way of raising trees for this purpose is called coppicing.

Certain plants are also being grown to produce different fuels for transport. Sugar cane in Brazil is fermented to produce alcohol, which is used instead of petrol. Other fuels which could be used to replace petrol in the future are also being studied.

Traditional English coppice

The trees are cut off just above the ground and left to sprout.

The new shoots grow very fast because the tree already has a good root system.

The shoots are cut every 4-5 years for firewood and other uses.

# Wind energy

The wind is one of the most promising of the renewable energy sources (see page 121). It can be used for a number of purposes, like producing electricity, or pumping water. Many countries are developing wind power technology, especially those whose geography means they get a lot of wind.

## Uses of wind energy

The wind has been used for thousands of years to power sailing ships and windmills. Today it is beginning to be used more and more, and for a variety of purposes, some of which are described here. The greatest potential for using the wind is for the production of electricity.

The wind is used on farms to pump water up from under the ground. There are over a million water pumps in use, mainly in the USA, Canada and Australia.

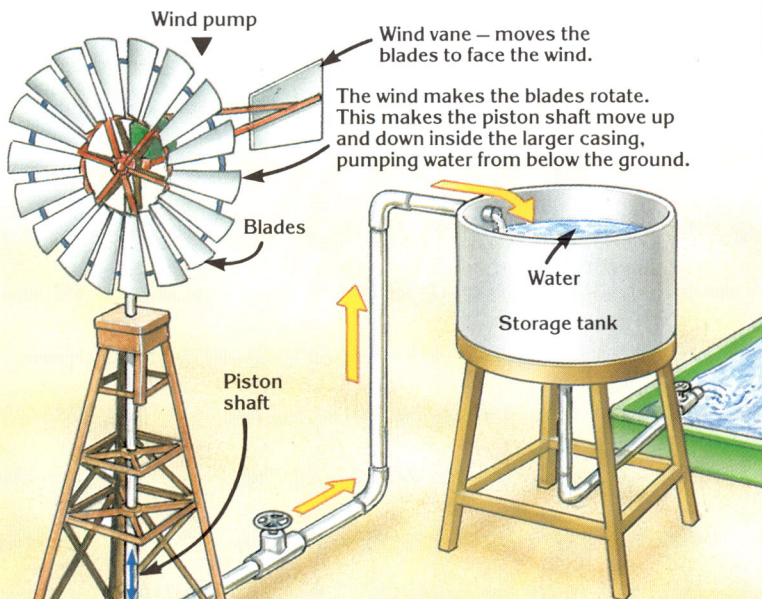

Wind pump ▼

Wind vane – moves the blades to face the wind.

The wind makes the blades rotate. This makes the piston shaft move up and down inside the larger casing, pumping water from below the ground.

Blades

Water

Storage tank

Piston shaft

A few modern ships are being fitted with sails (as well as engines) to harness the energy in the wind. This means they are able to save fuel.

Water-bearing rock

This Japanese cargo ship has two large metal and plastic sails.

A computer turns the sails so they are in the best position to catch the wind.

They can be folded up in very strong winds to protect them from damage.

## Making a wind-measuring device

It is quite easy to make a simple device for measuring wind speeds. It will work best where there is a steady wind. You will need two protractors, a table-tennis ball, a flat piece of wood or plastic (such as a ruler), about 15cm of stiff thread, a needle, some sticky putty and some glue.

Thread the needle with ▶ the thread, and push it right through the table-tennis ball. Remove the needle and tie a knot in the thread so that the ball cannot come off.

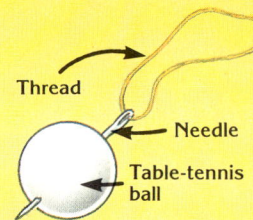

Thread

Needle

Table-tennis ball

Sticky putty

Hang the thread from the centre of the straight edge of one protractor, so that the ball hangs just below the curved edge. Stick the thread on with a small piece of putty or some glue.

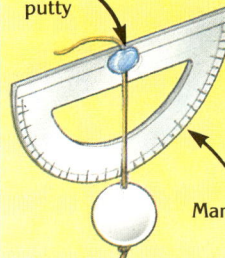

Marked sides of protractors

Now stick the other ▶ protractor to the first one with putty or glue, so that the thread is trapped inside.

Glue the wood or plastic to the back to make a handle.

If you are left-handed, stick the handle on this side.

Hold the device level, and parallel to the wind (see below). When the ball is blown upwards, read off the angle that the thread reaches, and work out the wind speed from the table on the right.

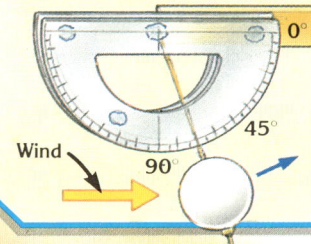

0°

Wind

45°

90°

| Angle (°) | Kilometres per hour |
|-----------|---------------------|
| 90 | 0 |
| 85 | 8-11 |
| 80 | 12-14 |
| 75 | 15-17 |
| 70 | 18-20 |
| 65 | 21-23 |
| 60 | 24-25 |
| 55 | 26-27 |
| 50 | 28-30 |
| 45 | 31-33 |
| 40 | 34-36 |
| 35 | 37-39 |
| 30 | 40-43 |
| 25 | 44-48 |
| 20 | 49-54 |

# Electricity from the wind

The most important use of the wind is to produce electricity. This was first done in Denmark during the 1890s. Today, it is becoming more and more common.

Wind power has great potential for the future, as it is relatively safe and pollution-free. It can also generate electricity at the same price as fossil fuels and nuclear power.

To produce electricity, the wind is used to turn the shaft of a turbine, which is attached to a generator. This is a smaller version of a power station generator, which is driven by steam (see pages 118-119).

There are two main forms of wind turbine. One type has blades which are fixed on a vertical axis. This means it can catch the wind from any direction (see right).

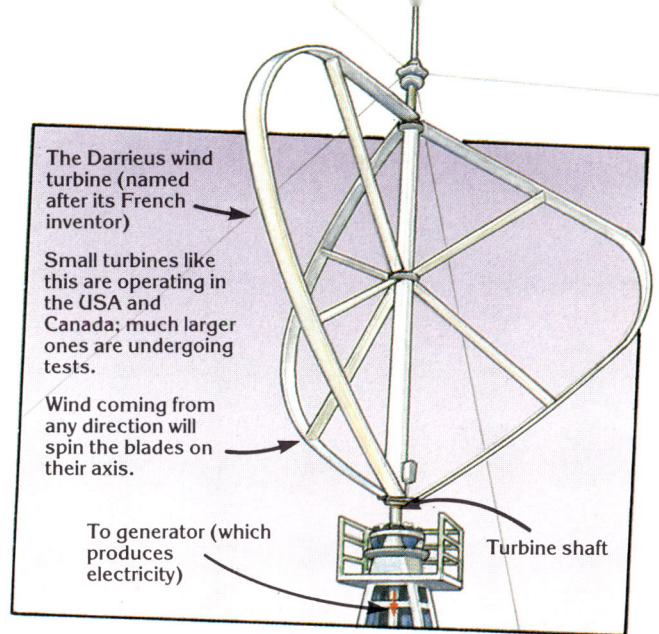

The Darrieus wind turbine (named after its French inventor)

Small turbines like this are operating in the USA and Canada; much larger ones are undergoing tests.

Wind coming from any direction will spin the blades on their axis.

To generator (which produces electricity)

Turbine shaft

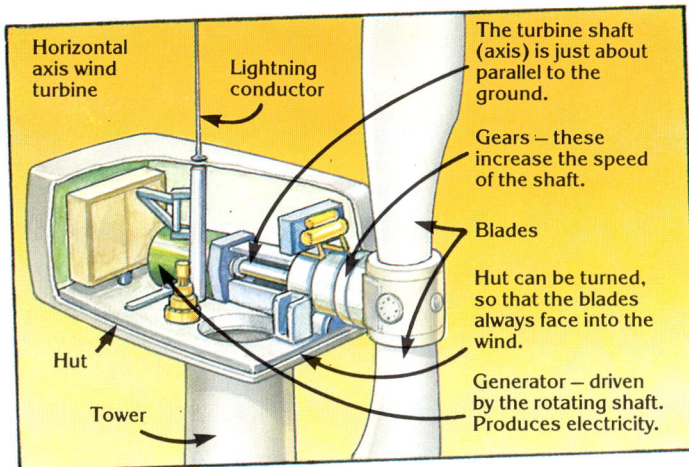

Horizontal axis wind turbine

Lightning conductor

Hut

Tower

The turbine shaft (axis) is just about parallel to the ground.

Gears – these increase the speed of the shaft.

Blades

Hut can be turned, so that the blades always face into the wind.

Generator – driven by the rotating shaft. Produces electricity.

◄ Most wind turbines now in use, though, are of the second type. They have horizontal axes (the shaft is parallel to the ground), which means they must be turned so that the blades face into the wind.

Most horizontal axis wind turbines have either two or three blades, and they differ greatly in size.

The best places to put wind turbines are where the wind is strongest and most consistent, such as on coasts and hilltops. However, this means they are very noticeable, and some people are opposed to them because of this. The machines also make a noise, so they cannot be placed close to houses.

# The future of wind turbines

At the moment, there are over 20,000 wind ► turbines producing electricity around the world. Most of these are in the USA, Denmark and Holland. Many other countries, like Sweden, the UK, Spain, India and Australia, are developing wind power technology and are building their own wind turbines.

Scientists are now designing and ► testing bigger wind turbines. Most of those used at the moment are 25-30m high and generate several hundred kilowatts of power, but the new ones can be over 50m high and generate 3-4MW (a megawatt is a million watts). Their blades can be 60-90m in diameter.

There are plans to build large wind turbines out at sea, where the winds are stronger and steadier and where they would be less noticeable.

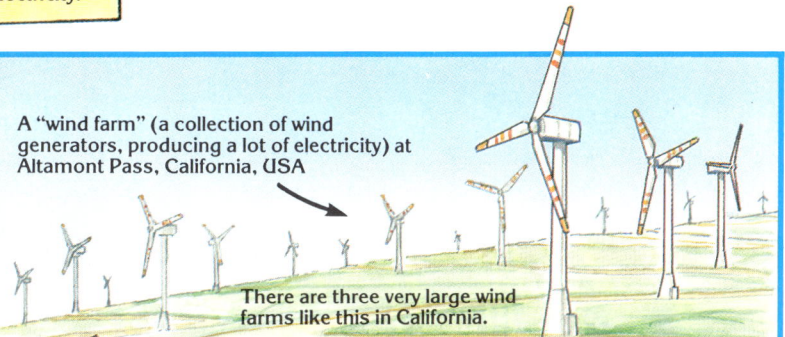

A "wind farm" (a collection of wind generators, producing a lot of electricity) at Altamont Pass, California, USA

There are three very large wind farms like this in California.

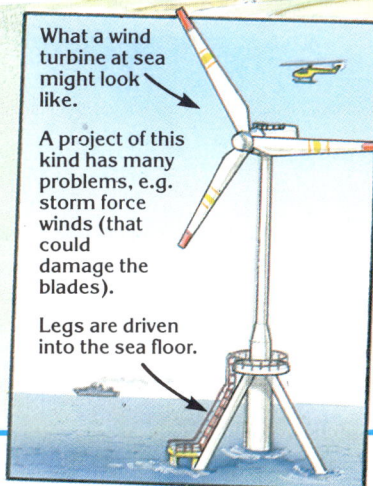

What a wind turbine at sea might look like.

A project of this kind has many problems, e.g. storm force winds (that could damage the blades).

Legs are driven into the sea floor.

Small wind turbines are important, too, especially for isolated farms and communities. Batteries are used to store the energy produced, for use when the wind is not blowing.

Over large areas, though, the wind is always blowing somewhere. By linking a lot of wind farms to the grid system, electricity can be sent from areas where the wind is blowing to areas where it is not, producing a more constant supply of electricity in all areas.

# Energy from water

The energy in moving water is one of the most widely used of the renewable energy sources. It supplies over 20% of the world's electricity through the use of hydro-electric power stations. Other forms of water energy, especially tidal and wave energy, also have great potential, but more research still needs to be done to make the technology efficient and inexpensive.

## Hydro-electric power

Hydro-electric power stations use the energy in moving river water to turn one or more turbines, producing electricity in generators (for more about turbine generators, see pages 118-119). Most rivers are capable of powering hydro-electric generators, but less than 10% of this potential is used in poor countries, and only about 30% in most richer ones. A few countries, though, such as Norway and Canada, already get a large part of their electricity from hydro-electric power stations.

## Inside a hydro-electric power station

Each hydro-electric power station is specially designed for its site, as no two rivers are the same size or flow at the same speed. The amount of energy available to the turbines depends on two things – the distance (height) between the surface of the water and the turbines (called the head of water), and the rate that the water flows through the turbines.

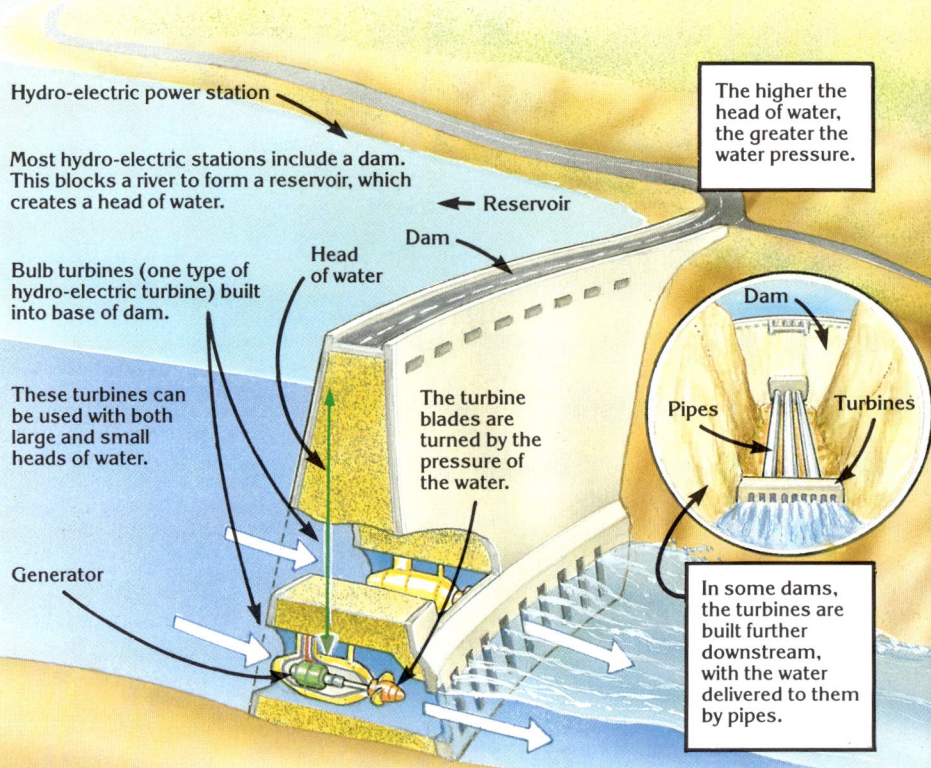

Hydro-electric power station

Most hydro-electric stations include a dam. This blocks a river to form a reservoir, which creates a head of water.

Bulb turbines (one type of hydro-electric turbine) built into base of dam.

These turbines can be used with both large and small heads of water.

Generator

Reservoir

Head of water

Dam

The turbine blades are turned by the pressure of the water.

The higher the head of water, the greater the water pressure.

Dam

Pipes

Turbines

In some dams, the turbines are built further downstream, with the water delivered to them by pipes.

## Tidal energy

Turbines like those used in hydro-electric power stations can also produce electricity from the rising and falling of the tide. There are already a number of systems (called tidal barrages) in operation, and several others are being considered, including one across the estuary of the river Severn, in England.

The largest working tidal barrage is in the Rance estuary, in France. Built in 1966, it is 750m long and provides up to 240MW of power.

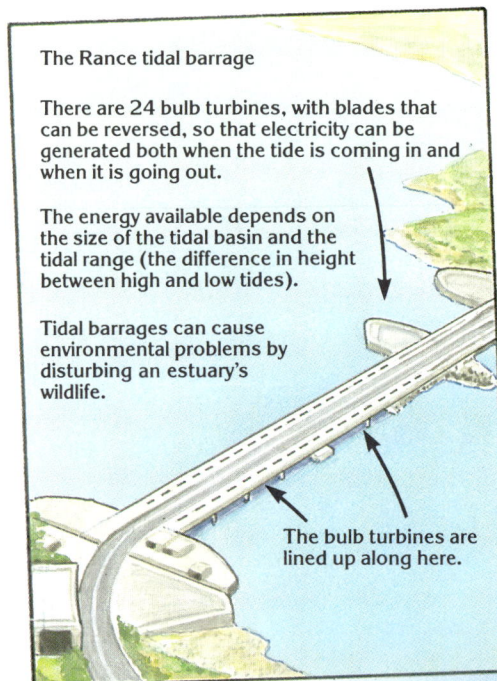

### The Rance tidal barrage

There are 24 bulb turbines, with blades that can be reversed, so that electricity can be generated both when the tide is coming in and when it is going out.

The energy available depends on the size of the tidal basin and the tidal range (the difference in height between high and low tides).

Tidal barrages can cause environmental problems by disturbing an estuary's wildlife.

The bulb turbines are lined up along here.

## Wave power

Some countries are looking at technology to harness the energy in the movement of ocean waves. This source of energy has huge potential. However, there are many problems to be tackled, such as dealing with high waves and strong winds in stormy weather.

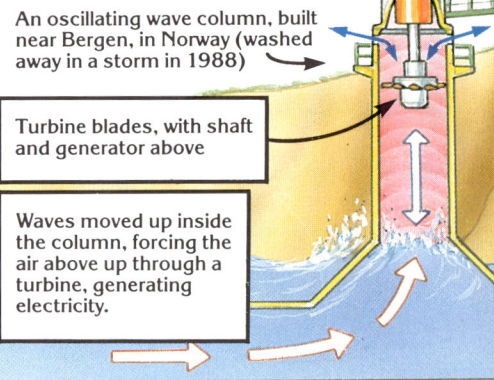

An oscillating wave column, built near Bergen, in Norway (washed away in a storm in 1988)

Turbine blades, with shaft and generator above

Waves moved up inside the column, forcing the air above up through a turbine, generating electricity.

## Problems with large dams

Building large hydro-electric dams can cause social and environmental problems.

Often a lot of land has to be cleared and flooded.

Many people may be forced to move from their homes.

Dams can become blocked by silt (soil carried by the river). In hot countries, they also bring an increase in diseases, like bilharzia, caused by tiny organisms in the still water.

Aerial view of dam and silted-up reservoir

Silt

Small dams are often a better choice than large ones, especially for supplying power to country areas. They cause less damage, and are easier to build. Almost 100,000 have been built in China since 1968 (providing over 5,000MW of power).

## Making a water wheel

Water wheels have been used for centuries to use the energy in moving water to do work.

Below is an example of a simple model water wheel you can make with basic materials.

◀ Cut out two circles of card, 20cm in diameter. Make a hole in the centre of each.

Cut up two egg cartons to make 12 small buckets. Paint or varnish these to make the outsides waterproof.

Stick or staple the buckets to the card, ▶ making the water wheel.

Place a 15cm nail through the holes in the card.

Tie some string very tightly to the nail and attach a weight (such as a pencil) to the end.

Buckets attached to card circles

Open ends should face outwards.

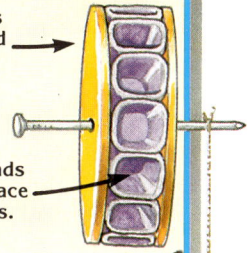

To attach the wire, make loops at both ends.

◀ Use a piece of wood (such as a ruler) and some wire to support the nail.

Put the wheel under a tap and watch it lift the weight.

Experiment with different water speeds from the tap.

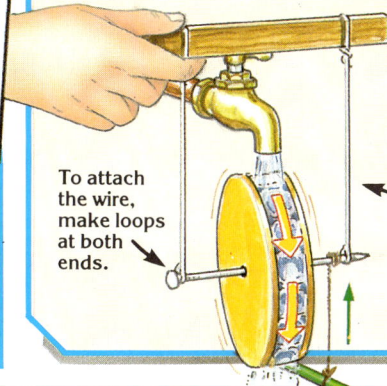

## OTEC

In hot, equatorial areas there is another potential means of gaining energy from the oceans, by using the temperature difference between the layers of water. The method, still being researched at present, is called Ocean Thermal Energy Conversion (OTEC).

OTEC devices use warm surface water to heat up and vaporize a fluid with a low boiling point, such as ammonia. The moving vapour drives a turbine, generating electricity. Cold water from deeper down is then used to cool the vapour and condense it back to ammonia for recirculating.

What a future OTEC machine might look like

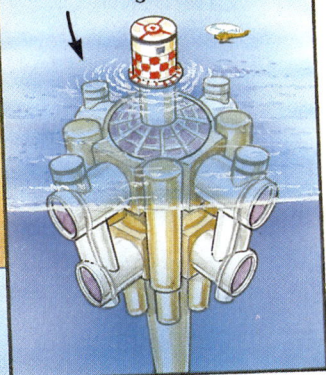

## Geothermal energy

Heat which comes from the earth itself is called geothermal energy. It is already used in some parts of the world, such as Iceland, where natural steam is produced as water passes over hot rock under the earth's surface. This steam is used to generate electricity.

Elsewhere, such as in France, warm water is pumped up from underground to heat blocks of flats.

Heat can also be gained from hot, dry rocks.

Two holes (wells) are drilled into hot rock several kilometres underground.

The rock is fractured (broken up) by pumping in water at very high pressure. Cold water is then pumped down one well into the cracks.

The water is heated up by the rock and is brought back up through the other well.

# Energy efficiency

Being energy-efficient means continuing to do most of the things we do today, but using less energy to do them. If we save energy, less is needed, and we reduce the damage to the environment caused by producing energy. Being energy-efficient is the cheapest and simplest way to start solving serious environmental problems. On the next four pages, you can find out about saving energy.

You may not be in a position yourself to make many of the changes suggested, but if you know about them you can make other people aware of them.

## Saving energy in the home

Many buildings, especially old ones, are very inefficient to heat, because they lose so much heat to the outside environment. By introducing a number of simple energy saving (conservation) measures, the cost of heating these buildings can often be cut by a half.

This shows where heat is lost from a house in winter, and how this heat loss can be reduced.

If you turn your heating down by a few degrees, you can save a lot of energy, and you probably won't notice the difference.

Insulating your hot water tank will make it heat up more quickly and stay hot for longer.

There are some more energy-saving ideas on page 119.

These energy-saving measures can also be used in larger buildings, such as schools and offices. Here, the amount of energy and money that can be saved is quite large. Find out if your school or community centre can put some of these measures into action. You could do your bit to help.

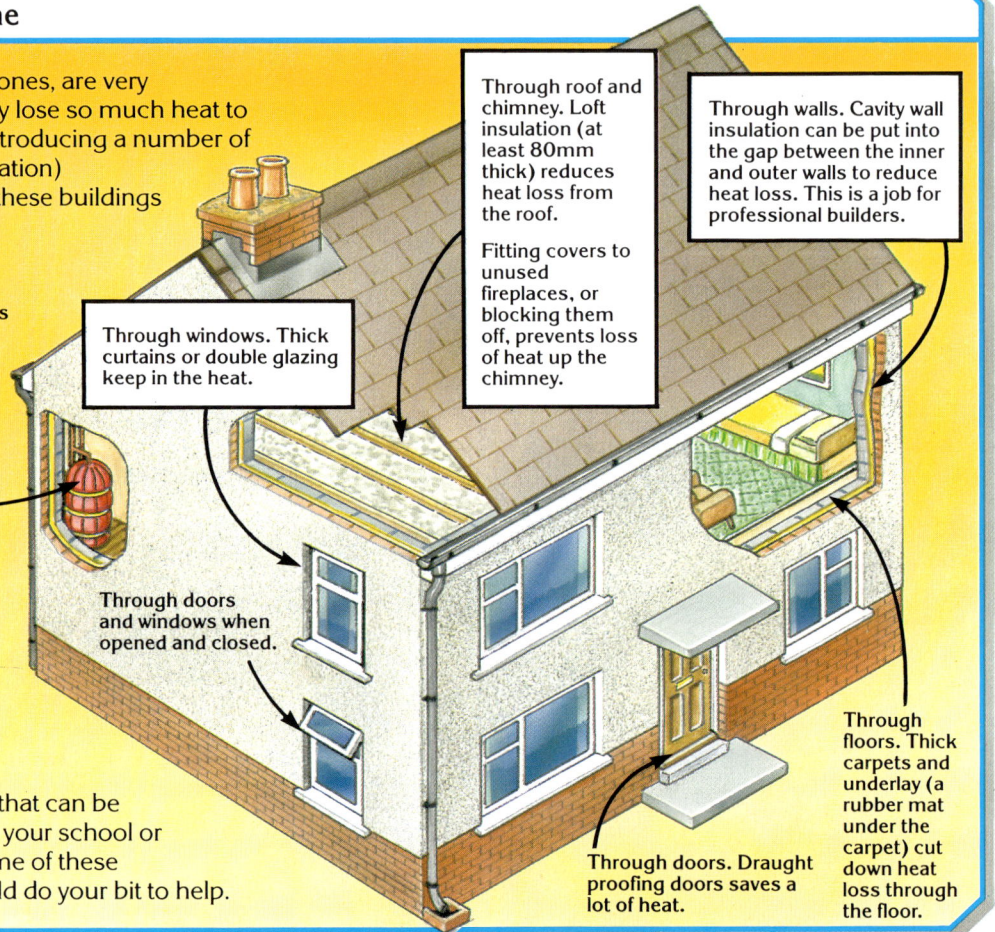

Through roof and chimney. Loft insulation (at least 80mm thick) reduces heat loss from the roof.

Fitting covers to unused fireplaces, or blocking them off, prevents loss of heat up the chimney.

Through walls. Cavity wall insulation can be put into the gap between the inner and outer walls to reduce heat loss. This is a job for professional builders.

Through windows. Thick curtains or double glazing keep in the heat.

Through doors and windows when opened and closed.

Through floors. Thick carpets and underlay (a rubber mat under the carpet) cut down heat loss through the floor.

Through doors. Draught proofing doors saves a lot of heat.

## Efficient heating

As well as preventing heat loss, it is important to make sure that the type of heating you use is as efficient as possible. There have been many developments in heating efficiency over the years, which have saved a great deal of energy and money for the people who have used them. Much more could still be done, though. The efficiency of a heating system varies according to the type of fuel it uses, whether it is in good or bad condition, and how sensibly it is used.

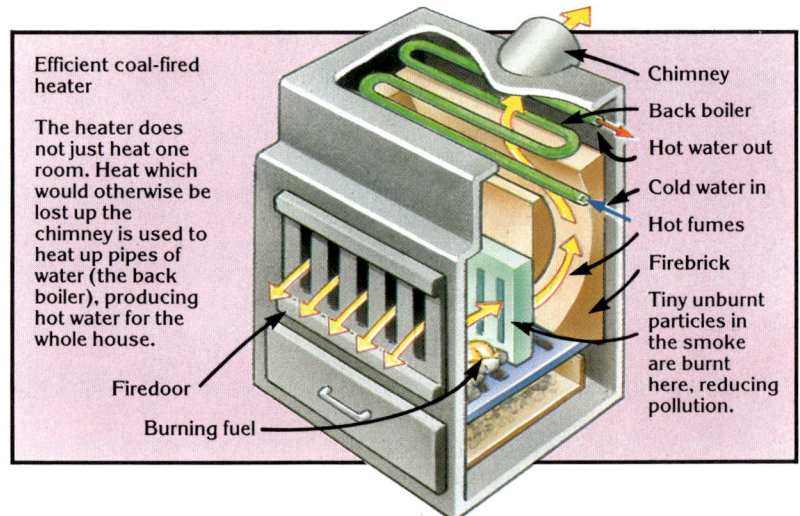

Efficient coal-fired heater

The heater does not just heat one room. Heat which would otherwise be lost up the chimney is used to heat up pipes of water (the back boiler), producing hot water for the whole house.

Chimney

Back boiler

Hot water out

Cold water in

Hot fumes

Firebrick

Tiny unburnt particles in the smoke are burnt here, reducing pollution.

Firedoor

Burning fuel

## Supplying energy to homes

One of the most efficient ways to provide heating in towns and cities where buildings are close together is known as district, or community, heating. Instead of each house and office burning fuel to provide its own heating, the heat for all the buildings is produced at a central point (such as a boiler or a power station).

Power stations which produce both electricity and district heating are called combined heat and power (CHP) stations. For more about CHP, see page 132.

CHP station in Denmark

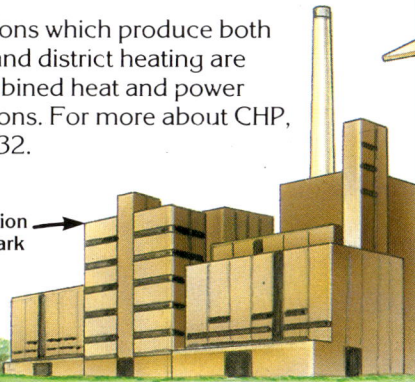

## Household appliances

There are big differences in the energy efficiency of different makes of electrical appliance (such as fridges, cookers and irons). Your family can save a lot of electricity, and money, by using the ones that are the most energy-efficient. Ask about the energy efficiency of different models when you are in the shop to make sure your parents buy the most efficient.

Some fridges now on sale use only a fifth of the electricity used by other fridges of the same size, and some now being developed will use just a tenth.

If everyone in the UK who bought a fridge in the next 15 years bought the most efficient type, the total saving would be 1,800MW (the power of 2 nuclear reactors).

## Slow cookers

A very energy-efficient way of cooking is to use a slow cooker – a large, well-insulated casserole dish which plugs into the mains and cooks food for 6-8 hours, using very little energy. Slow cooking itself is a very old cooking method, and is an excellent way to cook casseroles and soups. You can make an old-style slow cooker (a haybox cooker) very easily.

How to make and use a haybox cooker

Get a cardboard box that is large enough to fit a saucepan inside, with space around it.

Fill the box tightly with dry hay or straw, leaving a hole big enough for the saucepan.

Put the ingredients in the saucepan, put the lid on, and boil for 10 minutes (it is important to get the food very hot to start with). Then put the pan into the hole in the haybox, and cover it with another tightly-packed layer of hay or straw.

Close the flaps on the top of the box, and seal them with tape.

Food cooking in hot saucepan, insulated by haybox

Leave your food to cook for 6-8 hours. A meal put in the box in the morning will be cooked by the evening, and will only need to be reheated.

The hay acts as an insulating layer, keeping the heat in and the cold out.

You could try other insulating materials, such as crumpled-up newspaper or polystyrene.

## Energy efficient stoves

Many people in poor countries are not able to afford modern cooking and heating appliances, or the fuel that they burn. Many still burn wood on open fires and stoves, but, as more and more trees are cut down for fuel, whole areas are becoming deforested (losing all their trees).

This situation would improve if the open fires were replaced by low cost, energy-efficient ones, but care must be taken not to disrupt the people's way of life. Open stoves not only give them heat, but also lighting at night. They are also important as the centre of family life.

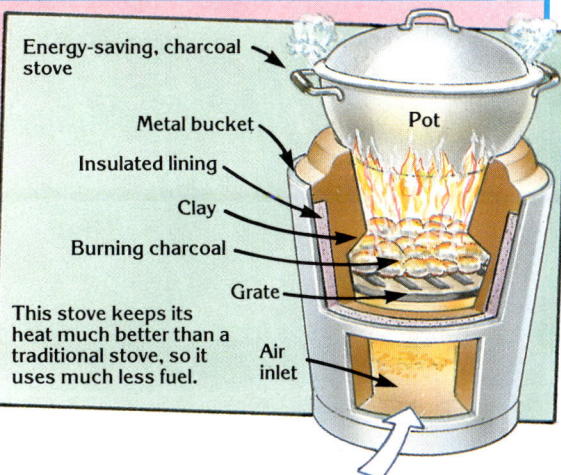

Energy-saving, charcoal stove

Metal bucket

Insulated lining

Clay

Burning charcoal

Grate

Pot

This stove keeps its heat much better than a traditional stove, so it uses much less fuel.

Air inlet

# Efficiency in industry

Many of the basic energy-saving measures used in the home can also be used in buildings where people work. The buildings and machinery used in industry, however, are much larger and more complex, so there are also different problems to be faced in order to improve energy efficiency. There are a number of ways to solve these problems, and these need to be used more widely.

## The heat wheel

The heat wheel is an energy-saving device used in industry. It uses the heat from warm air or hot fumes leaving a building or factory to warm up fresh, incoming air. A heat wheel recovers up to 80% of the heat in the outgoing air, saving a lot of energy.

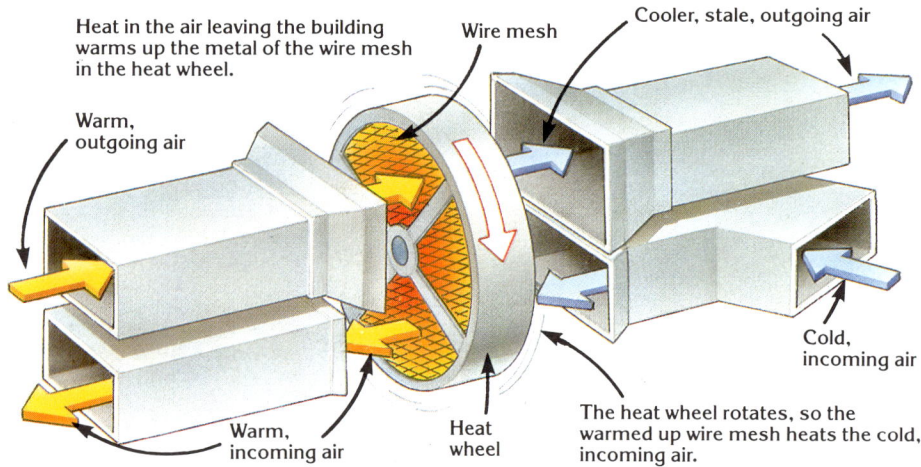

Heat in the air leaving the building warms up the metal of the wire mesh in the heat wheel.

Wire mesh

Cooler, stale, outgoing air

Warm, outgoing air

Cold, incoming air

Warm, incoming air

Heat wheel

The heat wheel rotates, so the warmed up wire mesh heats the cold, incoming air.

People in industry and business should be encouraged to introduce energy-saving devices and techniques to old buildings, or add them to new ones as they are built. They may be expensive to buy, but they can save money, as well as energy, in the long term.

## Combined heat and power

One important place to improve efficiency is in large power stations which use coal or oil. Only about 35% of the energy put in as fuel is converted into electricity. The rest is lost as heat. In the UK, for example, the heat lost from power stations is enough to heat every home in the country.

Ordinary power station

Cold water from a lake, river or the sea is used to cool steam in the condenser (see pages 118-119).

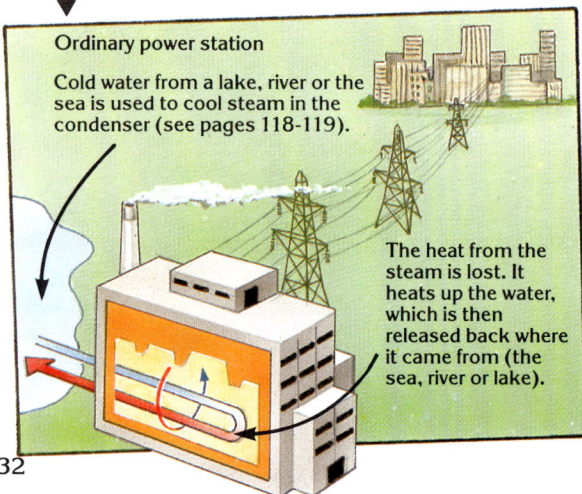

The heat from the steam is lost. It heats up the water, which is then released back where it came from (the sea, river or lake).

Combined heat and power (CHP) stations produce electricity and useful heat at the same time. Instead of being released, hot water from the production of electricity is piped to local buildings and used for space and water heating. This is known as district heating.

CHP stations produce slightly less electricity than ordinary power stations. But they use more of the heat produced, and can be twice as efficient overall (70-80% efficient).

## Embedded energy

In many industries, a lot of energy is used to make materials and goods – for example, to heat the furnaces in which steel and glass are made. This energy is sometimes known as embedded energy. If the materials, and the things which are made from them, are repaired, recycled and used again, then less energy needs to be used up in producing more materials and goods.

Any substance that is made using a lot of energy, such as steel or glass, has a lot of embedded energy.

Car          Glass windscreen and windows

Steel body

Any object that is made from these substances, such as a car, also has a lot of embedded energy.

CHP station

Well-insulated pipes (mostly underground) carry hot water from the condenser to local houses.

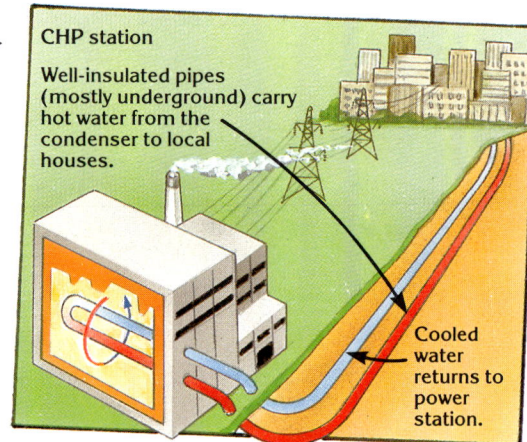

Cooled water returns to power station.

There are also much smaller CHP generators which produce both electricity and heat in the same way as the larger ones. These can be used in all kinds of industrial buildings.

# Efficiency in transport

About a quarter of all the energy used in some industrialized nations is used in transport. However, many means of transport are very inefficient, both as machines and as ways of carrying people and goods. By using new technology, we could produce machines which are more energy-efficient. Also, by changing our ideas about the way we use transport, we could create better, more energy-efficient transport systems and a more pleasant, less polluted environment.

## More efficient cars

Most cars are inefficient in the way they use energy. In the average car engine, only about 15% of the chemical energy stored in petrol is actually converted into the movement energy of the car. The rest is lost as heat. Engineers are now working on new, more efficient cars and engines for the future.

A more energy-efficient car of the future ▶

Streamlined car body means there is less friction between the air and the car. The air flows more smoothly over the body, so less energy has to be used up in moving against it.

Lighter bodywork (perhaps made of strong, hard plastic) means the engine has to do less work (it has to move less weight) and so uses up less energy.

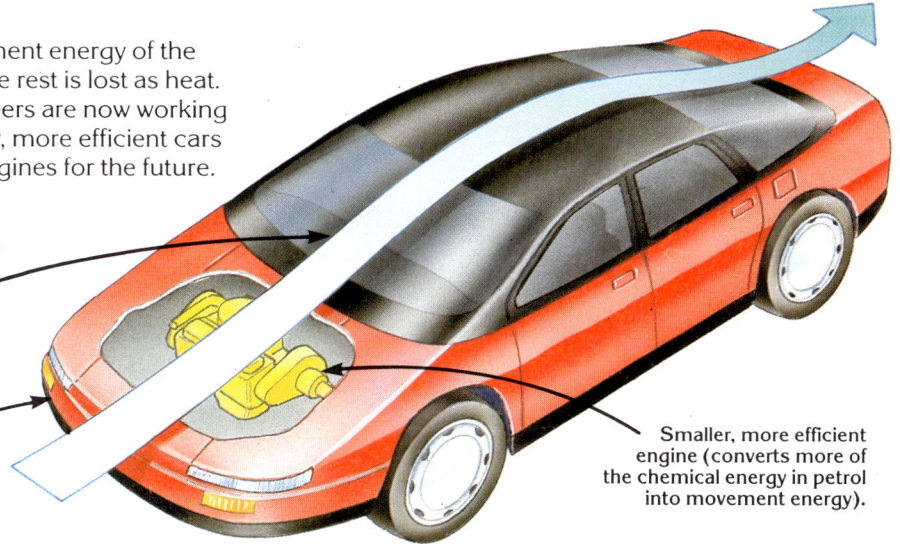

Smaller, more efficient engine (converts more of the chemical energy in petrol into movement energy).

## Cars and public transport

Although cars can be very useful, even energy-saving cars can be an inefficient means of transport. This is especially true in crowded areas, such as towns and cities. A car takes up road space and uses up a lot of energy, often to carry just one person.

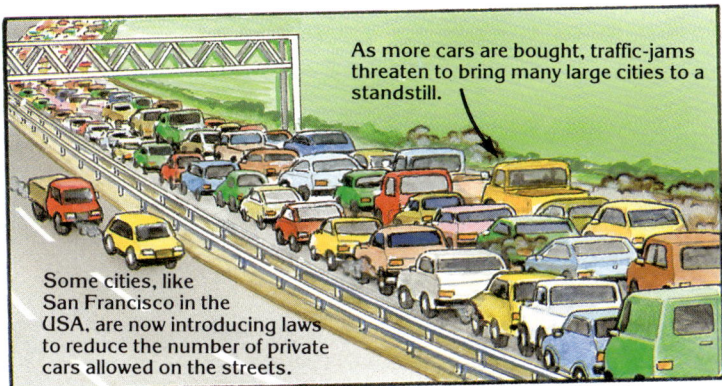

As more cars are bought, traffic-jams threaten to bring many large cities to a standstill.

Some cities, like San Francisco in the USA, are now introducing laws to reduce the number of private cars allowed on the streets.

Public transport is a much more energy-efficient way to move people around. Many people would like to see private cars banned from city centres, and replaced by much better public transport systems, with cheap, regular and extensive services. This would also reduce pollution from exhausts.

The number of heavy lorries on the roads could also be reduced, by introducing better rail systems. Trains are more energy-efficient for moving people and goods over long distances.

## Riding a bicycle

The bicycle is a very efficient machine. It takes little energy to travel comfortably over quite long distances. More people are now using bicycles, both for enjoyment and to keep fit. By not using petrol, they help to save energy and reduce air pollution. Below are some ideas to help make a bicycle work more efficiently.

Keep the tyres well pumped up. A flat tyre has more surface touching the road. This causes friction and slows you down.

Keep the moving parts well oiled. Oil reduces friction, making it easier to ride.

Oil at the points labelled below.
▼

Make sure the bicycle is the right size for you and the seat is at the correct height. If not, it will be harder to cycle (your leg muscles will not be working as efficiently as they could).

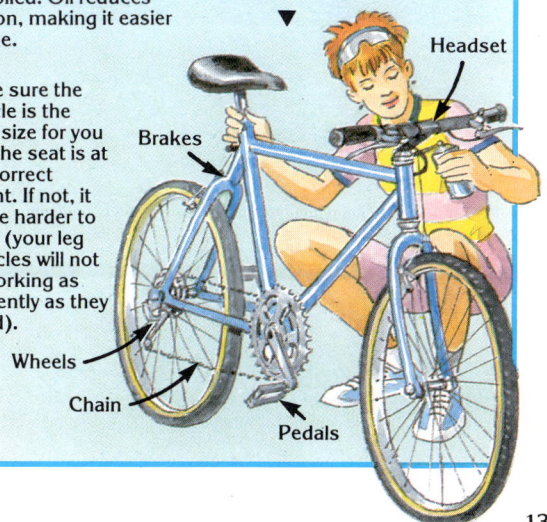

Headset

Brakes

Wheels

Chain

Pedals

# Energy in the future

Within the next few decades, there will have to be great changes in the way energy is used throughout the world. The way we produce and use energy at the moment is causing serious damage to the environment. At the same time, demand for energy is increasing as the world's population continues to grow, but there are only limited reserves of fossil fuels, which today provide about 80% of the world's energy. It is very important that everyone begins to use energy carefully and responsibly.

## The growth of pollution

When coal was first burnt in large quantities, during the Industrial Revolution in Europe in the 1800s, the pollution produced was mostly local. Towns and cities became very dirty and unhealthy.

Smog was a result of smoke from coal fires and factories mixing with fog.

Smog (a mixture of smoke and fog) in a large city in the 1870s.

Many people used to die from bronchitis and asthma when the smog was particularly bad.

Later, steps were taken to get rid of smog. Smokeless fuels were introduced and tall smoke stacks were built at power stations and factories to carry smoke away from local areas. But this meant that pollution was spread much further afield. For example, trees and lakes in Norway have been damaged by pollution from British power stations.

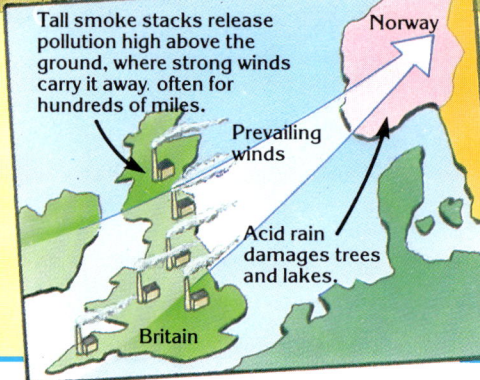

Tall smoke stacks release pollution high above the ground, where strong winds carry it away, often for hundreds of miles.

Norway

Prevailing winds

Acid rain damages trees and lakes.

Britain

As they grew wealthier, the industrialized countries burnt larger amounts of fossil fuels. This has resulted in a gradual build up of carbon dioxide in the atmosphere, which is one of the main causes of the greenhouse effect. This is a serious threat to the world's environment, and pollution has now become an international problem.

## Energy use in rich countries

In most rich countries, people's lifestyles are very wasteful of energy. This is because modern lifestyles developed when energy was cheap and plentiful, and few people realized the dangers of pollution. But we now know about these dangers, and can see that some of our energy resources will soon become more scarce. Because of these things, we must begin to change the way we use energy.

Some people believe that more and more energy must be used to improve living standards. However, this is only true in countries which are still building up their industries. In nations with a lot of modern industries, there is a much less direct link between energy use and living standards.

In the USA, the large, "gas-guzzling" car used to be very common. Today, far more Americans drive smaller, more energy-efficient cars.

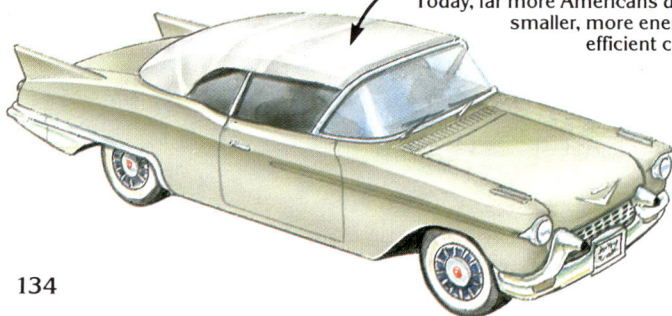

In Japan, the standard of living has continued to improve without an increase in energy use.

Japan used the same amount of energy in 1984 as it did in 1979, but there was a 23% increase in the country's wealth.

A lot of energy is saved by recycling materials and increasing energy efficiency.

An energy-efficient high-speed train in Japan

## Energy use in poor countries

Many of the world's poorest countries have very large, growing populations, but their use of energy sources per person is low compared to the rich countries.

However, a number of these countries have plenty of coal and want to develop their industries in the same way as the rich countries have, to improve the standard of living of their people. This would mean a vast increase in energy use and world pollution, and would greatly speed up the rate at which world resources are used up.

In 1988:

One person in China used 0.67 tonnes of oil or equivalent*.

One person in North America used 8.06 tonnes of oil or equivalent.

One person in the Middle East used 2.78 tonnes of oil or equivalent.

For more about world resources and energy consumption, see pages 136-139. See page 138 for more of these "per head" figures.

## Changes in energy use

Every few years something dramatic happens which changes the way people think about energy. These events affect the choices governments make about how to use energy in the future. For example, in 1973, the main oil-producing nations quadrupled the price of oil and threatened to stop supplying it to some countries. Then, in 1985, prices collapsed due to over-production. Another example is the nuclear accident at Chernobyl in the USSR in 1986, which changed many people's minds about the safety of nuclear power.

Scientific discoveries are also unpredictable. For example, newly-developed substances called high temperature superconductors, which conduct electricity very efficiently, are likely to improve greatly the efficiency of machines and cables. Events like these will continue to happen, making long-term planning very difficult.

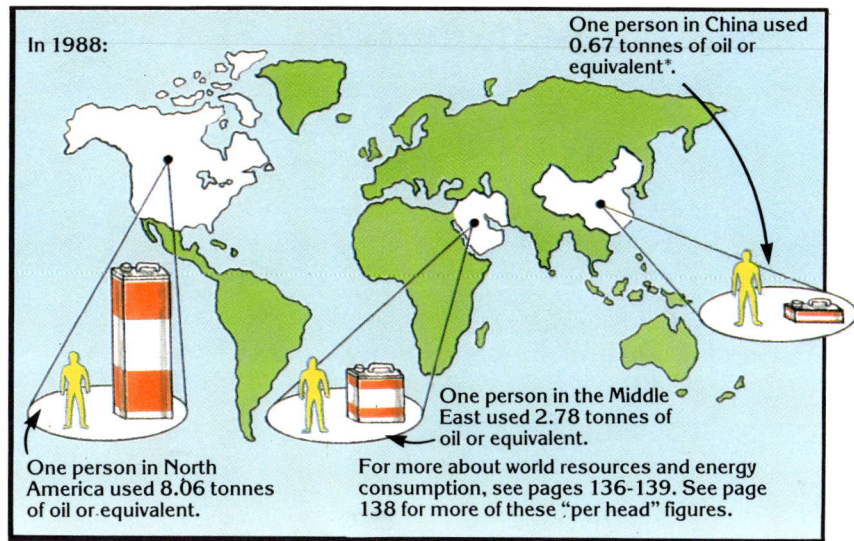

If oil prices are low, the car industry booms, and governments may build more oil-fired power stations.

If oil prices are high, governments may build more nuclear power stations, but fear of another accident like Chernobyl may mean a lot of public opposition.

A new, increasing awareness of environmental problems such as acid rain may mean governments take action to reduce pollution.

## Solutions to the energy question

We are surrounded by sources of energy that can be used to make our lives more comfortable and enjoyable. But all energy sources have a cost, in terms of money and environmental damage. If they are used sensibly, we can continue to have enough energy without destroying our environment. To achieve this, we will have to make some changes, such as those suggested here.

The wealthy ▶ countries must reduce their energy use, perhaps by 50% by the year 2020, by being more energy-efficient.

◀ They must also share their knowledge and technology with the poor countries, to help them develop their own efficient and appropriate ways of producing energy.

Laws must be passed, and help given, to make sure anti-pollution technology is introduced and used in all countries.

There must be more ▶ co-operation to tackle world problems such as the greenhouse effect.

◀ There must be more research into renewable sources of energy, and a gradual switch away from fossil fuels to these cleaner, safer sources.

Solutions must be found to the problems of nuclear waste and the safety of nuclear reactors, before there is a further increase in the use of nuclear power around the world. ▼

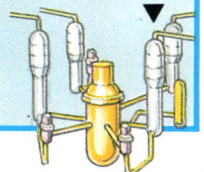

* See pages 136 and 137 for an explanation of "oil equivalent".

135

# World energy facts

On the next four pages there are some charts, maps and graphs which give an idea of the different amounts of energy produced and consumed in different areas of the world, and also the estimated reserves of these sources around the world.

## Production and consumption of fossil fuels

The charts below give the amounts of oil, natural gas and coal produced (brought out of the ground to be used or sold) and consumed (used) by different areas of the world in 1988.

Each area is a group of countries (the standard groups used in such statistics in 1988, before all the changes in the late 1980's and early 1990's). If the figure for a particular country within a group is significantly larger than the figures of the other countries in that group, it is given separately.

### Key to country groups

- North America (USA and Canada)
- Latin America (except Cuba, a socialist country)
- Western Europe
- Middle East
- Africa
- Asia (except socialist countries)
- Australia and New Zealand
- Socialist countries +

**Oil production, 1988 (million tonnes**)**

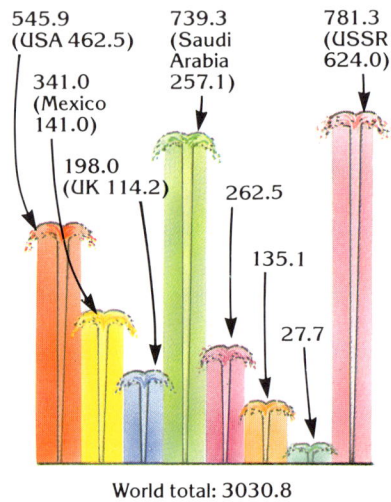

545.9 (USA 462.5)
341.0 (Mexico 141.0)
198.0 (UK 114.2)
739.3 (Saudi Arabia 257.1)
262.5
135.1
27.7
781.3 (USSR 624.0)

World total: 3030.8

**Oil consumption, 1988 (million tonnes)**

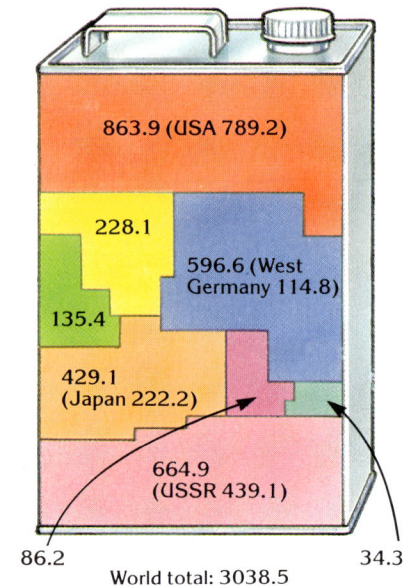

863.9 (USA 789.2)
228.1
596.6 (West Germany 114.8)
135.4
429.1 (Japan 222.2)
664.9 (USSR 439.1)
86.2
34.3

World total: 3038.5

The figures for gas and coal are given in units called "million tonnes of oil equivalent" ("mtoe"). These figures are arrived at by working out how much energy would be, or was, obtained from the total amount of gas or coal, and then giving the number of millions of tonnes of oil that would produce the same amount of energy.

**Natural gas production, 1988 (mtoe)**

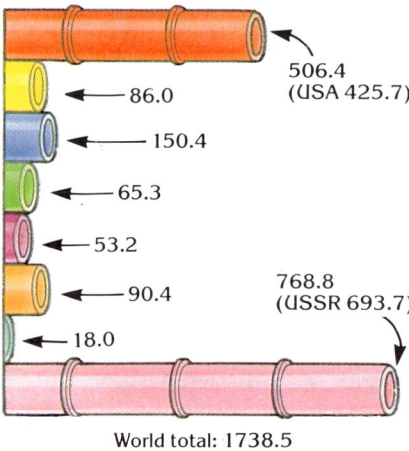

506.4 (USA 425.7)
86.0
150.4
65.3
53.2
90.4
18.0
768.8 (USSR 693.7)

World total: 1738.5

**Natural gas consumption, 1988 (mtoe)**

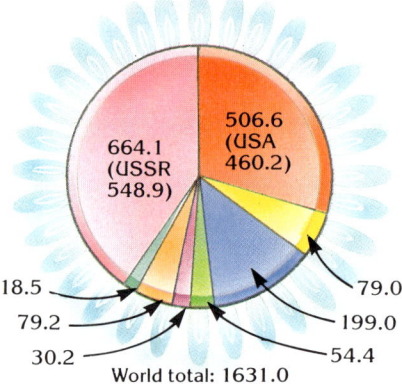

506.6 (USA 460.2)
664.1 (USSR 548.9)
18.5
79.2
30.2
79.0
199.0
54.4

World total: 1631.0

**Coal production, 1988 (mtoe)**

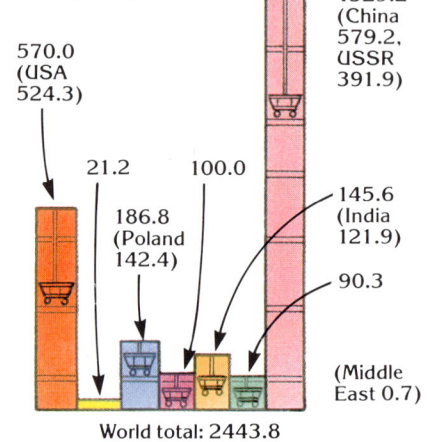

570.0 (USA 524.3)
21.2
186.8 (Poland 142.4)
100.0
1329.2 (China 579.2, USSR 391.9)
145.6 (India 121.9)
90.3
(Middle East 0.7)

World total: 2443.8

**Coal consumption, 1988 (mtoe)**

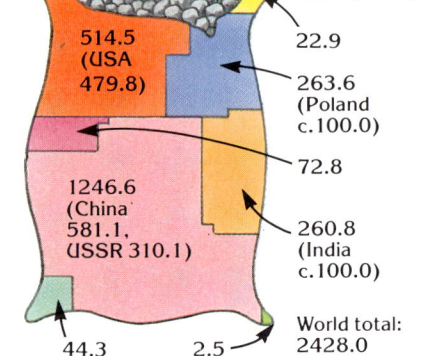

514.5 (USA 479.8)
22.9
263.6 (Poland c.100.0)
72.8
1246.6 (China 581.1, USSR 310.1)
260.8 (India c.100.0)
44.3
2.5

World total: 2428.0

Some interesting points can be made from looking at figures such as these. For instance, countries such as the USA consume far more oil than they produce. These countries must rely on buying oil from other countries. Also, you can see that the top five coal producers (the countries named) are also the top five consumers.

+ Albania, Bulgaria, China, Cuba, Czechoslovakia, East Germany, Hungary, Kampuchea, Laos, Mongolia, North Korea, Poland, Romania, USSR, Vietnam, Yugoslavia.

** One tonne (metric ton) = 1,000 kilograms or 0.98 tons (imperial tons)

# Nuclear and hydro-electric energy

Most of the world's energy comes from burning fossil fuels. But some energy is also produced by nuclear power stations and the various renewable sources. A complete picture of energy consumption is not possible without figures for these sources, but unfortunately some figures are incomplete and unreliable, in particular those for the burning of wood in Third World countries (in many cases, the main source of energy in these countries). The only clear international figures available for non-fossil sources are for electricity obtained from nuclear and hydro-electric power. As before, mtoe units are used, in this case being the amount of oil which would fuel an oil-fired power station to produce the same amount of electricity.

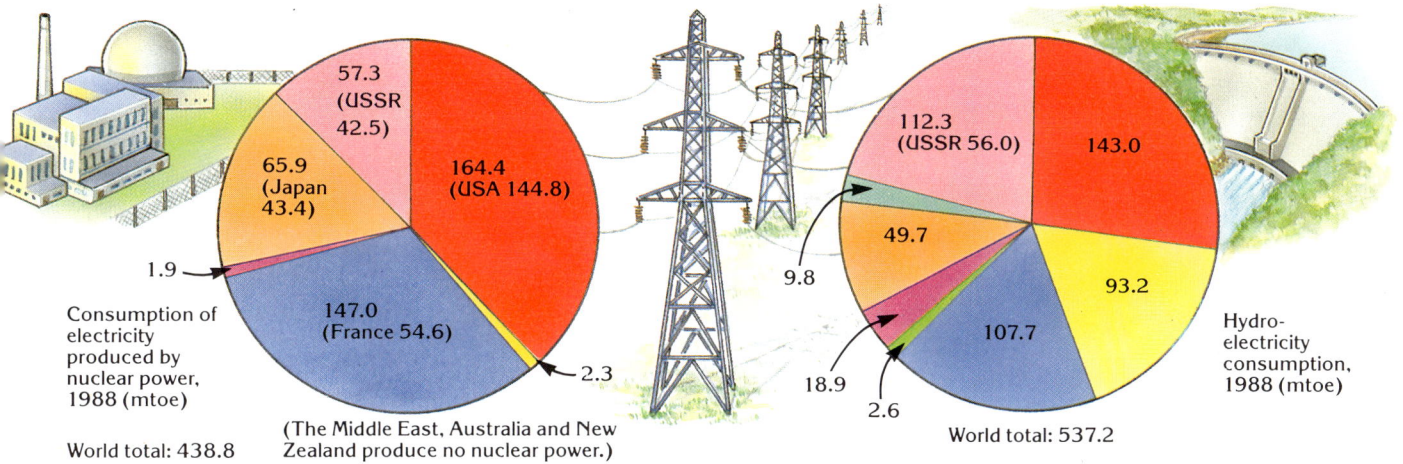

57.3 (USSR 42.5)

65.9 (Japan 43.4)

164.4 (USA 144.8)

1.9

147.0 (France 54.6)

2.3

Consumption of electricity produced by nuclear power, 1988 (mtoe)

World total: 438.8

(The Middle East, Australia and New Zealand produce no nuclear power.)

112.3 (USSR 56.0)

143.0

49.7

9.8

93.2

18.9

2.6

107.7

Hydro-electricity consumption, 1988 (mtoe)

World total: 537.2

# Primary energy figures

If, for each area, you add together the consumption figures for the five energy sources, you arrive at a "primary energy" consumption figure (in mtoe) for each area. Each of these charts breaks down this total (1988) figure (given below each chart) to show the percentages of the different sources consumed.

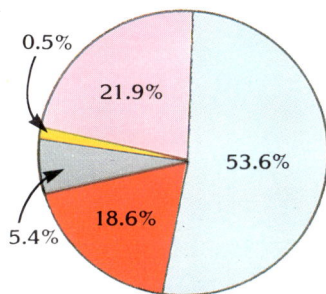

**Key**
- Oil
- Natural gas
- Coal
- Nuclear
- Hydro

6.5%

7.5%

23.5%

39.4%

23.1%

North America: 2192.4 (USA 1940.8)

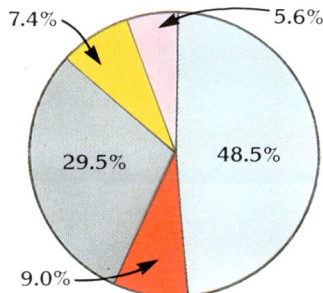

0.5%

21.9%

53.6%

5.4%

18.6%

Latin America: 425.5

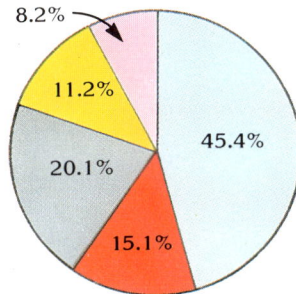

8.2%

11.2%

45.4%

20.1%

15.1%

Western Europe: 1313.9

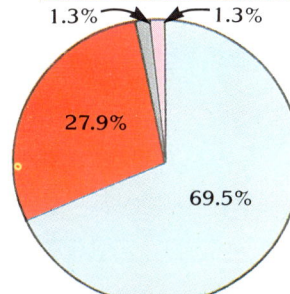

1.3%     1.3%

27.9%

69.5%

Middle East: 194.9

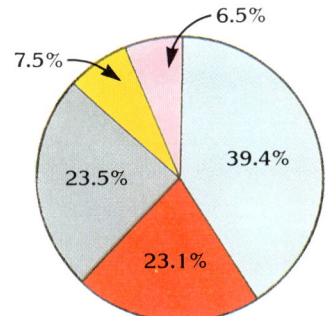

0.9%     9.0%

34.7%

41.0%

14.4%

Africa: 210.0

World total: 8073.5

7.4%     5.6%

29.5%

48.5%

9.0%

Asia: 884.7 (Japan 399.9)

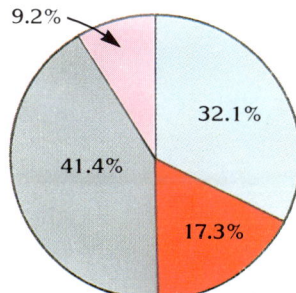

9.2%

41.4%

32.1%

17.3%

Australia and New Zealand: 106.9 (Australia 90.8)

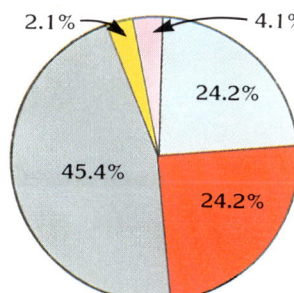

2.1%     4.1%

24.2%

45.4%

24.2%

Socialist countries: 2745.2 (USSR 1396.6)

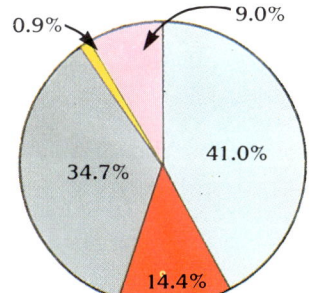

At the top of the next page, you can see figures which show how much energy each person in the different areas consumed in 1988.

137

## Energy use and population

This graph looks at the 1988 primary energy consumption figures, shown on page 137, in terms of how much energy (on average) was used per person in each of the areas. The figures are worked out by dividing the total primary energy consumption of each area by its population.

It must be remembered that the primary energy figures are based on the five "major" energy sources, and that other sources of energy, such as wood, animal waste and refuse, and also solar, wind and wave power, are not taken into account.

The area groups are the same as on pages 136-137 (for example, "Asia" still means non-communist Asia), but some countries have been separated out. You can see that there are some very large differences between the rich and poor areas of the world. One person in North America, for example, used over 23½ times more energy than a person in Africa.

Tonnes of oil or equivalent (see pages 136 and 137) used per head in 1988

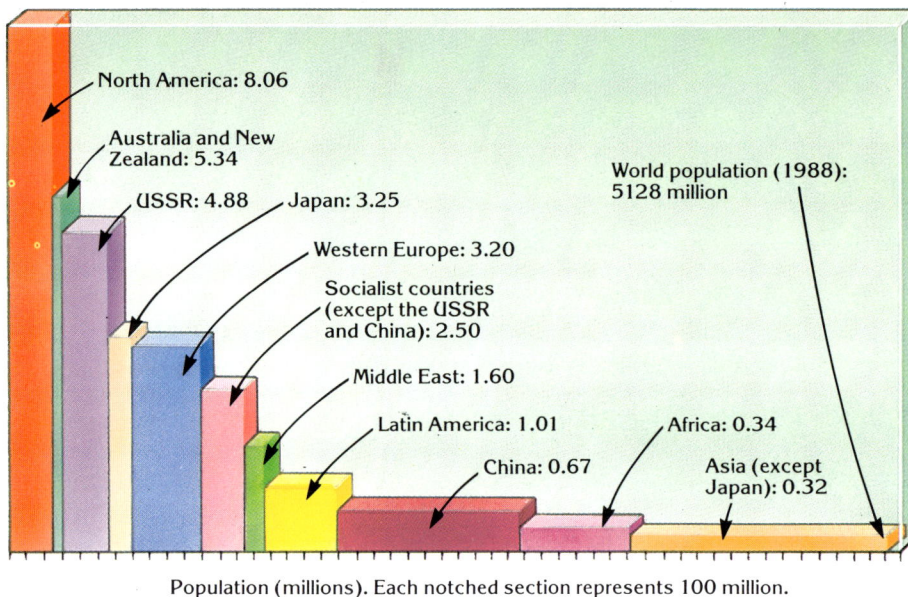

North America: 8.06

Australia and New Zealand: 5.34

USSR: 4.88     Japan: 3.25

Western Europe: 3.20

Socialist countries (except the USSR and China): 2.50

Middle East: 1.60

Latin America: 1.01

China: 0.67

Africa: 0.34

Asia (except Japan): 0.32

World population (1988): 5128 million

Population (millions). Each notched section represents 100 million.

Many of the countries which produce and use only a small amount of energy at the moment want to improve their living standards, but this would mean that they would greatly increase their energy use.

As you can see from the graph on the left, there were far more people using a small amount of energy in 1988 than there were using large amounts. If they all increased their energy use, the drain on the world's reserves would be enormous (and so would the increase in environmental damage). Below and at the top of page 139, there are some maps which show the state of the world's energy reserves.

## World fossil fuel reserves

These special maps are based on the area groups on pages 136-137 (though in two cases, Australia and New Zealand are put together with Asia, because their figures are too small to single out individually).

Most of the areas are in roughly the right geographical position, but their sizes are not their geographical sizes. The number of little squares each area occupies shows the known reserves of oil, gas and coal in that area in 1988. You can see how the Middle East dominates the oil map, the Middle East and the USSR dominate the gas map, and the USA, the USSR and China dominate the coal map.

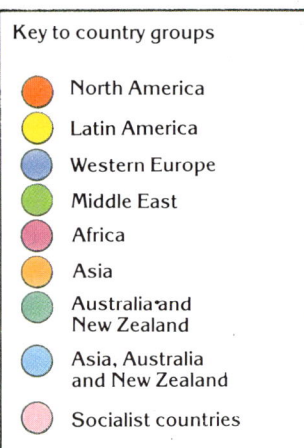

Key to country groups

- North America
- Latin America
- Western Europe
- Middle East
- Africa
- Asia
- Australia and New Zealand
- Asia, Australia and New Zealand
- Socialist countries

Known oil reserves in billion barrels (1 square = 1 billion barrels)

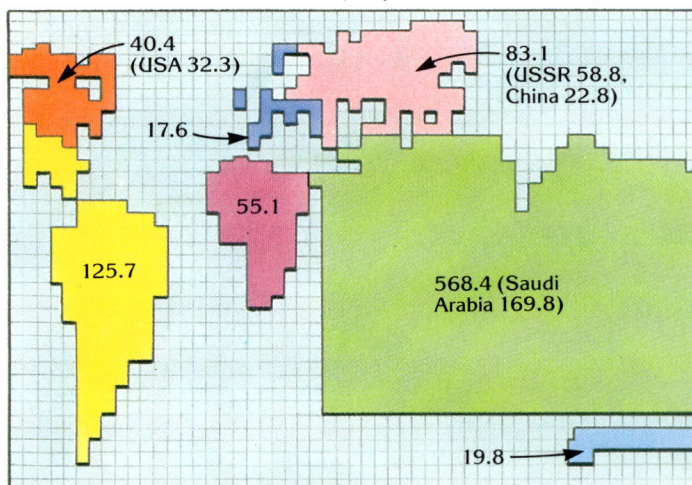

40.4 (USA 32.3)

83.1 (USSR 58.8, China 22.8)

17.6

55.1

125.7

568.4 (Saudi Arabia 169.8)

19.8

Known natural gas reserves in trillion cubic metres (1 square = 0.1 trillion cubic metres)

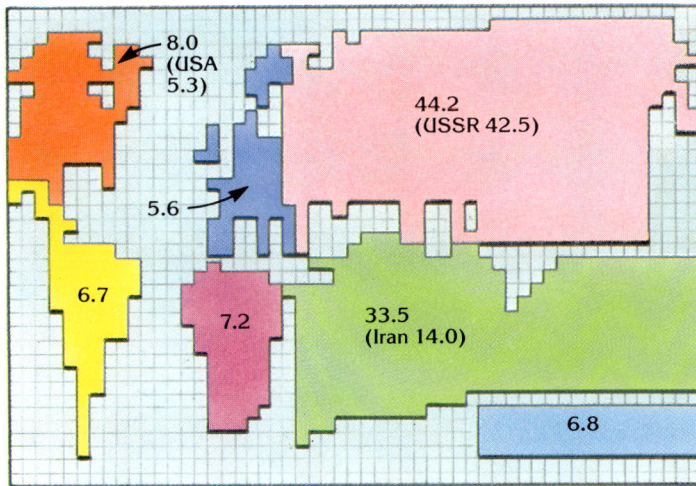

8.0 (USA 5.3)

44.2 (USSR 42.5)

5.6

6.7

7.2

33.5 (Iran 14.0)

6.8

Known coal reserves in billion tonnes (1 square = 1 billion tonnes)

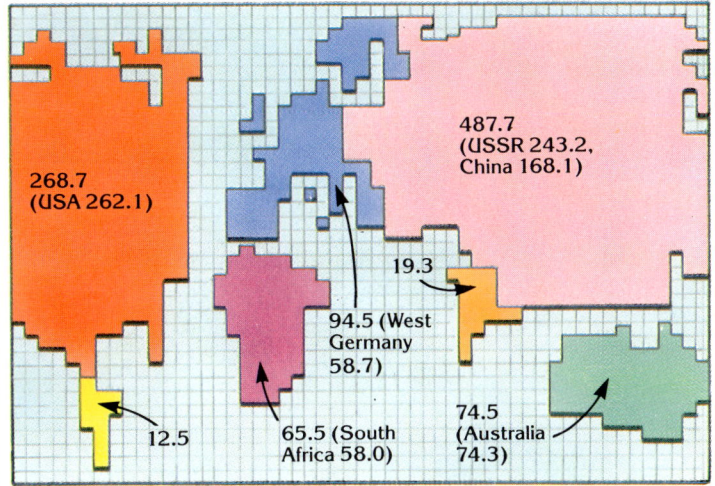

268.7 (USA 262.1)

487.7 (USSR 243.2, China 168.1)

19.3

94.5 (West Germany 58.7)

12.5

65.5 (South Africa 58.0)

74.5 (Australia 74.3)

The graphs below show how long the reserves of each area would last, if they continued to be produced (brought out of the ground) at the same (average) rate as that area produced them in 1988 (see page 136). The "whole world" figure shows how long world reserves would last if we continued to produce oil, coal and gas at the average 1988 rate (the average of the rates of all the countries).

The danger is that we will continue to increase our demand for energy and, because of this, our rates of production. This would mean that the reserves would not even last as long as these graphs show.

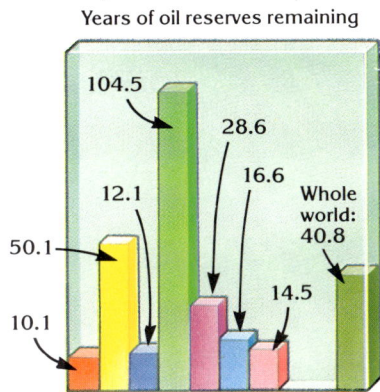

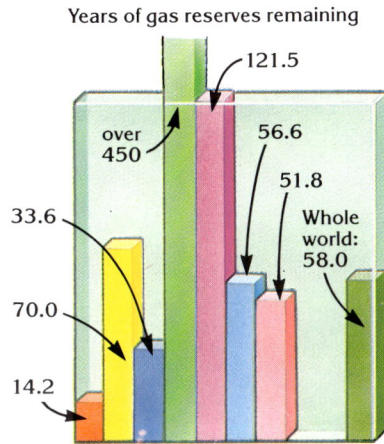

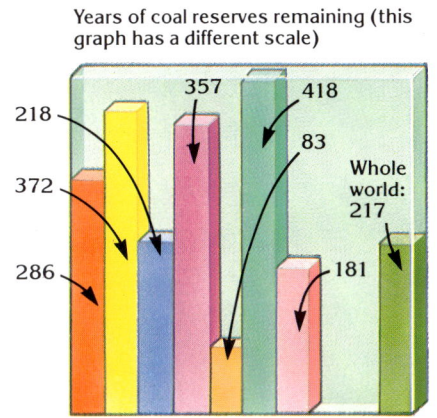

Years of oil reserves remaining

104.5

12.1

28.6

16.6

Whole world: 40.8

50.1

14.5

10.1

Years of gas reserves remaining

121.5

over 450

56.6

51.8

Whole world: 58.0

33.6

70.0

14.2

Years of coal reserves remaining (this graph has a different scale)

218

357

418

83

Whole world: 217

372

286

181

Although more oil, gas or coal may be discovered, we cannot rely on this. We must become much more energy efficient (use less energy in future years), so we can make the reserves last longer. In particular, the countries which use the most energy per head at the moment (see page 138) must drastically reduce their energy use, and help the poor countries build up their industries in the most energy-efficient way.

Another way we can secure enough energy in the future is to develop our use of renewable sources, such as the sun and the wind. This will also help to reduce the environmental damage caused by burning fossil fuels.

### Notes on units and numbers used on these pages

1. One tonne (metric ton) = 1,000 kilograms or 0.98 tons (imperial tons).

2. One barrel = 0.136 tonnes or 42 US gallons (35 imperial gallons).

3. One billion = one thousand million (1,000,000,000) and one trillion = one million million (1,000,000,000,000). These are USA values (in some countries, such as the UK, a billion is one million million, and a trillion is one million million million).

# The economics of energy

There are many costs and benefits involved in the production of energy. Large amounts of money are spent when a power station is built, and also to keep it working. If the power station has been planned properly, though, this expenditure should be balanced, and overtaken, by the amount of money earned from selling the energy, and from other sideline benefits.

There are also hidden costs and benefits involved in producing energy, and these may be difficult to measure in terms of money. People are now becoming more aware of such things as pollution and noise disturbance, and it is important that these factors are also considered. Below you can see these factors included in an economic plan of a refuse-burning power station (see pages 124-125).

Energy is produced in a refuse-burning power station by burning household and commercial refuse (waste). This would otherwise simply be buried in large tips, called landfill sites. An ideal, energy-efficient, refuse-burning power station would also be part of a CHP system (see page 132), so that the hot water it produces is not wasted.

**Other costs (not normally considered)**

Damage to the environment due to the release of gases (such as hydrogen chloride, carbon dioxide and sulphur dioxide), dust and particles of heavy metals (such as mercury and cadmium).

Disturbance to the local community, due to such things as noise, smells, soot and extra traffic.

**Benefits (normally considered)**

Money from selling electricity

Money from the local authority as a payment for taking away its refuse.

Money from selling metals and other materials extracted from the refuse.

Money from selling hot water (produced in the power station) as part of a CHP system (see page 132).

**Costs (normally considered)**

Paying the fees and wages of the architects, engineers and construction workers who designed and built the power station, and the management and workers who operate it.

Buying the land the power station is built on and the materials to build it with.

Buying basic supplies and paying for repairs and new machine parts needed to keep the power station running.

Paying for transport to bring the refuse and other supplies to the power station, and take away the ash.

Other costs, such as insurance, rates and possibly interest payments (extra payments that must be made if money was borrowed to help start up the power station).

**Other benefits (not normally considered)**

The amount of refuse to be buried is reduced to a relatively small amount of ash. This means the landfill site(s) will last longer and transport costs are lower because fewer lorries are needed.

There is less danger of pollution caused by poisonous substances seeping into local water from the landfill site(s).

Up to now, the other, "extra" costs have almost always been ignored during planning, because they are difficult to assess. It is also particularly true of power stations burning fossil fuels that pollution is very much accepted as a fact, and is not seen as a cost. So, from this point of view, there are not really any other "extra" benefits which can be gained from operating in a different way.

To work out the economics of a truly "environment-friendly" power station, the extra costs should be included, as far as possible, in the figures. For example, the release of harmful substances could be greatly reduced by spending more money on anti-pollution devices. So the price of these devices should be put in the "costs" column. It is very important that people begin to plan in this way, so that the true cost of producing energy can be calculated.

# Further information

Below are some addresses of organizations, groups and government offices which are concerned with energy resources and the production, consumption and conservation of energy. They will be able to provide you with further information.

If you want to find out about smaller, local groups that are concerned with energy issues, you could try asking at your local library or writing to the main offices of the organizations listed below, to see if they have local branches.

## International

International Energy Agency,
2, Rue Andre-Pascal,
75775 Paris Cedex 16, France

International Atomic Energy
Authority,
Wagramerstrasse 5,
P.O. Box 100,
A-1400 Vienna, Austria

Friends of the Earth International,
26-28 Underwood Street,
London N1 7JQ, England

Greenpeace International,
Keizersgracht 176,
1016 DW, Amsterdam
The Netherlands

## United Kingdom

National Power,
Sudbury House,
15 Newgate Street,
London EC1A 7AU

Powergen,
53 New Broad Street,
London EC2M 1JJ

Energy Efficiency Office,
1 Palace Street,
London SW1E 5HE

Association for the Conservation of Energy,
9 Sherlock Mews,
London W1M 3RH

UK Atomic Energy Authority,
11 King Charles II Street,
London SW1Y 4QP

National Centre for Alternative
Technology,
Machynlleth,
Powys SY20 9AZ

## United States of America

American Council for an Energy
Efficient Economy,
1001 Connecticut Avenue NW,
Washington DC 20036

Electric Power Research Institute,
3412 Hillview Avenue,
P.O. Box 10412,
Palo Alto,
California 94303

Solar Energy Research Institute,
1617 Cole Boulevard,
Golden,
Colorado 80401

World Resources Institute,
1735 New York Avenue NW,
Washington DC 20006

World Watch Institute,
1776 Massachusetts Avenue NW,
Washington DC 20036

Environmental Defense Fund,
257 Park Avenue South,
New York 10010

## Australia and New Zealand

Energy Information Centre,
139 Flinders Street,
Melbourne 3000,
Victoria

Energy Planning Office,
Energy Information Centre,
222 North Terrace,
Adelaide 5000,
South Australia

State Energy Commission,
465 Wellington Street,
Perth 6000,
Western Australia

## Canada

Atomic Energy of Canada,
344 Slater Street,
Ottawa,
Ontario K1A 0S4

Energy Resources Conservation
Board,
640-5 Avenue S.W.
Calgary,
Alberta T2P 3G4

Energy Probe Research Foundation,
100 College Street,
Toronto,
Ontario M5G 1L5

Department of Energy, Mines and
Resources,
580 Booth Street,
Ottawa,
Ontario K1A 0E4

Ontario Hydro,
700 University Avenue,
Toronto,
Ontario M5G 1X6

Australian Conservation Federation,
672B Glenferrie Road,
Hawthorn 3122,
Victoria

Victorian Solar Energy Council,
10th Floor,
270 Flinders Street,
Melbourne 3000,
Victoria

Ministry of Energy,
P.O. Box 2337,
Wellington,
New Zealand

# Glossary

**Atoms.** The "building blocks" of all substances. They are very tiny particles, each one made up of even tinier particles called **protons**, **neutrons** and **electrons**. The different amounts of these determine what substance the atom is.

**Biogas.** Gas produced by rotting material such as animal manure and other farm, household and industrial waste. The gas contains **methane** and can be used as a fuel to heat buildings or generate electricity.

**Biomass.** All types of organic (animal or plant) material. Biomass is a store of energy, which can be converted into other types of energy, e.g. wood, straw or animal dung can be burnt to produce heat and light energy.

**Chemical energy.** Energy stored in a substance and released during a chemical reaction. Fuels such as wood, coal, oil and food all contain chemical energy. The reaction when they are burnt (or digested) releases the energy, e.g. as heat and light energy.

**Conductor.** A material through which heat or an electric current can flow easily. Copper and iron are both good conductors.

**Conservation of energy.** When energy changes from one form to another (e.g. when fuel burns), the total amount of energy before the change is always the same as the total amount of energy after the change. The energy is always conserved. It cannot be destroyed.

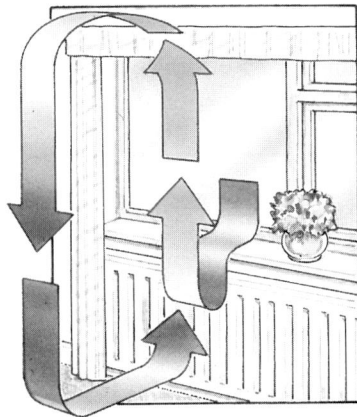

**Convection.** One way that heat travels through a liquid or gas. When heated, the **molecules** near the heat source gain more energy, moving faster and further apart. The heated liquid or gas then moves upwards, because it is now less dense and lighter. Cooler liquid or gas, with more densely-packed molecules, sinks to take its place.

**Distillation.** The process of separating a mixture of liquids by heating. The different liquids evaporate at different temperatures, the one with the lowest boiling point evaporating first. The separated gases are condensed back into liquids by cooling.

**Dynamo.** A machine which changes **kinetic energy** into electrical energy.

**Electromagnetic energy.** Energy which travels in waves, such as ultra-violet radiation. It can be thought of as a combination of electric and magnetic energy.

**Electromagnetism.** The effect whereby a magnetic field is produced around a wire when an electric current is passed through the wire. Electromagnets (see pages 119 and 120) use this principle.

**Electromotive force.** The force needed to drive an electric current in an electric circuit. It is measured in volts.

**Electrons.** Particles which form part of an **atom**. They move around its **nucleus**.

**Fission.** The splitting up of the **nucleus** of a heavy **atom** into two (or more) lighter nuclei. It releases huge amounts of energy.

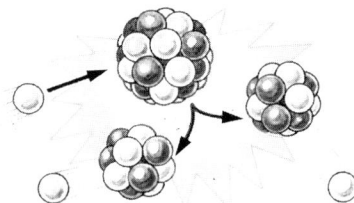

**Fossil fuels.** Fuels which result from the compression of the remains of living matter over millions of years. Coal, oil and natural gas are all fossil fuels.

**Friction.** The resistance between two touching surfaces (or one surface and the air) when they move over each other. This slows down the moving object(s). Some of the kinetic energy changes into other types of energy.

**Fusion.** The joining together (fusing) of the **nuclei** of two or more **atoms** into one heavier nucleus. It releases vast amounts of energy.

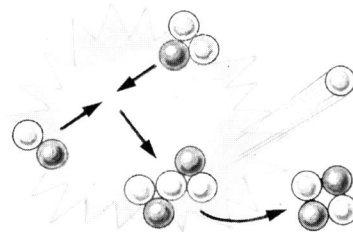

**Generator.** A device which turns **mechanical energy** into electricity. The mechanical energy may be provided by an engine or a **turbine**.

**Geothermal energy.** The heat energy which is produced by natural processes inside the Earth. It can be extracted from hot springs, reservoirs of hot water deep below the ground or by breaking open the rock itself.

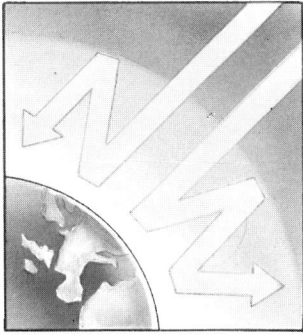

**Greenhouse effect**. The warming effect produced when radiation cannot escape to the atmosphere or space. A good example is what happens in a greenhouse (hence the name). Short-wave radiation from the sun penetrates the glass of the greenhouse, and is absorbed by the plants, but the long-wave radiation that the plants emit cannot get back out through the glass. Carbon dioxide and other gases in the atmosphere act like the greenhouse glass. The levels of these gases are increasing, so the climate is slowly getting warmer (called global warming).

**Grid system**. A network of cables which carry electricity from power stations, where it is produced, to the cities, towns and villages of a country.

**Hydrocarbons**. Chemical compounds which contain only carbon and hydrogen **atoms**. They are the dominant compounds in **fossil fuels**.

**Hydro-electricity**. Electricity which is produced from moving water. In a typical hydro-electric power station, the water turns **turbines**, which are attached to **generators**.

**Insulator**. A bad **conductor**, e.g. wood or plastic. These substances slow down the progress of electricity or heat energy.

**Joule (J)**. The unit of measurement of energy. One thousand joules equals one kilojoule (kJ). Kilojoules are normally used in measurements, since measured quantities are usually at least a thousand joules.

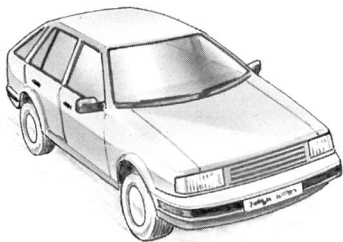

**Kinetic energy**. The energy of movement. The faster an object moves, the more kinetic energy it has. Also, the more mass a moving object has, the more kinetic energy it has.

**Methane**. A gas (a **hydrocarbon**) which is produced by organic (plant and animal) matter when it rots in the absence of oxygen. Natural gas is mainly methane.

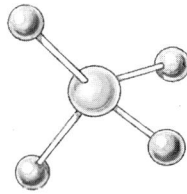

**Molecules**. Particles which normally consist of two or more **atoms** joined together, e.g. a water molecule is made up of two hydrogen atoms and one oxygen atom.

**Neutrons**. Particles which form part of the **nucleus** of an atom (**protons** make up the rest of the nucleus).

**Nucleus** (pl. **nuclei**). The central part of an **atom**, made up of tightly-packed **protons** and **neutrons**.

**Photosynthesis**. The process by which green plants make food (carbohydrates) from water and carbon dioxide, using the energy in sunlight. The food is a store of **chemical energy** inside the plants.

**Photovoltaic cell**. Another name for a **solar cell**.

**Potential energy**. Energy that is stored in an object due to its being within the influence of a force field, e.g. a magnetic or gravitational field.

**Power**. The rate at which energy is produced or used. It is generally stated as the rate of doing work or the rate of change of energy. Power is measured in watts (W). One watt equals one **joule** per second.

**Protons**. Particles which form part of the **nucleus** of an atom. The other particles in the nucleus are **neutrons**.

**Radioactivity**. A property of the **atoms** of certain substances, due to the fact that their **nuclei** are unstable. They give out energy in the form of particles or waves.

**Reactor**. Part of a nuclear power station – the structure inside which **fission** occurs in millions of atomic **nuclei**, producing vast amounts of heat energy.

**Renewable energy**. Energy from sources which are constantly available in the natural world, such as wind, water or the sun.

**Solar cell**. A device, usually made from silicon, which converts some of the energy in sunlight directly into electricity.

**Turbine**. A device with blades, which is turned by a force, e.g. that of wind, water or high pressure steam. The **kinetic energy** of the spinning turbine is converted into electricity in a **generator**.

# WEATHER & CLIMATE

Fiona Watt and Francis Wilson, Television Weatherman

Edited by Corinne Stockley

Designed by Paul Greenleaf

Illustrated by Kuo Kang Chen, Peter Dennis and Denise Finney

Additional designs by Stephen Wright

# Contents

147     About this book
148     Planetary weather
150     Heating the Earth
152     Pressure and winds
154     Moving air
156     Clouds
158     Water in the air
160     Highs, lows and fronts
162     Thunderstorms and hurricanes
164     Extreme weather conditions
166     Local weather
168     Monitoring the weather
170     Your own weather station
172     Analysing information
174     Weather forecasts
176     Worldwide climate
178     People and climate
180     Changing climates
182     Present-day climate changes
184     Pollution in the atmosphere
186     Predicting future weather
188     Record weather extremes
190     Glossary

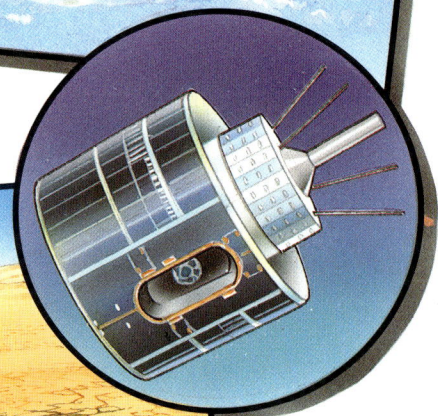

We are extremely grateful to the following organizations for their co-operation and assistance, and for the advice and up-to-date information they provided:

BBC Breakfast Time, Television Centre, Wood Lane, London W12 7RJ, The British Meteorological Office, London Road, Bracknell, Berkshire, RG12 2SY and

The London Weather Centre, 284-286 High Holborn, London WC1V 7HX.

# About this book

From pleasant sunny days to devastating storms, the weather is part of daily life for everyone in the world. This book explains how many of the different elements of the atmosphere combine to produce different types of weather. It also describes how different weather conditions produce the wide variety of climates which are found throughout the world.

The book examines the ways in which the weather is monitored all over the world, and the processes involved in gathering information in order to make accurate forecasts. It explores how climates have changed since the Earth was first formed, and what effect current environmental problems may have on the atmosphere, weather and climates in the future.

## Activities and projects

Special boxes like this one are used throughout the book for activities, projects and experiments. They will help you to understand the principles of different kinds of weather and its formation. You should be able to find most of the necessary equipment at home, but you may need to go to a hardware shop to buy a few of the items.

## Using the glossary

The glossary on pages 190-191 is a useful reference point. It gives detailed explanations of the more complex terms used in the book, as well as introducing some new words.

This scene shows a tropical cyclone, or hurricane. Hurricane winds can cause serious damage to buildings and trees and also create gigantic waves which crash onto shores. To find out more about hurricanes and how they are formed, see pages 162-163.

# Planetary weather

The Earth is one of a group of planets which make up the Solar System. Each planet is surrounded by a mixture of different gases which is called its atmosphere. The weather on each planet depends on its distance from the Sun and the movements of the gases in its atmosphere.

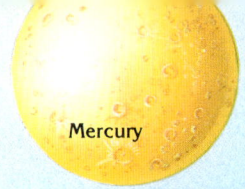

Mercury

## The Sun

The Sun sends out energy in the form of rays of heat and light called radiation. The amount of heat and light energy which reaches the planets in the Solar System depends on their distance from the Sun.

## The Sun's radiation

The Sun's radiation is made up of rays of different strengths of energy. Relatively speaking, they are all high-energy rays, but some are stronger than others. Some of these rays give us light, and they all heat up anything which absorbs them. Certain gases in the thermosphere and ozone in the stratosphere (see page 149) absorb some of the highest energy radiation (which is harmful). Clouds also absorb or reflect some of it. However, most of the Sun's radiation reaches the Earth's surface, where it is absorbed by the land or sea, or is reflected.

As it absorbs high energy radiation, the Earth warms up, and sends out lower energy radiation into the atmosphere Some of this radiation escapes into space, but some is absorbed by gases in the atmosphere, such as carbon dioxide. These gases then send out slightly lower energy radiation in all directions. Some of this reaches the Earth's surface where it is absorbed and again heats the surface.

High energy radiation from the Sun (solar radiation).

Most harmful radiation is absorbed by gases in the thermosphere and stratosphere (see page 149).

Some radiation is absorbed by, or reflected from clouds. Some is reflected from the Earth's surface (see page 151).

Most of the high energy solar radiation is absorbed by the Earth's surface, which is heated.

Earth's surface

The warmed Earth gives off lower energy radiation. Some is absorbed by gases in the lowest layer of atmosphere.

These gases send out radiation in all directions.

Some radiation returns to the Earth's surface which again absorbs it and is heated.

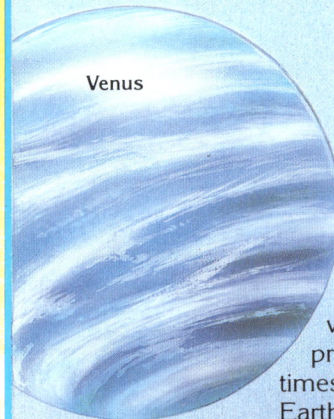

## Weather on different planets

Scientists have used information from space probes to work out what the weather may be like on other planets. The atmosphere of each planet in the Solar System is held to the planet by gravity and pushes down on its surface. This is called atmospheric pressure (known as air pressure on Earth). The planets have different atmospheric gases and pressures, which greatly affect the weather found on each one. The examples below are the planets nearest to the Earth.

Venus

### Weather on Venus

On Venus, the atmosphere is very dense, with pressure over 90 times greater than on Earth. The planet's atmosphere is mainly made up of carbon dioxide, which is very good at trapping heat. This makes temperatures as high as 475°C (887°F).

The Earth takes about 24 hours (a day) to rotate all the way round once.

Venus takes 243 Earth days to rotate.

Venus is surrounded by thick clouds containing droplets of sulphuric acid. These droplets may sometimes fall as rain, but they evaporate before reaching the ground and form clouds again. There are also continuous lightning storms.

The Earth

The Moon

## The Moon

The Moon is not a planet, but a satellite of the Earth. A satellite is any object in space which travels around, or orbits, a larger object such as a planet. Other moons orbit other planets. Mars, for instance, has two moons, and Jupiter has sixteen.

There is no water, wind and weather on the Moon, and it is covered with dust. There is also no atmosphere surrounding it, because the Moon's force of gravity is so weak that any gases cannot be held to its surface.

## Mars

The atmosphere on Mars is very thin with very low pressure. It is mainly made up of carbon dioxide with some nitrogen. There is no water on the surface, but there are areas of ice at the north and south poles. Temperatures are very low: -29°C (-20°F) during the day, falling to -85°C (-121°F) at night.

**From Mars, the sky appears to be pink. This is caused by dust from the red, rocky surface being blown into the air by strong winds.**

## Jupiter

Jupiter's atmosphere appears to be a mass of swirling gases, which surround a solid centre, or core. The gases are thought to be hydrogen and helium. Temperatures on the planet are thought to be very low, not rising above -130°C (-200°F).

**The Great Red Spot on the surface of Jupiter's atmosphere is thought to be a massive storm.**

# The Earth's atmosphere

The Earth's atmosphere is divided into layers (see below) according to temperature, although there are no solid boundaries separating each layer. The Earth is the only planet in the Solar System which has large amounts of water, both in its atmosphere, and on or below its surface.

The magnetosphere is the uppermost layer. It contains no gases, but forms a barrier which stops many particles from space entering the Earth's atmosphere. Most weather satellites (see page 169) are found way up beyond this layer.

The air in the exosphere is extremely thin as it contains very few gases. The top of this layer is about 900km (560 miles) from the ground. Some polar orbiting weather satellites (see page 169) are found in this layer.

The thermosphere contains gases which absorb some of the harmful solar radiation, and so heat up this layer. The temperature at the top, which is about 450km (280 miles) from the ground, may be as high as 2000°C (3632°F), but it decreases as you go down.

The mesosphere reaches a height of about 80km (50 miles). It is coldest at the top, about -100°C (-148°F), but warms up towards the bottom because of the warmer stratosphere below.

The top of the stratosphere is about 50km (31 miles) from the ground. Ozone gas forms a separate layer within it. This absorbs some of the Sun's harmful rays, heating up the layer. The temperature is highest at the top, about 0°C (32°F), cooling down towards the troposphere below. Jet aircraft fly here, where the air is still, or stable.

The troposphere varies in height between 10km (6 miles) and 20km (12 miles). Its lowest temperature is at the top, about -50°C (-58°F), but the air warms up the nearer you get to the surface. All the things which combine to make our weather are found in this layer.

Earth's surface

# Heating the Earth

The way that the Sun's rays strike the surface of the Earth is important in determining the temperature of an area. In turn, the amount of heat received by any given area has a direct influence on the weather, as it affects the temperature of the air lying immediately above it.

## The Sun's heat and the seasons

Not all places on the Earth's surface receive the same amount of heat from the Sun. The Earth is tilted at an angle, and its surface is curved, so the parallel rays of the Sun strike some areas full on, and others at more oblique angles.

As the Earth travels around the Sun in its orbit, the effect of its tilt is gradually to change the area which receives the most direct heat. At the start of each orbit, one hemisphere is tilted towards the Sun. After half the orbit (6 months later), the opposite hemisphere is in that position. The change in temperature due to this effect causes the seasons.

Near the equator, the seasons do not have great differences in temperature. The Sun's rays strike almost full-on all year round, so the temperature remains high.

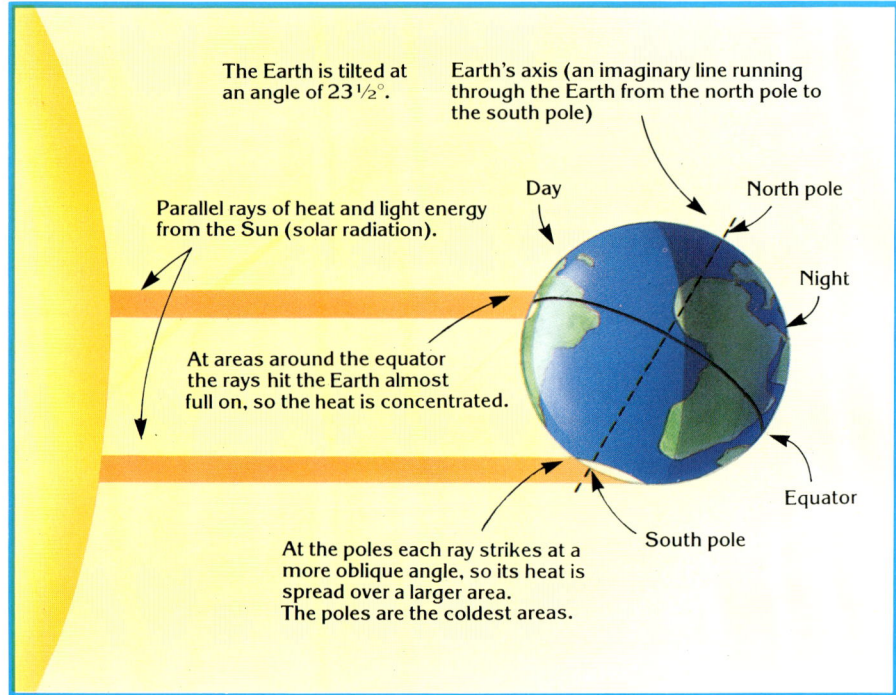

The Earth is tilted at an angle of 23½°.

Earth's axis (an imaginary line running through the Earth from the north pole to the south pole)

Day

North pole

Parallel rays of heat and light energy from the Sun (solar radiation).

Night

At areas around the equator the rays hit the Earth almost full on, so the heat is concentrated.

Equator

South pole

At the poles each ray strikes at a more oblique angle, so its heat is spread over a larger area. The poles are the coldest areas.

The further away from the equator a place is, the lower its summer and winter temperatures in comparison with places at the equator.

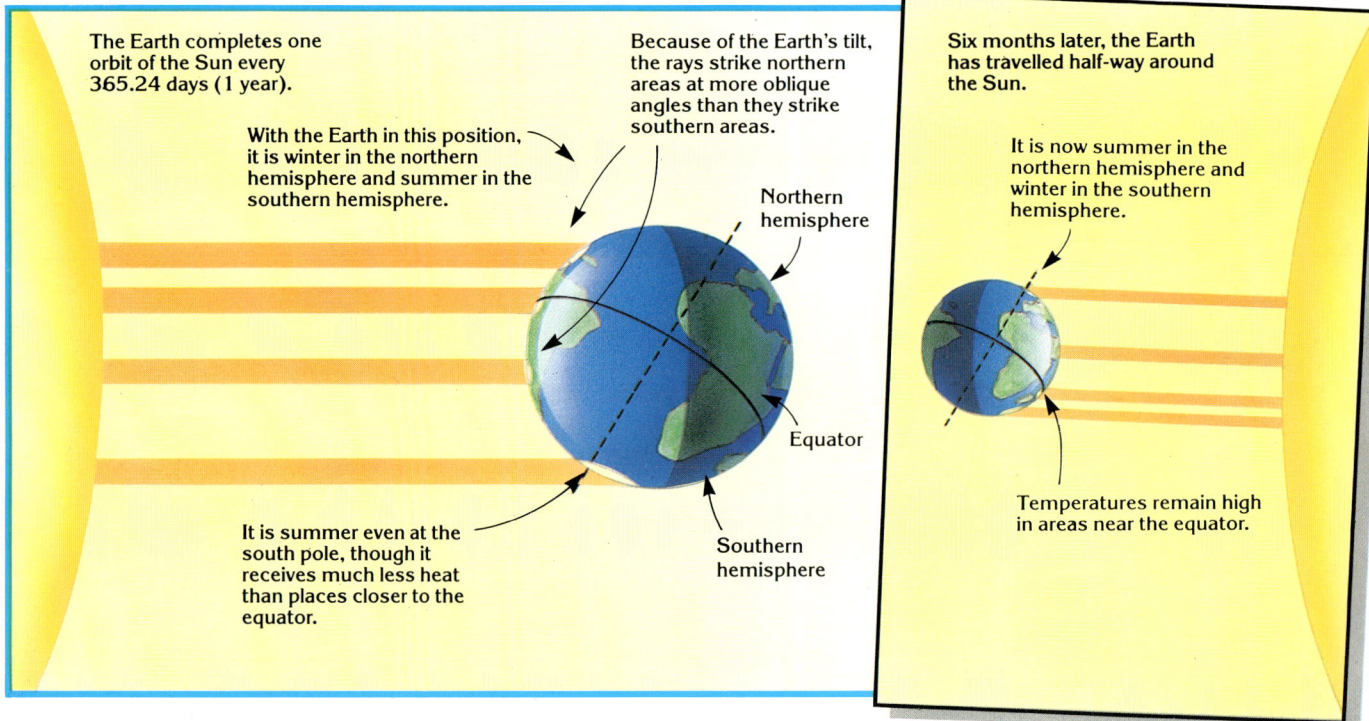

The Earth completes one orbit of the Sun every 365.24 days (1 year).

With the Earth in this position, it is winter in the northern hemisphere and summer in the southern hemisphere.

Because of the Earth's tilt, the rays strike northern areas at more oblique angles than they strike southern areas.

Northern hemisphere

Equator

It is summer even at the south pole, though it receives much less heat than places closer to the equator.

Southern hemisphere

Six months later, the Earth has travelled half-way around the Sun.

It is now summer in the northern hemisphere and winter in the southern hemisphere.

Temperatures remain high in areas near the equator.

## Surface temperatures

As well as some places receiving more solar radiation than others, there are also differences in the amount of this radiation which is absorbed by different surfaces. Forests, sand and bare soil absorb more radiation than surfaces such as snow and ice, which reflect most of it. The temperature of the air in contact with a surface depends on the temperature of that surface.

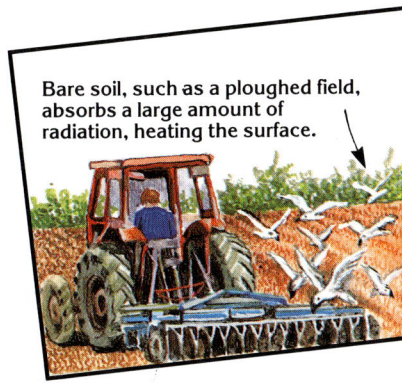

Bare soil, such as a ploughed field, absorbs a large amount of radiation, heating the surface.

Snow and ice absorb very little solar radiation. Most of it is reflected into the atmosphere.

Air temperatures remain low.

## A bottle fountain

A bottle fountain shows how heated air expands. To make one, you will need a glass bottle with a plastic screw-top, a corkscrew, some food colouring, a straw, some sticky putty* and a needle.

### What to do

1. Make a hole in the bottle top using a corkscrew (be careful with the sharp point).

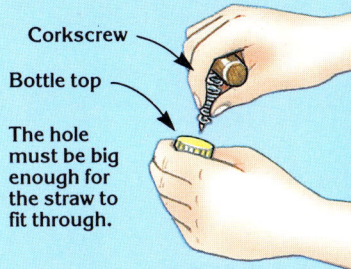

Corkscrew

Bottle top

The hole must be big enough for the straw to fit through.

Food colouring

Bottle

Water

2. Half fill the bottle with cold water. Add a few drops of food colouring.

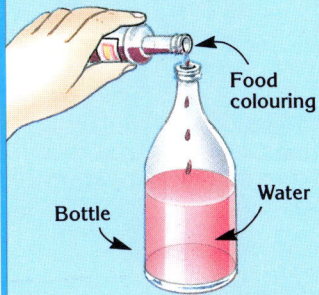

Needle

Hole

Sticky putty

Straw

Bottle

Make sure the end is in the water.

3. Screw the top tightly onto the bottle. Push the straw through the hole and seal around it with some sticky putty. Make a plug of sticky putty in the top of the straw. Use a needle to pierce a hole down through the plug.

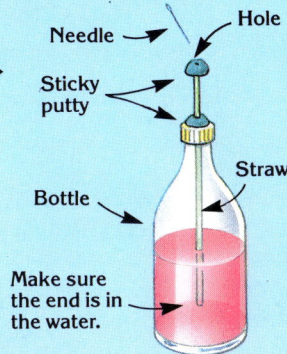

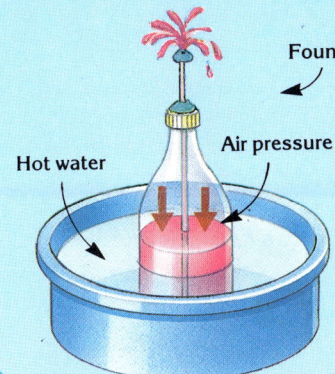

Fountain

Hot water

Air pressure

4. Carefully put the bottle in a deep bowl of very hot water. As the air in the bottle is heated, it expands and pushes down on the water, forcing water out of the straw.

## Air temperatures

The Earth's surface is mainly heated by the absorption of solar radiation (see page 148). Where areas of the surface are warmer than the layer of air immediately above them, this air is heated.

Warmed air expands, becomes less dense and rises. Surrounding cooler air moves in to replace the rising warm air. The warm air cools as it rises, becomes denser again and eventually stops rising. It sinks back to Earth, where it may be heated again if the surface is still warmer than the air above. This circulation of warm and cold currents of air is called convection, and the currents are convection currents.

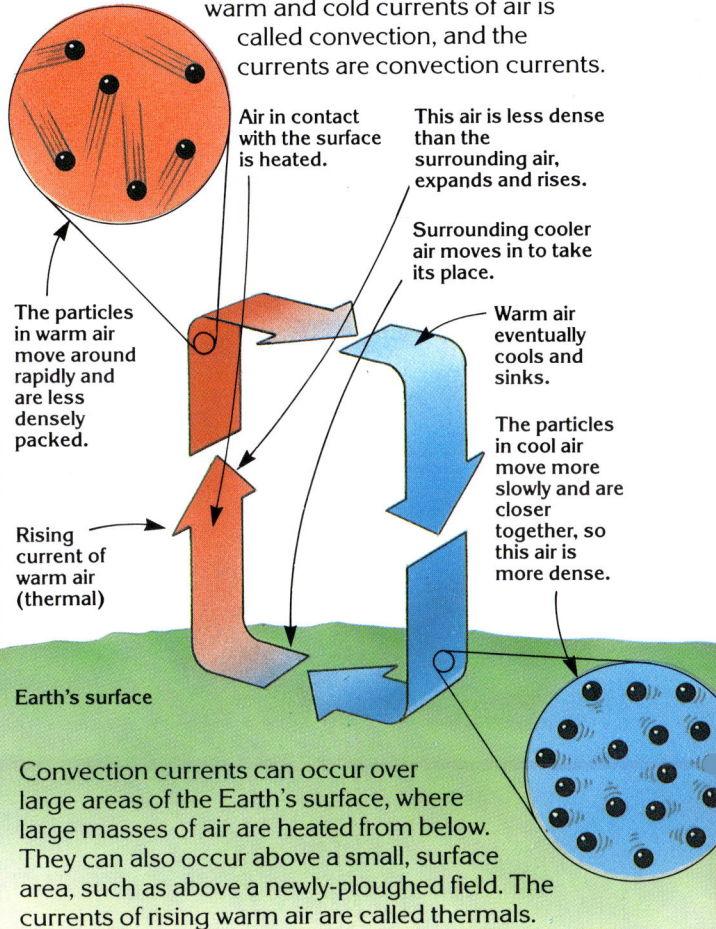

Air in contact with the surface is heated.

This air is less dense than the surrounding air, expands and rises.

Surrounding cooler air moves in to take its place.

Warm air eventually cools and sinks.

The particles in warm air move around rapidly and are less densely packed.

The particles in cool air move more slowly and are closer together, so this air is more dense.

Rising current of warm air (thermal)

Earth's surface

Convection currents can occur over large areas of the Earth's surface, where large masses of air are heated from below. They can also occur above a small, surface area, such as above a newly-ploughed field. The currents of rising warm air are called thermals.

* Sticky putty is used for sticking paper or posters to walls.

# Pressure and winds

The pressure of the air on the Earth's surface is different in different places. This is partly due to the different amounts of heat they receive. Pressure differences cause the movement of air (winds).

Air pressure also decreases with altitude (height above sea level), because there is a greater amount of air pushing down on the surface at sea level than higher up, for instance on a mountain.

## Differences in air pressure

When air rises, it leaves behind an area of lower pressure, because the upward-moving air is not pressing down so hard on the surface. Areas of high pressure are formed where air is sinking back down, and so pushing down harder.

If a pressure difference exists, air moves from the higher to the lower pressure area, in order to even out the pressure.

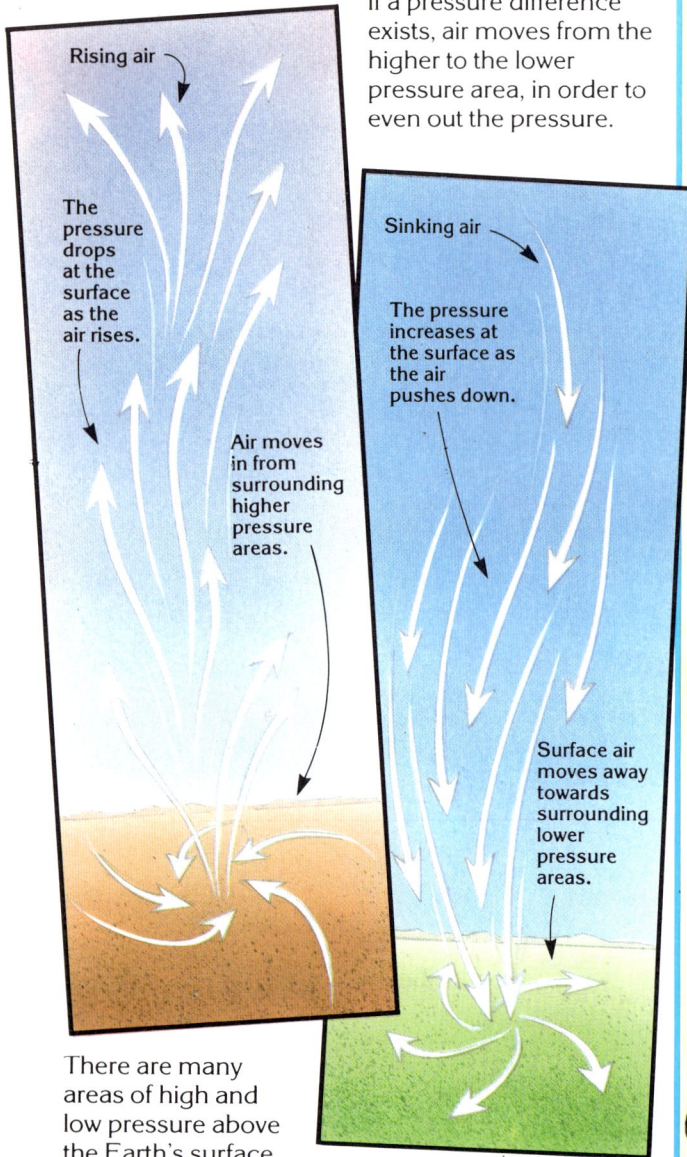

Rising air

The pressure drops at the surface as the air rises.

Air moves in from surrounding higher pressure areas.

Sinking air

The pressure increases at the surface as the air pushes down.

Surface air moves away towards surrounding lower pressure areas.

There are many areas of high and low pressure above the Earth's surface, due to such things as uneven surface heating. Air moves between these, forming surface winds.

## Measuring air pressure

Air pressure is measured in millibars* on a barometer. You can make a model barometer using a large, narrow, plastic bottle, two rubber bands, some cardboard and some water.

### What to do

1. Cut a 2.5cm (1in) strip of thin cardboard and draw a scale along one edge. Attach the cardboard to the bottle using the rubber bands.

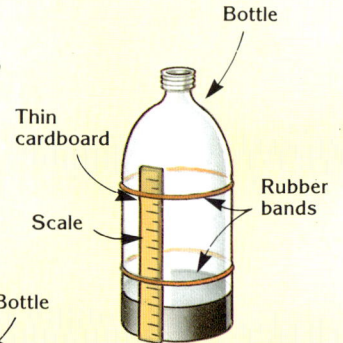

Bottle

Thin cardboard

Rubber bands

Scale

Try not to get the scale wet

Bottle

Bowl    Water

2. Fill the bottle with water so it is three quarters full. Also fill the bowl nearly to the top with water.

3. Place your hand over the top of the bottle and turn it upside-down. Put your hand into the bowl so that the neck of the bottle is under the water. Remove your hand from under the bottle and stand it in the bowl.

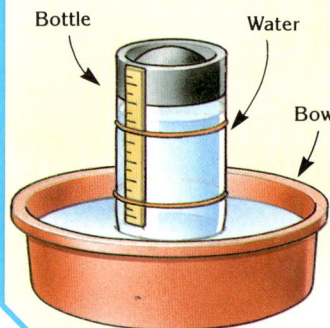

Turn the bottle over carefully.

Try not to let any water out.

Bottle    Water

Bowl

4. The water level in the bottle will rise and fall with the air pressure, as more or less air pushes down on the water in the bowl.

Mark the water level on the day you make your barometer (you could find out what the air pressure is, and write this too).

# Major pressure areas of the world

Around the Earth, there are several major bands where high or low pressure predominates (although in each band individual areas of different pressure may occur - see page 154). There is a general pattern of air movement from the high to the low pressure areas.

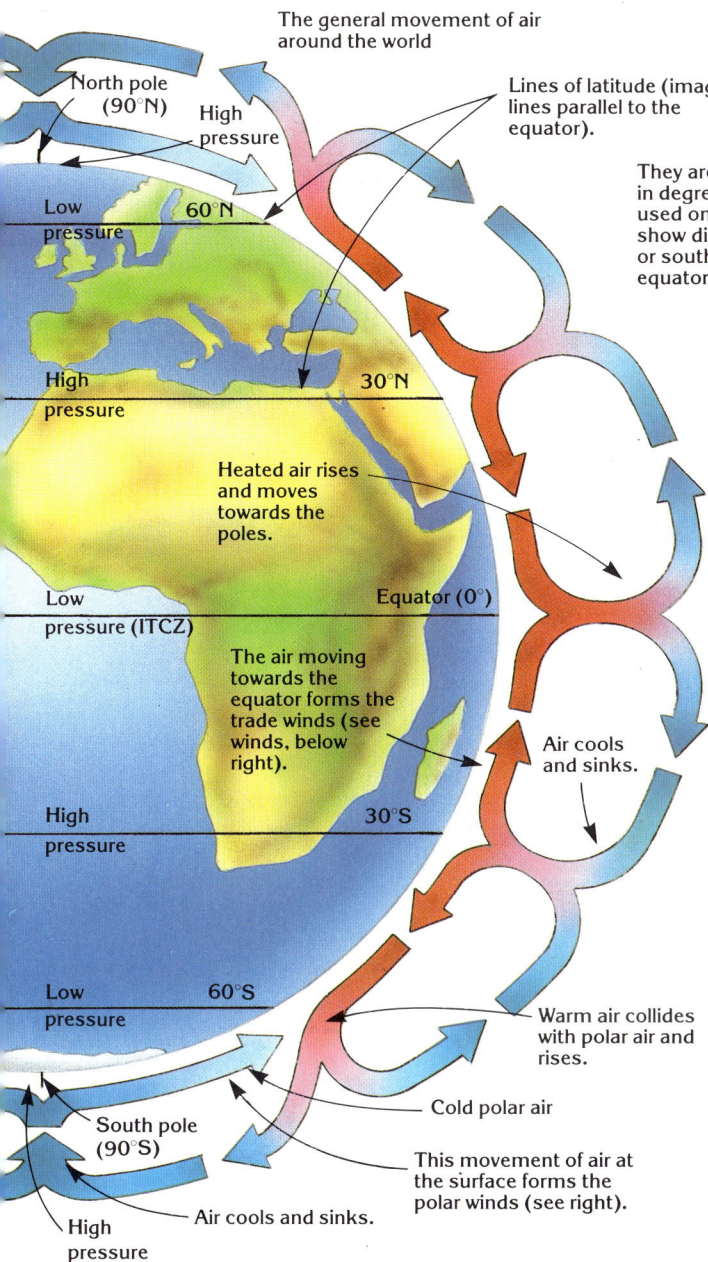

The Earth's surface receives the most solar radiation around the equator. The land greatly heats up the air immediately above it, and this vast amount of air rises, leaving a band of predominately low pressure, called the Intertropical Convergence Zone (ITCZ), at the surface. This sets up all other air movements.

The general movement of air around the world

North pole (90°N)

High pressure

Lines of latitude (imaginary lines parallel to the equator).

They are measured in degrees and are used on maps to show distance north or south of the equator.

Low pressure    60°N

High pressure    30°N

Heated air rises and moves towards the poles.

Low pressure (ITCZ)    Equator (0°)

The air moving towards the equator forms the trade winds (see winds, below right).

Air cools and sinks.

High pressure    30°S

Low pressure    60°S

Warm air collides with polar air and rises.

Cold polar air

South pole (90°S)

This movement of air at the surface forms the polar winds (see right).

Air cools and sinks.

High pressure

The warm air rising above the equator spreads out and cools, sinking around latitudes 30° north and south of the equator. The sinking air pushes down on the surface, creating a band of high pressure, so when it reaches the surface, the air moves north and south towards areas of lower pressure.

## The Coriolis effect

When air moves from high pressure to low pressure, the winds do not take the most direct possible route. They "try" to, but are deflected sideways. This is due to the rotating movement of the Earth, and is called the Coriolis effect.

The forces involved have the effect of deflecting the winds in the northern hemisphere to the right of their "intended" direction, and those in the southern hemisphere to the left. The Coriolis effect acts on the world's main air movements (see left) to determine the directions of the world's main winds.

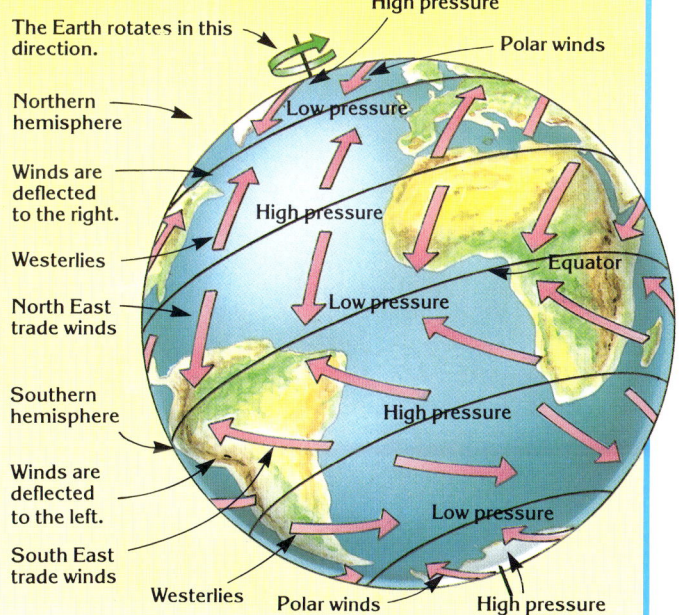

The world's main winds

The Earth rotates in this direction.

High pressure

Polar winds

Low pressure

Northern hemisphere

Winds are deflected to the right.

High pressure

Westerlies

North East trade winds

Low pressure

Southern hemisphere

High pressure

Winds are deflected to the left.

South East trade winds

Equator

Low pressure

Westerlies    Polar winds    High pressure

At about 60°N and 60°S, cold air moving away from the poles meets the warmer air from nearer the equator. The warmer air is less dense and is forced to rise, forming areas of low pressure at the surface. This air cools and sinks again around the poles, forming a band of high pressure.

# Moving air

The air around the world is on the move all the time. The main high and low pressure bands (see page 153) set up the general, long-term pattern of air movements. However, individual, small or very large high and low pressure areas are also constantly being created over different places on the surface. This causes surface movements of air (winds) between them. On any particular day, these may blow in a different, even opposing, direction to the main, general movement of the air.

## Pressure differences

The creation of different highs and lows in different places is mainly due to fast high-level winds which blow around the Earth in the direction of its spin (from west to east). The strongest ones travel around at high levels roughly above 60°N and 60°S where the high-level polar air is met by warmer air (see page 153). There are also weaker ones at 30°N and 30°S.

The strong winds follow wavy paths, formed because the warmer air makes more progress towards the pole over some areas than others. The winds travel fastest where the warm air pushes the greatest distance into the polar air, so they have uneven speeds, slowing down and speeding up as they travel. At their fastest they are called jet streams.

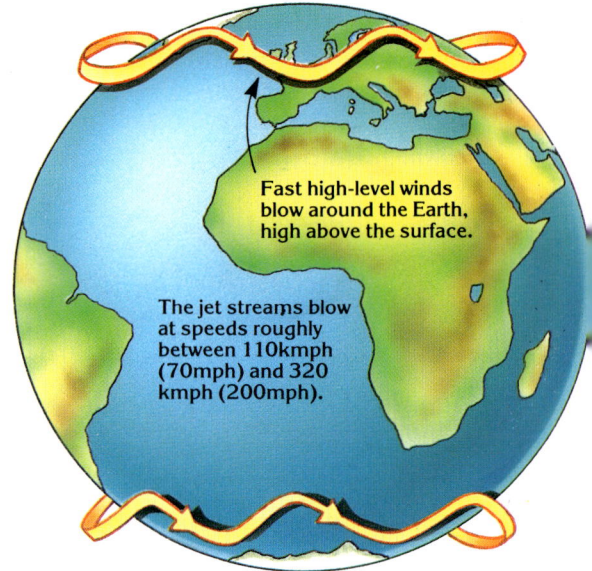

Fast high-level winds blow around the Earth, high above the surface.

The jet streams blow at speeds roughly between 110kmph (70mph) and 320 kmph (200mph).

The wavy paths (see below) and uneven speeds of the winds disrupt the air around and below them. In some areas, the air gets squashed together, so some gets pushed down, creating higher pressure at the surface. In others, the air thins out, so underlying air moves up to to fill up the space, creating lower surface pressure.

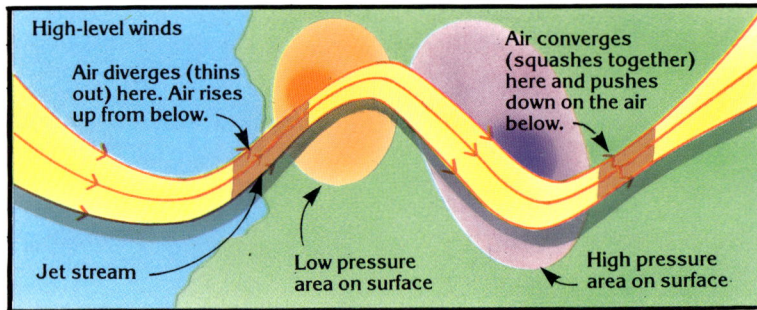

High-level winds

Air diverges (thins out) here. Air rises up from below.

Air converges (squashes together) here and pushes down on the air below.

Jet stream

Low pressure area on surface

High pressure area on surface

Because the air is disrupted, low pressure areas may form in a general high pressure band, and vice versa. The air which then moves in or away to even up the pressure may move in a different direction to the general pattern. This is because these closer pressure differences have the strongest influence.

All these air movements have a "knock-on" effect. Air becomes disrupted elsewhere, and this leads to the irregular day-to-day pattern of air movements around the globe.

## Moving areas of pressure

Surface winds are always blowing from the centres of high pressure areas towards the centres of low pressure ones, but, in addition, these centres themselves are also moving. Having been created over one particular place on the Earth's surface, they are moved around by the high-level winds above them.

As the centres move, they influence each other. The closer they are, the greater this influence. If the pressure difference between a high pressure centre and its surroundings is not that great, the air moving out of the high does not move very fast. So high pressure areas, with no other influences, have slow surface winds.

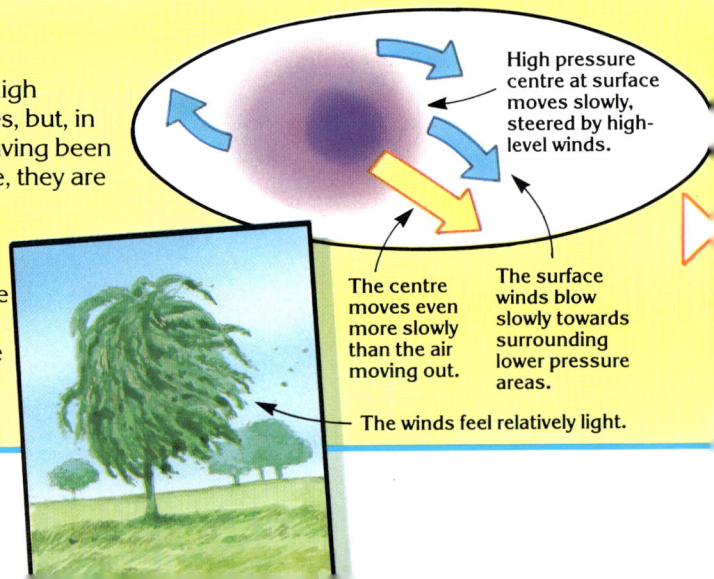

High pressure centre at surface moves slowly, steered by high-level winds.

The centre moves even more slowly than the air moving out.

The surface winds blow slowly towards surrounding lower pressure areas.

The winds feel relatively light.

## Temperature and humidity

A mass of air may be warmer or colder, drier or more humid (contain more water vapour) than the air in the area it moves into. If so, it will bring a change of weather with it. Its characteristics depend on where it has come from and the type of surface it has travelled over, but also on its speed. Slow-moving air has more time to be affected by the surfaces it passes over.

Air temperature is influenced by surface temperatures. At places such as the poles and the equator, these are obviously very different, but they may also differ in areas which are quite close. One reason for this may be the different types of land which the Sun's rays fall on (see page 151), another that the areas are land and sea. At different times (in a daily cycle or a longer seasonal one), the sea may be warmer than the land, or vice versa.

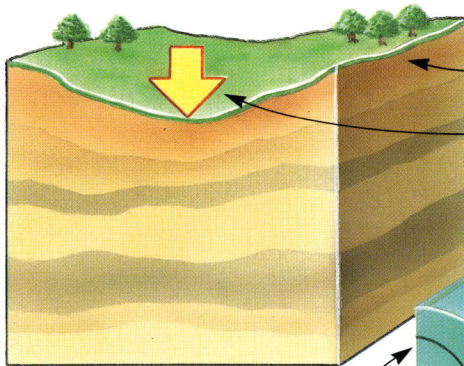

Land heats up quickly, because just the surface is heated.

Sun heats land only to a shallow depth.

This means it cools down quickly as well.

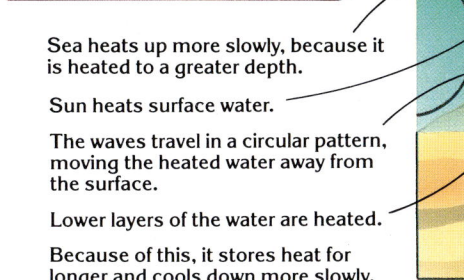

Sea heats up more slowly, because it is heated to a greater depth.

Sun heats surface water.

The waves travel in a circular pattern, moving the heated water away from the surface.

Lower layers of the water are heated.

Because of this, it stores heat for longer and cools down more slowly.

The humidity of a mass of air is greater if it is travelling over the sea, as water evaporates from the sea into the air. Air which has travelled far over land tends to contain little water vapour.

## Classifying air masses

Air masses are classified according to the area they originally came from, called their source.

Air masses which form over seas and oceans are called maritime (m) air masses.

A tropical maritime (mT) air mass develops over warm seas. It is warm and moist.

A polar maritime (mP) air mass forms over the sea near the poles. It is cold and moist.

Continental (c) air masses form over land.

A tropical continental (cT) air mass develops over hot, dry land. It is warm and dry.

Polar continental (cP) air masses develop over land near the poles. They are cold and dry.

If a high pressure centre is close to a low pressure centre, though, the pressure difference between the two areas is more acute, and the air moves faster. The larger the pressure difference, the faster the air will move, so the stronger the surface winds.

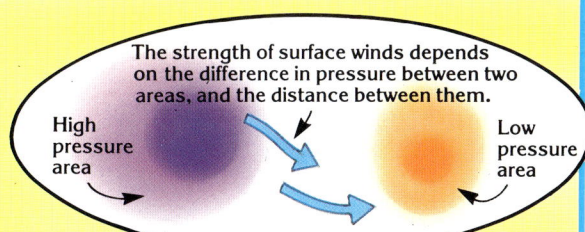

The strength of surface winds depends on the difference in pressure between two areas, and the distance between them.

High pressure area

Low pressure area

The closer two areas of different pressures are, the faster the winds will blow between them.

Strong winds mean a large pressure difference. The air moves to even it out.

# Clouds

Clouds are made up of millions of tiny droplets of water or ice crystals, formed when air is cooled. Clouds are formed in several ways and are named according to their shape, height and size. They help to forecast the type of weather which may follow. They are often associated with precipitation (rain, snow, sleet or hail), but not all clouds lead to this kind of weather.

## Water vapour

Water is found in the air as an invisible gas called water vapour. This is formed when water in rivers, lakes, seas and oceans is heated. The heat makes the water evaporate (turn into vapour), and it rises into the air. The humidity of the air is the amount of water vapour it contains.

The humidity of the air varies from place to place and with temperature. When air can hold no more water vapour it is said to be saturated.

The very hot air in tropical areas (see pages 176-177) often holds a large amount of water vapour.

The air here is said to be very humid or "sticky".

## How clouds are formed

Air contains millions of microscopic particles of dust. When moist air rises, expands and cools, any water vapour it contains condenses (turns back into a liquid) onto the surface of the particles. This forms minute water droplets which group together to make clouds. The temperature at which this happens is called the dew point. If the cloud temperature falls below freezing, the water droplets freeze to form ice crystals.

There are several reasons why air rises and clouds are formed.

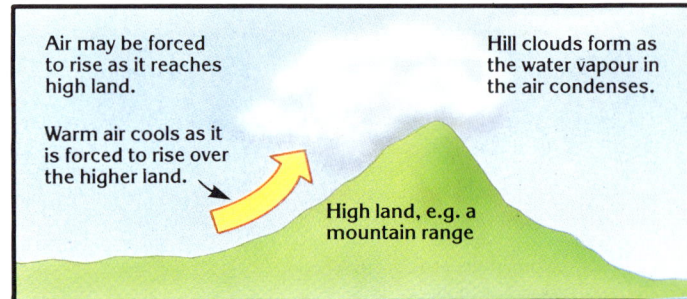

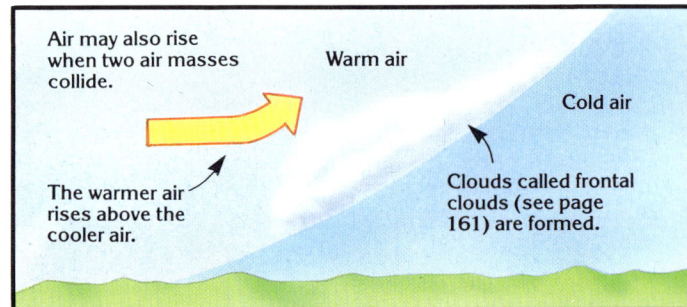

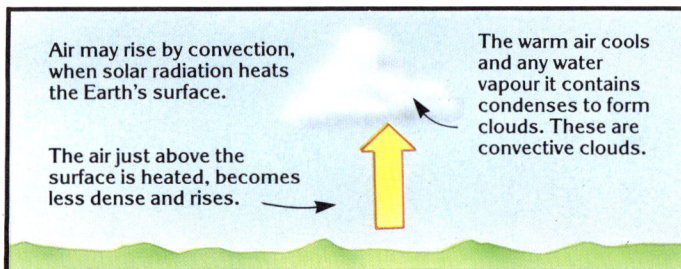

Air may be forced to rise as it reaches high land.

Hill clouds form as the water vapour in the air condenses.

Warm air cools as it is forced to rise over the higher land.

High land, e.g. a mountain range

Air may rise by convection, when solar radiation heats the Earth's surface.

The warm air cools and any water vapour it contains condenses to form clouds. These are convective clouds.

The air just above the surface is heated, becomes less dense and rises.

Air may also rise when two air masses collide.

Warm air

Cold air

The warmer air rises above the cooler air.

Clouds called frontal clouds (see page 161) are formed.

## Making a "cloud"

This experiment shows how clouds are formed as warm air is cooled. You will need a large glass jar, a small metal baking tray and some ice.

Do not use boiling water as this may crack the glass.

**What to do**

1. Pour 2.5cm (1in) of hot water into the jar.

Metal baking tray

Large glass jar

2. Place some ice cubes in the baking tray and put the tray on top of the jar.

Ice cubes

Jar

3. As the air inside the jar rises and is cooled by the ice, the water vapour it contains condenses into droplets.

Water vapour condenses in the jar to form a "cloud".

## The main cloud types

The main types of cloud are recognized by their shape and height. There are three main cloud types called cirrus, cumulus and stratus. There are many combinations of these clouds and different types may exist in the sky at the same time.

Cirrus clouds are high level clouds, usually found above 6000m (20,000ft). They are made up of ice crystals and have a feathery, wispy appearance.

Cumulus clouds are found at different heights. They are individual, rounded clouds with fairly flat bases. They are often seen on dry, sunny days.

Stratus clouds form a layer or sheet across the sky. They are found at low levels, below 500m (1,650ft) and often produce light rain and drizzle.

Many different cloud patterns are formed from combinations of the main cloud types. Their names refer to the types of clouds or the height at which they are found. For instance, the word 'alto' in a cloud type indicates that the clouds are middle level clouds, found between 2000m and 6000m (6,500ft and 20,000ft). Stratus means layered, and nimbus indicates rain or snow is falling from the cloud.

Cumulonimbus clouds are like massive cumulus clouds. They have flat tops and may extend to great heights. They are associated with heavy rain and thunder (see page 162).

Cirrus clouds

Cirrostratus clouds are cirrus clouds which form a thin, almost transparent, layer over the whole sky. They often bring rain.

Cirrocumulus are a combination of cirrus and cumulus clouds. They are individual clouds of ice which are sometimes arranged in rows.

Altostratus clouds normally form a grey sheet of cloud across the sky. Sunlight can usually be seen filtering through this.

Altocumulus are small grey or white cumulus clouds of roughly the same size, often lying in rows and sometimes joined together.

Nimbostratus clouds are a thick layer of grey clouds with an uneven base, which blot out the Sun completely.

Stratocumulus clouds form a sheet of rounded cumulus clouds which are almost joined together.

Cumulus clouds

Stratus clouds

## Measuring cloud cover

The number of clouds covering the sky is measured in oktas. The number of oktas indicates how much of the sky is covered by clouds. Oktas are measured on a scale of 0 to 8 (8 oktas means that the sky is completely covered). For example, a weather forecaster may describe the sky as having four oktas of cloud, which means that half the sky is obscured by clouds.

A sky with 3 oktas of cumulus cloud.

Aircraft trails are artificial cirrus clouds made up of ice crystals.

## Aircraft trails

High-flying aircraft sometimes leave a white trail behind them when the air is very cold. The aircraft's exhaust system sends out a mixture of hot gases, containing large amounts of water vapour. The water vapour cools, condenses and freezes in the cold air, forming thin "cloud" trails. These are called contrails.

# Water in the air

Water is found in the air as water vapour or as water droplets and ice crystals in clouds (see page 156), depending on the temperature of the air. The temperature of the air also determines the type of precipitation (rain, snow, sleet or hail) which may fall from the clouds.

## Rain and snow

The temperature of the air in clouds determines the way that rain and snow are formed. In areas such as tropical areas, where the cloud temperature is mainly above the freezing point of 0°C (32°F), rain is formed by a process called coalescence. The clouds are made up of millions of minute droplets of water and as these droplets collide, they join together, forming larger droplets.

Gradually the droplets increase in size until they are too heavy to be kept up in the cloud by air currents and fall as raindrops.

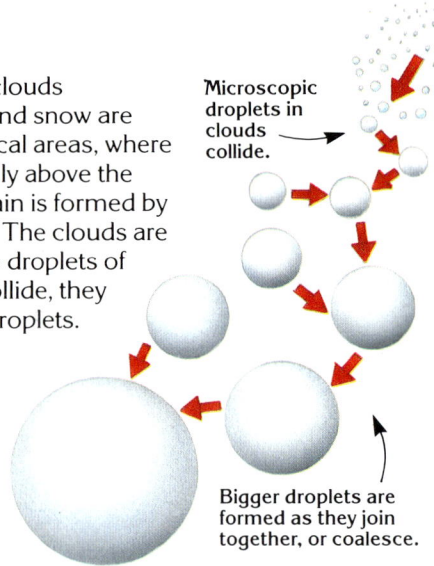

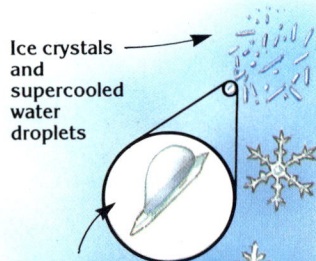

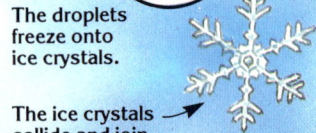

Microscopic droplets in clouds collide.

Bigger droplets are formed as they join together, or coalesce.

Ice crystals and supercooled water droplets

The droplets freeze onto ice crystals.

The ice crystals collide and join together to form snowflakes.

Scientists think that the shape of snowflakes depends on the height and temperature at which they are formed.

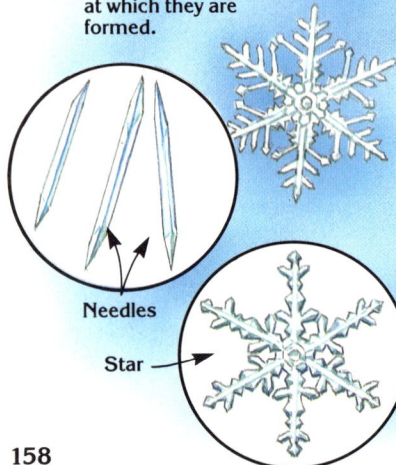

In cooler areas, clouds may stretch up into air which is below freezing. These clouds are a mixture of water droplets, lower down, and ice crystals and special supercooled water droplets higher up. These droplets exist as water even though the temperature is below freezing.

As well as coalescence at the bottom, a process called accretion happens higher up in these clouds. The ice crystals attract the supercooled droplets, which freeze onto them. As the crystals grow and stick to others, snowflakes form. When they become too heavy to be held up, they fall.

In areas where the air temperature near the ground remains below freezing, snow falls, but if the temperature is above freezing, the flakes melt and fall as rain. Sleet is a mixture of snowflakes and raindrops.

Needles

Star

Plates

## Hail

Hail forms in cumulonimbus clouds (see page 157), which have strong upward and downward currents of air moving within them. The temperature at the top of these clouds is well below freezing. As ice crystals rush around the cloud, they collide with supercooled water droplets and are rapidly coated with layers of ice.

More ice layers are added as the hailstones are swept up and down and tossed about in the cloud. They eventually fall when they are too heavy to be held up by the air currents within the cloud.

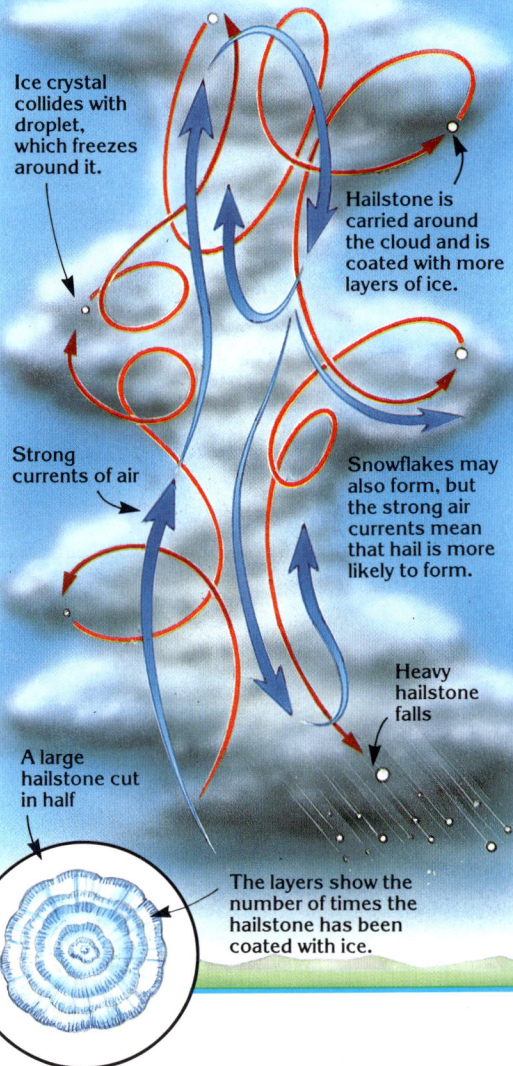

Ice crystal collides with droplet, which freezes around it.

Hailstone is carried around the cloud and is coated with more layers of ice.

Strong currents of air

Snowflakes may also form, but the strong air currents mean that hail is more likely to form.

Heavy hailstone falls

A large hailstone cut in half

The layers show the number of times the hailstone has been coated with ice.

## Mist and fog

Mist and fog are "surface clouds", made up of minute droplets of water. Like clouds, they are formed when water vapour in the air condenses as it cools below its dew point. Clouds form when air is cooled as it rises, whereas fog forms when a deep layer of air is cooled by the underlying surface. Sea fog is formed when warm, moist air is cooled over a cold sea (see page 166).

The difference between mist and fog is determined by the density of the "cloud". This affects the distance which can be seen ahead, or the visibility. Fog is more dense, resulting in poorer visibility than in mist (see page 171).

The surface is cooler than the air.

Water vapour condenses.

Fog forms above the surface.

## Dew

Dew forms when air immediately in contact with a cold surface is cooled to its dew point. The water vapour condenses into dew droplets on the surface. Dew is always found when there is fog, but it may also form on a clear night when the layer of air touching the surface reaches its dew point, but the air immediately above does not.

Air directly in contact with surface cools below its dew point.

Water vapour condenses into droplets of dew on cold surfaces.

## Measuring rainfall

The amount of rain or snow which falls can be measured on a rain gauge. To make a rain gauge you will need a tall plastic bottle (with a flat, clear bottom) and a ruler.

### What to do

1. Use a sharp pair of scissors to carefully cut around the plastic bottle, about 10cm (4in) from the top.

No lid

Plastic bottle

Scissors

Flat, clear bottom

Top piece or funnel

2. Fit the top piece of the bottle upside-down in the bottom piece. These form the funnel and collecting jar. The funnel directs rain into the collecting jar and also forms a barrier to stop any of it evaporating.

Bottom piece or collecting jar

Rain gauge

Remember to empty the rain gauge after each measurement.

Ground

3. Sink the base of the bottle in the ground in an open area, away from trees and buildings. Use a ruler to measure the amount of rain which falls in a given time. You could make a daily record.

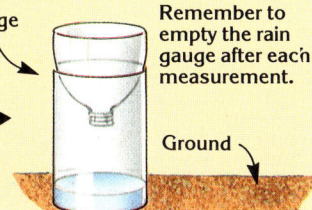

If you are measuring snow, you may not need the funnel. About 12cm (4½in) = 1cm (⅓in) of water.

## Frost

Frost occurs when the ground temperature is below freezing. The most common type is known as hoar frost. It is made up of tiny ice crystals. Some of these are frozen dew, others form when water vapour turns directly into ice as it comes into contact with a freezing surface. This happens without the water vapour passing through the stage of condensing into water droplets (dew).

On a cold winter morning, white hoar frost is often seen covering the ground.

The ground may freeze (a ground frost) without there being any white covering, if there is not enough moisture in the air.

# Highs, lows and fronts

Areas of high and low pressure are constantly moving across the Earth's surface, with air moving between them (see pages 154-155). Air moving into an area brings with it the characteristics of where it has come from. Where two air masses with different characteristics meet, the air does not mix easily, but forms a boundary, called a front.

## Movement of air around highs and lows

Meteorologists refer to areas of high pressure as highs or anticyclones, and areas of low pressure as lows, depressions or cyclones.

As surface winds blow into a low, and away from a high, the Coriolis effect (see page 153) makes them circulate around the pressure centre.

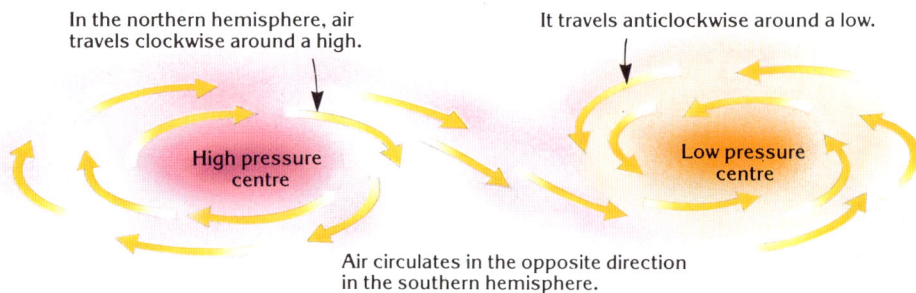

In the northern hemisphere, air travels clockwise around a high.

It travels anticlockwise around a low.

**High pressure centre**

**Low pressure centre**

Air circulates in the opposite direction in the southern hemisphere.

## Highs and lows on a weather map

Weather maps (see page 172) show air pressure readings at sea level. On these maps, places of equal pressure are joined by lines called isobars. Surface winds do not blow from high to low pressure directly across the isobars. Instead, they blow almost parallel to the isobars. This is because the air spirals into and out of the high and low pressure centres (see above).

The average pressure of the atmosphere has been set as 1013mb (29.91psi)*. However, areas are not marked as high or low in relation to this, but in relation to the pressure in surrounding areas. For instance, a pressure of 1008mb is marked as a low when the surrounding areas are 1032mb, but as a high when the surrounding areas have readings of 996mb.

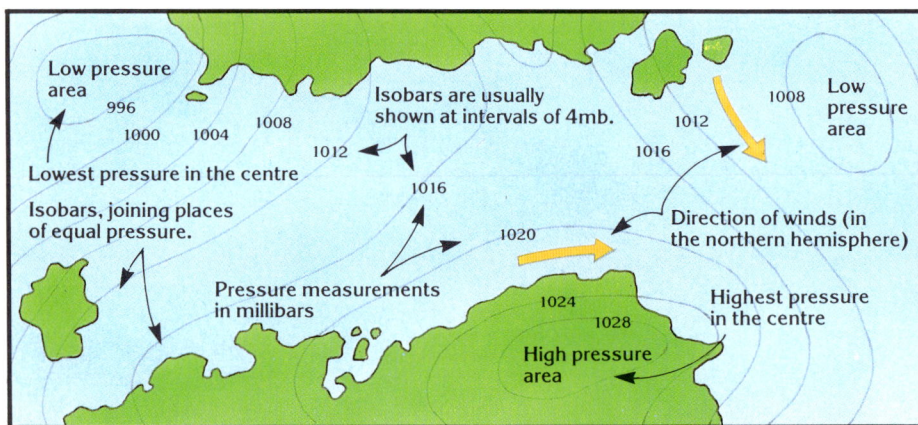

Low pressure area
996
1000    1004    1008
Lowest pressure in the centre

Isobars, joining places of equal pressure.

Isobars are usually shown at intervals of 4mb.

1012
1016
1020

Pressure measurements in millibars

1008
1012
1016

Low pressure area

Direction of winds (in the northern hemisphere)

1024
1028
High pressure area

Highest pressure in the centre

## The Buys-Ballot law

The Buys-Ballot law states that in the northern hemisphere, if you have your back to the wind, there will be lower pressure on your left and higher on your right. In the southern hemisphere, low pressure is found on the right.

## Fronts

A front is the boundary between two masses of moving air with different temperatures and humidity. The main front is called the polar front and is found around latitudes 60°N and 60°S, where cold polar air meets warmer tropical air coming from towards the equator. In some places along the polar front, the warm air mass bulges into the cold air and in others the cold air pushes out into the warm air. This is because there are uneven pressure differences along the front.

In some places the cold polar air pushes into warmer air.

60°N (latitude)

Polar front

In others, the warmer tropical air bulges into the colder air.

In general along the front, the warm air rises over the cooler air. It rises at different speeds in different places, forming areas of low pressure. The greater the temperature difference between the warm and cold air, the faster the warm air will rise. The greatest differences in temperature occur at the points where one mass of air has pushed furthest into the other. High-level winds (see page 154) may also be causing air to rise in certain places, speeding it up even more.

* mb = millibars, psi = pounds per square inch. To convert millibars to pounds per square inch, multiply by 0.02953.

## Fronts and pressure

Wherever air is rising along the polar front, there is a fall in pressure. However, individual centres of low pressure are formed where the air is rising most quickly as these are the points which have the lowest pressure compared with those on either side of them. Because of these individual centres, the polar front is never seen as a continuous line, but as a series of individual fronts, occurring at the low pressure centres. These are known as frontal depressions. The surrounding warm and cold air moves towards them, because they have the lowest pressure. Winds do not blow directly into areas of low pressure, though (see page 160), so the air circulates around them as it moves in.

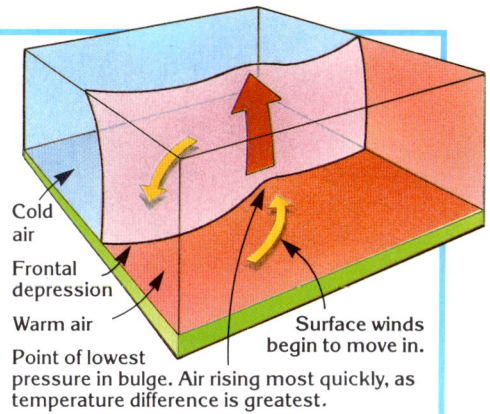

Cold air

Frontal depression

Warm air

Point of lowest pressure in bulge. Air rising most quickly, as temperature difference is greatest.

Surface winds begin to move in.

## Warm and cold fronts

As the winds circulate around a frontal depression, they bring warm air into an area where there is colder air, and vice versa. This movement of air forms warm and cold fronts (as shown in the diagram below).

Where cooler air moves into a warmer area, it is known as a cold front. The cool air pushes under the warm air, forcing it to rise.

Where warm air advances into an area to replace cooler air, it is known as a warm front. The warm air rides up over the cooler air.

Original bulge forms a wave shape.

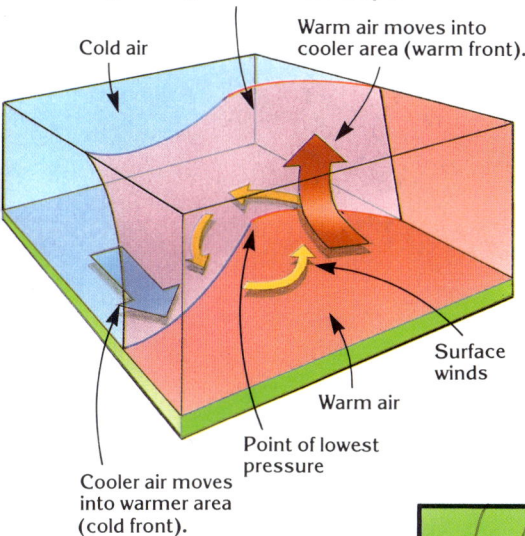

Cold air

Warm air moves into cooler area (warm front).

Surface winds

Warm air

Point of lowest pressure

Cooler air moves into warmer area (cold front).

A cold front

Cool air mass

Frontal clouds form where cooler air forces warmer air to rise.

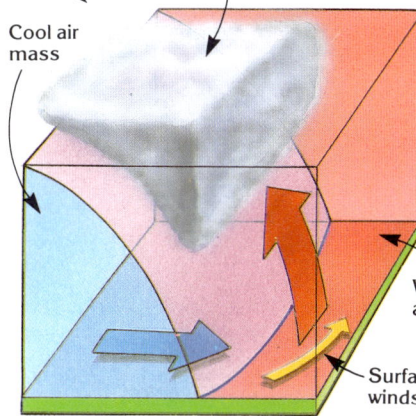

Warmer air mass

Surface winds

On a weather map, a cold front is marked by a line with triangles along it.

A warm front

Frontal clouds form as the air rises and cools.

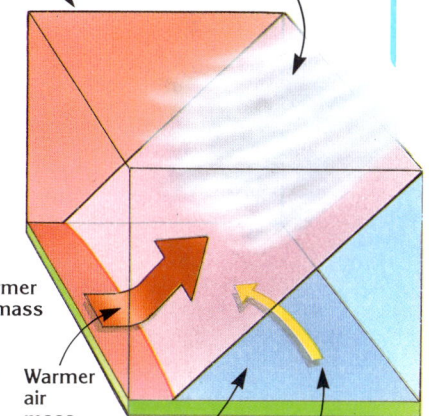

Warmer air mass

Cool air mass

Surface winds

A warm front is marked by a line with semicircles along it.

## Occluded fronts

A cold front gradually moves towards a warm front and may eventually catch it up. If it does so, it undercuts the warm air and lifts it right off the ground. The front is then described as an occluded front. This extra "push", as the cold air moves in and lifts the warm air, can produce huge clouds and very heavy rain.

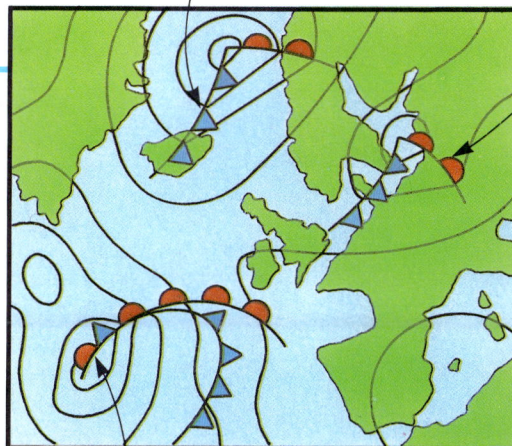

Occluded fronts on weather maps are lines with both semicircles and triangles.

## Changing weather

Like all pressure areas, frontal depressions are not stationary, but are moved by high-level winds. They bring a general pattern of unsettled weather to places they pass over. Cirrus clouds are usually the first sign that a depression may be approaching, followed by a sequence of other clouds and rain. However, no two depressions produce exactly the same sequence of weather.

# Thunderstorms and hurricanes

Storms are a combination of strong winds and heavy rain, snow or hail, and form in low pressure areas. Under certain conditions, minor storms can develop into thunderstorms or hurricanes, which can cause much damage to areas where they occur.

## Thunderstorms

Thunderstorms form when particularly warm, moist air rises into cold air above land or sea. As the humid air rises to a great height, water vapour condenses, forming huge cumulonimbus clouds.

Water droplets and ice crystals in the clouds bump together and break up as they rub against each other in strong currents of air. This action builds up positive electrical charges at the top of the clouds and negative charges at the base.

When the charge at the base of the cloud gets to a certain strength, electrical energy is released and passes through the air to another point with the opposite charge, such as the ground. This release of energy is called the leader stroke and forms a path of charged air for the main stroke to travel along. The main stroke travels back up to the cloud and produces a flash of lightning.

At the same time as the main stroke travels up, it heats the air, causing it to expand very quickly. This expansion of air produces the sound we hear as thunder.

Cumulonimbus cloud

Leader stroke forms a charged path.

Main stroke follows path back up to cloud and produces a flash of lightning.

The air expands very quickly, producing thunder.

If the storm is directly overhead, the thunder will be heard at the same time as the lightning is seen.

If not, the lightning is seen several seconds before the thunder is heard, as the speed of light is faster than the speed of sound.

Thunderstorms die out once the charges in the clouds have evened out.

## Hurricanes

In tropical areas, thunderstorms may develop into violent storms with torrential rain, and wind speeds reaching as much as 300km per hour (186mph). Meteorologists call these storms tropical cyclones, but they are more commonly known as hurricanes. They are also given other names in different countries around the world, such as typhoons in S.E. Asia and willy-willies in Australia.

Hurricanes form only above tropical seas between the latitudes 5° and 20° north and south of the equator, where the sea temperature is above 27°C (80°F), and so the conditions of heat and moisture are at their most extreme.

Main areas where hurricanes develop

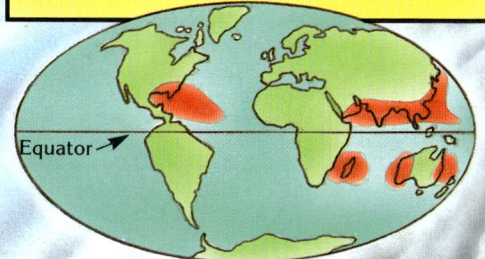

Equator

A section through a hurricane

Rings of cumulonimbus clouds form around a hurricane's centre. They join at the top, which may reach the top of the troposphere (see page 149).

A hurricane may have a diameter of 500km (300 miles), covering a much greater area than a thunderstorm.

Thunder and lightning often occur during hurricanes.

## The development of a hurricane

It is not fully understood why a hurricane develops, as moist air is always rising above warm seas, but it is thought that an "extra" low pressure area moving in over the sea may set them off.

As the pressure falls rapidly, strong surface winds area formed as air is sucked in towards the centre of the low. At the centre, the air speeds up and spirals upwards. Vast quantities of water vapour in the rising air condense to form massive cumulonimbus clouds. As the water vapour condenses, enormous amounts of heat are given out which makes the air rise even faster, and in turn increases the speed of the surface winds moving in.

## Naming hurricanes

Lists of alternate male and female names are drawn up each year. As soon as a storm becomes hurricane strength with wind speeds over 199km/h (74mph), it is given the next name on the list.

Hurricane Gilbert in 1988 caused severe damage to islands in the Caribbean.

Air at the centre rises rapidly, forming a spiralling column.

As the vapour condenses, heat is given off, making the air rise faster.

## The eye of the storm

Down the centre of the storm there is a column of air 30-50km (20-30 miles) wide, called the eye. The air here is slowly sinking and the winds are light. As the eye passes overhead, the wind and the rain stop for a short time, only to start again as the other side of the hurricane passes over.

Strong surface winds

Warm sea

## Tracking hurricanes

Like all storms, hurricanes do not stay in one place, but travel away from the area where they form. Their path is influenced by the movements of high-level winds (see page 154) and the direction of warm sea currents. A hurricane dies out when it reaches an area where there is no longer the necessary warmth and moisture, such as when it reaches a cool sea, or land.

Satellite images are used to detect where a storm may develop into a hurricane.

Meteorologists try to predict the path which a hurricane may take, and issue warnings to people who are at risk from the storm.

A satellite image of a hurricane

# Extreme weather conditions

Extreme weather conditions, such as floods or droughts, sometimes interrupt the usual pattern of weather in some areas. In other places, extreme conditions are experienced each year as part of the seasonal pattern.

## Droughts

A drought occurs when there is less than 0.2mm ($\frac{1}{100}$in) of rain, or other type of precipitation, over a period of at least fifteen days. Droughts may occur because of a high blocking the passage of rain-bearing lows across an area (see page 165). They also occur when areas of land are cleared of vegetation in areas which are already very dry (see pictures, right).

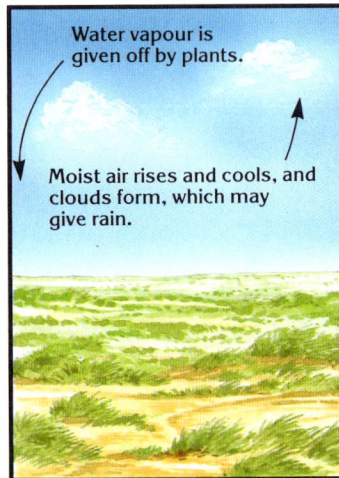

Water vapour is given off by plants.

Moist air rises and cools, and clouds form, which may give rain.

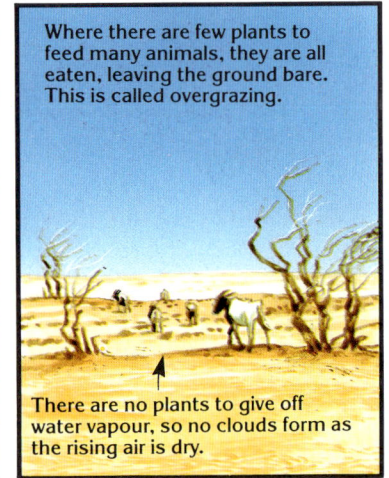

Where there are few plants to feed many animals, they are all eaten, leaving the ground bare. This is called overgrazing.

There are no plants to give off water vapour, so no clouds form as the rising air is dry.

## Flooding

Flooding may occur for several reasons, for instance, if large amounts of rain fall and there is too much water to drain away. Flooding also occurs when sea levels rise, when the land is swamped by waves caused by storms, or when snow on land melts as temperatures rise rapidly, causing rivers to overflow.

When more than 15mm ($\frac{6}{10}$in) of rain falls in 3 hours, meteorologists describe the conditions as a "flash flood".

When a flash flood occurs, there is too much water to drain away. It flows rapidly across the surface, flooding areas in its path.

## Monsoons

The term monsoon describes winds which blow, in tropical areas such as India and S.E. Asia, from roughly opposite directions in different seasons. The combination of the extremes of temperature and pressure in these areas, and the position of the land and the sea, produces extreme weather conditions.

This scene shows the extremely heavy rain which falls during the wet monsoon season.

One of the two winds is dry, while the other brings extremely heavy rain, so there is a dry monsoon, which creates a dry season, and a wet one which brings a rainy season.

For example, in India, the wet monsoon blows when the Sun lies almost directly overhead, and the equatorial band of low pressure, called the ITCZ (see page 153) is furthest north. The land is heated intensely, causing vast amounts of air to

rise, forming even lower pressure on the surface. Very moist winds blow in from the Indian Ocean, to replace the rising air. Many places receive as much as 3,000mm (118in) of rain during the rainy season.

The dry season occurs when the sun is no longer directly overhead and the ITCZ is furthest south. This low pressure zone causes winds to blow from high pressure over the land towards the ITCZ. These winds are dry as they have travelled a large distance over the land.

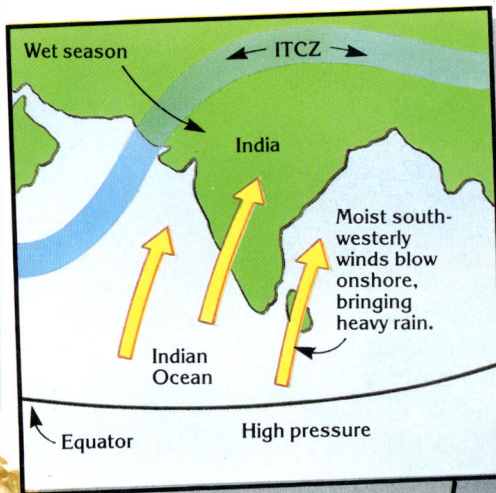

Wet season — ITCZ →

India

Moist south-westerly winds blow onshore, bringing heavy rain.

Indian Ocean

Equator — High pressure

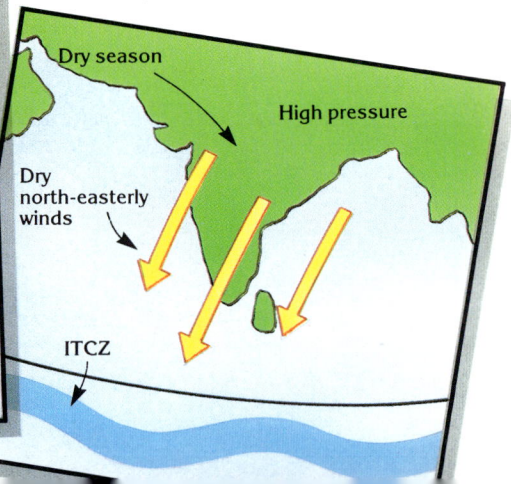

Dry season

High pressure

Dry north-easterly winds

ITCZ

## Measuring air humidity

During the wet monsoon, the humidity of the air (see page 156) is extremely high. Humidity is sometimes measured on wet and dry bulb thermometers. To make these you will need two thermometers, with scales roughly ranging from 0°C to 35°C (32°F to 95°F), some cotton wool, two rubber bands and a small bowl of water.

### What to do

1. Wrap the bulb end of each thermometer in equal amounts of cotton wool. Secure each piece with a rubber band.

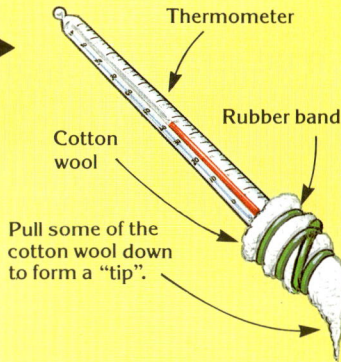

Thermometer

Cotton wool

Rubber band

Pull some of the cotton wool down to form a "tip".

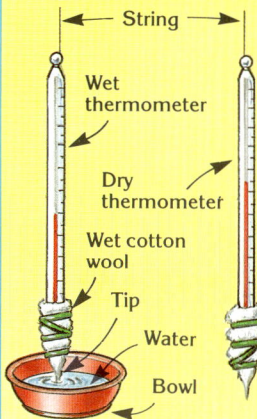

String

Wet thermometer

Dry thermometer

Wet cotton wool

Tip

Water

Bowl

2. Stick a piece of thin string to the other end of each thermometer. Use drawing pins to hang the thermometers outside in the shade. Put a bowl of water below one of the thermometers so that its tip is in the water.

3. After 30 minutes, read each thermometer. Work out the difference between the two temperatures. Use the chart to calculate the humidity of the air.

Heat is given off as water evaporates from the cotton wool, so the temperature shown on the wet thermometer will be lower than that on the dry one. If the air contains large amounts of water vapour, less water evaporates, so the temperature difference between the thermometers will be smaller, and the humidity measurement higher.

Humidity is measured as a percentage. 100% humidity is very humid and the air feels sticky.

| Temperature on the dry thermometer ▼ | Difference between wet and dry bulb thermometers | | | | | | | | | |
|---|---|---|---|---|---|---|---|---|---|---|
| | 1°C 2°F | 2°C 3°F | 3°C 5°F | 4°C 7°F | 5°C 9°F | 6°C 11°F | 7°C 13°F | 8°C 14°F | 9°C 16°F | 10°C 18°F |
| 10-14°C (50-57°F) | 85 | 75 | 60 | 50 | 40 | 30 | 15 | 5 | 0 | 0 |
| 15-19°C (59-66°F) | 90 | 80 | 65 | 60 | 50 | 40 | 30 | 20 | 10 | 5 |
| 20-25°C (68-77°F) | 90 | 80 | 70 | 65 | 55 | 45 | 40 | 30 | 25 | 20 |

Humidity (%)

## Blocking highs

Areas around 60° north and south of the equator usually experience changeable weather as areas of high and low pressure are moved across them by the high-level winds (see page 154). The wavy pattern of these winds, and the position of the waves, changes frequently, bringing highs and lows which change the weather.

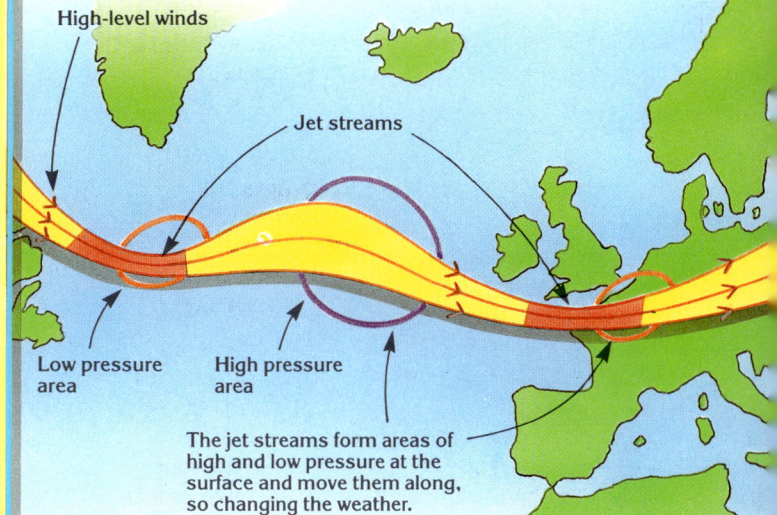

High-level winds

Jet streams

Low pressure area

High pressure area

The jet streams form areas of high and low pressure at the surface and move them along, so changing the weather.

Occasionally, the movement of the low pressure areas is "blocked" by an area of high pressure which remains in one place for a long period of time and prevents any change in the weather for several days or weeks. These areas of high pressure are known as blocking highs.

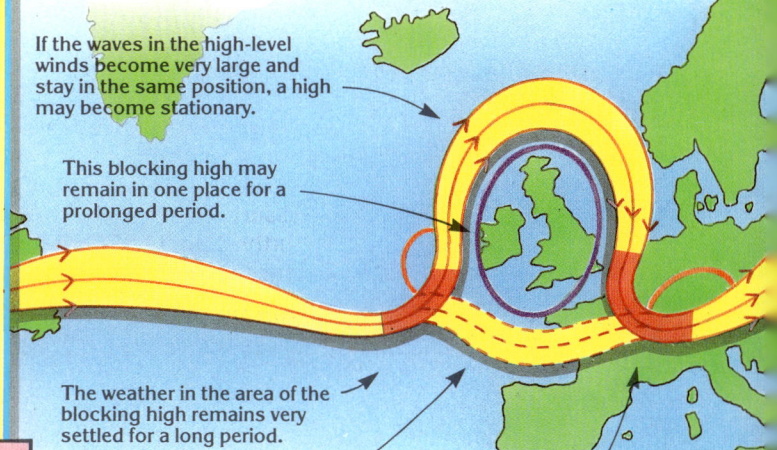

If the waves in the high-level winds become very large and stay in the same position, a high may become stationary.

This blocking high may remain in one place for a prolonged period.

The weather in the area of the blocking high remains very settled for a long period.

It diverts the flow of the high-level winds, and the lows are steered around it.

Other areas experience unsettled weather because of these diverted lows.

Blocking highs can persist for several days or even weeks. They may produce prolonged cold weather, with ice and snow in winter, or very hot, dry weather in summer, which may lead to a drought.

# Local weather

Coastal and mountain areas often experience local variations in winds, temperature and rainfall, which seem to have no relation to the overall weather pattern of the larger area surrounding them. Cities also frequently have different types of weather from their surroundings (see page 178).

## Land and sea breezes

Coastal areas often experience land and sea breezes, which form a local circulation of air affecting areas up to 30km (20 miles) inland. The breezes may blow in a different direction from the wind blowing across the rest of the country that day.

Land and sea surfaces heat up and cool down at different rates (see page 155). Sea breezes are formed on days of high pressure when the land heats up quickly. Air rises from the land, forming a local area of relatively low pressure. This air spreads out as it meets high pressure air which is sinking. At the surface, air moves in from the sea to replace this rising air. This movement of air at the surface forms sea breezes.

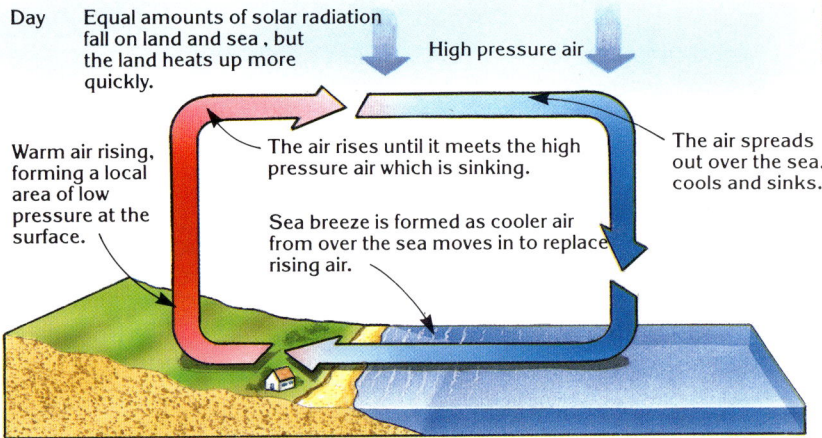

Day — Equal amounts of solar radiation fall on land and sea, but the land heats up more quickly.

High pressure air

The air rises until it meets the high pressure air which is sinking.

Warm air rising, forming a local area of low pressure at the surface.

The air spreads out over the sea, cools and sinks.

Sea breeze is formed as cooler air from over the sea moves in to replace rising air.

At night, the circulation is reversed as lower pressure forms over the warmer sea and air moves out from the land.

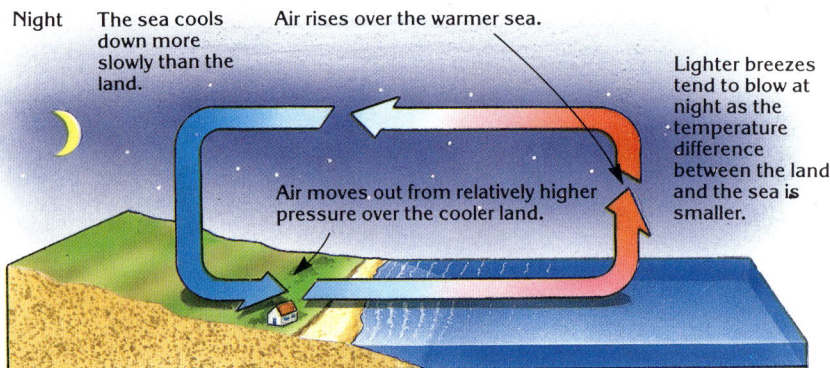

Night — The sea cools down more slowly than the land.

Air rises over the warmer sea.

Lighter breezes tend to blow at night as the temperature difference between the land and the sea is smaller.

Air moves out from relatively higher pressure over the cooler land.

Land and sea breezes do not form every day. For instance, on cloudy days, land and sea surfaces receive little solar radiation. This means that the temperature difference between the two surfaces is too small to start the circulation of air.

## Coastal fog

Fog may be found at the coast, when there is sunshine only a short distance inland. Sea fog is formed when winds, blowing towards the coast from a warm source region, pass over the cold surface of the sea. The warm air is cooled below its dew point, forming fog (see page 159).

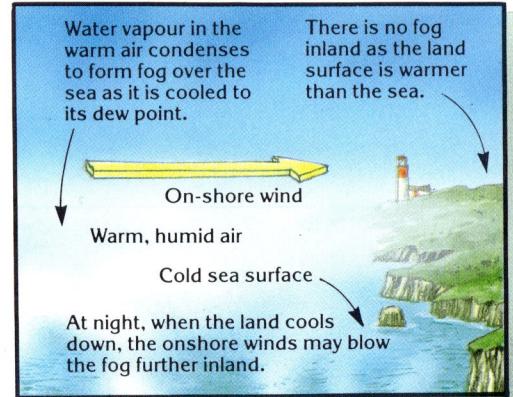

Water vapour in the warm air condenses to form fog over the sea as it is cooled to its dew point.

There is no fog inland as the land surface is warmer than the sea.

On-shore wind

Warm, humid air

Cold sea surface

At night, when the land cools down, the onshore winds may blow the fog further inland.

## Ocean currents

Water travels around the world's oceans in currents, generally following the pattern of the prevailing winds which form them (see page 153). When a wind blows steadily in one direction for a long period, the moving air drags the surface of the water along, forming a current. The winds help to keep the currents moving in a steady flow.

Ocean currents can be either warm or cold, depending on where they were formed. They change the temperature of the air above them, bringing warm or cold air to places in their path.

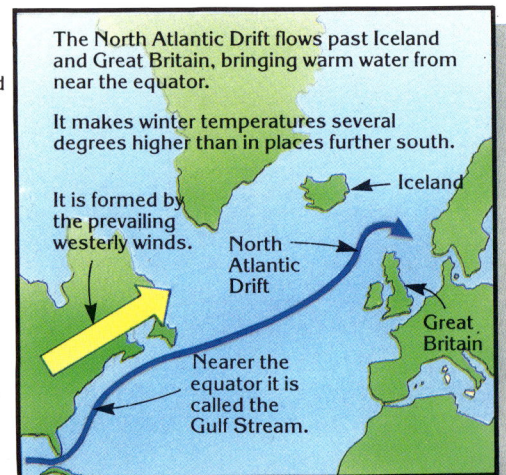

The North Atlantic Drift flows past Iceland and Great Britain, bringing warm water from near the equator.

It makes winter temperatures several degrees higher than in places further south.

It is formed by the prevailing westerly winds.

Iceland

North Atlantic Drift

Great Britain

Nearer the equator it is called the Gulf Stream.

## Valley winds

Valleys often experience different weather from their surroundings. On clear, calm nights, for instance, fog often forms in valleys and light winds may blow down the mountain or hill slopes into the valley bottom. During the day, local winds may form which blow the other way, up the valley slopes.

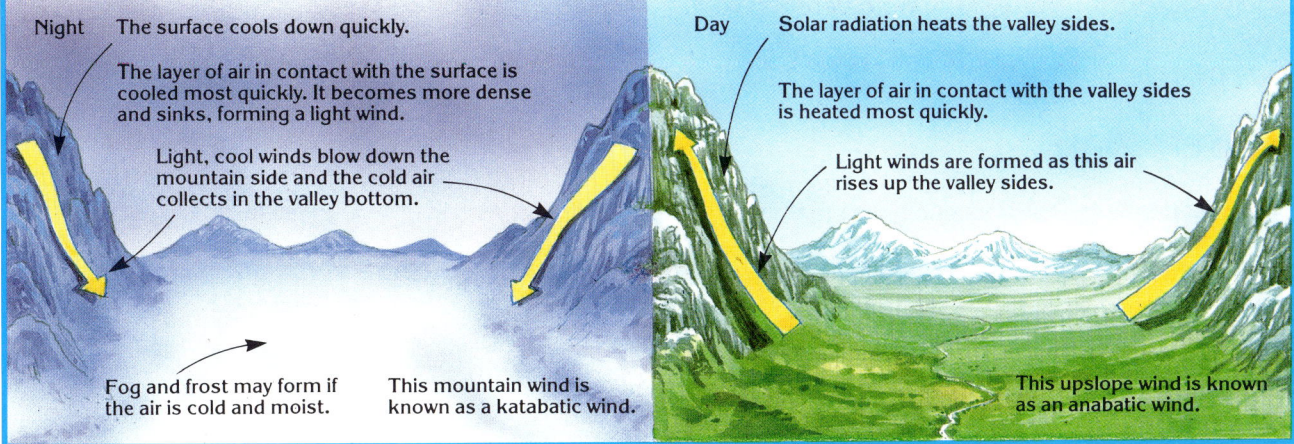

Night — The surface cools down quickly.

The layer of air in contact with the surface is cooled most quickly. It becomes more dense and sinks, forming a light wind.

Light, cool winds blow down the mountain side and the cold air collects in the valley bottom.

Fog and frost may form if the air is cold and moist.

This mountain wind is known as a katabatic wind.

Day — Solar radiation heats the valley sides.

The layer of air in contact with the valley sides is heated most quickly.

Light winds are formed as this air rises up the valley sides.

This upslope wind is known as an anabatic wind.

## Rainbows

A rainbow is an isolated optical effect caused by the Sun's rays being refracted (bent) and reflected as they pass through millions of raindrops. For a rainbow to occur there needs to be bright sunshine and rain occurring at the same time.

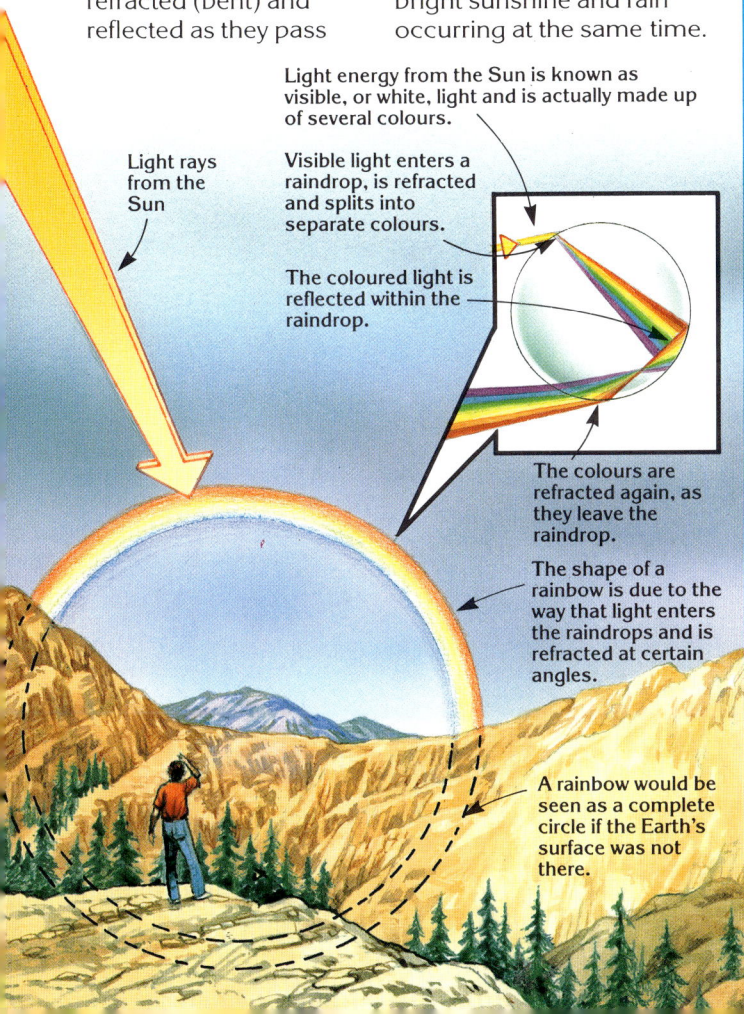

Light energy from the Sun is known as visible, or white, light and is actually made up of several colours.

Light rays from the Sun

Visible light enters a raindrop, is refracted and splits into separate colours.

The coloured light is reflected within the raindrop.

The colours are refracted again, as they leave the raindrop.

The shape of a rainbow is due to the way that light enters the raindrops and is refracted at certain angles.

A rainbow would be seen as a complete circle if the Earth's surface was not there.

## A rainbow effect

It is possible to split the Sun's visible light into its separate colours, producing a rainbow effect. For this you will need a bowl of water, a piece of white cardboard, a small mirror and a very bright, sunny day.

### What to do

1. Place the bowl of water in a very sunny position. Put the mirror into the bowl and lean it against the side.

Put a stone into the water to stop the mirror from slipping.

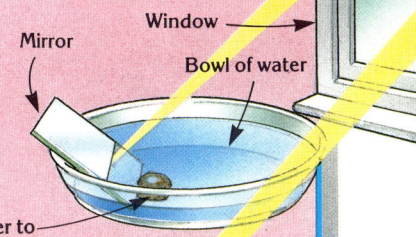

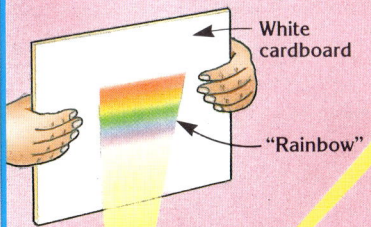

Mirror

Window

Bowl of water

White cardboard

"Rainbow"

2. Adjust the angle of the mirror so that a strong beam of sunshine falls on its surface. Move the cardboard around in front of the bowl, until a reflected "rainbow" appears on it.

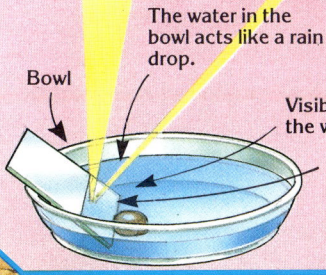

The water in the bowl acts like a rain drop.

Bowl

Visible light is refracted as it enters the water.

It is then reflected by the mirror and refracted again as it leaves the water, producing a rainbow effect.

# Monitoring the weather

In order to forecast the weather, meteorologists use information collected around the world. This information is based on observations made at the same time every day, at weather stations and elsewhere, using a variety of methods.

Thermometers

## Weather stations

At weather stations, observers use a variety of instruments to monitor such things as wind speed, clouds, air temperature and pressure. They also record the general weather, such as if it is raining or foggy.

The methods and equipment used at every station are standardized, so the weather is monitored in exactly the same way.

Air temperatures are measured on the thermometers inside a Stevenson screen. The shuttered sides allow air to flow freely, but keep the thermometers out of direct sunlight.

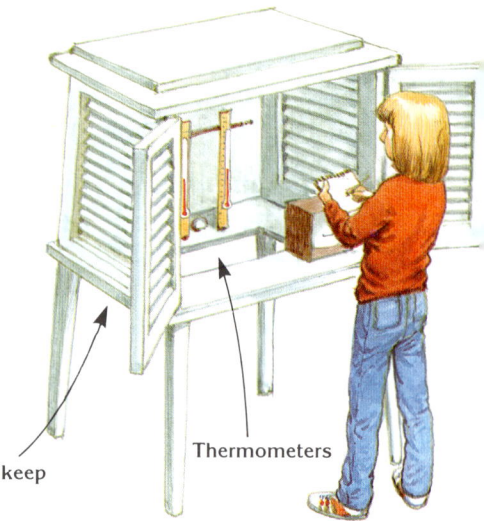

## Aircraft and ships

Many aircraft and ships provide weather information about areas where there are no weather stations. Like automatic weather stations on land (see below), they have equipment which records different weather conditions along their routes.

Many aircraft fly at an altitude of between 10-13km (30,000-40,000ft).

They provide useful information about high-level winds.

Ships provide information about weather conditions at sea.

This information is sent via satellite to a processing station on shore.

## Automatic weather stations

Automatic weather stations are positioned in areas such as mountains or polar regions, where it would be difficult to have an observer permanently monitoring the weather. Computers are programmed to take readings from the weather instruments every hour.

An automatic weather station in Antarctica

Automatic stations are unable to provide information about cloud types, current weather conditions or visibility.

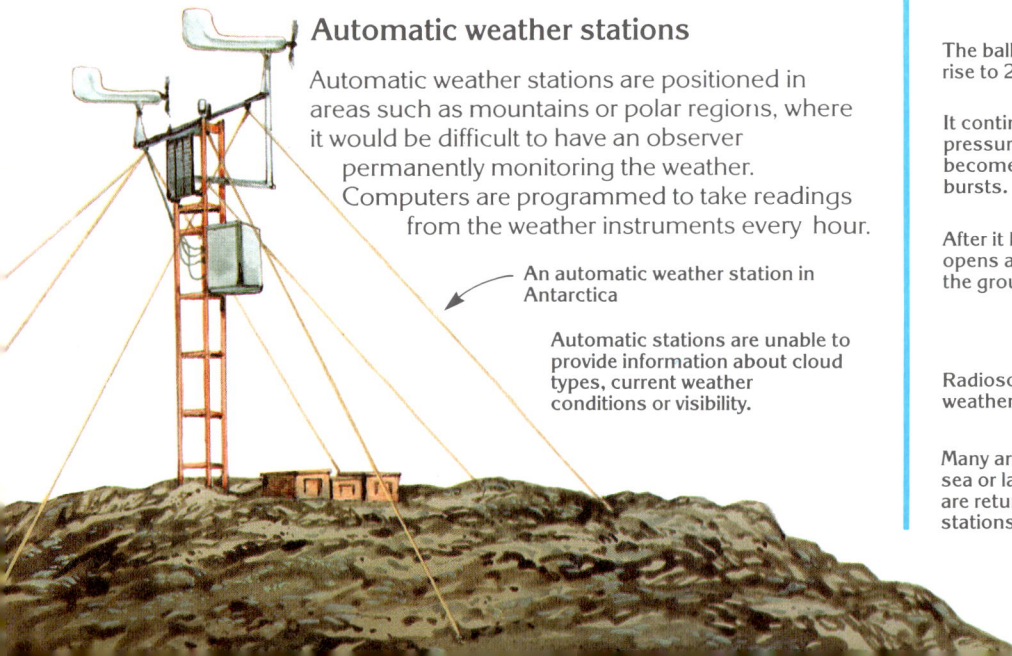

## Radiosondes

The temperature, humidity and pressure at different heights above the ground are recorded by instruments called radiosondes. These are carried high into the air by balloons.

Balloon

The speed, direction and rate of ascent of the rising balloon indicate the strength and direction of the wind. As the balloon rises through the air, the temperature, humidity and pressure readings are taken by the radiosonde. Signals from radiosondes are transmitted to places called processing stations on the ground.

The balloon takes about an hour to rise to 20km (60,000ft).

It continues to rise until the pressure of the surrounding air becomes so low that the balloon bursts.

After it bursts, a small parachute opens and the radiosonde falls to the ground.

Radiosonde

Radiosondes are released from weather stations twice a day.

Many are lost, as they fall into the sea or land in remote areas. Some are returned to the weather stations by people who find them.

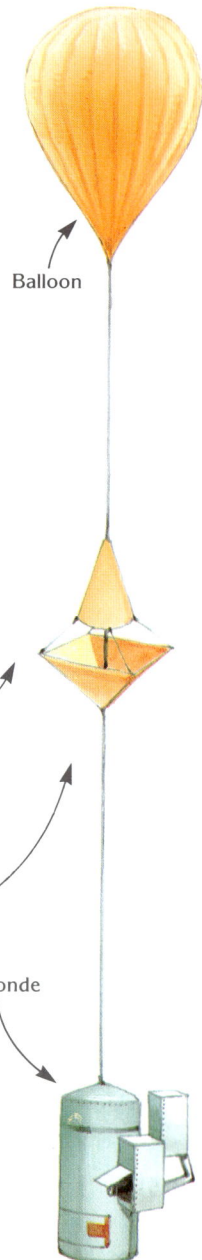

## Weather satellites

Weather satellites provide essential information about the location and movement of weather systems, and the pattern of clouds around the Earth. Two types of weather satellite orbit the Earth.

Geostationary satellites orbit at a height of 36,000km (22,400 miles) above the equator.

Geostationary satellites orbit the Earth once every 24 hours, the same time the Earth takes to spin around its axis. This means that they always monitor the weather above the same place on the Earth's position.

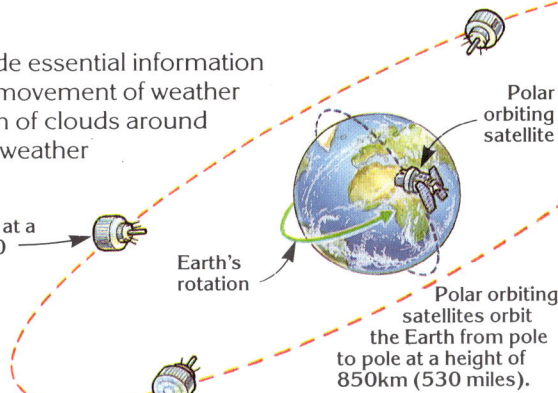

Polar orbiting satellite

Earth's rotation

Polar orbiting satellites orbit the Earth from pole to pole at a height of 850km (530 miles).

Polar orbiting satellites take about 100 minutes to complete one orbit, passing over both the Arctic and Antarctica. Each time they complete one orbit, the Earth has rotated by 25° longitude. This means a different strip of the Earth's surface is monitored on each orbit.

## Satellite images

Weather satellites carry instruments called radiometers, which sense the intensity of reflected light or heat. This information is turned into images (pictures) at processing stations. The satellites are useful in locating and tracking the paths of weather systems, particularly over large oceans.

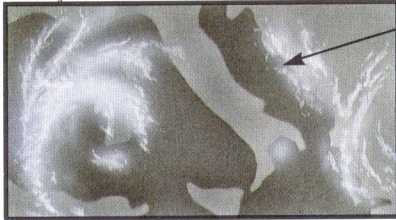

A visible satellite image

Different surfaces, such as cloud tops, land, water and ice reflect different amounts of sunlight. These different amounts show up as different shades of white or grey. These images cannot be produced at night as there is no light.

An infrared satellite image

Infrared images are produced from measurements of heat, not light. The temperatures of different surfaces are recorded to produce these images. Infrared images of the Earth can be produced during the day and at night.

## Radars

Weather radars are used to show where there is rain, hail or snow and how heavily they are falling. Radar systems work by sending out waves of radiation which bounce off rain drops and are reflected back, like echoes, to a receiving dish. The information is then sent, often via a satellite, to a processing station where it is turned into an image.

Radar images are colour-coded to show where the heaviest precipitation is occurring.

White lines are coastlines

The heaviest rain is coloured yellow.

## A wind vane

All weather stations have a wind vane which indicates the direction of the wind. To make a wind vane you will need some thin cardboard, adhesive book covering film, 1m (40in) of 5mm (⅕in) dowel, glue, strong sticky tape, two cable clips and a pen lid.

### What to do

1. Draw out the wind vane on the cardboard and cut it out. Cover one side with the film and score a line down the centre.

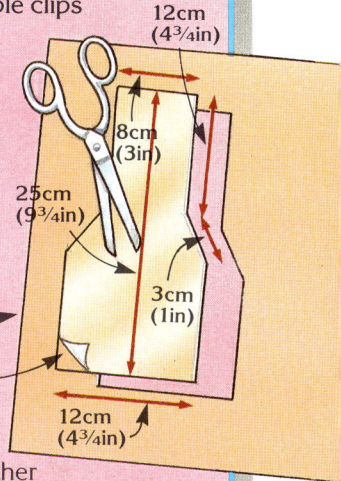

Cardboard

Covering film (for waterproofing)

12cm (4¾in)

8cm (3in)

25cm (9¾in)

3cm (1in)

12cm (4¾in)

2. Fold the vane in half. Stick the folded halves together (covered sides outwards) and cut across the narrow end to make a pointer. Use the tape to stick the pen lid to the vane.

Pen lid

Fold in half along the scored edge.

Pointer

3. Get someone to hold the dowel against a wooden post and attach it with the cable clips, so that the dowel does not turn.

Place the vane on top of the dowel. Make sure it spins freely.

Wind

Dowel

Cable clips

4. Find reference points, such as trees or walls, for north, south, east and west, using a map or compass. The wind turns the vane until the pointer is pointing in the direction the wind is blowing from.

Remember, a wind is always named by the direction it blows from.

If the pointer is pointing to the east, the wind is blowing from east to west, so an easterly wind is blowing.

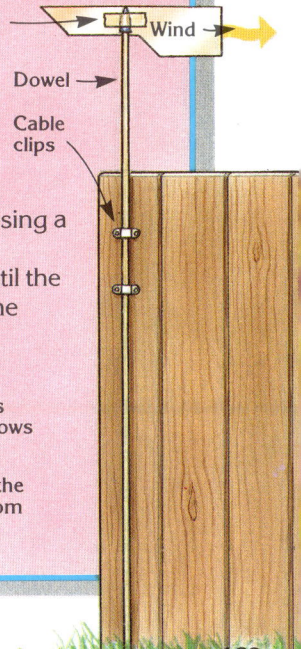

# Your own weather station

Professional observers at weather stations around the world (see page 168) make regular observations to record weather conditions. By making daily observations and using simple equipment, you can set up your own weather station and begin a logbook to record your local weather.

## Choosing a site

It is very important that the equipment used for recording different weather conditions is not affected by its surroundings. It is best to place the equipment in a relatively open area, such as a garden, but away from trees and tall buildings.

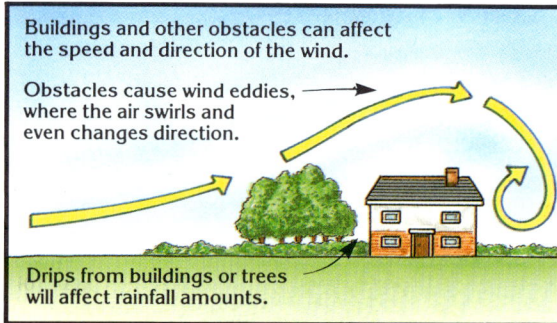

Buildings and other obstacles can affect the speed and direction of the wind.

Obstacles cause wind eddies, where the air swirls and even changes direction.

Drips from buildings or trees will affect rainfall amounts.

## Temperature

Temperatures which are recorded at weather stations are taken in the shade (see page 168). You can make recordings by hanging a thermometer on a fence or a wall which is in the shade.

## Wind direction and speed

Wind direction is monitored on a wind vane (see page 169), which needs to be sited away from any obstacle. Wind speed is usually measured by an anemometer (but see below).

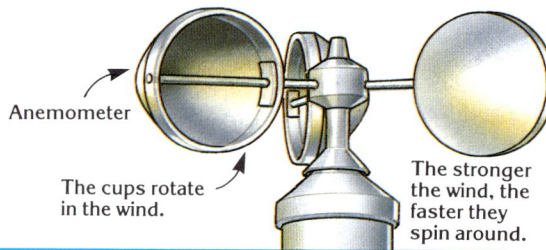

Anemometer

The cups rotate in the wind.

The stronger the wind, the faster they spin around.

The highest and lowest temperatures can be recorded on maximum and minimum thermometers. You can buy these at a garden centre.

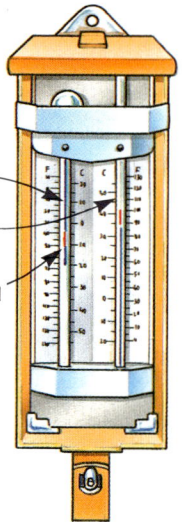

Minimum thermometer

Maximum thermometer

As the temperature rises or falls, the liquid in each thermometer moves an indicator. The indicator will remain at the highest (maximum thermometer) or the lowest (minimum thermometer) temperature reached.

## Measuring wind speed

In order to measure wind speed at your weather station, you could make a simple wind box. You will need a shoe box, sticky tape, some thin cardboard, a knitting needle, a protractor, plastic film and a fine, permanent-ink pen.

Protractor

Scale

Pen

Plastic film

### What to do

1. Using the protractor and the permanent-ink pen, mark the angles for a wind-speed scale, at 5° intervals between 0° and 90° on the plastic film.

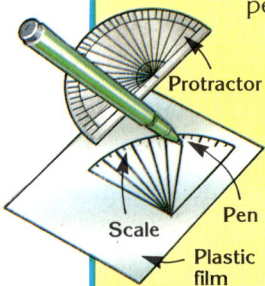

2. Cut the ends off the shoe box and lid, and stick them together. Cut a hole in one side of the box, near to one end (see below), and stick the scale inside, so it is displayed through the hole.

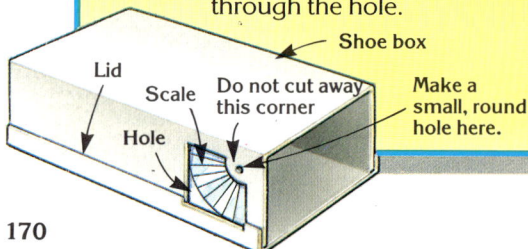

Lid

Scale

Hole

Shoe box

Do not cut away this corner

Make a small, round hole here.

3. Push the knitting needle through the small, round hole (see previous picture), and wiggle it about until it rotates freely. Cut out a cardboard flap, slightly smaller than the end of the box. Stick it to the needle.

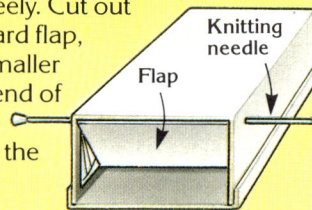

Knitting needle

Flap

4. Hold the box so the flap faces into the wind. Look at the angle of the flap and work out the wind speed from the table below.

| Angle (°) | Km/h | Angle | Km/h |
|-----------|------|-------|------|
| 90 | 0 | 40 | 34-36 |
| 85 | 8-11 | 35 | 37-39 |
| 80 | 12-14 | 30 | 40-43 |
| 75 | 15-17 | 25 | 44-48 |
| 70 | 18-20 | 20 | 49-54 |
| 65 | 21-23 | | |
| 60 | 24-25 | | |
| 55 | 26-27 | To convert km/h | |
| 50 | 28-30 | to mph, multiply | |
| 45 | 31-33 | by 0.621 | |

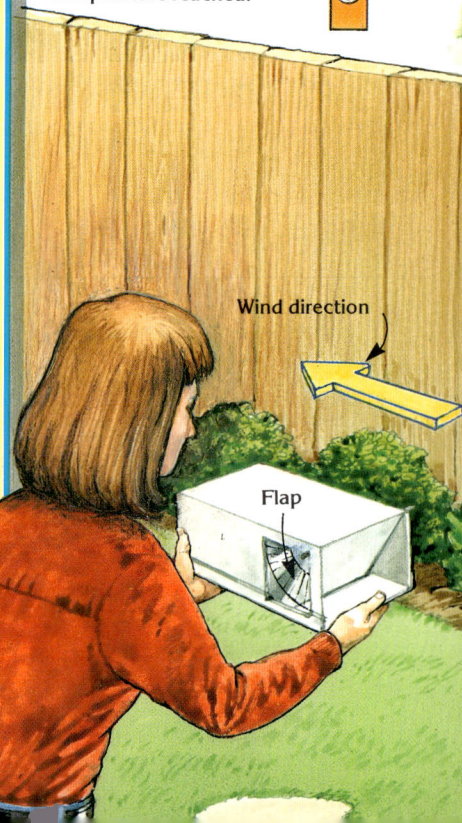

Wind direction

Flap

## Visibility

Visibility is recorded as the distance a person can see. On a clear day, write down various landmarks you can see, such as a church or some hills. If your own weather station is in an area where the view is restricted, you could use a local open space to record the visibility. Use a map of your area (your local library should have one) to measure the distance from your recording point to each landmark.

Estimate the visibility by recording the furthest landmark you can see that day.

When visibility is less than 1km (3,000ft), it is said to be foggy.

Visibility is poor when you can see for between 1-5km (3,000ft-3 miles).

## Clouds

Weather observers record the cloud types. They also record the cloud cover measured in oktas (see page 157).

Abbreviations are used to indicate each cloud type.

| | |
|---|---|
| Cirrus – Ci | Stratus – St |
| Cirrocumulus – Cc | Altostratus – As |
| Cirrostratus – Cs | Stratocumulus – Sc |
| Cumulus – Cu | Nimbostratus – Ns |
| Altocumulus – Ac | Cumulonimbus – Cb |

Visibility is said to be moderate when you can see for 5-10km (3-6 miles).

Visibility is said to be good when you can see for more than 10km (6 miles).

## Pressure

Air pressure is measured on a barometer which should be placed inside a building. You can use your home-made barometer (see page 152) to record whether the pressure is rising or falling. You could also find out the exact pressure reading from your local weather centre.

The barometer should be placed away from direct sunlight. It should also be placed away from sources of heat, such as radiators and fires.

In your logbook, use arrows to indicate whether the pressure is rising or falling, or remaining the same.

## Humidity

The humidity of the air is measured on wet and dry bulb thermometers (see page 165), which should be placed in the shade.

Wet and dry bulb thermometers

## Precipitation

You can measure rainfall and other types of precipitation with your rain gauge (see page 159). Make sure it sits well away from trees and buildings.

## A weather logbook

Try to take your observations at the same time each day. Start a logbook in which you can record all your readings. Also record the general weather, such as if it is raining or sunny. You could use the weather symbols on page 172 to record your observations.

| Date | Time | Pressure Rising or Falling | Wind Speed | Wind Direction | Cloud Oktas | Cloud Type | Visibility | Temp | Humidity | Precipitation | General weather |
|---|---|---|---|---|---|---|---|---|---|---|---|
| 1st Jan | 08.00 | ↓ | 8-11 km/h | SW | 8 | Ns | poor | 4°c | 100% | 2mm | rain |
| | | | 12-14 | W | | | poor | 6°c | 95% | 0.5mm | drizzle |

# Analysing information

Weather observations, taken at weather stations all over the world (see page 168), are gathered together and distributed by special communication links to national weather centres in many countries, where all the information is analysed and weather maps are produced.

## Incoming information

The information received at national weather centres includes observations made at manned and automatic weather stations, and on ships and aircraft, as well as information from processing stations, such as radiosonde readings, and satellite and radar images.

Some of these observations are turned into weather maps called synoptic charts, such as the one above right.

These use many different symbols to show the different readings. The key on the right shows the main symbols.

Every day, in addition to producing synoptic charts, the centres produce a computer model of the atmosphere (see page 173), based on the information they receive. After all their analyses are complete, they make the results available to those who need them.

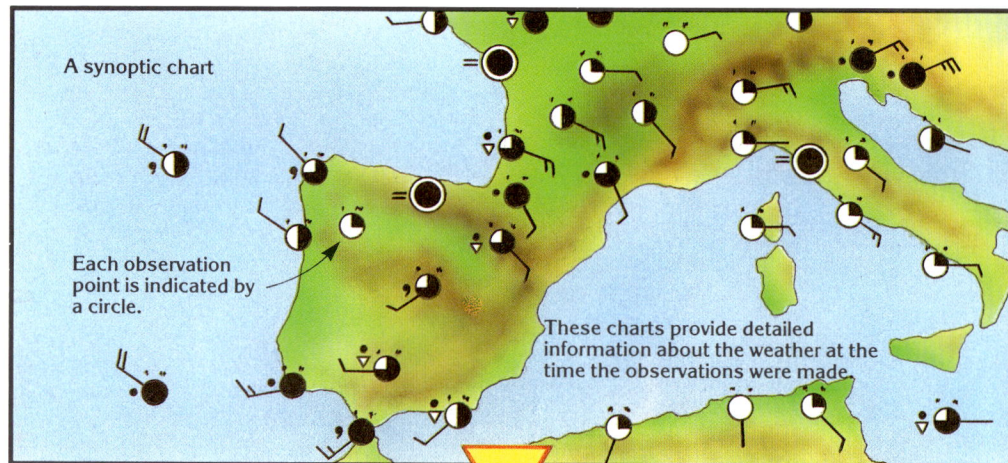

A synoptic chart

Each observation point is indicated by a circle.

These charts provide detailed information about the weather at the time the observations were made.

## Key

Temperature (in °C)

Present weather conditions (see below)

Cloud cover (see below)

2

92

Wind "arrows" indicate the direction from which the wind is blowing.

A north-easterly wind

Marks on the arrow show the wind speed. Each whole mark shows a wind speed of 18km/h (12mph). Half marks show a speed of 9km/h (6mph). The appropriate number of marks are added to the arrow to add up to the wind speed.

Pressure is shown by the last two numbers of the measurement. This is all that is needed, because of the normal range of pressures (very rarely below about 950mb or above 1040mb).

Cloud cover is measured in oktas (see page 157) and shown by the amount of the circle which is shaded. This shows there were 4 oktas of cloud. An extra white ring around the circle, and no wind arrow, means it was calm.

### Key to symbols for weather conditions

| Mist | = | Snow | ✱ |
| Fog | ≡ | Hail | ▲ |
| Rain | ● | Thunderstorm | ↯ |
| Drizzle | ❜ | The "showers" symbol is always shown with one, or more, other symbols: | |
| Showers | ▽ | Snow shower | ✱▽ |

## Plotting observations

If you set up your own weather station (see pages 170-171), you could use the symbols shown on this page to show your observations. Show the symbols for temperature, cloud cover, present weather, wind speed and direction.

In this example the temperature is 10°C.

The pressure of 1008mb is shown by the last two figures of the measurement.

The present conditions show a rain shower (see symbols chart).

10    08

There are 6 oktas of cloud.

The wind speed is 18kmph (12mph) and is blowing from the south-west.

# Computer models

Meteorologists use computers to predict what may happen to the weather for a period of time ahead. Using information from observations, calculations are made on computers to produce a model of the atmosphere as it was at the time when the observations were made. This model uses numbers to represent all the values for temperature, humidity, wind and pressure at different levels in the atmosphere.

## Grid points

In order for the computer to predict what may happen to the atmosphere, all the different readings made at different levels have to be arranged in a regular pattern in the model. Imaginary lines of longitude and latitude divide the Earth's surface into a grid. The points where the lines meet are called grid points, and the readings are assigned to these points. In most cases, the actual observations were not made at places exactly on these grid points, but the readings are allotted to the grid point nearest to where they were made.

In areas where there is little or no information, the computer estimates conditions using readings from surrounding grid points and past information about the weather.

There are 40,000 imaginary grid points covering the Earth's surface.

The computer has readings for temperature, pressure, winds and humidity, not just for each grid point, but also for points at many levels directly above it.

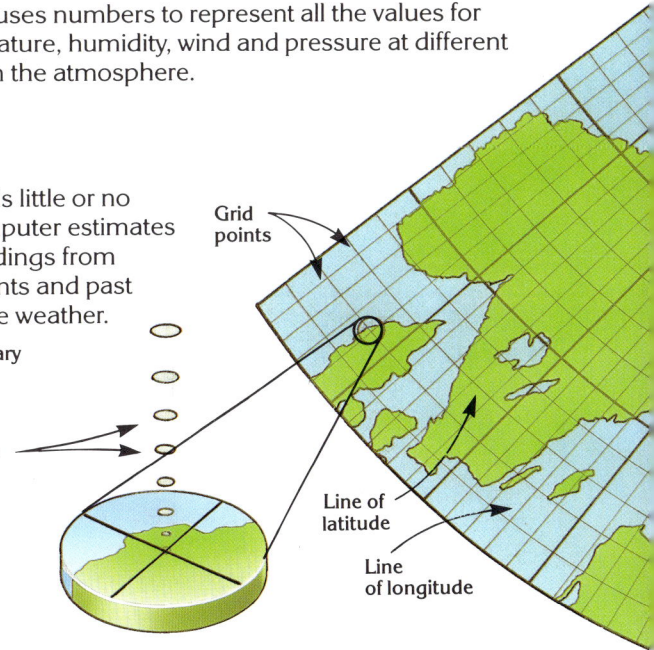

Grid points

Line of latitude

Line of longitude

## Predictions

To make a prediction, the computer calculates changes that should occur to each set of grid point numbers in a short space of time ahead, usually ten minutes. This produces a new set of numbers for the computer to use. This "time-step" process is repeated many times, until the computer predicts, for instance, what the temperature and winds will be like twelve hours ahead. This whole process takes only a few minutes and then computer maps and charts are produced, based on the predictions, which weather forecasters can use.

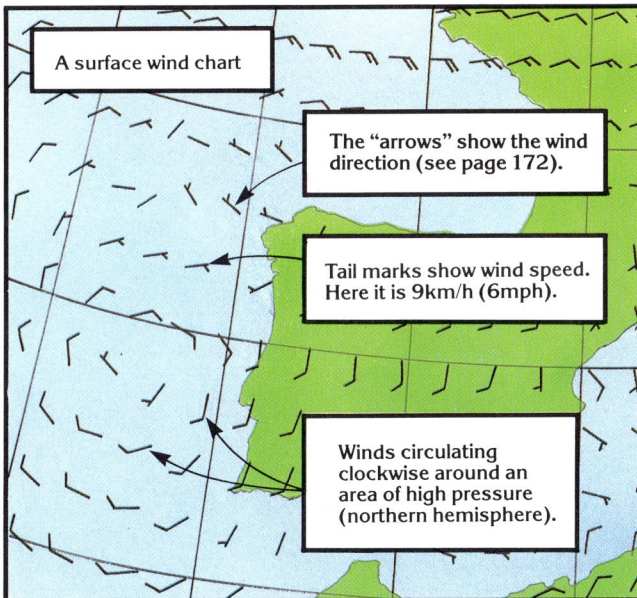

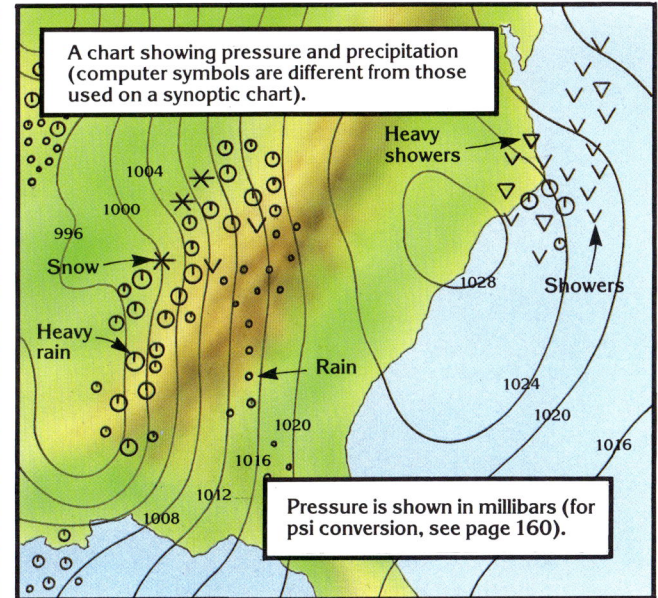

A surface wind chart

The "arrows" show the wind direction (see page 172).

Tail marks show wind speed. Here it is 9km/h (6mph).

Winds circulating clockwise around an area of high pressure (northern hemisphere).

A chart showing pressure and precipitation (computer symbols are different from those used on a synoptic chart).

Heavy showers

Snow

Showers

Heavy rain

Rain

Pressure is shown in millibars (for psi conversion, see page 160).

Computer predictions about the weather twelve hours and twenty-four hours ahead are produced at national weather centres twice a day. The time-step process is usually continued to give predictions for up to a week ahead. These predictions may not be very accurate, however, because each time the time-step process is repeated, any small errors, which were present in the original grid point calculations, will reappear and become magnified. This is the reason why many long-term weather forecasts are often unreliable.

# Weather forecasts

In order to predict the weather for the hours and days ahead, forecasters analyse information they receive from national weather centres (see pages 172-173). They look at the computer predictions but also use the observation maps and satellite images to make their own predictions. Forecasts reach the public via television, radio, newspapers and telephone information lines.

## Weather forecasters

Weather forecasters work in many different places, such as the national weather centres themselves, or at separate city weather centres or meteorological offices at military and public airports.

They study all the information they receive and look closely for things such as fronts, highs and lows, which may bring a change to weather patterns. They also often add their knowledge of frequent local weather conditions, such as coastal fog (see page 166).

Forecasters at city weather centres have direct contact with some public services.

Severe weather conditions, such as fog, snow and ice greatly affect road transport.

When ice is expected, the relevant department can be alerted, so the roads can be sprayed with salt.

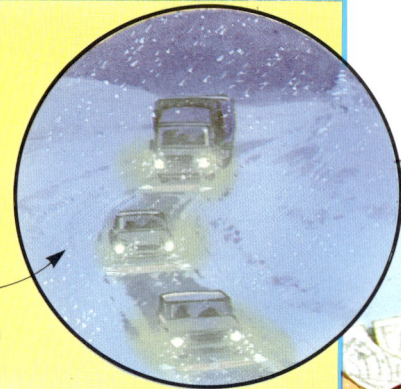

## Television forecasts

Many weather forecasters on television are trained meteorologists. They make their own forecasts, using the large variety of information sent to them directly from a national weather centre. Other forecasters are television presenters who read out forecasts provided by a weather centre. The forecaster's predictions for the day ahead are presented as a sequence of weather maps, which have been drawn up on computers in the graphics department of the television centre. These weather maps may show, for example, temperatures, winds or a summary of the expected weather conditions. The forecasters also use "movies" (individual geostationary satellite images joined together) to show the movement of weather systems.

The maps (seen by the viewers) are changed by the forecaster, either with a hand-held remote control or by using certain "cue" words, as a sign for someone else to change the image.

The technique of changing background images is called colour separation overlay.

During a weather broadcast, the forecaster stands in front of a blank screen, which is brightly coloured, for instance green.

The studio camera films the forecaster and the screen.

The viewers see the forecaster and a series of weather maps on their screen, but the forecaster sees only the blank screen.

This is because, while the camera is filming, anything green is being replaced electronically by the computer weather maps.

Studio camera

The forecaster cannot wear any green clothes as they would "disappear" and the weather chart would appear in their place.

## Radio and newspaper forecasts

Meteorologists at national and city weather centres provide radio stations and newspapers with information for their weather reports. National radio stations give a very generalized forecast for the whole country. Local radio stations, like local television stations, provide a more detailed forecast for their particular area. Newspaper forecasts are not as up-to-date, as the information they use has been issued at midday on the day before it appears in the newspaper.

A meteorologist analysing satellite images, charts and maps.

A television monitor next to the camera shows the forecaster what the viewers are seeing, and helps him point to the correct places on the blank screen.

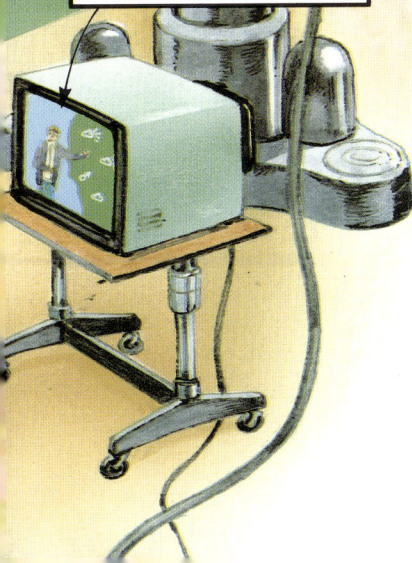

Stormy conditions, such as high seas, create dangers for people who work at sea, so detailed advance warnings are needed. Some radio stations broadcast a specialized shipping forecast. These give warnings of severe weather conditions along with the expected wind speed and direction.

Up-to-date weather forecasts are particularly important for people who work at sea, e.g. on ships and oil rigs.

## Who uses forecasts?

Weather forecasts are used by many specialized services, as well as being of interest to the public. Forecasts of approaching bad weather, such as storms or poor visibility, are of particular importance to aircraft, airports, shipping and fishing boats. Destinations can be changed, or routes diverted, to avoid bad weather conditions.

Specialized farming forecasts are broadcast on some television and radio stations. Farmers need to know if there is likely to be a severe frost, or if it is going to rain when they sow, harvest or spray their crops.

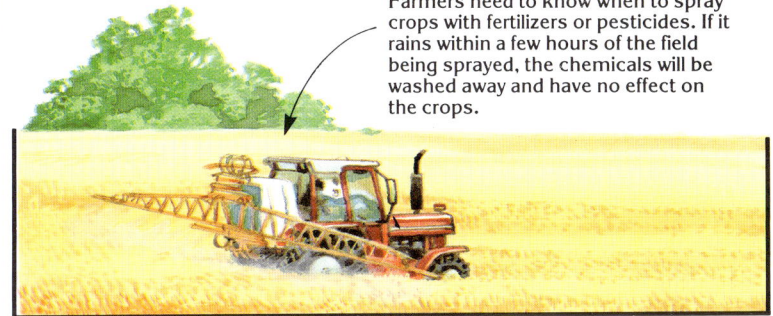

Farmers need to know when to spray crops with fertilizers or pesticides. If it rains within a few hours of the field being sprayed, the chemicals will be washed away and have no effect on the crops.

## How accurate are forecasts?

Weather forecasters try to be as accurate as possible, but their predictions are not always correct. You could compare the forecasts given for your area, over a period of days. Make a chart for recording the accuracy of forecasts from newspaper, television, radio and telephone.

Record your own weather observations (see pages 170-171) and compare your records with the forecasts.

A forecast is fairly accurate if the wind speed is within 8km/h (5mph) and the temperature is within 2°C (4°F) of your readings.

Mark your chart with ticks or crosses depending on whether you think the forecast is accurate.

| | | Actual measurements | Newspaper | | T.V. | | Radio | | Telephone | |
|---|---|---|---|---|---|---|---|---|---|---|
| Sunday | Temp. | 17°C | 16°C | ✓ | 16°C | ✓ | 17°C | ✓ | 14°C | ✗ |
| | Wind | 12 km/h | 14 km/h | ✓ | 15 km/h | ✓ | 12 km/h | ✓ | 15 km/h | ✓ |
| | General weather | rain | showers | ✓ | showers | ✓ | clear | ✗ | rain | ✓ |
| Monday | Temp. | | | | | | | | | |
| | Wind | | | | | | | | | |
| | General weather | | | | | | | | | |

# Worldwide climate

The climate of a particular area is the average pattern of weather which it experiences, measured over a long period. There are many different types of climate in different areas around the world, and these have a great effect on the vegetation and animals found there.

## Climates around the world

World climates are classified into different types, mainly by latitude and temperature. Within each main type, variations may occur. For instance, coastal areas have maritime or mediterranean climates, whereas places in the centre of large continents have continental climates. When naming a climate, these variations are combined with the main types. For instance, a coastal area in the tropics has a tropical maritime climate.

### The world's main climate types

Arctic or polar. Very cold and dry, strong winds. Summer temperatures may be 10°C (50°F) near coasts, but much lower inland. Some areas also classified as deserts.

Cold. Short summer, warmest month between 10°C (50°F) and 15°C (59°F). Cold winter, averaging −20°C to −30°C (−4°F to −22°F). Low rainfall, usually in summer.

Mountain. Temperature and rainfall depend on the latitude and change according to height.

Cool temperate. Between one and five months of temperatures below 6°C (43°F). Rainfall throughout year. Warm summers but cold winters, often below freezing.

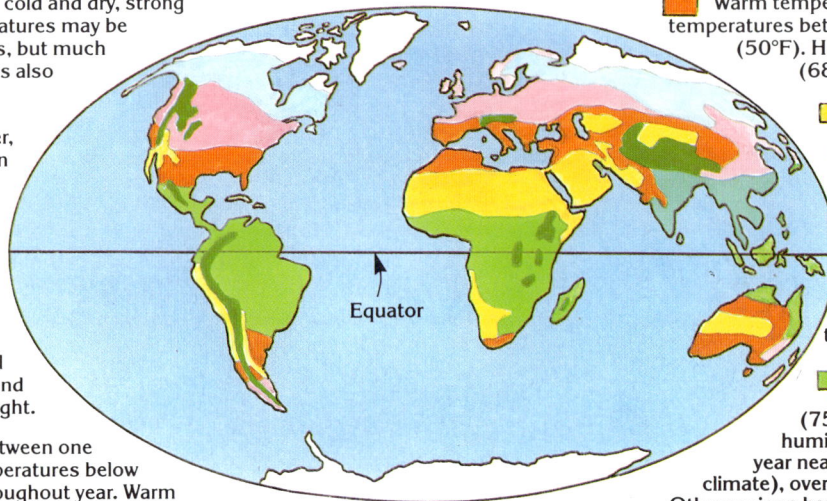

Warm temperate. Mild, wet winters with temperatures between 4°C (39°F) and 10°C (50°F). Hot summers, 20°C to 27°C (68°F to 81°F), with little rain.

Desert. Annual rainfall below 250mm (10in). In hot deserts, temperatures during the daytime may exceed 52°C (125°F).

Monsoon. A hot, wet season and a cool dry season, caused by winds which change with the season (see page 164).

Tropical. Temperatures high all year, between 24°C (75°F) and 27°C (81°F). High humidity. Heavy rain throughout year near equator (called equatorial climate), over 2,000mm (80in) per year. Other regions have most rain in one season.

Equator

## Water loss from plants

Plants take in water through their roots and use it to make their food, but some water evaporates through tiny pores in their leaves.

To show that plants from different climates lose water vapour at different rates you need two 2 litre (2 quart) clear plastic bottles, a house plant, a cactus, two polythene bags, wire bag ties and plates, and some petroleum jelly.

**What to do**

House plant, e.g. geranium

Cactus

Wire tie

Polythene bag

Pot

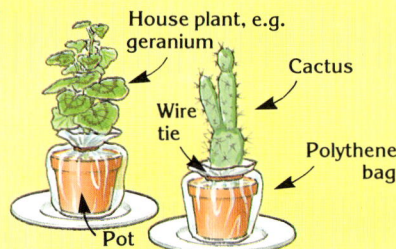

1. Give each plant 90ml (approx. 3 fl.oz) of water. Place each pot in a bag and fasten around the base of each plant with the wire ties. Place each plant on a plate.

2. Using a pair of scissors, carefully cut the base off each bottle.

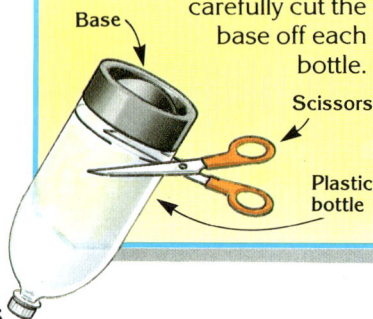

Base

Scissors

Plastic bottle

3. Place a bottle over each plant. Smear a thick layer of jelly around the base of each bottle.

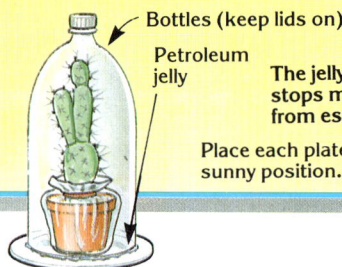

Bottles (keep lids on)

Petroleum jelly

The jelly stops moisture from escaping.

Place each plate in a light, sunny position.

4. After three days, you should see water droplets on the inside of the bottles. These have condensed from water vapour given off by the plants.

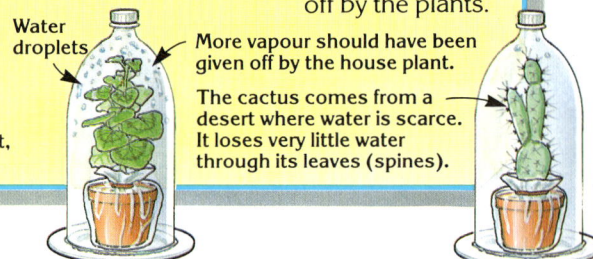

Water droplets

More vapour should have been given off by the house plant.

The cactus comes from a desert where water is scarce. It loses very little water through its leaves (spines).

# Climate and living things

Plants and animals are found in all areas of the world, each type adapted to the climate of its area. The fewest species are found where conditions are harshest, such as at the poles, and the greatest number in areas with much kinder climates. The most variety occurs in the warm, wet tropical areas.

## Tropical rain forests

Rain forests are found in tropical areas near the equator, where there is over 2,000mm (80in) of rain a year. Temperatures are high as, because of their position, these areas receive most solar energy (see page 150). Over half the Earth's species of plants and animals live in rain forests.

In tropical rain forests, it rains in short, heavy showers nearly every day. The warm, humid conditions provide the ideal living conditions for plants and animals.

## Surviving in deserts

In hot deserts, daytime temperatures are very high as there is hardly any cloud cover to protect the surface from the Sun's rays. It cools down quickly at night as heat radiates into space. There is little rain each year but fog and dew may form when the air cools at night. The few plants and animals which live in these regions have developed ways of surviving the intense heat and scarcity of water.

Some animals, such as the head-standing beetle, rely on fog or dew for water. The fog condenses on to its body, and it tilts forwards, so the droplets run into its mouth.

Many desert animals, including the head-standing beetle, escape the fierce heat by burrowing under the surface.

Many desert plants can store water in special cells when it rains. This means they can survive through the long, dry periods.

Leaf succulents have leaves which swell up to hold water.

Cacti store water in their stems. They also have spines instead of leaves. These have a much smaller surface area, so lose less water through evaporation.

Scarlet macaw

Ocelots hunt for their prey in forest trees and on the ground.

Toucan

Squirrel monkey

Plants known as bromeliads grow on the trunks and branches of trees.

Red-eyed tree frogs live in the rainwater which collects in their leaves.

Emerald tree boa

## Surviving freezing temperatures

There are relatively few species of animals or plants living near the poles, where the temperature is nearly always below freezing.

In Antarctica, temperatures may fall below −40°C (−40°F).

Penguins are protected from the freezing temperatures by very dense feathers and a thick layer of fat under their skin.

Giant armadillo

# People and climate

People live in all the different climates of the world, ranging from the polar areas to the equator. In order to live a comfortable life, particularly where the climate is harsh, they have designed their houses, clothes and lifestyles to fit the conditions of their particular climate.

## Building design

Most buildings are designed to make living in a particular climate as comfortable as possible. In temperate climates, with seasonal variations in temperature, many buildings have thick walls which trap the heat which builds up inside them. Many of these buildings are heated artificially in winter by fires and central heating. Windows are designed to let in maximum amounts of sunlight in winter and let out excess heat which builds up during the day in summer.

In temperate areas, houses are designed to keep heat in during the winter.

Large windows are often positioned on the sunniest side of the house to allow in as much sunlight as possible in the winter. These can be opened in summer to allow heat to escape.

Thick curtains help to keep in the heat in winter.

In hot climates, houses are designed for coolness. Most have few walls or partitions, to allow the maximum amount of air to circulate. Some buildings have window shutters, which are closed during the hottest part of the day, to keep the hot air out, and opened in the early morning and evening to allow cool air to circulate around the building.

In tropical areas, many houses have few inside walls. This allows air to circulate freely inside the building.

In areas of heavy rain, roofs are often built with a steep pitch (angle) to allow the water to drain off easily.

Houses are built on stilts in tropical areas to avoid being flooded during heavy rain.

## City climates

Cities tend to have a different climate to their surrounding area because of their high concentration of buildings. They tend to be warmer at night, and may also get more rain in summer. The amount of pollution in the air also tends to be higher in cities (see page 184).

Tall buildings act as barriers to the wind. This either forces the wind upwards, or funnels it along the streets between buildings.

If the air rising over the city is exceptionally warm and humid, it may cool to form clouds, which may give short bursts of rain.

Building materials, such as bricks, stone and concrete, absorb a great deal of heat during the day.

At night, this heat is given off slowly, forming a "heat island", which makes a city up to 5°C (9°F) warmer than its surroundings.

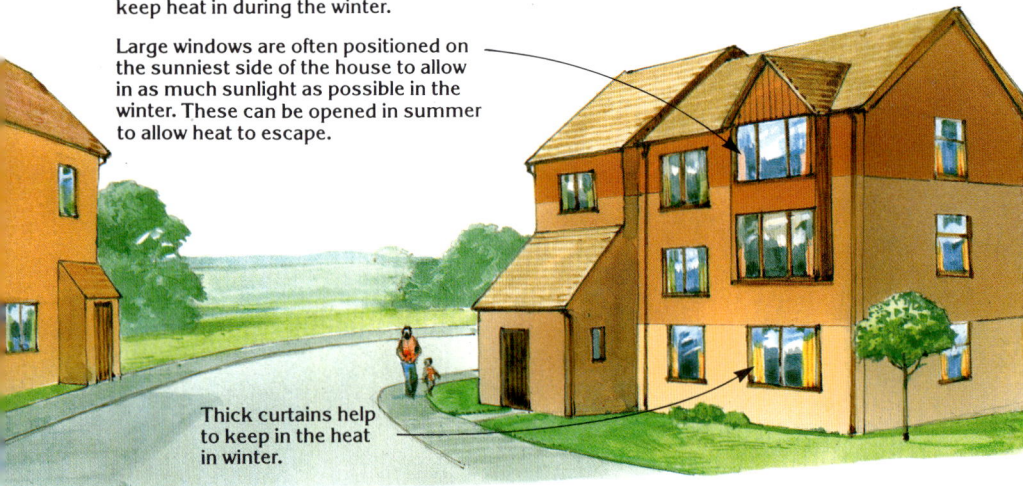

## Reflecting the Sun's heat

Different surfaces absorb and reflect different amounts of solar energy (see page 151). Light-coloured and shiny surfaces reflect the Sun's rays and so reduce the amount of heat which materials absorb.

In countries with a hot, sunny climate, buildings are often painted white, to reflect heat away. People also often wear light-coloured clothes to reduce the amount of heat their bodies receive.

In hot climates, buildings are white-washed to reflect the heat and help keep them cool.

People who live in extremely hot climates, such as deserts, wear long robes to protect them from the Sun and from wind-blown sand.

Just as few walls help air to move around inside a house, flowing robes help to circulate air around a body, keeping it cool.

## The body and temperature

The human body reacts to different temperatures with various mechanisms which help it adjust its own temperature. Normally a person's body gives off heat, as it is warmer than the surrounding air. This heat is lost from the blood in blood vessels just under the surface of the skin.

When a person gets very hot, extra body heat is given off by sweating. As water evaporates from the skin, the body temperature is lowered. More heat is also lost from the skin's blood vessels, as these widen to allow more blood through.

When it is very cold, the blood vessels constrict, or become narrower, letting less blood through, so less heat is lost from the body. In extremely cold conditions, the supply of blood to some parts of the body, usually fingers and toes, may stop completely.

The blood travels into the surface blood vessels from the main arteries, and out of them via the veins.

The blood is pumped around all the blood vessels by the heart, and picks up heat as it travels.

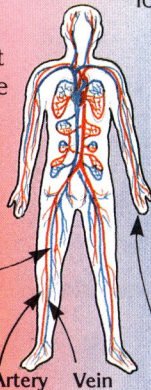

Artery    Vein

If fingers and toes receive no blood, they receive no heat. The skin "dies". This is known as frostbite.

## Making a radiometer

A radiometer is an instrument which uses reflection and absorption to measure solar energy. To make a simple radiometer, you need a black pen, a chewing gum wrapper, a jam jar, a pencil, some foil, strong glue, thread and a used matchstick.

**What to do**

Black surface
Chewing gum wrapper
Foil

1. Colour the paper side of the wrapper with the black pen. Cut it into four pieces, each 2cm x 2.5cm (¾in x 1in).

Matchstick
Shiny surfaces
Stick 12cm (5in) thread to the other end.

2. Stick the pieces of paper to one end of the matchstick (see right), with the shiny surfaces facing the same way.

Pencil
Sticky tape
Thread
Jar
Radiometer

3. Wrap the loose end of thread around a pencil and secure it with some sticky tape. Suspend the radiometer in the jar.

4. Place the jar in a very sunny position.

The radiometer turns as solar energy is absorbed by the black surfaces and reflected by the shiny surfaces.

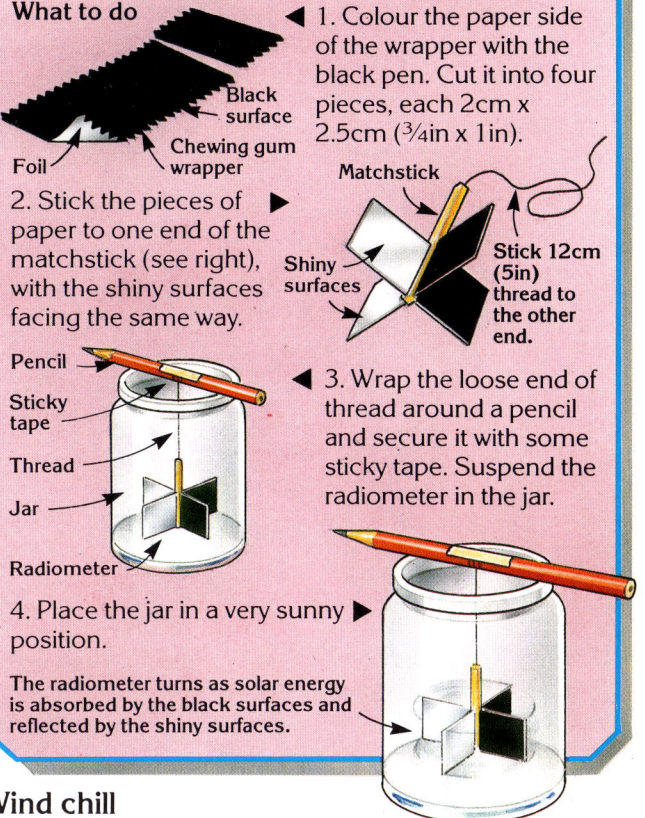

## Wind chill

The wind can make the air temperature feel colder than it actually is. This is called the wind chill factor. Normally, a thin layer of warm air surrounds your body, but if the wind is strong, this warm air is blown away, making you feel colder.

If the air temperature is 0°C (32°F) and a gentle breeze is blowing, the wind chill factor makes it feel like −3°C (27°F). If the wind speed increases to a strong breeze, the temperature feels like −10°C (14°F).

Scientists who work at the poles wear several layers of clothes to help insulate their body against freezing temperatures and the wind.

The clothes trap air which is warmed by the scientists' body heat, keeping them warm.

# Changing climates

The Earth was formed about 4,600 million years ago, but the climate has not always been as it is today. At certain times, covering periods of thousands of years, it was much warmer than it is now. At other times, it was a lot colder, with much of the land covered in ice.

## The first atmosphere

When the Earth was first formed, the atmosphere as we know it did not exist. The Earth's surface was a mass of liquid rocks which cooled to form a solid crust. As it cooled, the primitive atmosphere was formed from steam and poisonous gases, given off by erupting volcanoes.

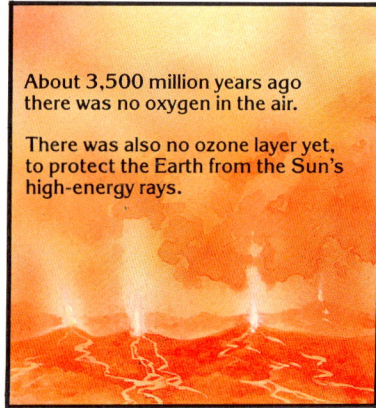

About 3,500 million years ago there was no oxygen in the air.

There was also no ozone layer yet, to protect the Earth from the Sun's high-energy rays.

About 2,000 million years ago, tiny organisms appeared. They lived in water and produced oxygen, which entered the atmosphere.

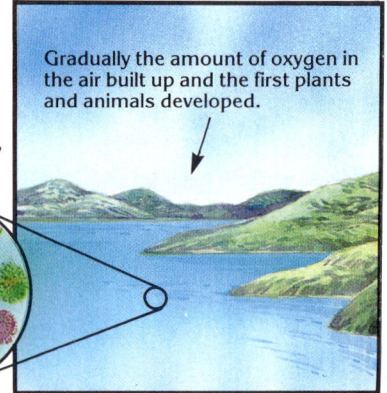

Gradually the amount of oxygen in the air built up and the first plants and animals developed.

## Ice ages

In the past, the Earth has gone through periods of time, called ice ages, when the climate was much colder and ice sheets covered huge areas of the surface. At the moment, ice sheets are found at the poles, but at times, ice has covered much larger areas.

Present-day ice sheet

Scientists think that ice ages have occurred about every 100,000 years and that they last for about 75,000 years. At the moment, the climate is between ice ages. This is called an interglacial climate.

Ice sheets are still found in the Arctic and Antarctic.

There are several theories which try to explain why ice ages occur. In the past, some scientists believed that the climate became colder because at certain times the amount of energy given off by the Sun decreased.

Ice ages have also been explained by a change in the Earth's angle of tilt on its axis and a change in the path of the Earth's orbit around the Sun.

The ice which forms the ice sheets has built up over thousands of years.

## Climate change due to moving continents

The climate of each continent may have also changed because its position gradually changes. This is because the Earth's crust is made up of several pieces, called plates, which move very slowly, carrying the continents with them. Millions of years ago, many countries may have had a different climate because they were not found in the same latitude as they are today.

200 million years ago scientists believe there was one "supercontinent" called Pangea.

Antarctica was in much warmer latitudes.

India was much further south.

Gradually the continents moved to their present-day positions.

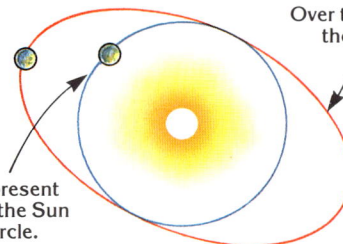

The Earth's present orbit around the Sun is almost a circle.

Over thousands of years the shape of the orbit may have gradually changed to an ellipse (oval) and back to a circle. This would have changed the amount of solar energy the Earth received. When the orbit changed to an ellipse, an ice age may have occurred as the Earth became cooler.

## Volcanic eruptions

Scientists believe that erupting volcanoes may affect world climates. When a volcano erupts, fine volcanic dust may be thrown high into the atmosphere. The dust acts as a screen, reflecting more solar radiation back into space and preventing it from reaching the Earth.

It is thought that when the Earth was first formed, thousands of volcanoes covered the surface. Poisonous gases and dust, thrown out as the volcanoes erupted, greatly affected the climate.

Large volcanic eruptions still occur today, but they are very rare and their effect on the climate is short-term. Records show that the weather may be affected for two or three years following a huge eruption.

When Tambora in Indonesia erupted in 1815, volcanic dust was flung high into the atmosphere.

Dust from Tambora was spread around the world by high-level winds. Temperatures fell as the amount of solar radiation reaching the Earth decreased.

## Climate change and the extinction of the dinosaurs

About 65 million years ago more than half the species of plant and animal life, including the dinosaurs, became extinct. Scientists believe that a sudden change in climate could have caused the mass extinction.

Dinosaurs existed on Earth for over 150 million years. During that time, the climate was believed to be warm and humid.

Some scientists believe that many species became extinct due to a massive volcanic eruption which blocked out the sunlight. This caused green plants to die, as they need sunlight to produce their food. In turn this meant many plant-eating animals died out.

Other scientists believe that a massive asteroid (immense rock in space), with a diameter of about 15km (9 miles), may have hit the Earth. The impact sent huge amounts of dust into the atmosphere, blocking out solar radiation.

## Counting tree rings

Scientists work out climatic changes by studying the layers in rocks. In a similar way, by looking at the growth rings in the trunk of the tree which has fallen or died, it is possible to work out what the weather may have been like when it grew.

Each year the water-carrying tubes, or xylem, add new layers of cells in the centre of the tree's trunk, pushing the trunk outwards. In a year which has a warm, wet growing season more layers of cells will be added, producing a wide growth ring. In a season which has been dry or cold, the growth ring will be narrow.

You can work out the age of the tree by counting the rings.

A narrow growth ring shows that the growing season was cold and dry.

A wider growth ring indicates that the weather in that year was probably warm and wet.

This tree was 16 years old.

## Geological evidence

Most rocks are formed in layers, and by studying these layers, geologists (scientists who study rocks and their formation) are able to work out what the climate may have been like when each layer was formed.

Geologists use other methods to work out the age of the layers. By studying the minerals which make up a rock, they can date when rocks were formed. Once they have dated the layers, they can work out when climatic changes took place.

Rocks formed in warm climates contain a greater variety of fossils, compared with those formed in cooler times.

Rocks which lay at the surface during ice ages show evidence of being eroded, or worn away, by glaciers, or masses of moving ice.

# Present-day climate changes

At present, many scientists believe that world climates may be changing. They think this is due to the weather being affected by rising temperatures, caused by a build-up of certain gases in the atmosphere.

## The greenhouse effect

The greenhouse effect is the term used to describe how the Earth is kept warm by heat trapped by gases in the lower atmosphere. It has been occurring for millions of years. Without the greenhouse effect, it is thought that the average temperature on the Earth's surface would be $-15°C$ ($5°F$).

The gases, such as carbon dioxide and water vapour, are known as greenhouse gases, as they act like greenhouse glass. They let the Sun's high-energy radiation pass down through them to heat the Earth's surface, but absorb the lower energy radiation which the Earth sends back up. They then send out even lower energy in all directions. Some of this reaches the Earth, which receives extra heating.

High-energy radiation travels in through the glass of a greenhouse.

This is absorbed by the objects inside, which heat up. They send out lower energy radiation, which the glass absorbs.

The glass sends some radiation back, giving the objects extra heat.

In a similar way, the Earth's surface receives extra heating as greenhouse gases absorb and send out lower energy radiation.

## Global warming

At present, average temperatures around the world are gradually rising. This is known as global warming. There could be a number of reasons for this, but many scientists link it with a known increase in greenhouse gases. They believe this has led to more heat being trapped, and that it is mainly due to man's activities.

The amount of carbon dioxide in the air has increased by 25% in the last hundred years.

Power stations and factories which burn fossil fuels (coal, oil and gas), give off carbon dioxide as they produce power.

Carbon dioxide is also given off as forests are cleared and burned, to make way for farmland and building.

The scientists believe that if the amount of greenhouse gases continues to rise at its present rate, average temperatures will increase by between $1.5°C$ and $4°C$ ($3°F$ and $7°F$) in the next fifty years. Many people agree with them, and are trying to reduce the amount of greenhouse gases released into the atmosphere.

## Other greenhouse gases

Carbon dioxide and water vapour are the main greenhouse gases, but other gases, such as chlorofluorocarbons (CFCs), nitrous oxides and methane, also absorb out-going radiation. The amount of these gases is also increasing.

CFCs are given off by aerosol sprays and refrigerators.

CFCs are also thought to destroy ozone in the stratosphere (see page 184).

## The effects of global warming

If world temperatures continued to rise, it would greatly affect world climates and the lives of people and wildlife.

There would be more rain in tropical areas, as the extra heat would increase the amount of water vapour in the air. Areas which receive little rain would receive even less, and turn into deserts, so people and animals would have to move away.

Sea temperatures would rise and this might lead to flooding in low-lying areas and an increase in the number of severe storms.

Nitrous oxides come from car exhaust fumes and from fertilizers used on fields.

Methane is given off from rotting vegetation and swamps. Growing rice in water-filled paddy fields to feed millions of people has meant creating man-made swamps which give off more methane.

Many animals kept for food give off methane as a waste gas.

The amount of rubbish people produce has increased. Methane is given off from rotting rubbish in refuse dumps.

If temperatures rose, many animals would not be able to adapt to the climate changes.

Many plants would die for lack of water, and animals would have to migrate, or move to other areas, in search of food and water.

If many plants die due to rising world temperatures, many species of animals could die out.

## Rising sea levels

If world temperatures increase, sea levels may rise, for two main reasons. Firstly, when water is heated it becomes less dense and expands. If the sea temperature rose, its level would rise as the water expanded.

Secondly, higher temperatures could melt some of the ice which permanently covers some land, such as Antarctica and certain mountains. The water would eventually flow into the sea, making it rise. The melting of ice floating in the sea, however, would not add to rising sea levels.

The Arctic ice-cap is a huge, floating sheet of ice.

Like Antarctica, the Arctic is surrounded by floating icebergs.

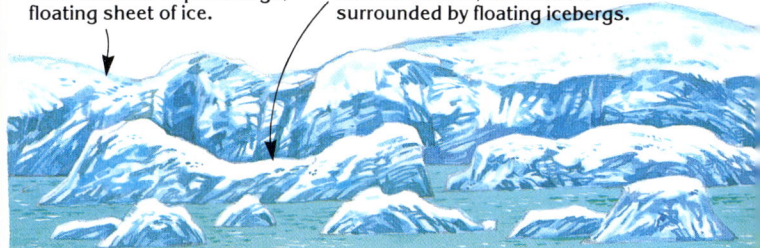

Even if all the ice in the Arctic melted, it would not cause a rise in sea levels. This is because when ice melts, the water which is left occupies less space than it did as ice.

## Melting ice

The Arctic ice-cap floats on the sea. It would have little effect on the sea level if it melted. To carry out an experiment to show this, you need some ice cubes, a large glass bowl and a ruler.

### What to do

1. Half-fill the bowl with water. Add ten ice cubes, and measure the water height.

Make sure all the ice cubes are floating in the water.

Ice cubes

Bowl

Ruler

Water

2. Wait for the ice cubes to melt.

3. Once the ice cubes have melted, measure the height of the water again.

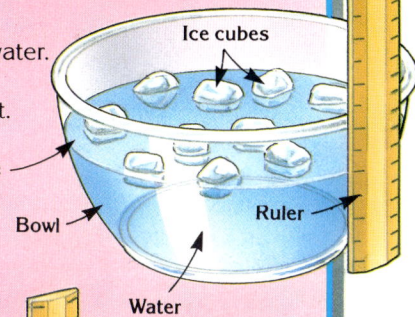

The level of the water should be less than before the ice cubes melted. This is because the frozen water of the ice cubes took up more space. Now the cubes have melted, their volume as water is less than it was as ice.

# Pollution in the atmosphere

Air pollution is caused by any undesirable substance which enters the atmosphere and upsets the natural balance. These substances may be gases, liquids or solids, and are known as pollutants. Most pollutants are given off into the air as a result of human activities.

## The ozone layer

Ozone is a gas, found throughout the Earth's atmosphere, but concentrated particularly in a layer in the stratosphere (see page 149). This layer is important because the molecules of gas stop harmful high-energy solar radiation from reaching the Earth's surface. Scientists have discovered that the ozone layer is getting thinner.

They think that substances in man-made gases called CFC s (see page 182) are rising into the stratosphere and breaking down the ozone molecules and that, if this continues, more and more harmful radiation will reach the Earth's surface. Exposure to harmful high-energy radiation can cause some forms of skin cancer.

Above Antarctica, scientists have discovered a "hole" where the ozone layer is thin.

They monitor the amount of ozone in the atmosphere using instruments attached to balloons.

## Temperature inversions

In certain unusual conditions, a layer of warm air may trap colder air beneath it for several days at a time. This is called a temperature inversion.

When a temperature inversion occurs above a city, it greatly affects the build-up of pollutants, such as smog (smoke and fog). Normally, pollutants are dispersed, or scattered, through the atmosphere by moving air. The inversion prevents the air from rising, and traps the polluted air at a low level.

Smog is formed as water condenses onto tiny particles, given off as fossil fuels are burned.

The air cannot rise as it is trapped beneath the warm air, so the pollution builds up.

Smog is not as common as it used to be. This is due to fewer buildings being heated by coal fires, and fewer power stations in cities.

Smog affects people with asthma and other breathing problems.

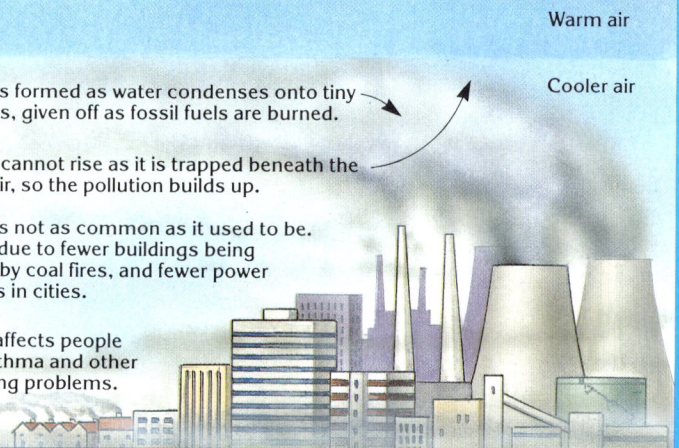

Warm air

Cooler air

## Surface ozone and photochemical smog

Some ozone, known as surface ozone, is found at ground level. It is a form of pollution and can cause health problems. It is formed by the chemical reaction of different pollutants with strong sunlight. The main pollutants in this case are nitrogen oxides and hydrocarbons from exhaust fumes.

When a large quantity of surface ozone builds up, it is known as photochemical smog. This is virtually invisible at street level, but can be seen as a brown haze hanging above a city.

Photochemical smog is an increasing problem in large cities in the summer.

Pollutant gases build up in the air at low levels and react with sunlight to produce surface ozone (photochemical smog). It causes people to suffer from eye irritations and sore throats.

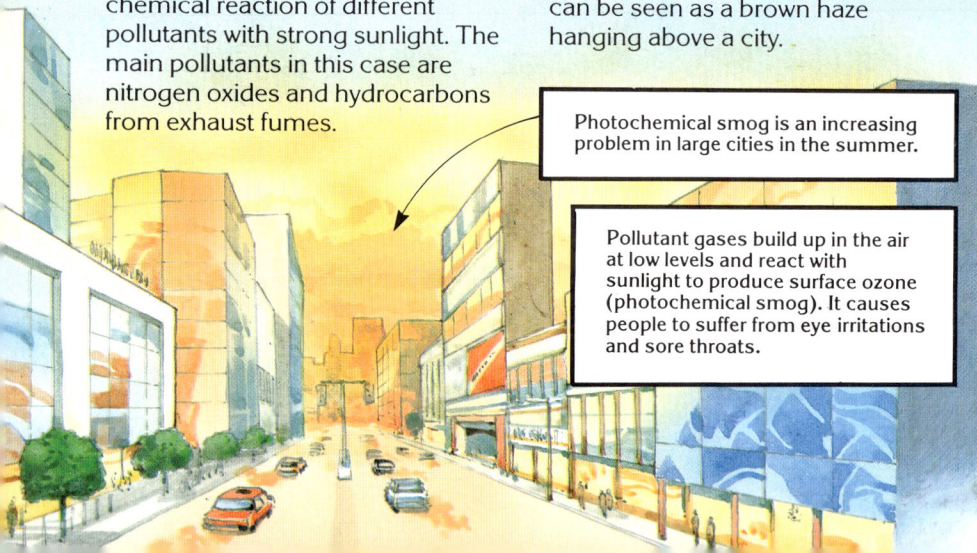

## Lead pollution

Lead is another air pollutant. It enters the air as particles from exhaust fumes, and is found much more in cities than in rural areas. Scientists believe that if people are exposed to large amounts of lead, it will build up in their blood and cause brain damage.

Lead-free petrol is now widely used to cut down on the amount of lead which pollutes the air.

# Acid rain

Rainwater normally contains tiny amounts of acid, but this causes little damage. When mixed with some pollutants, though, it becomes much more acidic, and produces harmful rain known as acid rain.

Many animals cannot survive the higher acid levels, for example in lakes and rivers. Trees and other plants suffer as the acid makes them less resistant to frost and to attack by insects and diseases.

Acid rain also eats into and dissolves the surfaces it lands on, such as rocks. Harmful minerals are washed out of some rocks, and these do further damage to animals and plants (see picture, below).

Pollutants such as sulphur dioxide and nitrous oxide make rainwater more acidic. They enter the air in exhaust fumes, and when fossil fuels are burned.

Acid rain clouds may be blown for long distances before the rain falls.

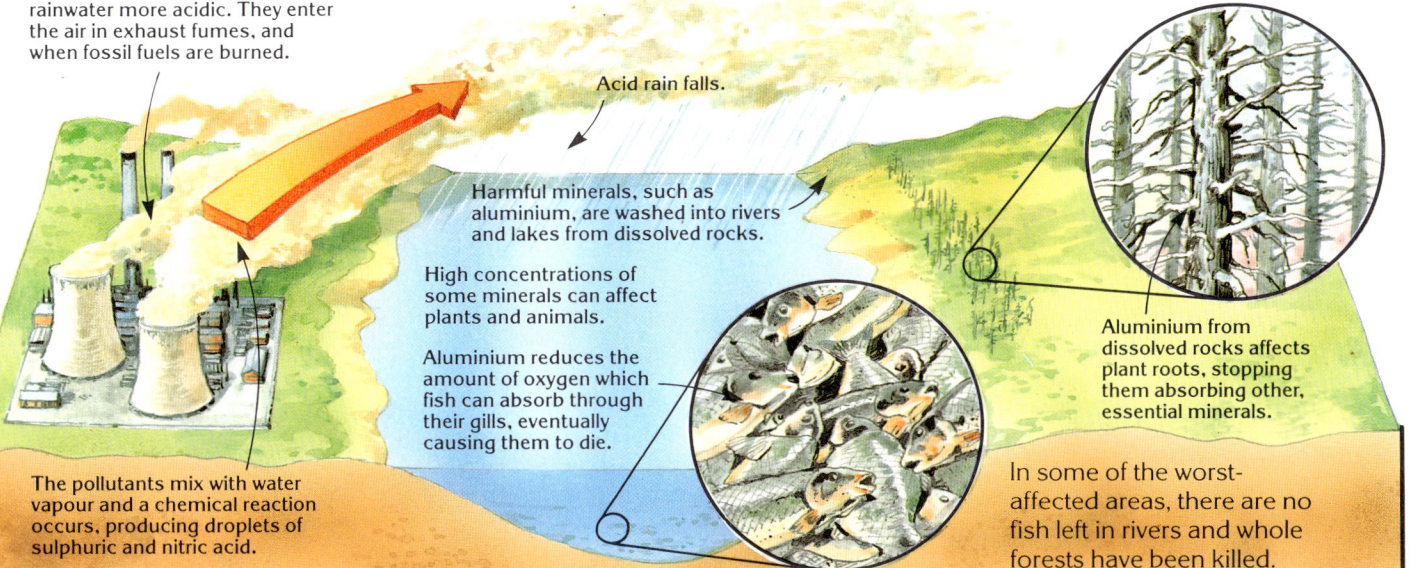

Acid rain falls.

Harmful minerals, such as aluminium, are washed into rivers and lakes from dissolved rocks.

High concentrations of some minerals can affect plants and animals.

Aluminium reduces the amount of oxygen which fish can absorb through their gills, eventually causing them to die.

The pollutants mix with water vapour and a chemical reaction occurs, producing droplets of sulphuric and nitric acid.

Aluminium from dissolved rocks affects plant roots, stopping them absorbing other, essential minerals.

In some of the worst-affected areas, there are no fish left in rivers and whole forests have been killed.

## Acid rain indicator

Most rainwater is slightly acidic. To make an indicator to see how acidic your rain is, compared with other substances, you need some red cabbage, white vinegar, bicarbonate of soda, a jug and some jars.

### What to do

1. Collect some rainwater in a jar. Chop up 3 large cabbage leaves. Put them into a saucepan with ½l (1 pint) of tap water. Boil them gently for ten minutes.

2. Let the mixture cool, then pour the liquid through a sieve into the jug.

3. Test your indicator liquid by pouring 1cm (½in) depth into two jars. Add a few drops of vinegar to one and ½tsp of bicarbonate to the other.

4. In the same way, use your indicator to test some rainwater to see how acidic it is.

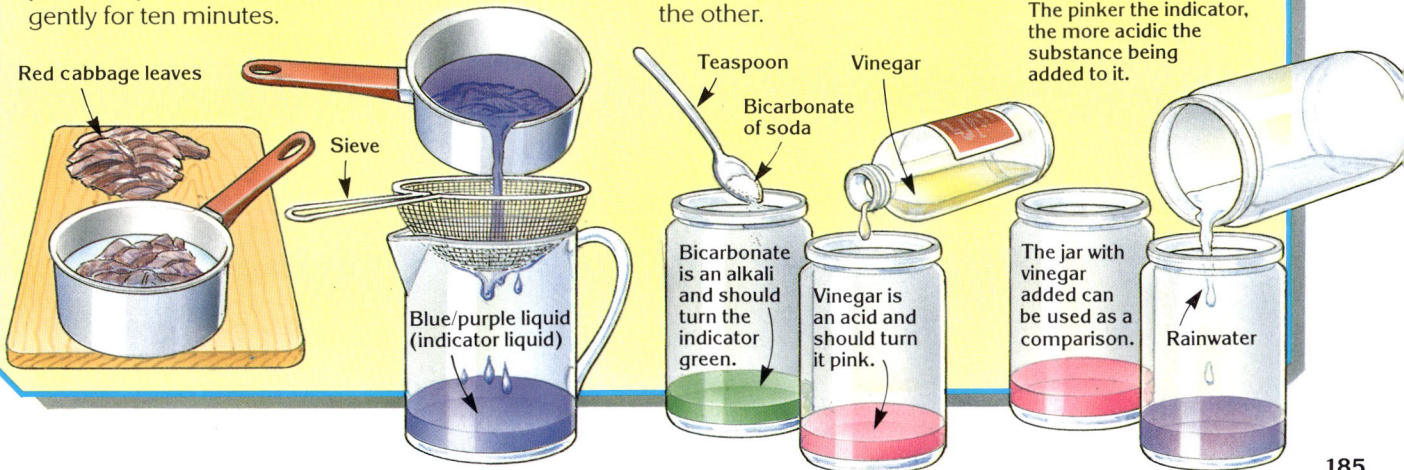

The pinker the indicator, the more acidic the substance being added to it.

Red cabbage leaves

Sieve

Teaspoon

Vinegar

Bicarbonate of soda

Blue/purple liquid (indicator liquid)

Bicarbonate is an alkali and should turn the indicator green.

Vinegar is an acid and should turn it pink.

The jar with vinegar added can be used as a comparison.

Rainwater

# Predicting future weather

With the current concern about global warming (see page 182), meteorologists are trying to predict what effect rising temperatures may have on weather and climates around the world in the future. They use computer models to work out future climates, in a similar way to forecasting daily weather (see page 173).

## General circulation models

Scientists use computer models, called general circulation models, or GCMs, to predict future weather patterns. Their computers contain vast amounts of information about the atmosphere, such as its composition of gases, average surface and upper air temperatures and humidity, as well as information about oceans.

By changing particular pieces of information, for instance by adding more greenhouse gases, scientists can create new models which show what effect global warming may have on weather in the future.

GCMs have predicted that in continental regions, such as in North America, rainfall may increase in winter and temperatures may rise by 2-4°C (4-7°F) in the next fifty years.

There could also be a 2-3°C (3-5°F) temperature rise in summer, with less rain.

This change in climate could greatly affect the amount of wheat which is grown in the vast areas of North America, known as the prairies.

## Uneven temperature increases

Using general circulation models, scientists have predicted that there may be an average temperature rise of 1.5°C (2.7°F) by the year 2050. They think that temperatures will rise unevenly, though, with the greatest rise at the poles. This will have an increase of up to 4°C (7°F), compared to 1°C (1.8°F) in tropical areas.

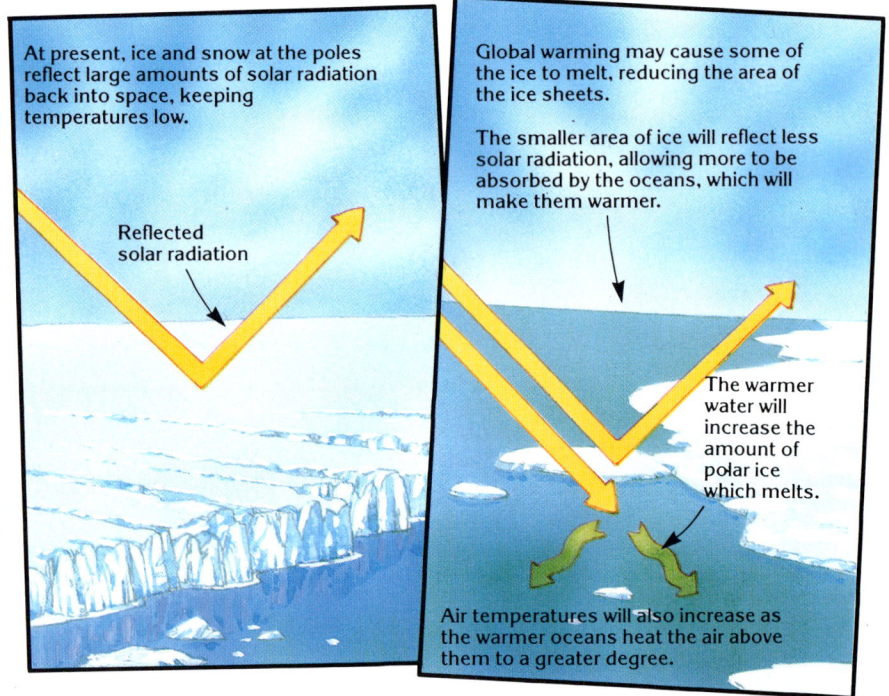

At present, ice and snow at the poles reflect large amounts of solar radiation back into space, keeping temperatures low.

Reflected solar radiation

Global warming may cause some of the ice to melt, reducing the area of the ice sheets.

The smaller area of ice will reflect less solar radiation, allowing more to be absorbed by the oceans, which will make them warmer.

The warmer water will increase the amount of polar ice which melts.

Air temperatures will also increase as the warmer oceans heat the air above them to a greater degree.

### Predicted temperature increases around the world

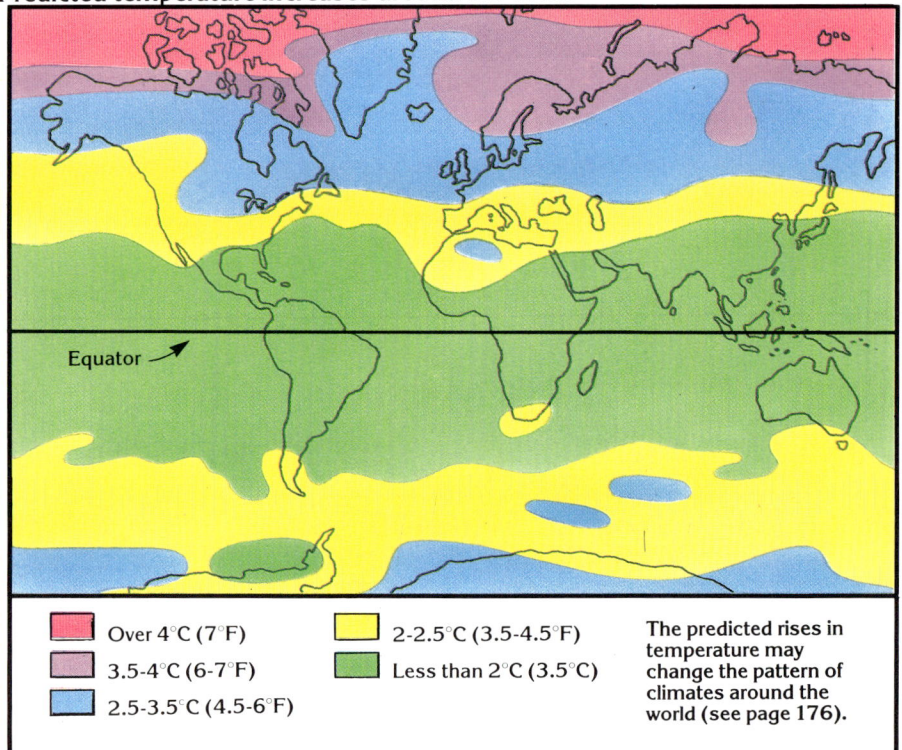

Equator

| | | |
|---|---|---|
| ■ Over 4°C (7°F) | ■ 2-2.5°C (3.5-4.5°F) | |
| ■ 3.5-4°C (6-7°F) | ■ Less than 2°C (3.5°C) | |
| ■ 2.5-3.5°C (4.5-6°F) | | |

The predicted rises in temperature may change the pattern of climates around the world (see page 176).

186

## Changing cloud cover

Some scientists believe that in a warmer world there would be more clouds, as greater amounts of water would evaporate from seas. This could lead to many areas having more rain than they do now. Also, some types of cloud reflect solar radiation, while others absorb radiation from the Earth's surface. Depending on the type and amount of "new" cloud, the rate at which global warming occurs could be affected.

If the number of clouds increases, the rate of global warming may be reduced, or even halted, but it may also be increased. Whether temperatures increase or decrease may depend on the type of clouds which are formed.

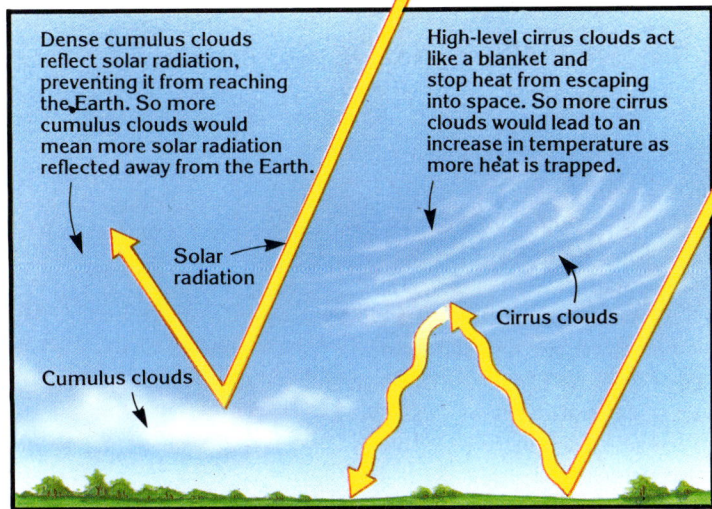

## More storms?

Some scientists believe that extreme weather conditions, such as storms, hurricanes and floods could become more frequent in a warmer world, particularly in tropical areas. Even though the temperature increase in tropical areas may be small, the warmer temperatures could lead to more hurricanes, as there would be a greater area of sea with temperatures above 27°C (80°F) (see page 162).

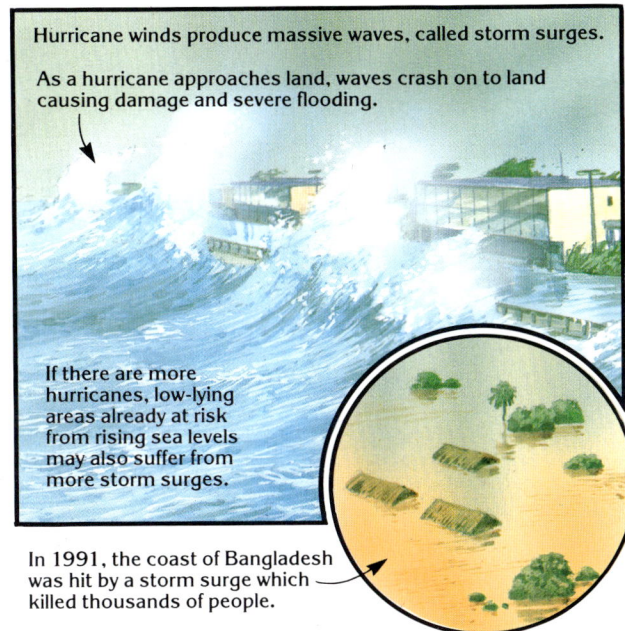

Hurricane winds produce massive waves, called storm surges.

As a hurricane approaches land, waves crash on to land causing damage and severe flooding.

If there are more hurricanes, low-lying areas already at risk from rising sea levels may also suffer from more storm surges.

In 1991, the coast of Bangladesh was hit by a storm surge which killed thousands of people.

Other scientists believe that storms could become less frequent, particularly in temperate areas. Areas of low pressure, which lead to storms, develop because of the large temperature difference between polar and tropical air (see page 160). Due to the predicted uneven increase in world temperatures, this difference would become smaller, so, according to these scientists, fewer severe storms would occur.

Dense cumulus clouds reflect solar radiation, preventing it from reaching the Earth. So more cumulus clouds would mean more solar radiation reflected away from the Earth.

High-level cirrus clouds act like a blanket and stop heat from escaping into space. So more cirrus clouds would lead to an increase in temperature as more heat is trapped.

Solar radiation

Cirrus clouds

Cumulus clouds

## A bottle hurricane

Winds within a hurricane rise in a spiral motion, known as a vortex. It is possible to create your own vortex in a bottle. For this you will need two identical clear plastic bottles (also with plastic tops), some very strong glue and a corkscrew.

### What to do

1. Use the glue to stick the two bottle tops together, flat surfaces together.

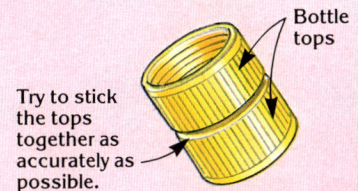

Try to stick the tops together as accurately as possible.

Bottle tops

2. Let the glue dry, then make a hole through the lids using a hammer and a nail.

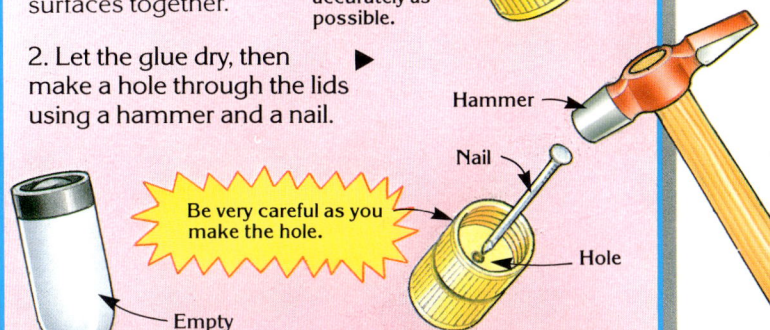

Be very careful as you make the hole.

Hammer

Nail

Hole

Empty bottle

Double top

3. Fill one bottle with water so it is three-quarters full. Screw the double top on tightly, and then the empty bottle.

Water

4. Turn the bottle upside down and start the water rotating by giving it a gentle swirl.

The water creates a vortex as it pours into the other bottle.

# Record weather extremes

Record-breaking weather and climate conditions have been monitored by meteorologists all around the world.

## The rainiest climate

The wettest place in the world, with the highest number of rainy days each year, is Mt. Wai-'ale-'ale on the island of Kauai in Hawaii. It rains on as many as 350 days each year.

The Hawaiian islands lie in the Pacific Ocean. The south-east trade winds blow here, all year. These winds are warm and moist.

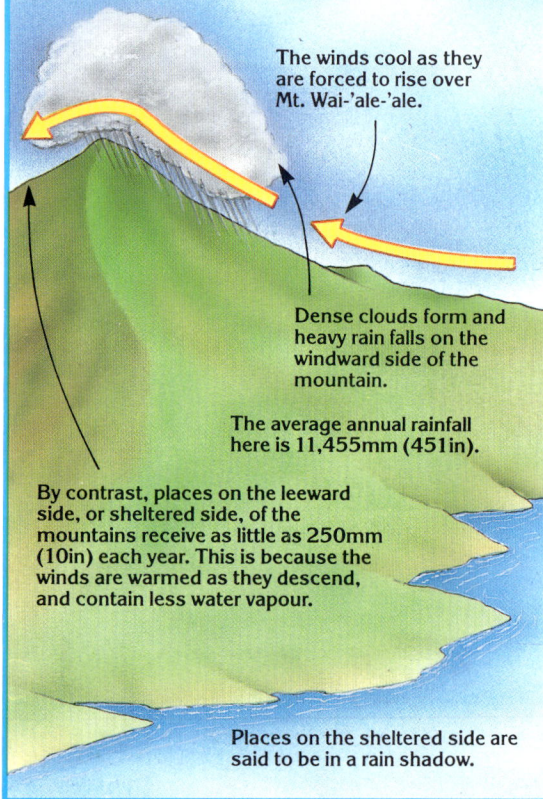

The winds cool as they are forced to rise over Mt. Wai-'ale-'ale.

Dense clouds form and heavy rain falls on the windward side of the mountain.

The average annual rainfall here is 11,455mm (451in).

By contrast, places on the leeward side, or sheltered side, of the mountains receive as little as 250mm (10in) each year. This is because the winds are warmed as they descend, and contain less water vapour.

Places on the sheltered side are said to be in a rain shadow.

## Longest drought

The driest place in the world, which has also experienced the longest drought, is Calama in the Atacama Desert in Chile. It is said that up until 1971 there had been no rain there for 400 years.

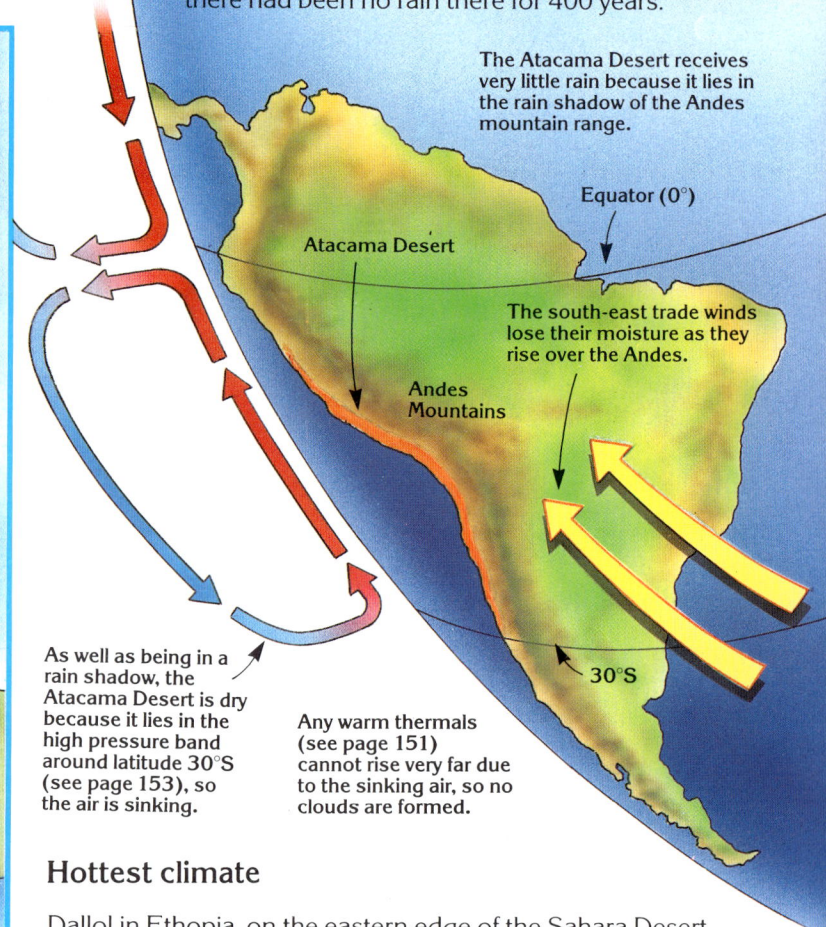

The Atacama Desert receives very little rain because it lies in the rain shadow of the Andes mountain range.

Equator (0°)

Atacama Desert

The south-east trade winds lose their moisture as they rise over the Andes.

Andes Mountains

As well as being in a rain shadow, the Atacama Desert is dry because it lies in the high pressure band around latitude 30°S (see page 153), so the air is sinking.

Any warm thermals (see page 151) cannot rise very far due to the sinking air, so no clouds are formed.

30°S

## Hottest climate

Dallol in Ethopia, on the eastern edge of the Sahara Desert, has an average annual temperature of 34.4°C (93.9°F), making it the hottest place in the world.

Clouds greatly affect the amount of solar radiation which reaches the Earth's surface (see page 187).

Few clouds are found above the Sahara Desert, which lies in the band of permanent high pressure at roughly 30°N (see page 153).

Here, air from tropical regions further south sinks towards the Earth's surface.

The air becomes warmer as it sinks, so any water vapour it contains does not condense to form clouds.

The hot surface greatly heats the air above it.

The highest air temperature ever recorded was at Al 'Aziziyah in Libya, which is also at the edge of the Sahara Desert. The temperature reached 58°C (136.4°F) in the shade (meteorologists always measure temperatures in the shade – see page 168).

## Coldest climate

The coldest climate in the world is in Antarctica. Scientists at the Plateau research station in Antarctica have kept records which show the average annual temperature to be −56.6°C (−69.8°F).

The lowest air temperature was also recorded in Antarctica, at the Russian research station in Vostok. The temperature fell to −89.2°C (−128.6°F).

Snow reflects over 90% of solar radiation back into the atmosphere.

The surface receives very little heating, so the air above remains very cold.

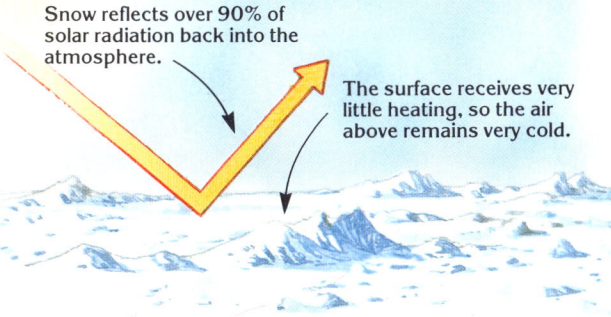

The lowest numbers of hours of sunshine is also found at the south pole. The Sun does not rise for 182 days each year, due to the tilt of the Earth (see page 150).

## Air pressure and wind speed

The highest recorded air pressure occurred in Agata, in northern Siberia. The pressure of the air at sea level reached 1083.8mb (32 psi).

The lowest air pressure, which measured 870mb (25.69psi), was recorded in the centre of Typhoon (hurricane) Tip, which occurred above the Pacific Ocean in 1979. A U.S. Air Force aircraft flew into the eye of the hurricane (see page 163) to measure the pressure.

The highest recorded surface wind speed of 450km/h (280mph) was caused by a tornado in Texas, USA.

The lowest pressure which occurs may never be measured as it will probably occur at the very centre of a tornado (see page 191).

It is unlikely that a barometer could be positioned at exactly the right place to measure the pressure.

It is also unlikely that any instrument would survive the incredibly strong winds caused by tornados.

## Observing wind speed

The speed of the wind is usually measured on an anemometer, but it can be estimated using a scale called the Beaufort scale. The scale is based on the effect of the wind at different speeds.

Force        Description        Speed

0. Calm. Smoke rises vertically.

0km/h (0mph)

1. Light wind. Wind direction shown by smoke.

1-5km/h (1-3mph)

2. Light breeze. Wind felt on face, leaves rustle.

6-11km/h (4-7mph)

3. Gentle breeze. Leaves and twigs constantly move, flags begin to flutter.

12-19km/h (8-12mph)

4. Moderate breeze. Dust and paper blown about, small branches on trees move.

20-29km/h (13-18mph)

5. Fresh breeze. Small trees sway, small waves on lakes.

30-39km/h (19-24mph)

6. Strong breeze. Large branches on trees move, difficult to use an umbrella.

40-50km/h (25-31mph)

7. Near gale force. Whole trees sway, difficult to walk against the wind.

51-61km/h (32-38mph)

8. Gale. Twigs broken off trees, very difficult to walk.

62-74km/h (39-46mph)

9. Severe gale. Chimney pots and roof tiles break off.

75-87km/h (47-54mph)

10. Storm. Seldom occurs away from coasts, trees uprooted, buildings damaged.

88-101km/h (55-63mph)

11. Violent storm. Very rarely occurs, widespread damage.

102-117km/h (64-73mph)

12. Hurricane. Total devastation.

118+km/h (74+mph)

# Glossary

**Acid rain.** Rain which contains water droplets that have absorbed pollutants from the atmosphere and become unusually acidic. The term is also used to describe dry pollutants which fall on to surfaces from the air.

**Anemometer.** An instrument used for measuring the speed of the wind. ▼

**Anticyclone.** An area of relatively high air pressure, also known as a high.

**Atmospheric pressure (air pressure).** The weight of air pushing down on a planet's surface.

**Barometer.** An instrument which measures air pressure.

**Beaufort scale.** A scale used for measuring the strength of the wind, based on observations.

**Blocking high.** A high pressure area which remains stationary and diverts the normal path of lows across an area of the Earth's surface.

**Climate.** The weather conditions experienced in an area over a long period.

**Cold front.** The boundary between a mass of cold air and a mass of warmer air where the cold air is moving in to replace the warmer air.

**Computer model.** A representation of the atmosphere created by a computer, used by meteorologists to produce a weather forecast.

**Condensation.** A process by which a gas or vapour changes into a liquid.

**Convection.** The upward movement of air which has been heated by the land or sea surface below.

**Coriolis effect.** The effect caused by the Earth's rotation which appears to deflect air as it moves between two places.

**Cyclone.** An area of low pressure. It may also be called a low or a depression.

**Dew point.** The temperature at which water vapour condenses to form water.

**Evaporation.** A process by which a liquid changes into a gas or vapour.

**Front.** The boundary that separates two masses of air of different temperature.

**Geostationary satellite.** A weather satellite which stays above the same place on the Earth's surface.

**Global warming.** An overall increase in world temperatures which may be caused by additional heat being trapped by greenhouse gases, such as carbon dioxide and CFC's.

**Greenhouse effect.** The heating effect caused by gases in the atmosphere trapping heat (radiation) from the Earth's surface.

**Humidity.** The amount of water vapour in the air.

**Ice ages.** Periods of time when ice covered large areas of the Earth's surface.

**Intertropical Convergence Zone (ITCZ).** A band of low pressure, formed around the equator, where warm air ▼ rises and is replaced by air moving in from the northern and southern hemispheres.

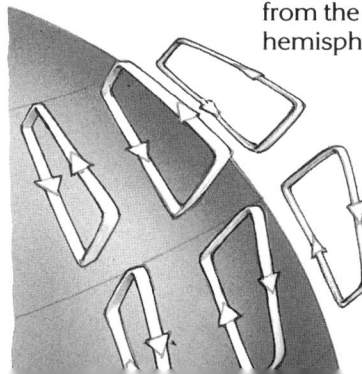

**Isobar.** A line on a weather map joining places which have equal atmospheric, or air, pressure.

**Jet stream.** The strongest currents of the high-level winds which circle the Earth between 10km and 16km (6 miles and 10 miles) above the surface.

**Meteorologist.** A scientist who studies all the elements of the atmosphere which combine to form the weather.

**Monsoon.** A wind which blows from different directions at different times of the year, creating a wet, or rainy season, and a dry season.

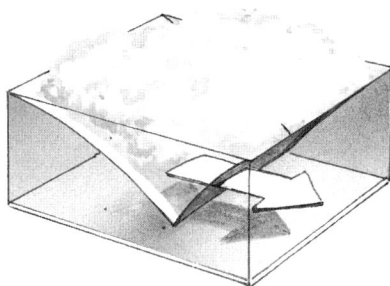

**Occluded front.** A front which occurs where a cold front moves in and undercuts a warm front, lifting the warm air away from the surface.

**Ozone layer.** A layer of ozone gas, found in the upper atmosphere, which absorbs harmful solar radiation.

**Polar front.** The boundary where cool air moving in from polar regions meets warm tropical air.

**Polar orbiting satellite.** A weather satellite which travels over both the north and south poles each time it completes one orbit of the Earth.

**Precipitation.** Any form of moisture, such as rain, snow, sleet or hail, that falls to the ground from a cloud.

**Prevailing wind.** The most common wind which tends to blow in any given location.

**Radiosonde.** An instrument, attached to a balloon, which monitors pressure, temperature and humidity at different heights above the Earth's surface.

**Smog.** Fog mixed with air pollutants, such as smoke, which cause the fog to become more dense.

**Solar radiation.** Heat and light energy from the Sun.

**Synoptic chart.** A chart which shows various elements of the weather, such as temperature and pressure, monitored in different places at the same time.

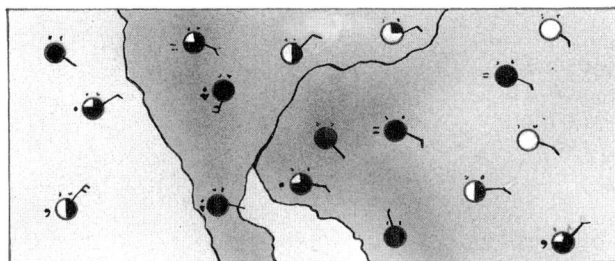

**Temperature inversion.** A situation which arises where a layer of warmer air lies above cooler air, making the temperature increase or stay the same, rather than decreasing, with height.

**Thermal.** A rising current of warm air which is caused by a local area of the Earth's surface heating up more than its surroundings.

**Tornado.** A violently rotating column of air which may extend from the base of a cumulonimbus cloud. It is thought to be formed by strong upward currents of air which exist within the cloud.

**Tropical cyclone.** A severe storm, with torrential rain and strong winds, formed over warm seas between 5° and 20° north and south of the equator. It may also be called a hurricane or a typhoon.

**Warm front.** The boundary between a mass of warm air and a mass of cooler air, where the warm air moves in to replace the cooler air.

**Wind.** Air moving from high pressure areas to areas of lower pressure.

# Index

**Acid rain**, 23, 63, 82, 94, 113, 185, 190
**Adaptation** (animal), 64-65, 72, 94
**Aestivation**, 77
**Air** (atmosphere), 5, 14-15, 46, 148-149, 180
  —movement (winds), 152, 153, 154, 155, 156, 160, 161
  —pollution, 15, 23, 63, 73, 104, 113, 134, 184-185
  —pressure, 14, 15, 148, 152-153, 154-155, 160-161, 165, 166, 168, 171, 172, 173, 189, 190
  —temperature, 14, 149, 151, 155, 158, 159, 160-161, 166, 168, 170, 179, 184, 186, 189
**Anabatic wind**, 167
**Anemometer**, 170, 190
**Antarctica**, 15, 24, 32, 40-41, 44, 65, 83, 177, 180, 184, 189
**Anticyclones**, see **High pressure areas**
**Appropriate technology**, 83, 94
**Aquifers**, 28, 46
**Arctic**, 9, 15, 32, 65, 180
**Arête**, 25
**Atmosphere**, see **Air**
**Atoms**, 104, 106, 142
**Automatic weather stations**, 168, 172
**Axis (Earth's)**, 4

**Backwash**, 46
**Barometer**, 152, 171, 190
**Batteries**, 105, 127
**Beaufort scale**, 189, 190
**Biogas**, 125, 142
**Biomass**, 124, 142
**Biomes**, 56, 94
**Bird(s)**,
  feeding—, 70
  —table, 70, 87
  —watching, 87
**Blocking highs**, 165, 190
**Buys-Ballot law**, 160

**Cacti**, 33, 64, 177
**Camouflage**, 65, 94
**Carbohydrates**, 55
**Carbon cycle**, 60
**Carbon dioxide**, 15, 61, 113, 134, 148, 182
**Carnivores**, 34, 35, 57
**Catalytic converters**, 63, 73
**Charcoal**, 124
**Chemical energy**, 100, 102, 103, 104, 105, 111, 142
**Chemicals** (in farming), 63
**Chemical weathering**, 22
**Chlorofluorocarbons (CFCs)**, 15, 77, 94, 182, 184
**Cirque**, 25
**Cities**, 18, 36-37, 72-73, 131, 133, 134, 178

**Climates**, 18-19, 24, 46, 54, 76-77, 94, 176-183, 188, 190
  changes in—, 24, 76-77, 180-183
  city—, 18, 178
**Climax community**, 76, 94
**Clouds**, 16, 17, 156-157, 158, 161, 162-163, 171, 172, 187, 188
  acid rain—, 23, 113, 185
  frontal—, 161
  hurricane—, 162-163
  thunderstorm—, 17, 157, 162
**Coal**, 23, 38, 39, 104, 111, 112-113, 136-139
**Coastal (sea) fog**, 159, 166
**Cold fronts**, 161, 190
**Colonies** (animal), 68
**Combined heat and power stations (CHPs)**, 81, 94, 131, 132, 140
**Commensalism**, 69
**Community** (natural), 35, 53, 94
**Conduction** (heat/electricity), 107, 108
**Conductors**, 107, 108, 142
**Conservation groups** (nature), 45, 71, 92-93, 141
**Conservation of energy** (energy saving), see **Energy efficiency**
**Conservation of energy** (Law of), 102, 142
**Consumers** (food chain), 34, 35, 55, 56, 57, 94
**Continental plates**, 6, 10, 12, 46
**Continents**, 6, 46
**Contrails**, 157
**Convection**, 107, 142, 151, 156, 190
**Co-operation** (animal), 69
**Coriolis effect**, 153, 160, 190
**Crop rotation**, 63, 94
**Crystals**, 20
**Cyclones**, see **Low pressure areas**

**Dams**, 128-129
**Darwin, Charles**, 79
**Debris**, 22, 23, 24, 25, 30, 32, 46
**Decomposers**, 34, 56, 57, 94
**Deforestation** (tree destruction), 37, 42, 75, 81, 94, 124
**Deltas**, 27, 36, 46
**Depressions**, see **Low pressure areas**
**Desertification**, 42, 46, 64, 82, 94
**Deserts**, 19, 28, 32-33, 37, 42, 44, 46, 56, 64-65, 176, 177, 188
  frozen (icy)—, 19, 32, 40, 65
**Development aid**, 42, 83
**Dew**, 159,
  —point, 156, 159, 190
**Distillation**, 114, 142
**Droughts**, 17, 37, 46, 164, 165, 188
**Drumlins**, 25
**Dust bowls**, 23, 55
**Dykes** (volcanoes), 12
**Dynamo**, 118, 142

**Earthquakes**, 10, 11
**Ecosystems**, 34, 35, 46, 53, 56-57, 94
**Electrical energy/Electricity**, 38-39, 81, 102, 105, 108, 109, 118-119, 122, 124, 126, 127, 128, 129, 162
**Electromagnetic energy**, 102, 109, 110, 142
**Electromagnetic spectrum**, 109
**Electromagnetism**, 142
**Electromagnets**, 118, 119, 120
**Electromotive force (emf)**, 108, 142
**Electrons**, 104, 142
**Embedded energy**, 132
**Endangered wildlife**, 71, 82
**Energy,**
  embedded—, 132
  —chains, 103
  —consumption & production figures, 135, 136-138
  —economics, 140
  —efficiency, 81, 103, 130-133
  —in food chains, 34, 55, 56, 57
  —quality, 109
  renewable—, 38, 39, 47, 81, 95, 121-129, 143
  —reserves, 138-139
**Environment**, 34, 37, 42, 46, 52, 54-55, 80, 81, 82
**Environmental groups**, 45, 71, 92-93, 141
**Erosion**, 22, 23, 25, 26, 27, 29, 30, 32, 37, 46, 76
  —by glaciers, 25
  —by rivers and streams, 26, 27, 29
  —by waves, 30
  soil—, 23, 37, 42
**Erratics**, 25
**Eskers**, 25
**Estuaries**, 31, 39
**Evolution**, 78-79, 94
**Exfoliation**, 22
**Export crops**, 80, 82
**Extinction**, 71, 94

**Faults** (rock), 10, 46
**Fertilizers**, 63
**Fetch**, 46
**Fishing**, 42, 59
**Fission** (nuclear), 105, 116, 142
**Flooding**, 11, 17, 25, 27, 36, 164, 187
**Flood plain**, 27, 46
**Fog**, 159, 166, 167
  —in valleys, 167
  sea (coastal) —, 159, 166
**Folds** (rock), 10, 46
**Food chains and webs**, 34, 35, 40-41, 46, 56, 57, 94
**Forecasts** (weather), 174-175
**Forest farms**, 125
**Forestry**, 66

Fossil fuels, 15, 23, 38-39, 46, 61, 63, 81, 111, 112-115, 118, 135, 136-139, 142
Fossils, 6, 7, 78, 79
Fractionating column, 114
Fractures, see Faults
Freeze-thaw action, 22, 25
Friction, 24, 103, 142
Fronts, 160-161, 190
    cold–, 161, 190
    occluded–, 161
    polar–, 160, 191
    warm–, 161, 191
Frontal clouds, 161
Frontal depressions, 161
Frost, 159, 167
Fuels, 38-39, 81, 104, 111, 112-115, 117, 124, 125, 135-139
Fusion (nuclear), 105, 110, 116, 142

Gaia hypothesis, 79
Gas (natural), 38, 39, 104, 111, 114-115, 136-139
Gas (town), 115
General circulation models (weather), 186
Generators, 118, 142
    turbine–, 116, 118-119, 124, 127, 128, 129
Genetic engineering, 83, 94
Geostationary satellites, 169, 174, 190
Geothermal energy (underground heat), 39, 81, 111, 129, 142
Glaciation, 24-25
Glaciers, 23, 24-25, 44, 46
Global warming, 15, 25, 27, 46, 113, 182-183, 186, 190
Gravitational potential energy, 105, 106
Greenhouse effect, 15, 38, 46, 61, 82, 95, 113, 134, 143, 182, 190
Grid system (electricity), 119, 127, 143
Ground water, 28-29, 46

Habitats, 53, 82, 95
    destruction of–, 71
    marine–, 58
Hail, 17, 158
Heat (thermal) energy, 102, 103, 104, 106-107, 111, 121-123, 130, 131, 132, 133
Heat wheel, 132
Herbivores, 34, 57
Hibernation, 77
High-level winds, 154, 160, 161, 163, 165
High pressure areas (Anticyclones), 152-153, 154-155, 160, 164, 165, 166, 188, 189, 190
    blocking–, 165, 190
Human population, 36-37, 42, 71, 80, 138
Humidity, 46, 155, 156, 165, 171, 190
Humus, 54

Hurricanes (Tropical cyclones), 8, 47, 147, 162-163, 187, 191
Hydraulic action, 26, 30
Hydrocarbons, 114, 115, 143
Hydro-electric power/Hydroelectricity, 38, 47, 111, 128-129, 137, 143

Ice, 22, 23, 24-25, 40, 151, 156, 158, 159, 180, 183, 186
    –ages, 24, 25, 76, 180, 181, 190
    –bergs, 24
    –crystals (in clouds/frost), 156, 157, 158, 159
    –sheets, 24, 47, 180
Igneous rock, 20, 47
Impermeable rock, 21, 28, 47
Infra-red radiation, 107, 109, 110
Insulation (in the home), 81, 130
Insulators (heat/electricity), 107, 108, 143
Intensive farming, 63, 95
Intertropical Convergence Zone (ITCZ), 153, 164, 190
Irrigation, 37, 42, 43, 47, 95
Isobars, 160, 190

Jet streams, 154, 165, 191
Joules (J), 101, 143

Katabatic wind, 167
Kinetic energy, 100, 102, 103, 106, 107, 143

Land breezes, 18, 166
Landfill sites, 115, 140
Latitude (lines), 44, 153
Lava, 12, 47
Light energy, 102, 103, 109, 110
Lightning, 17, 162
Limestone caves, 29
Longitude (lines), 44
Longshore drift, 30, 31
Low pressure areas (Depressions/Cyclones), 152-153, 154-155, 160-161, 164, 165, 166, 187, 189, 190

Magma, 12, 20, 21, 47
Magnetic energy/Magnetism, 109
Magnetic potential energy, 105
Marginal land, 64, 95
Meanders, 27
Mechanical energy, 106, 107, 118
Mechanical weathering, 22
Metamorphic rock, 21, 47
Metamorphosis (butterfly), 77
Methane, 115, 125, 143
Migration, 77
Mimicry, 65
Minerals, 20-21, 41, 47, 54, 55
Mist, 159
Molecules, 104, 106, 143

Monsoons, 164, 176, 191
Moon (atmosphere of), 149
Moraine, 25
    terminal–, 25
Mountain(s), 19, 21, 24, 26, 44, 188
    –climates, 19
    fold–, 10
    underwater–, 8, 9

Natural cycles, 60-63
Natural selection, 79, 95
Neutrons, 104, 143
Niches, 35, 70, 95
Nitrogen cycle, 61
Nuclear energy/power, 39, 81, 102, 105, 116-117, 137
Nucleus, 104, 105, 143

Oases, 28
Occluded fronts, 161, 191
Oceans and seas, 6, 8-9, 18, 30-31, 35, 42, 44, 58-59, 166
Oil, 23, 38, 39, 81, 104, 111, 114-115, 135, 136-139
    –refining, 114-115
Omnivores, 35, 57
Organic, 95
Organic farming, 63, 95
OTEC, 129
Ozone (gas), 15, 148, 149, 184
    surface–, 15, 184
Ozone layer, 15, 40, 47, 77, 82, 95, 149, 184, 191

Parasites, 69
Permeable rock, 21, 28, 47
Pervious rock, 21
Photochemical smog, 15, 184
Photosynthesis, 5, 34, 55, 95, 111, 143
Photovoltaic cells, see Solar cells
Planets, 4-5, 148-149
Plankton, 58
Plant galls, 69
Pocket parks, 73, 90-91
Polar climates, 19, 65, 176
Polar orbiting satellites, 149, 169, 191
Pollution, 15, 23, 27, 42, 59, 62, 63, 73, 82, 95, 104, 113, 115, 133, 134, 135, 184-185
Pond, 53, 84-85
    –building, 84-85
Population,
    animal–, 70
    human–, 36-37, 42, 71, 80, 138
Porous rock, 21
Potential energy, 102, 105, 143
Power, 101, 143
Power stations, 109, 116-119, 124-125, 131, 132
Precipitation, 16, 17, 47, 156, 158, 159, 171, 173, 191

Predators, 47, 70
Pressure (air/atmospheric), 14, 15, 148, 152-153, 154-155, 160-161, 164, 165, 166, 168, 171, 172, 173, 189, 190
Prevailing winds, 191
Prey, 47, 70
Producers (food chain), 34, 55, 56, 57, 95
Protons, 104, 143

Quality of energy, 109

Radars, 109, 169
Radiation,
    infra-red—, 107, 109, 110
    (process), 107
    (result of radioactivity), 39, 117
    solar— (Sun's energy), 4, 15, 18, 109, 110, 111, 113, 148, 150, 151, 153, 166, 167, 179, 182, 184, 186, 187, 188, 189
    ultra-violet—, 15, 109, 110
Radioactive waste, 39, 81, 117
Radioactivity, 39, 81, 117, 143
Radiosondes, 168, 191
Rain, 16, 17, 156, 157, 158, 159, 169, 176, 178
    acid—, 23, 63, 82, 94, 113, 185, 190
    —forests, 5, 19, 34, 35, 44, 74-75, 82, 177
    —shadows, 188
Rainbows, 167
Reactors (nuclear), 116, 143
Recycling, 62, 90-91
Refuse (burnt for energy), 81, 124-125, 140
Renewable energy, 38, 39, 47, 81, 95, 121-129, 143
Rivers, 23, 26-27, 44, 128
Rock, 20-21, 22, 23, 24, 25, 26, 28, 29, 30, 32
    impermeable—, 21, 28, 47
    permeable—, 21, 28, 47
    pervious—, 21
    porous—, 21

Satellite(s), 149, 163, 169, 190, 191
    —images, 163, 169, 174
Sea breezes, 18, 166
Sea (coastal) fog, 159, 166
Seas and oceans, 6, 8-9, 18, 30-31, 35, 42, 44, 58-59, 166
Seasons, 16, 19, 76, 150
Sedimentary rock, 21, 47
Sediments, 21, 26, 27, 31, 47
Seeds, 65, 86, 90
Sills (volcanoes), 12
Sleet, 158
Smog, 134, 184, 191
    photochemical—, 15, 184

Snow, 151, 158, 189
Social groups (animal), 68, 70
Soil, 54, 55
    —erosion, 23, 37, 55, 82, 95
Solar cells, 122, 143
Solar (flat plate) collector, 122
Solar energy (radiation), 4, 15, 18, 47, 109, 110, 111, 113, 148, 150, 151, 153, 166, 167, 179, 182, 184, 186, 187, 188, 189, 191
    uses of—, 38, 81, 121-123
Solar heating, 121-122
Solar power, see Solar energy (uses of)
Solar System, 4, 148
Sound energy, 102, 107
Spits, 31
Springs, 26
Stalactites, 29
Stalagmites, 29
Static electricity, 108
Stored energy, 100, 104-105
Storm(s), 17, 162, 163, 187, 189
    —surges, 187
Strain energy, 100, 103, 105
Stratosphere, 14, 149, 184
Succession, 72, 76, 95
Sun, see Solar energy (radiation)
Super-organisms, 68
Sustainable development, 95
Swash, 47
Symbiosis, 69
Synoptic charts, 172, 191

Temperature(s), 106
    air—, 14, 149, 151, 155, 158, 159, 160-161, 166, 168, 170, 179, 184, 186, 189
    body—, 179
    —inversions, 184, 191
    main climate—, 176
    planet—, 4-5, 148-149
    surface—, 151, 155, 159, 169, 182, 183, 186, 188, 189
Terminal moraine, 25
Territory (animal), 70, 95
Thermals, 151, 188, 191
Thunderstorms, 17, 162
Tidal barrages, 39, 128
Tidal energy/power, 39, 81, 111, 128
Tidal waves, see Tsunamis
Tides, 30, 31, 111
Tornadoes, 17, 47, 189, 191
Town gas, 115
Traffic calming, 73
Transformers, 119
Transport, 42, 73, 133, 134
Trophic levels, 57, 95
Tropical cyclones (Hurricanes), 8, 47, 147, 162-163, 187, 191
Tropical rain forests, see Rain forests
Tsunamis (tidal waves), 11, 47

Tundra, 19, 56, 65
Turbine, 118, 143
    —generators, 116, 118-119, 124, 127, 128, 129
Typhoons, see Tropical cyclones

Ultra-violet radiation, 15, 109, 110
Urban areas, 18, 36-37, 72-73, 133, 134, 178, 184

Valley winds, 167
Visibility, 159, 171
Volcanoes, 7, 9, 12-13, 20
    underwater—, 9
Voltage/volts, 108, 119

Warm fronts, 161, 191
Waste,
    burning of—, 81, 124-125, 140
    radioactive—, 39, 81, 117
    recycling—, 62, 82
Water,
    —cycle, 16, 59, 60, 110-111
    —energy/power, 38, 39, 81, 110-111, 128-129
    erosion by—, 21, 23, 26, 27, 29, 30, 37
    —falls, 26
    —in deserts, 28, 32, 33, 64, 177
    —loss from plants, 176
    —pollution, 23, 27, 42, 59, 63, 113, 115, 185
    underground—, 13, 28-29
    —vapour, 7, 16, 155, 156, 158, 159, 162, 163, 164, 165
Watts, 101
Wave(s), 23, 30-31
    —energy/power, 81, 111, 128
    —erosion, 23, 30
    tidal—, see Tsunamis
Weather,
    —forecasts, 173, 174-175
    —observations, 168-171, 172
    —stations, 168, 170-171, 172
Weathering, 22-23, 47, 54
Whaling, 93
Wind(s), 15, 54, 110, 152, 153, 154, 155, 160, 161, 166, 170, 172, 173, 189, 191
    anabatic—, 167
    —chill factor, 179
    —energy/power, 38, 39, 81, 110, 126-127
    —erosion, 23, 32
    high-level—, 154, 161, 163, 165
    hurricane—, 163, 187
    katabatic—, 167
    monsoon—, 164
    —pump, 126
    —turbines, 127
    valley—, 167
    world's main—, 153